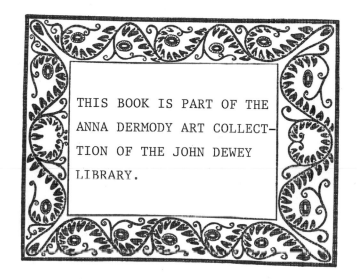

The Life and Works of

THOMAS SULLY

The Life and Works of
THOMAS SULLY

By Edward Biddle and Mantle Fielding

Da Capo Press • New York • 1970

This edition of
The Life and Works of Thomas Sully
is an unabridged republication of the first edition published
in Philadelphia in 1921 in an edition limited to five hundred copies.

Library of Congress Catalog Card Number 74-77716

SBN 306-71354-3

Published by Da Capo Press
A Division of Plenum Publishing Corporation
227 West 17th Street, New York, N.Y. 10011

The Life and Works of
THOMAS SULLY

Painted by Thomas Sully

Engraved by John Sartain

THOMAS SULLY.

From the original picture painted by him in 1856, for
Mr. Ferdinand J. Dreer.

Yr friend & obt Svt
Thos Sully

The Life and Works of

THOMAS SULLY

[1783-1872]

By
Edward Biddle
and
Mantle Fielding

Philadelphia
1921
Wickersham Press
Lancaster, Pa.

TB 1838.

PREFATORY NOTE

WE have been very much aided in what we may have been able to accomplish in the following biographical chapters, by the readiness to put at our disposal letters and papers remaining in the possession of members of the Sully family. Especially has this been so with Mrs. Albert Sully, the widow of Dr. Albert Sully (grandson of Thomas Sully) and now a resident of Brooklyn (N. Y.).

Miss Julia Sully of Richmond (Va.), a great-niece of the artist, has also shown much interest.

The descendants of Thomas Sully's step-daughter, Mary Chester Sully, who married John Neagle the distinguished portrait painter, have been very ready to assist us. They are residents of Philadelphia and possess some very charming family portraits from Sully's brush. In their parlor hangs the large painting by the Artist of his wife, with the pet dog of the family " Ponto " at her side.

To Dr. I. Minis Hays of the American Philosophical Society we are indebted not merely for official aid, but for very cordial support and valuable suggestions.

The Pennsylvania Historical Society through its executive staff has afforded us every facility during the progress of the work.

The Pennsylvania Academy of the Fine Arts in the same way has been most ready to aid and forward our wishes.

To all of these we make our sincere acknowledgments.

LIST OF ILLUSTRATIONS

THOMAS SULLY

CHAPTER I

BIRTH AND PARENTAGE—REMOVES TO CHARLESTON, S. C., WITH PARENTS—
ENTERS BROKER'S OFFICE—SOON ABANDONS IT—BECOMES A PUPIL OF
M. BELZONS—PARTS FROM HIM—GOES TO RICHMOND, VA.—DEATH OF
HIS BROTHER LAWRENCE—SULLY ASSUMES FRESH RESPONSIBILITIES—
PAINTS HIS FIRST MINIATURE.

AT the mention of Thomas Sully's name the average reader will be apt to conjure up a mature if not an aged artist. No doubt the more familiar likenesses of Mr. Sully have helped to foster this impression. The portrait picturing him at the age of 73 is the familiar likeness, and the one he painted of himself when scarcely in middle life is rarely noted. But there was a young and vigorous Sully, full of buoyant determination and high ambitions; and in this biographical Memoir we shall attempt to bring him before our readers in a rejuvenated form.

The period of life lending itself best to special description is from the entrance of our embryo artist into the practice of his art, when about 16 or 17 years old, and for forty (40) years thereafter. This embraces Sully's two visits to Europe, that is, to England; for whatever advantages he might have gained from wider foreign study and observation, they were denied him. But young Sully made such good use of his opportunities at his very first English visit, that it is doubtful whether further travel would have contributed anything to his after-success as a portrait painter. He had the advantage of coming immediately under the direction and influence of Benjamin West, the "American patriarch of painting," who advised him to "study portraiture in England, above all schools."

West exhibited great interest in Sully, and writing to a friend in Philadelphia under date of Nov. 3rd, 1809, he expresses himself as follows :

" Philadelphia I cannot name without being interested in all that has a connection with that city ; this, my good Sir, alludes to a young gentleman now studying painting under my direction as a Professor of that Art, whose talents only want time to mature them to excellence, and I am apprehensive that his means of support are too slender to admit his stay at this seat of Arts that length of time to effect what I could wish, as I understand it is doubtful whether it cannot be longer than the beginning of next summer. . . . The young gentleman I allude to is Mr. Sully. I find him every way worthy and promising. I could not refrain from thus giving you my sentiments, when the success of Mr. Sully in his profession as a painter is so much to be desired."

We shall return to this highly significant period in Sully's career, but must needs turn back to an earlier date in order to give the events of his life in chronological order.

Our artist was of English parentage, the son of Matthew and Sarah Chester Sully, who were actors. They came to this country from England in 1792, bringing their family with them, and settling at Charleston, S. C. It was a numerous family, consisting as it did of four sons and five daughters. Thus in the order of their births, we name the sons, Lawrence, Matthew, Chester, and *Thomas ;* and the daughters, Harriet (married Prof. Porcher of S. C.), Elizabeth (m. Middleton Smith of Charleston, S. C.), Jane (m. J. B. LeRoy), Mary, and Sarah. Of the two latter, one married Mons. Belzons, a French refugee living at Charleston. Thomas, the subject of our memoir, was about 9 years of age when he reached this country, his birth having occurred in the month of June, 1783, at Horncastle, in Lincolnshire, England.*

* Mrs. Ravenel, in her book on Charleston, mistakenly names Sully as a *Carolinian.*

2

Matthew Sully, the father, was brother-in-law to a Mr. West, then managing theatres in the south. Charleston was about to open a new theatre, and it was doubtless in view of that event that the Sullys were drawn to the southern town.

Charlestown, as it had always been called down to 1783, had now blossomed forth as the City of *Charleston*. Its growth was becoming marked, a number of causes contributing towards it. A Huguenot settlement had been early formed there, and so a French foundation existed which attracted later settlers of that nationality. At this particular juncture the dreadful upheaval at St. Domingo (1792) brought numerous French refugees, escaping the horrors of their devastated island homes. Being kindly received and welcomed by the Charleston people, they were afforded opportunities of earning livelihoods. They brought an atmosphere of gaiety and gallic vivacity to the life of the city, soon to be reflected in the diversions and amusements of the place. Music and dancing were made accessible, through the knowledge and teaching of the newcomers.

The new theatre evidently introduced a fresh and welcome diversion as may be gathered from the following quotation : " The opening of the theatre in January, 1793, was quite an event in the history of Charleston. Theatricals had been so long discontinued here that the rising generation were strangers to the fascination of the stage ; and I can never forget the delight which this new amusement produced in all classes of our community. The box office was thronged of a morning ; and in the evening of representation, the doors of the theatre were besieged by crowds long before the hour of opening them. The stage was the general subject of conversation ; and so enchanting was its influence that the ladies were heard to say that they could *live* in the theatre!" So writes Fraser in his "Reminiscences of Charleston."

For theatrical people this promised well, but there was another branch of art for which our youthful Sully thirsted that had as yet but few votaries. No doubt young Thomas' parents, when placing him in

3

business with an insurance broker, were influenced by prudential motives, and swayed doubtless by a feeling that artists are apt to have, that *any* occupation but their own is best for their offspring. The boy Sully was about 12 years of age when the parents decided on this step. An amusing anecdote has come down that the broker in question soon complained that although his youthful assistant was "very industrious in multiplying figures, they were figures of *men and women*, and that if the broker took up a piece of paper in the office he was sure to see a face staring at him!" In short, that "Tom spoiled all the paper that fell in his way, or that he could lay his hands on." The broker ended by advising Tom's father that "the boy should be made a *painter*."

Young Sully's artistic tastes had been kindled while at school. Charles Fraser, afterwards well known as a miniature painter, and somewhat older than our youthful artist, attended the same establishment and although then a mere beginner, Sully afterwards said "he was the first person that ever took the pains to instruct me in the rudiments of the art, and although himself a mere tyro, his kindness, and the progress made in consequence of it, determined the course of my future life."

Another influence also, was the fact that his own elder brother, Lawrence, was a miniature and device painter. The latter never attained any wide celebrity, but to the younger brother, with his inborn tastes, one so near and familiar to him engaged in such a pursuit must have proved a constant spur.

When young Sully parted from his insurance patron, it was at last determined to put him in the way of becoming a painter. Shortly before the period we are dealing with, a Mr. Belzons, a Frenchman, had married one of young Sully's sisters. Mr. Belzons had practiced art as an amateur abroad, and coming to Charleston had set up there as a miniature painter.* It was arranged that young Tom should take instructions from this gentleman, who had by marriage become his brother-in-law.

---

* In the Charleston Directory for the year 1797 appears " Mons. Belzons, Miniature Painter, 28 Church St."

4

There is nothing to show that Mr. Belzons' abilities were in any way extraordinary, no doubt indeed very moderate. But what does seem well-established is that he did not possess the patience requisite for the rôle of a teacher. So it was not long after, following a violent scene, in which the brother-in-law's temper appears to have been much at fault, that the relations of pupil and instructor were abruptly ended. This came about, when Sully was 16 years of age (1799). It was a serious crisis in the youth's outlook in life. His parents were no longer living, his elder brother Lawrence had removed to Richmond, Va., and worse still, he was without means. The story goes that after the rupture at Belzons', his late pupil spent the first night in a public refuge, so determined was he not to seek a reconciliation. The next day, meeting a friend, he related what had occurred and asserted his determination not to return to his brother-in-law's house. The friend sympathized in these feelings, and better still was able to offer him some temporary protection. Then Mr. Read, a Navy agent, became interested in the youth's difficulties, and offered his interest to procure a midshipman's birth for him. The offer was accepted, and our future painter came near becoming a sailor. But fortunately for the cause of art, his brother Lawrence got into communication with him and proposed that he should come to Richmond and become his pupil. Some difficulties were experienced in arranging for transportation to Richmond, but happily these were overcome through the liberality of a sea-captain, who carried young Sully to Norfolk in his own ship. Here he tarried a few days at Capt. Leffingwell's house until his brother remitted funds, with which he was enabled to discharge his debt to the captain and pay for a passage on the James River to Richmond.

His brother Lawrence, at this time a man of some 30 years of age, and in whose house he now came to live, had some years previously married Sarah Annis, of Annapolis, Md. Two children had been born of the marriage, and the birth of a third daughter, still further increased the family, in the following year. With this considerable household the two brothers later determined to remove to Norfolk. Here it was, on May 10th, 1801, that young Thomas Sully painted his first miniature from life, being a likeness of his brother Chester Sully.

That invaluable "Account of Pictures", for so he himself styles it rather than a "Register," and which Sully so sedulously kept, was begun at this time, and the first entry in its pages is one describing the miniature just mentioned. It is interesting to follow the entries throughout the book, but a peculiar halo seems to hover over these opening pages. They appear to foreshadow the success that was to follow, and to be eloquent of a steady tenacity of purpose. The youthful Sully evidently feels that he has entered upon his rightful career. It is to be no haphazard adventure, but a steady and increasing employment. He rules his book in columns, enters first the date at which any likeness is begun, followed by the size of the picture, then the sitter's name with perhaps some explanatory note attached, and finally the price or value of the portrait, and the date of its completion. These succeeding entries, carried through each year, form a most illuminating commentary on the growth of Sully's powers, and the favor with which the efforts of his brush became increasingly rewarded.

6

Date	Size	For whom painted	Price	Finished
18	Kit Cat	Gov'ner painted Sister Mary —	150	Sept 22
27	Head	Messrs Downes & Co Downingsville	150	Oct 3rd
Jan'y 25	Bust	Ship E. Bates, painted in London 40/ Bust	2.50	Dec'r 26
Dec'm 5	Bust	John Tottenham Merchant at 40/ Frame	2.50	Oct. 26
1838 28	Bust	Sam'l Davison Esq'r for Experiment —	2.00	Feb'y 13
Jan'y 9	Kit Cat	Mr Stephen Price —	3.50	Sept 9
11	Kit Cat	"Charity," an original composition	3.50	[September]
March 13	Bust	"Sleeping Girl" copy from Reynolds	3.00	June
22	Kit Cat	Victoria, Queen of England — the head only	5.00	May 15
April 5	Head	"Strawberry Girl" copy fr: Picture & Frame	3.00	April 20
21	Head	"Girl & Bird" copy after Reynolds — Ditto	3.00	May 2
May 23	Kit Cat	Full length Queen Victoria for Holyrood Ground	1000	June 24
Sept'm 30	Whole length	Queen Victoria for the St George's Society	1000	Jan 14
Octob'r 2	Whole length	Queen Victoria for myself	2000	Decm 20
Dec'm 27	Head	Leonard Girl copy after the Purchase'r Mr Nov — 20	150	Sept 2

CHAPTER II

"First attempt in oil colors"—Meeting with Thomas Abthorpe Cooper—Removes to New York City—Paints numerous portraits of dramatic people—Visits Gilbert Stuart in Boston—Removes to Philadelphia—Sails for England.

ADDRESSING ourselves, therefore, to these records, we find that in 1801 he painted "10 pieces," valued at $180. The year that followed was meagre of results, but Sully signalized its passage by his "first attempt in oil colors," painting a small portrait of William Armistead.

1803 proved a much better year in the amount of work produced, but an event followed towards its close that was to bring with it grave and unlooked-for responsibilities. This was the death of his brother Lawrence. (The latter had moved back to Richmond with his family, and Thomas had followed him there.) This unexpected calamity, instead of overwhelming and stifling young Sully's art ambitions, appears only to have moved him to greater effort. Now he displayed that steady fortitude which distinguished him in after life, for without a moment's hesitation he at once undertook the support of his brother's orphaned children and their mother. Here we may anticipate our story by relating that some two years following this event, Thomas married the widow. She was some four years his senior, but the union turned out a most happy one. No fewer than nine children were the issue of this marriage, and the ties uniting the children of Lawrence and those of his brother Thomas appear to have been of the closest and most affectionate nature. Sully's domestic life was distinguished by all that nice regard for the duties and responsibilities of parenthood that are sometimes lacking in those "married to Art." His life was well ordered and benevolent, thoughtful and considerate in its relations with all men; and we shall find this bearing fruit in the esteem in which he was held in his lifetime, as well as the affectionate regard paid his memory.

Just previous to his brother Lawrence's death our youthful artist, ever seeking for means of improvement, had planned to go abroad with a view of study. Of course this had to be abandoned; but fortunately he was enabled to carry out the project a few years later, as we shall discover in the course of our story.

Sully's exertions during the next two years produced only moderate gains; thus in 1805 he notes having painted " 30 pieces ", valued at $680, while in 1806 the number, estimated at only 18, brings rewards amounting to $527.

It was in the month of November of this year that he removed to New York City. Its coming about was the result of a meeting with Thomas Abthorpe Cooper, the distinguished English actor, then on a theatrical tour of the South, and stopping for a while at Richmond. Dunlap,* when recounting their meeting, merely states that Cooper, sitting to Sully for his portrait, formed a friendship for the painter, etc., etc.; but the tradition preserved among the descendants of the English actor is that Cooper, learning of young Sully's tribulations, sought him out, and, after sitting to him for his portrait, advised and encouraged him to seek a wider and more promising field. It is entirely probable that this is the true story, for to a generously disposed man, as Cooper appears among his contemporaries, knowledge that a young fellow-countryman of talent was in difficulties through lack of patronage, would be likely to prompt him in seeking him out, as he is reported to have done. At any rate, the fact is indisputable that it was Cooper who advised and planned for Sully's removal to New York, and this with Cooper's assistance, was carried out a few months following the Richmond meeting. It proved a

---

* History of Rise and Progress of Arts of Design in U. S., by Wm. Dunlap.

turning-point in Sully's career; Cooper at once introduced him to members of his own profession, and the entries in Sully's "Account of Pictures" attest that his new friend and patron gave practical expression to his generous feelings. In November, Sully records having painted John Harwood, of New York Theatre, "for Cooper," and Mrs. Twaits of New York Theatre, "for Cooper"; in December Mrs. Darley of New York Theatre, "for Cooper." Later followed portraits of Mr. Darley, "for Cooper." Also Mrs. Villars, in the character of Lady Macbeth, and Mrs. Warren, of the Philadelphia Theatre; evidencing that the painter's introduction to the actor and his circle carried with it substantial benefit.

In fact, at the end of 1807, our artist, now 24 years of age, is able to count "pieces" painted to the number of 70, and his receipts at $3,203 (!)

But, as there is no bright light that has not its corresponding shadow, we find entered also, "The Embargo was put in force at the close of this year, 1807; which greatly injured my prospects." It was in this same year, 1807, that our newly launched Sully first had an opportunity of meeting Gilbert Stuart, then at the height of his fame, and settled in Boston.

Armed with a letter of introduction from Cooper to Mr. Andrew Allen, of Boston, he visited that city, and through the latter was introduced to Stuart. It happened very fortunately that at the very time of Sully's advent Allen was fulfilling an engagement to sit to Stuart for his own portrait. They went together, therefore, to Stuart's studio, and Sully, when describing the meeting and his experience, relates: "I had the privilege of standing by the artist's chair during the sitting, a situation I valued more at that moment than I shall ever again appreciate any station on earth" (!) Then a still happier circumstance occurred, for while lingering in the painting room there entered there Isaac P. Davis, a well-known and liberal Bostonian, and an attached friend of Gilbert Stuart's. Following mutual introductions, an arrangement was made that Mr. Davis should sit to Sully, and that Stuart would pass upon the

9

portrait when finished, with a view of giving helpful criticism. We can readily enter into Sully's feelings when, having finished the picture, he carried it to Stuart. We had best quote his own description of what occurred.

"He looked at it for a long time, and every moment of procrastination added to my torment. He deliberated and I trembled. At length, he said, 'keep what you have got, and get as much as you can.'" (!) Of course, the "keep what you have got" must have fallen like a benediction upon Sully's ears. Coming from Stuart, it meant everything. The latter followed up his favorable criticism by added encouragement, and communicated to Sully his own arrangement of colors when painting, and the manner he had of using them. He offered advice and recounted his own experience. It is small wonder that Sully retained to the end of his career a warm admiration of Stuart's genius. In some recollections that he jotted down in 1869, and but three years preceding his own death, he takes occasion to vindicate Stuart's memory against certain charges circulated, touching his personal habits.*

Following his Boston visit, and at the instance of his friend Mr. Benjamin Chew Wilcocks, Sully determined to take up his residence in Philadelphia. We can approximate the time through a portrait painted of Mr. Wilcocks' sister, which he began on December 9, 1807.† This

---

*Sully expressed himself to the following effect: " He (Stuart) has been called a man who drank too much, but I never saw him the least disguised by liquor. I have been with him in company, but never witnessed the slightest impropriety." (*Recollections of an Old Painter. Hours at Home*, Vol. X.)

† He did not settle in Philadelphia until the following year (1808), painting the portrait of Miss Wilcocks at his first visit. When coming to Philadelphia from New York at this time he bore the following letter addressed to *Miss Rebecca Gratz* by his friend Washington Irving:

" I hardly need introduce the bearer, Mr. Sully to you, as I trust you recollect him perfectly. He purposes passing the winter in your city, and as he will be ' a mere stranger and sojourner in the land,' I would solicit for him your good graces. He is a gentleman for whom I have a great regard, not merely on account of his professional abilities, which

painting has the distinction of being the first portrait coming from Sully's brush in the opening of his new career in Philadelphia. It was to be followed, as we know, by a succession of portraits, the list of which alone indicates the immense vogue that he gained, and the growing demand, that the features of Philadelphia's loveliest women, and her most distinguished men, should be perpetuated by Thomas Sully's pencil.

Sully was now receiving what in these days seems an almost ludicrously small sum for the work he was doing. Fifty dollars was his regular price for a bust portrait. When the size ran somewhat larger, approaching a half-length, $80 was paid him. Of course he was still a very young man, only now about entering his twenty-fifth year. But as one looks at these early pictures one cannot help envying the fortunate recipients of so much enduring art. After the lapse of more than a hundred years, and in spite of the famous names in portraiture that have emerged in that period of time, they continue, in the opinion of connoisseurs, to rank as among the loveliest counterfeit presentments, to be found either in this country or abroad.

The injury to his art prospects by the Embargo Act, which our readers will recall Sully's allusion to at the close of 1807, necessitated some sacrifice, on his part, and we find him, at the opening of 1808, enenengaging to paint portraits for a list of subscribers at the reduced price of $30 to each sitter. His friends interested themselves in this plan, and Sully's written records show that he painted the portraits of at least 26 sitters on these terms, a " Dr. E. Griffiths" heading the list of those who sat to him in the series of what in the language of the day will be termed "thrift" portraits.

are highly promising, but for his amiable character and engaging manners. I think I cannot render him a favour for which he ought to be more grateful than in introducing him to the notice of yourself and your connections. . . . Excuse the liberty I have taken, and believe me with the warmest friendship. Ever yours,

WASHINGTON IRVING.

NEW YORK, NOV. 4TH, 1807.

A yearning for opportunities of greater improvement had again set it, and in this year Sully looks about for means to visit England, where in London, he feels sure, the surroundings he seeks will not be lacking. It was at this juncture that his Philadelphia friend and patron, Mr. Benjamin Chew Wilcocks, came especially to his aid. This gentleman going about among his intimates secured the adhesion of six sympathizing friends, who with himself agreed to subscribe $200 each towards the proposed journey, and fortunately on terms which enabled Sully to accept of the offer, seeing that he could honorably discharge the debt.

In repayment, it was agreed that Sully should furnish each of the subscribers with a copy of some master, to be painted while in London and shipped at his own expense to Philadelphia. This entire transaction shows Sully in a most favorable light. He might have been very well content to forego all such extraordinary effort. He was, with the powers already at his command, in a position where he could in normal times, feel sure of employment, and, with a reputation that, to one less spurred by the highest ambition, might have seemed sufficient. It is likewise evidence of the regard felt for his capacities, that these gentlemen were willing to encourage him in his more ambitious plans.

It was no light task, however, that he undertook, and when mentioning this period of his life to a friend, his comment was, "I will not dwell upon the slavery I went through nor the close economy used, to enable me to fulfill my engagement; but although habitually industrious, I never passed nine months of such incessant application." This alludes to his experiences in London of which we shall speak in the next chapter.

On the 17th day of May, 1809, by a decree of the Court of Common Pleas of Philadelphia, Thomas Sully was admitted to American citizenship, and in anticipation of his voyage abroad he secured a government passport, bearing date June 3, 1809. On the 10th of June he set sail from the Delaware, and after a voyage just short of five weeks, landed in Liverpool on July 13th (1809).

12

CHAPTER III

SULLY'S alacrity in settling to his task is clearly proven, when we find him in less than two weeks' time setting up his easel in London. He had taken the precaution of arming himself with a number of letters of introduction. To Benjamin West he bore a letter from Mr. Wm. Rawle, of Philadelphia. His experience with the veteran American painter in London, was to prove very much the same as when coming under Gilbert Stuart in Boston. At their very first interview, West remarked, "I can't teach you until I know what you can do. Paint a head and show it to me." So we find, by an entry in Sully's "Register," that already on July 25th he has painted a likeness "Head-size" of his friend and fellow-artist, Charles B. King, "as a specimen to show West." West appears to have detected an indecision on Sully's part in expressing the anatomy of the head, betraying some lack of knowledge of the internal structure. He therefore advised the young painter to study osteology assiduously. Sully was not slow in acting on this valuable advice, and there can be little doubt that his having followed it, played an important part in the marked development shown at the end of his English visit, and when renewing his portrait painting in Philadelphia. His method of study in London was to copy anatomical engravings at night; in addition to which he and his friend King studied from a model hired to stand in their painting room.

Charles B. King, the artist just mentioned, and to whom Sully became greatly attached, was the first person whom Sully had sought out

13

after his arrival in London. King had already been in London some years, and was therefore familiar with art affairs in the English capital, such knowledge proving of great use to Sully. These kindred spirits at once discovered an interchange of sympathy, and therefore agreed to share an apartment between them, and occupy a painting-room together. Long after, Sully, when referring to this episode, remarked, "I resided under the same roof with him (King) and our painting-room was in common during my stay in London ; an intimacy of twenty years enables me to testify to qualities of heart and correctness of conduct rarely equalled for purity or usefulness." *

West had by this time abandoned portrait painting. He had proved himself a very good portrait painter, but apparently historical composition was the form in which he preferred to express himself; and which he conceived stood upon a higher plane than the other. This is brought out very clearly in a letter addressed to Charles Willson Peale at very nearly the same time we are describing. The elder Peale's son Rembrandt was about embarking for France to study painting, and collect the portraits of eminent men. After expressions of kindly interest, West writes: "Although I am friendly to portraying eminent men, I am not friendly to the indiscriminate waste of genius (!) in portrait painting ";† he then goes on to lay particular stress on the young man's approaching opportunity for the study of classical examples in Paris, and to urge his taking advantage of it. He was equally outspoken with Sully, and after re-

---

* This estimable man was a native of Newport, and passed his summers there and his winters in Washington. During a period of forty years his studio at the Capital was filled with the portraits of the political and other celebrities of the day,—not remarkable for artistic superiority, but often curious and valuable as likenesses, especially the Indian portraits. His industry and simple habits enabled him to acquire a handsome competence, and his amiable and exemplary character won him many friends. He died at Washington, D. C., March 18, 1862, at the age of seventy-six. (Henry T. Tuckerman, " Book of the Artists.")

† Gilbert Stuart took the opposite view, saying that " no man ever painted history, if he could obtain employment in *portraits*."

14

marking that he did not paint portraits himself any longer, told him to go about and see what portraits he liked best. From what followed it seems certain that the paintings of Sir Thomas Lawrence particularly attracted Sully. He made this distinguished artist's acquaintance, and was highly pleased at the reception accorded him. His own account gives some interesting details of the interview, and mentions the particular source from which he had secured a letter of introduction. We shall therefore quote Sully's own words :

"A miniature painter named Miles, who used to be in the employ of the Emperor Paul of Russia, upon Paul's death came to America and taught drawing. He gave me a letter (letters?) to a number of painters, among whom was Sir Thomas Lawrence. He received me very warmly on Miles' account, but was too much of a gentleman not to add, 'and on your own also.' So when West said to me, 'I don't paint portraits myself, go about and see whose portraits you like best,' I availed myself of Lawrence's instruction. . . . Lawrence was one of the most finished gentlemen I ever met. . . . He made a good deal of money, but was too generous to grow rich, for if a beggar asked him for five pounds he would give him fifty (!)."

Sir Thomas Lawrence was a great friend of the Kembles, and there are pleasant accounts of that intimacy to be found in Fanny Kemble's "Record of a Girlhood." * Sully himself was later to come into most amicable relations with the spirited author of those biographical Records. She came to the United States in 1832 with her father, Charles Kemble. Sully's portraits of her made at the time of this visit are charming examples. He painted the much fêted and admired young actress in a number of the characters that she assumed on the stage, as "Beatrice," "Bianca," "Juliet," etc., as well as portraying her in the likeness of her natural self. The portrait of her in Shakespeare's "Beatrice" and which

* She pays Lawrence the following compliment apropos of a knowledge of the stage and acting : "Sir Thomas Lawrence is the only unprofessional person I ever heard speak upon it whose critical opinion and judgment seemed to me worth anything."

15

hangs at the Academy of Fine Arts in Philadelphia is probably the most effective of those he painted of her in character. It is the one that Fanny Kemble herself expressed a preference for.

Sully has sometimes been called the "Sir Thomas Lawrence of America" and it is not to be denied that there are enough points of resemblance between the two to suggest such a comparison. The English artist, while painting a goodly number of masculine portraits, and in many instances with marked success, was undoubtedly at his best when portraying the galaxy of lovely women distinguished both by birth and beauty that flocked to his easel during the height of his success.

Sully, in the same way, has no small number of effective portraits of men to his credit. They comprise the likenesses of distinguished soldiers, statesmen, actors and literati, prominent in their day and generation, and many of these portraits are extremely impressive. But his forte lay in delineating the softness and charm of female character.

It may be objected by some of Sully's many admirers that the linking of his name in a comparison with that of Lawrence is not the meed of praise they would seek to have bestowed. Since Lawrence's death, or rather following close upon it, it has been the fashion to detract from his living reputation as a painter. Mrs. Kemble touches upon it in her "Recollections," and while admitting that "of his merit as a painter an unduly favorable estimate was taken during his life," concludes that "since his death his reputation has suffered an undue depreciation." She then goes on to speak in admiration of "his lovely head of Mrs. Nugent, the splendid one of Lady Habberton, and the noble picture of my grandmother" (Mrs. Siddons). Among the male portraits she prefers his likeness of Canning, the portrait of Lord Aberdeen, and of her uncle, John Kemble.

In estimating Lawrence's art, it should be remembered that he succeeded a school of portraiture that perhaps has never been excelled. To tread upon the heels of Gainsborough, Reynolds and Romney, paint contemporaneously with such masters as Raeburn and Hoppner, and yet establish the high reputation that Sir Thomas did, is distinction in itself.

Benjamin West thought highly of Lawrence's art. To a friend who expressed regret that Sir Thomas did not more often employ his time in works similar to his celebrated " Satan " and "less to portraiture", West replied, "Do not confound his pictures with mere portraits; painted as his are they cease to be portraits in the ordinary sense; they rise to the dignity of history . . . his reputation must last as long as the arts shall be valued by mankind." *

Both the English and the American artist felt tenderness toward children and in the happy delineation of childhood Lawrence was thought to excel. Can any question exist as to Thomas Sully's charming accomplishment in the same field? The sprightly smiling faces that he painted with so much tender grace are the very embodiment of innocence and happy childhood. Fortunate indeed are possessors of such canvasses from Sully's brush.

Some idea of the immense zeal shown, and the self-denial practiced by our student while in his English surroundings may be gathered from the following anecdote. It is related that at his first interview with C. B. King, the artist, in London, the latter inquired as to his proposed length of stay, and as to how much money he had brought for the purpose. When Sully answered, "Four hundred dollars," King replied, "Why, my good sir, that is not enough for three months! I'll tell you what. I am not ready to go home, my funds are almost expended, and before I saw you I had been conning a plan to spin them out and give me more time. Can you live low?" "All I want is bread and water," replied Sully. "Oh! then you may live luxuriously, for we will add potatoes and milk to it. It will do! We will live in these rooms, they

---

* Judging by the prices paid now for Lawrence's pictures, West's estimate and prediction are both being realized. His portrait of Miss Farren, afterwards Countess of Derby (in a white silk dress lined with fur), sold at Christie's in London in 1897 for 2415 guineas.

will serve us both. We will buy a stock of potatoes, take in bread and milk daily, and . . . work away like merry fellows." And this they decided bravely to do, and as it turned out, with happy results.

It was through Benjamin West's thoughtfulness that Sully was put in the way of beginning almost immediately, the execution of the copies promised his friends and patrons in Philadelphia. He soon discovered that while permission to *view* private collections of paintings in England might be forthcoming, no opportunity would be granted for *copying* any of the pictures. He then considered the advisability of going to France, where he was told a more liberal spirit prevailed. Before making a decision, however, he thought it well to take Mr. West into his confidence, and it was well that he did so. West showed the greatest sympathy, and is reported to have spoken as follows:

"I understand that your object on your return is portrait painting; then stay in England. You wish to fulfill an engagement and improve yourself by copying some pictures. My collection, old and new, is at your service. There are specimens of the ancient masters and of the moderns. Take them as you want them, and come to me for my advice when you want it."

How nobly the old painter lives up to his reputation of benignity and generosity! By "take them" West actually authorized Sully to carry the picture he might be copying to his own painting room,—an immense advantage, both facilitating and expediting the work he was so anxious to accomplish. After such an experience, it seems but natural that the first picture Sully should undertake to copy would be one from his benefactor's brush. He chose the latter's painting taken from the story of "Pylades and Orestes." This is said to have been Benjamin West's first venture in the special field of composition he had marked out for himself. The picture had attracted much attention and was finally purchased by Sir George Beaumont, who included it in a gift of pictures to the British Government. Dunlap, in 1834, when describing the picture, notes that "there is an admirable copy of it in this country (U. S. A.), painted by Mr. Sully." *

His second work was the "Holy Family" after Correggio, begun in September and finished in October. Then followed a picture which is now in Philadelphia, Raphael's "Madonna della Sedia." It was begun and completed in the month of December. This charmingly executed copy is in the possession of Mrs. Alex. D. Campbell, a daughter of Mr. Benj. Chew Wilcocks, for whom it was painted. This lady is fortunate in the possession of a fair-sized gallery of Thomas Sully's works, which from their variety and excellence form a most attractive collection.

Our untiring artist followed up his Madonna with a copy of Sir Joshua Reynolds' "Holy Family." This was a large canvas, as was the succeeding one, "Telemachus in the Island of Calypso," † after Benjamin West. These last two works were begun in January (1810) but not completed until March 1st and 2nd respectively, or about a week before Sully's sailing from England on his return voyage to America.

He had also executed some half-dozen landscapes on an order from a gentleman in Philadelphia,‡ so that he had kept his promise for the classical copies, and painted these works in addition.

Sully had been abroad nine months ; that is, allowing for the voyage over, he had been able to devote something like eight months to the prosecution of his plan for study and improvement. The reader, we hope, from our recital, will have been able to measure the spirit of ardor and devotion shown. It may be recalled that following the young student's arrival he very soon discovered that the means at his command would not permit of a longer stay than the period just coming to a close. West's letter, already quoted and written to a friend in Philadelphia, foreshadowed the financial difficulties in the way. These obstacles seem

* Exhibited at Pennsylvania Academy of fine Arts in 1811.
† Exhibited at Pennsylvania Academy of Fine Arts in 1811.
‡ Mr. John Coates.

19

only to have had the effect of rousing all Sully's faculties and of filling him with a determination to make even the short period of probation fulfill the expectations of his friends.

Happily we shall find that in none of these hopes were they to be disappointed. He exhibited a marked advance in his art at his return, and the portraits painted in the years that immediately followed, placed him in the very front rank of living portraitists. It was on the 10th of March (1810) that he set sail for home, and he so noted it in his Records. Under what different conditions shall we find him revisiting England when in middle life, to paint his well-known portrait of Queen Victoria in her coronation robes!

CHAPTER IV

TRADITION has it that on Sully's return to Philadelphia he occupied a house jointly with Benjamin Trott, the justly celebrated miniature painter. Doubtless they were intimate, but careful examination fails to discover proof of this reported arrangement.

Sully, before going abroad in 1809, was established at "162 Mulberry Street," afterwards renamed "Arch Street." Following the old numbering on Chestnut Street, this would place his dwelling at 5th and Arch Streets. In that same year (1809) and in the following year (1910) Trott's address appears in the Directory as at the "Corner of 6th and Minor Streets." Sully's address in the last mentioned year is quoted as at "56 South 11th Street." It was doubtless therefore at the latter domicile that we find him resuming his brush, on April 24th, 1810, and painting the bust of a Mr. Dalmatia. He is careful to note that "It is the first on my return to Philadelphia." A month or two later he paints a portrait of Mrs. Dalmatia. (Just who these sitters were we have not discovered.) To Mr. Dalmatia succeeds "Mr. Dwyer, Comedian," showing that the dramatic profession had not forgotten Cooper's earlier protégé. Dwyer was an Irishman, enjoying considerable celebrity, and we find him noted in Wm. B. Wood's "Recollections of the Stage," where he speaks of him as being "much admired."

Then follows a portrait of E. Hudson (Dentist). The latter was an Irishman by birth also, and coming to Philadelphia in 1805, ultimately rose to prominence in his profession. James Gardette was the only dentist of note in the city at that period, so that the field was open to a man of ability, which Hudson soon proved himself to be. The portrait reveals a spirited figure, the countenance bespeaking alertness and force. It would make a good companion picture to the well-known likeness of Dr. Thomas Parke that hangs at the Library Company of Philadelphia, and which Sully painted 12 years later. Dr. Hudson's portrait remains in the possession of a lady descendant, connected through marriage, and residing at Burlington, N. J.

Sully now feels sufficient confidence in his powers to undertake the painting of a whole-length figure. His sitter for this portrait is Wm. B. Wood, the popular actor-manager, in the character of "Charles de Moor," from Schiller's celebrated play of "The Robbers." This painting is in Philadelphia, and we have had recent opportunity for examining it. The scene depicted is the Camp of the Robbers at sunrise. In the foreground is seen the half-recumbent figure of Von Moor, the bandit chief, surrounded by three or four of his satellites, to whom their leader is evidently giving commands. Pistols are at his belt, and the turbaned banditti gathered about him appear intent upon his orders. The coloring is excellent, and the entire composition well carried out.

This play of Schiller's entitled "Die Raüber," was written when its author was but 19 years of age. It had great success in the dramatist's native land, and found favor in other countries in translated form. Here in Philadelphia, in its English translation, it became a favorite play, and was frequently performed.

The dramatic portrait just described was soon to be followed by another, that attracted greater attention, and is still cited with high approval whenever Sully's powers as a portrait painter are under review. This was the likeness, life-size, of George Frederick Cooke in the rôle of Richard III. The coming of this English actor to our shores was an event in theatrical annals, and many anecdotes of his genius, as well as of his eccentricities, have been preserved. While playing many parts, Sir Pertinax in "The Man of the World," being accounted one of his best, among his Shakespearian rôles the character of Richard appears to have found most favor. He had played it abroad with success, and he made his American début in the part. In performing it, as far as costume was concerned, he never resorted to the usual practice of wearing an artificial "mountain on my back," nor "legs of an unequal size," although these personal points are so strongly marked in the text. Wm. B. Wood, in his "Recollections," when discussing the matter, remarks that "his uniform costume while acting in our theatres, is preserved in Sully's fine picture now in the Academy of Fine Arts at Philadelphia." He refers again to the portrait when writing of Cooke's demise in the following year. "The greatest event at this time connected with the Drama . . . was the death of George Frederick Cooke, who died in the City of New York. A special tribute to his extraordinary dramatic genius was considered to be due him. The stage was arrayed in mourning; *and the fine full-length portrait of him by Mr. Sully was exhibited.*"

Some time previously we find Washington Irving writing from Philadelphia to his friend Henry Brevoort in New York about the picture. "Sully has finished a very fine and careful portrait of Cooke, and has begun a full-length picture of him in the character of Richard. This he is to receive $300 for, from the gentlemen of Philadelphia who opened a subscription for the purpose which was filled up in an hour."

Sully has left on record his meeting with Cooke and the impression made upon him by his acting: "I painted Cooke the actor about two weeks after he came to Philadelphia. I made 3 pictures of him—a full-length in the character of Richard III, now in the Philadelphia Academy; one dressed as a gentleman, owned by Mr. Edwin Forrest, and a head which I learn has recently been sold in New York. He was a *bon-vivant* and a wonderful actor. When I first saw him act in Philadelphia it was very difficult to get into the house. In the first scenes I was disappointed, but as the play advanced I grew enthusiastic. Mr. Benjamin

Wilcox was with me, and our seat was a carpenter's horse. When he wanted to applaud he would cry, 'Get off, Sully, get off,' and then he would pound away vigorously with both ends of our seat."

During the next succeeding years, Sully was to paint portraits which for vigor and truthfulness show him at his best. Two of these were painted in 1813, one being a half-length of James Ross of Pennsylvania, now hanging at the Pennsylvania Academy of the Fine Arts, and the other a whole-length of Samuel Coates, President of the Pennsylvania Hospital. The latter was a gift by Sully to this institution, and not, as it has been made to appear elsewhere, for a payment of $400. Sully, in his "Account of Pictures," places a value on it of that amount,* but the Minutes of the Hospital show very clearly that no money payment whatever entered into the transaction; thus:

"At a meeting of a number of the Contributors to the Pennsylvania Hospital, held the third day of the fifth month 1813, it having been stated that Thomas Sully had *presented* to the institution a likeness of Samuel Coates, President of the Board of Managers, the following Resolution being moved and seconded was unanimously adopted:

Resolved, That the thanks of this meeting be communicated to Thomas Sully for his valuable present of a likeness of Sam'l Coates, Prest. of the Board of Managers.

In connection with the full-length picture painted of Commodore Stewart, at this same period, Sully tells an amusing anecdote. After remarking that "As a class, Friends are the most patient sitters, and sailors the most impatient," he continues: "The most patient sailor I ever painted was 'Old Ironsides,' then Capt. Stewart . . . he called to arrange the time for a sitting and was just going away when I said to him, 'But, Captain, you have not told me the size.' 'Oh,' he replied, 'the old woman (his mother) wants me, and she shall have me *altogether.*'"

* As we pointed out in an earlier chapter, Sully invariably placed a *valuation* on everything he painted.

24

We can hardly suppose that DuMaurier laid this anecdote under contribution when relating the career of "Trilby" (!).

Sully's experience when painting Decatur for the municipality of New York was of a very different character, for he notes that "he (Decatur) was a very impatient sitter, although a most gentlemanly man," remarking also that "he had very much of a French face, with a long nose." The portrait has never been regarded as a particularly happy effort of Sully's brush, and this restlessness on the part of Decatur during the sittings may be the explanation for its shortcomings.*

Sully's reputation had now become firmly established, and in the next few years sitters will come to him in increasing numbers. A glance at the list which is a part of this biography will confirm the statement. His income begins to show a gratifying increase, and a calculation of his gains during the next 10 years discloses an average yearly income of four thousand dollars ($4,000). Not wealth, certainly; but enabling the recipient to maintain his family in comfort, while free himself from pecuniary anxieties.

But Sully is not a man to wrap himself up in his own success, and turn his back on others less fortunate.† He has a ready sympathy for aspiring talent, and becomes active in all movements for the promotion of Art and encouragement of those engaged in its practice. He joins the Society formed by a body of artists looking to the development of the then recently established Academy of Fine Arts, and who were associated as "Pennsylvania Academicians." He was shortly after appointed

---

* Not the least interesting of Sully's notes connected with this portrait is the following: "About this time I saw a great deal of Irving. When I had done with Decatur, Irving carried me up to West Point; thence we went to Livingston and there parted. When I went out sketching he used to accompany me, and would employ his time in writing.

† Sully mentions meeting Eichholtz at Lancaster, Pa., in 1809, when the latter was struggling hard to acquire the rudiments of painting, "I gave him during my stay in Lancaster *all the professional information I could impart.*"

to, and served on, a Committee "to organize a system for the management of the Schools of the Academy," and there can be little doubt that his views exercised a controlling influence in any plan adopted.

His readiness to aid and encourage younger artists is exhibited by the generous instruction given young Leslie (C. R.). The latter recounts the incident himself in his Memoirs, and we cannot do better than transcribe his own account of it. "Before I left Philadelphia, Mr. Sully, with whom I had become acquainted, gave me the first lesson I received in oil painting.* He began a copy of a picture in my presence, and then put his palette and brushes into my hand, telling me to proceed in the same way with a copy of my own. The next day he carried his work further, and I again followed him, and so on, until the copies were both finished ; thus explaining to me at once the processes of scumbling, glazing, etc."

This youth to whom Sully showed so much kindness, had through his skill in drawing, and especially by a sketch made of George Frederick Cooke, the actor, attracted the attention of a group of art connoisseurs in Philadelphia. They determined that the embryo artist should be afforded an opportunity for further developing his talents abroad. Under the lead of Samuel T. Bradford, the leading bookseller in the Philadelphia of that day, by whom young Leslie had been employed, a fund was subscribed for the purpose. The distinguished career that came to Leslie, following this start, fully justified the high opinion formed of his capacities.

Before his departure, Sully had playfully rallied him on his entire ignorance of painting in oil, at the same time offering to instruct him. Leslie very gratefully accepted the offer, as we have seen, and expressed so great a sense of obligation that Sully, to lighten the burden, said that he wanted no return except *in kind*, when he should demand it of him. To give Sully's own account, written later in life: "He laughed at this, and ridiculed the idea of his ever teaching me anything. But I knew

* Entry in Sully's Register : " Begun Octr. 4, 12 x 10. Study of an old man's head in the style of Rembrandt, to instruct Charles Leslie in the management of oil colors. Finished Octr. 8th."

where he was going to and assured him I was not joking. . . . When I went to London (this refers to the year 1837, when Sully went to England and painted Queen Victoria) I said, 'Now, Leslie, remember the promise you gave me.' I then made him tell me frankly my leading fault. 'Your pictures look,' he said 'as if you could blow them away.' 'Ah!' I replied, 'you mean that they lack strength?' 'Yes,' said he, 'that is it.' After I had labored on and, as I thought, corrected this fault, I asked him to tell me what other weakness he could see in my painting. He said he had no other suggestion to offer, and bid me go on my own way. Whenever he introduced me abroad, he would say, 'This is the gentleman who taught me how to paint.' He did me many acts of kindness. If I could put in money all the returns poor Charles made me, it would amount to hundreds of dollars."

What has just been related was jotted down when Thomas Sully was very far advanced in years, and long after Leslie had passed away. The anecdote has been given here at some length, for the reason that an impression appears to exist in certain quarters that Leslie had repaid Sully with downright ingratitude. It is evident that Sully himself harbored no feeling of injury as an outgrowth of Leslie's critical remark. Even so sympathetic a writer and admiring a critic as Tuckerman has adverted to Sully's "fairy-like, unsubstantial manner," qualifying this, however, by adding that "there are subjects and sitters to which such a style is exclusively adapted." But as between artists much must be allowed for, and no better proof could be forthcoming than the anecdote that Sully relates himself touching his own criticism of Benjamin West. The latter, having invited him to point out any defects he might see in his painting, Sully did not hesitate to tell the great man that he thought "his outlines were too hard" (!). Here was as outspoken a criticism as Leslie's reported expression, and addressed by one so young to so venerable a master might well have seemed presumptuous; but it was taken in good part, West even taking the trouble to explain that he did it purposely, "as a guide to the engravers," which Sully comments upon as being a mistake in his judgment.

Sully, while essentially identified with portraiture, still adhered to the title of "History and Portrait Painter," apparently adopted when setting up his easel in Philadelphia. In fact, as late as 1829 we find him registered under that title, as also his daughter Jane, afterwards Mrs. Darley. It is not surprising, therefore, to find him putting this title to the proof when an opportunity presented itself.

In the fall of 1818 he was applied to by the Legislature of North Carolina for two full-length portraits of Washington. His reply was, a proposition that, instead of these, he should paint one historical picture representing some prominent action in which General Washington had taken part; and suggesting that the scene should be the crossing of the Delaware for the attack on Trenton.

This offer was accepted, and Sully then wrote asking for information as to the size of the place for which the picture was intended. Not receiving an answer, he proceeded with the work in a canvas of unusual dimensions (actually 17′ 4″ x 12′ 5″). He was engaged for a very considerable time in painting this picture—Dunlap speaks of years—and had the extreme disappointment, after it was finished, of being informed that, owing to its great size, there was no place fitted to receive it, and so the picture was thrown back on his hands. Ultimately he was able to dispose of it for $500, to a frame-maker in Boston, who in turn sold it to the Boston Museum.* This institution ceased to exist in 1892, but we are happy to find that this picture passed into the possession of the Boston Museum of Fine Arts, where quite recently the large canvas has been unrolled, put in order and placed on view.

Another historical piece, finished somewhat earlier, was the "Capture of Major André." It is said to have been painted for Kearney, the engraver, and the supposition followed that an engraving was to have been made from it. This, however, does not appear to have been done. An engraving of the "Washington Crossing the Delaware" was made by W. Humphrys and G. S. Lang, and published in Philadelphia in 1825.

---

* This was the old museum and theatre.

CHAPTER V

A T the opening of the previous chapter we adverted to the localities
in Philadelphia where Sully had carried on his painting, previous
to going abroad, and immediately following his return. Two
years after the latter event, his address has changed to the " Philosophical
Hall ", and here we shall find him pursuing his Art undisturbed for the
next ten years.

The records of the Philosophical Society have aided us in establishing this fact, as well as of noting the relations of goodwill that existed on
the part of the Society and its members towards the subject of our
biography. At a meeting held on March 6, 1812, the question of leasing
certain rooms to Mr. Sully was brought up, and the " Committee was
empowered to execute a lease to Mr. Sully." Apparently this was for
two rooms on the second floor of the building, across from the large room
on the same floor, which has been invariably devoted to the uses of the
Society itself. At the time of which we write, there appear to have been
three rooms occupying the space now taken up by the single large room
on the north side of the second floor. At a meeting held two months
later, the Society is careful to note in its minutes that " The N. E. Room
2nd Story is ordered reserved *for the Society* in lease to Mr. Sully."
The room retained under this limitation appears to have been known as
the " Engravers' Room." Five years later further accommodations in
the Hall are granted the artist. Under date of February 17, 1817, is an
entry to the effect that " Mr. Sully's proposition to lease the unoccupied
rooms is acceded to." These " unoccupied rooms " were undoubtedly

on the first floor, and Sully's object in obtaining them would seem to be made clear through the following advertisement, appearing shortly afterwards :

T. Sully's
Gallery of Pictures
is opened
For the Reception of Visitors
at his Residence in the Philosophical Hall
South Fifth Street
Admittance 25 cents

Just what success attended this venture is not ascertainable. We are rather led to suppose that from a money-making standpoint it did not make a very good return. William Dunlap, journeying south in the autumn of 1819, stopped with Sully for a day or two. He notes that " He was at this time painting his great picture of the crossing of the Delaware and occupied the Philosophical Hall adjoining the State House. . . . He had (built) opened an exhibition gallery with little profit." These were dull times in portrait painting, and Dunlap mentions that Sully told him " he had not had a portrait to paint for Philadelphia since May last."

At this historical and familiar locale our artist was to continue down to the year 1822. A note written in that year indicates that a change was then impending. We quote the letter in full, as besides reflecting Sully's amiable traits ; it shows his delicate sense of obligation towards the fulfillment of any promise made.

* March 26th, 2 O'clock.

N. BIDDLE, ESQ.

Dear Sir : When I called on Mr. Brintinal last Saturday for the purpose of engaging your house in Chestnut St. I had not been allowed to inspect the upper

* On the back of the letter is endorsed, " T. Sully, March 26, 1822."

floor. On visiting it this morning, by appointment for that purpose, I discovered that the front room was so much obscured *by the trees on the opposite side of the street* as to render the light unfit for the purpose.* I am therefore obliged with much disappointment and mortification to decline renting the house.

If I have been the occasion of any injury by my precipitancy, I will most cheerfully make amends. Respectfully,

Yr. Obt. S'v't.

THOS. SULLY.

Not having succeeded in establishing himself on Chestnut Street, as we have just seen, Sully in 1823 and 1824 is to be found at 49 George Street, which address answers to Sansom Street of the present day. In 1825 he has migrated to the corner of Fifth and Minor Streets, while during 1826 and 1827 we find him established at 116 Chestnut Street. This address, under the new system of numbering, introduced a few years later, became 320 Chestnut Street. At the time of Sully's occupancy we find it described as "a fine old-fashioned three-storied brick dwelling— and which had a garden in its rear with outlets upon Hudson's Alley and upon Carpenter's Court."

It is pleasant to reflect that our artist, when relinquishing so agreeable a site, was not compelled to drop back into anything inferior. On the contrary, we shall find that his next move placed him in most congenial surroundings, and that through the consideration and nice feeling of his new landlord, special facilities were provided him for the prosecution of his art. Stephen Girard had acquired property in Chestnut Street, just below Fifth Street, included now in the Lafayette Building, belonging to the Girard Estate. In 1827 he made certain improvements to the property by demolishing some old structures on the Chestnut Street front and erecting on their sites three substantial four-storied brick buildings. Whether the house on Fifth Street afterwards known as 11 South 5th Street was erected at this time, or already stood upon

---

* We see that 100 years ago our city still preserved one feature of a "green country towne."

the ground, seems difficult to determine. One account is to the effect that the house was "specially built for Mr. Sully by Stephen Girard with a suitable painting room, expressly for the purpose in the back part of the house," while the other is to the effect that "the house belonged to Stephen Girard and Girard made alterations in it to suit Mr. Sully's desires." In either event, the arrangement showed a friendly and appreciative regard for the comfort of the artist, and stands out as an agreeable incident in the life of the Merchant-Mariner. When painting the portrait of a Dr. Aitkin, begun on October 24, 1828, Sully is careful to note that it is "1st work in Girard's house." This would seem to settle pretty accurately the time of his having taken possession.

At this abode we shall find that he continued for the remainder of his life; a period of not less than 44 years. The painting-room appears to have been admirably situated and arranged. It has been described as "very large and lofty, lighted by a single window extending from floor to ceiling—which gave the painter a flood of light—regulated by easily adjusted curtains."

There was also in the house an exhibition room. A gentleman still living, who was on intimate terms with the artist and his family during the later period of their occupancy, states that "at the head of the first flight of stairs leading into the back building of the Sully house was the exhibition room, which served also as an anteroom to the studio." In addition to all these interior advantages, exterior ones were not wanting, as there appears to have been a good-sized yard included in the northern portion of the Sully lot, which insured to the studio a good northerly light.*

After the death of Stephen Girard, which occurred in 1831, Mr. Sully's leasehold was continued by the executors as later also by the

---

* This is confirmed through a list of Mr. Girard's property, *filed in 1832*, where occurs the following: "A lot of ground in the east side of Fifth street between Market and Chestnut Streets, north of the property occupied by *Mr. Sully*. *Mr. Sully has the use of this lot for a garden.*"

Commissioners of the estate. There are references from time to time of renewals of the lease, as also changes in the amount of the annual rent. Thus in June, 1842, " Mr. Sully solicits a reduction of rent," and in the same month follows : " Mr. Sully's rent was reduced from $665 to $555 per annum." In 1861, when the Civil War had begun, there was a further reduction to $450 per annum " until better times."

Towards the close of his long tenancy, a gratifying mark of the regard felt for him in the community in which he had so long lived and labored, was the decision by the municipal authorities that certain changes in the City plan, involving the removal or diminution of the premises leased, should be deferred during Thomas Sully's lifetime. This was in 1867, when the building of a large market house (where the Bourse now stands) was about being inaugurated. An ordinance had been passed for the opening of Ranstead Street to the south of the building from Fourth to Fifth Street. This carried with it the necessity of demolishing the house occupied by Mr. Sully. The City Councils were appealed to by influential citizens in support of Mr. Sully's prayer to be left undisturbed in his old home in the closing years of his life. As the artist naively pleaded, referring to his wife and himself, " We shall not trouble you long." * To the lasting credit of City Councils, this appeal was not unheeded, and the width of the street opening at the 5th Street end was so reduced as to leave unscathed and intact the domicile in which Sully was to pass the remaining years of his life.

* There seems to have been something prophetic in this, for *Mrs.* Sully died on July 25th of the same year, and but a few months following her husband's prediction.

33

CHAPTER VI

THE farewell visit paid to the United States in 1824–5 by the Marquis de la Fayette was an event that thrilled and roused to enthusiasm the entire country. Without attempting to minimize the hearty reception accorded the distinguished Frenchman in every part of the Union, it is safe to say that in no other State or city was greater affection shown his person than through the tributes paid him by the inhabitants of Pennsylvania and the citizens of Philadelphia. Preparations to welcome him in the city were promptly set on foot, through a " Committee of Arrangements " appointed by the City Councils. This body began its meetings almost immediately on the announcement of the arrival of General Lafayette upon our shores.

The Committee's first effort was directed towards ascertaining the date at which the distinguished guest might be expected to arrive in Philadelphia. For this purpose two members were delegated to visit New York, where General Lafayette had landed on August 15, 1824. At a formal meeting of the Committee on the morning of August 18, it was stated that, apprehending "the General might arrive unexpectedly in this City", with the concurrence of the Mayor, they had engaged rooms at the Mansion House for the General. The Mayor stated that he had forwarded to the General the invitation and resolutions of this city. At an evening session more exact and reassuring news was brought by Mr. Brown, of the Committee, who stated he had been present in New York at the delivery of the letter from the Mayor of this city to General Lafayette, and that the General contemplated visiting here

34

from the 10th to 15th of September. As it turned out ultimately, the Marquis after landing, made a journey through New York State, traveling as far as Albany, and it was therefore not until towards the latter end of September that he set out from New York on his visit to Philadelphia. The Marquis had desired, on quitting Trenton (N. J.), to travel to Bordentown (N. J.), pass the night at Point Breeze with the Comte de Survilliers (Joseph Bonaparte), and resume his journey on the following morning by steamboat to Bristol (Pa.). The Committee, on the other hand, had planned that he should cross the bridge over the Delaware at Trenton, and be received by the deputations and military escort at Morrisville (Pa.). The following letter confirms the determination of the latter arrangement, and exhibits the amiable disposition shown by the Marquis in yielding to the solicitations of the citizens of Pennsylvania. The letter is addressed to a member of the Committee of Arrangements at Philadelphia by A. H. Brown, representing the Committee.

" *My dear Sir :*

I have just had a private interview with General (La) Fayette, he says he is ready to carry into full effect any arrangement the Committee have or may make. After hearing our arrangement, he says it is very good, and to him pleasing. He is now gone to dinner and will see me again in the morning, he goes to church tomorrow, in the afternoon visits J. Bonaparte, returns to Trenton in the evening, and will be ready for us on Monday morning at 10 o'clock. I have seen Govr. Williamson, he says he will deliver the General to us on Monday morning at whatever place we may designate. I said, on the line of Pennsylvania, he said, that it would be awkward to the General to change from one carriage to another at the bridge, but would accede to any arrangement we pleased to make. Bispham says our quarters are all prepared, the General is at the same house.

Yrs truly
A. A. BROWN.

Saturday evening 6 o'clock."

On the journey from Morrisville to Philadelphia on the following Monday, a stop was made at Frankford, where quarters had been prepared at the Arsenal for the General's suite. The night was spent there, and on the following morning the Marquis proceeded on his march to Philadelphia. The venerable Judge Peters drove over from Belmont and sat beside him in the carriage. It is not our province to record in detail the incidents of the entry into Philadelphia and of the events that followed. We propose rather to pass to an event linking Sully's name with that of the distinguished guest, and to give some account connected with the splendid full-length portrait that still ornaments the building in which the citizens of Philadelphia paid homage to the former trusted and beloved companion-in-arms of General Washington. An opportunity to have his likeness perpetuated through the genius of Thomas Sully was eagerly seized upon, and on October 2nd the following note was addressed to General Lafayette:

" Oct. 2, 1824.

Dear Sir :

A number of our most respectable citizens are desirous of presenting to the city of Philadelphia your portrait by Sully, should you consent to sit for it. This we most respectfully request in their behalf, knowing the very high esteem in which the possession of such a portrait would be held by our fellow-citizens.

Mr. Sully will consult your own time for the purpose both here and else-where. We are, most respectfully,

Your obd't,

J. S. LEWIS
W. RUSH
J. M. SCOTT
A. A. BROWN
JAS. WILMER
BENJ'N TILGHMAN."

To GEN'L LAFAYETTE.

It is stated elsewhere that an original study of Lafayette by Sully was executed at this time in *Philadelphia*. This we are inclined to doubt, and will state our reasons for it. Sully, in his reminiscences, states: "Lafayette I painted from life in *Washington* for the City of Philadelphia," and adding, "He invited me very cordially to visit him in France."

In the request made by the Committee that the General should sit to Sully for his portrait, the concluding lines are to the effect that "Mr. Sully will consult your own time for the purpose *both here and elsewhere.*" The note conveying the request to sit to Sully is dated only 3 days before General Lafayette's departure from Philadelphia, which occurred on October 5th, 1824. It is more than likely, therefore, that with the various engagements and occupations incident to his visit, the General should have preferred to postpone sittings until a time of less stress and demand upon him. It was doubtless with a view of gaining his consent to sit that the Committee worded its request as it did, not making it incumbent upon him to sit at Philadelphia. It seems probable therefore that the study of the head of the Marquis now owned by a gentleman in Philadelphia,* was painted not at Philadelphia but at Washington, D. C.

The history of the full-length portrait is well worth reciting, and more especially as the circumstances surrounding it are more clearly ascertained than heretofore.

Sully's entry in his "Account of Pictures" is to the effect that it was "painted by subscription." He values the painting at $600. The writers have been unable to discover any list of subscribers and further researches lead them to suppose that nothing of a formal character was drawn up. It is probable that the Committee had intended soliciting subscriptions, but that in some way the plan miscarried. Certain it is that the portrait remained under Sully's control for a number of years after it was finished. That the Committee recognized its responsibility, there is evidence in a balance paid over to Sully from funds left after the expenses of the Lafayette Ball. In the account of Henry D. Gilpin, Treasurer, appears the following entry:

*Mr. Herbert Welsh.

37

" Investment of Col. Prevost,
rec'd back & paid to Mr. Sully, $235.68 "

and the following receipt:

" 1827, Feby 21st Rec'd of H. D. Gilpin fifteen dollars and 77 cents, which
with $235.68 stock transferred to me on the 4th of Jan'y
1827, making together $251.45 is in full of the above balance
paid to me by the Managers of the Lafayette Ball, towards
the painting of Gen'l Lafayette.

THOS. SULLY."

Just what the "stock" may have been is not made clear, but as the artist gives his receipt for so much money, the inference would seem to be that it was convertible into cash. This payment of a sum little over $250 is the only evidence of any remuneration having been received by Thomas Sully for the full-length life-size likeness of General Lafayette, now hanging in the Hall of Independence. At a subsequent period he presented the portrait to the Pennsylvania Academy of Fine Arts, and this institution in the year 1848 and with the artist's consent, passed it over to the City of Philadelphia in exchange for a picture by Benjamin West.

Of course the Hall of Independence is its appropriate resting place, and both the Academy and the artist were well advised, when arranging for its transfer there.

It is not surprising to discover evidences of true friendship having been established between the artist and his distinguished sitter; for we shall find this feeling invariably animating those with whom he had to do. We have already alluded to the invitation given Sully by Lafayette to visit him at La Grange, which the former records himself. In a letter from that place of date January 1, 1827, to a correspondent in Washington, the Marquis sends this message: "If Mr. Sully comes to Washington, or when you write, be pleased to mention me very affectionately to him."

CHAPTER VII

Paints a portrait of Judge Hopkinson for Dartmouth College—
   Friendship formed with Fanny Kemble and portraits painted
   of her on her visit to this country with her father, Charles
   Kemble—Paints the latter in character.

WE now approach a period when Sully came to occupy a position of
still greater prominence, and to be recognized as the most eminent
portrait painter in the United States. The year 1827 had witnessed the death of both Gilbert Stuart and Charles Willson Peale. Each
of these had continued practising his art almost until the end. Peale had
been succeeded by his son Rembrandt, while Stuart left no male descendant of his name to succeed him. His daughter Jane studied under him,
and made creditable copies of her father's works. His nephew, Gilbert
Stuart Newton, painted in England and attained considerable reputation.
Henry Inman, born in 1801, was prominent until 1839, while his eccen-
tric but distinguished instructor, John Wesley Jarvis, died in that year.
Other names survived,—Trumbull and Vanderlyn, living respectively
down to 1843 and 1852. But Trumbull, living to a great age, was an
octogenarian when Sully was but in middle life, and Vanderlyn passed
much of his time abroad. John Neagle, in Philadelphia, who had married
Sully's stepdaughter Mary, was recognized as a painter of great merit,
but he never gained the vogue enjoyed by Sully. And so our artist's
gifts as a portrait painter came to be adjudged superior to any of his
contemporaries.

Thus, the authorities of Dartmouth College, when requesting Judge
Joseph Hopkinson to sit for his portrait, pass a resolution reciting as
follows :

" Whereas Steuart (Stuart) has died since the original vote (of Dartmouth College) was passed and whereas Sully is believed in this section of the United States to be unsurpassed by any living artist within reach, I therefore now respectfully inquire—if you will permit the College by their Agent to employ Mr. Sully to paint your portrait.

GEO. C. SHATTUCK.

Boston, Jan'y 4th, 1835."

This same year witnessed his election to membership in the American Philosophical Society. The form of proposal and the names attached to it speak for themselves :

" The undersigned beg leave to recommend as a member of the Society, Thos. Sully, Esq., one of the most distinguished painters of the United States.

CONDY RAGUET

C. N. BANCKER

S. V. MERRICK

HENRY C. CAREY

HARTMAN T. BACHE

CH. D. MEIGS

[Judge] J. K. KANE

JOHN VAUGHAN

ALEX. DALLAS BACHE "

We shall find that not very long after this the most important commission probably of his career was to follow, and that the painting of the young Queen Victoria, from life sittings, marked a summit to his fame, as well as a lasting memorial of his genius. It seems appropriate, and forms a gratifying reflection, that our city is happily linked with this highwater-mark of Sully's genius, through the possession of the portrait by the Society in Philadelphia for whom the commission was originally executed.

So, when, a short time before, the Kembles, father and daughter, arrived on our shores (1832), and came to Philadelphia, it was only natural that Sully's brush should be the one invoked to paint their portraits. Fanny Kemble, in her lively and witty "Recollections", tells of sitting to Sully, and of the sympathetic relations established between the artist and herself. Writing two or three years later from the United States to an intimate friend in England, she comments on his amiability and high sense of honor:

"BRANCHTOWN [near Philadelphia], MAY 27TH, 1835.

*Dearest H————: ***

. . . "I am extremely vexed at all the trouble you and Emily have taken about my picture, for the artist himself, (Mr. Sully of Philadelphia) is not satisfied with it himself, and I am sure would be rather sorry than glad that it was exhibited. That artist is a charming person, and I must tell you how he proceeded about that picture. When your letter came, acknowledging the receipt of it, he asked how you were satisfied. I told him the truth, and what you had written on the subject of the likeness. He did not appear stupidly annoyed, but sorry for your disappointment, and told me that he had been from the first dissatisfied with it as a likeness himself. He pressed upon my acceptance for you, a little melancholy head of me, an admirable and not too much flattered likeness; but as he had given that to his wife, of whom I am very fond, of course I could not deprive her of it, and there the matter rested. But when, some time after some pictures he had painted for us were paid for, he steadfastly refused the price agreed upon for yours, because it had not satisfied him *himself*. He said that had you been even less pleased with it, he should not therefore have refused the money, but his own conscience, he added, bore witness to the truth of your objections, and when that was the case, he invariably acted in the same way and declined to receive payment for what he didn't consider worth it. As he is our friend, we could not press the money upon him, but we have got him to undertake a portrait of Dr. Mease,† and I have added several grains more to my regard for him. As to the likeness, had you seen me about three months after my marriage you would have thought better of it."

* Harriet St. Leger (pronounced Sellenger!)

† Father of Pierce Butler, who married Fanny Kemble, and a man of distinction in the Philadelphia of that day.

In printing this letter Mrs. Kemble comments as follows :

"The portrait in question painted for my friend, and now I believe still at Ardgillan Castle, was one of six painted of me at various times, the best likeness of them all being one that he took of me in the part of Beatrice, for which I did not sit."

Three years later, when addressing the same correspondent, Mrs. Kemble writes :

"Touching my picture, my dearest Harriet, I am desired to say that your spirited defence of your right to it (whether you like it or not) is admirable, that it certainly shall not be taken from you by force, and that there was no intention whatever of infuriating you by the civil proposal that was made to relieve you of it, by sending you a more satisfactory one, under the impression that you are not satisfied with what you have. . . . Sully is now in England. I wish there were any chance of your seeing him, but after remaining there long enough to paint The Queen, he intends visiting Paris for a short time and then returning home.* He is a great friend of mine, and one of the few people here that I find pleasure in associating with. As his delicacy about being paid for the picture arose from the idea that, not being satisfied with the likeness, you probably did not care to keep it, I have no doubt that, the present state of your regard for it being made clear to him, he will not object any more to receiving the price of it.
"Phila., Saturday, March 18, 1838."

The portrait of Fanny Kemble in the character of "Beatrice", hanging at the Academy of Fine Arts in Philadelphia, and the one that she herself preferred to any other of Sully's, reflects all the charm and animation that descriptions of her have sought to convey.

"Ever since Fanny Kemble burst upon the world at the age of twenty she

---

* If there was no meeting with Miss St. Leger, the "dearest Harriet" in the correspondence (which we think there must have been), another friend was more fortunate, for in a letter to "Mrs. Jameson" in London, written from Philadelphia May twenty-seventh, 1838, occurs : "I am glad you like Sully, because I love him."

has been an object of interest to the English Race in both hemispheres. . . . Mrs. Kemble lacked the stature and perfect symmetry of Mrs. Siddons, but she had the noble head, the effulgent eyes, the sensitive mouth and flexible nostrils, the musical voice, the dignified and graceful gestures, which distinguished her Aunt; and in addition, the sense of humor, the mobile temperament quick as flame, the poetic sensibility, which characterized her mother."

So wrote a gentleman in Boston,* recalling the impressions of his youth.

At the time of her American début she was just 23 years of age. She notes it in a letter to her intimate friend, Miss St. Leger:

"Thursday, Nov. 27th.

"This is my birthday—In England always one of the gloomiest days of this gloomy month; here my windows are all open and the warm sun streaming in. . . . I am to-day three and twenty. Where is my life gone to? As the child said, "Where does the light go when the candle is out? . . ."

She seemed to hold a fascination for both young and old. Daniel Webster, writing from Washington to an intimate friend, adds a post-scriptum to this effect:

"Fanny Kemble is here, turning everybody's head. I went to see and hear her, last Eve', and paid for it by a tremendous cold. I hear that the Venerable Judges go constantly."

And in confirmation we find Judge Story writing his wife:

"We have had little to do this week in Court. . . . Having some leisure on our hands, the Chief Justice and myself have devoted some of it to attendance upon the theatre to hear Miss Fannie Kemble, who has been in this City the past week."

A play that she often appeared in, and with which the American

* The late Henry Lee.

43

tour was opened, was Milman's "Fazio", in which her father usually took the title part. Sully painted him in the character, and this portrait also hangs in the Academy. She herself depicted "Bianca," and her grave and anxious air in the picture from Sully's brush forms a striking foil to her smiling and arch "Beatrice." In England, when appearing in the play, she writes of it:

"Next Wednesday week I am to come out in Bianca, in Milman's 'Fazio.' Do you know the play? It is very powerful, and my part is a very powerful one indeed. I have hopes it may succeed greatly. Mr. Warde is to be my Fazio, for, I hear, people object to my having my father's constant support, and wish to see me act alone; what geese, to be sure—I wonder whether they think my father has hold of strings by the means of which he moves my arms and legs".

And on her American tour she writes of the character:

"'Bianca,' which they have everywhere chosen for my opening part; and it is a good one for that purpose, as I generally act and look well in it and it is the sort of play that all sorts of people can comprehend."

John Sartain [the noted engraver], in his "Reminiscences, "* mentions having been present in Sully's studio when Charles Kemble sat to him for the portrait of "Fazio."

"I was introduced to Mr. Kemble in Sully's painting-room, going there by appointment for the purpose. When the sitting was over, Mr. Kemble stepped down from the raised platform and, looking at the picture, remarked that the face appeared large. Sully said, 'You have a large face.' To which Kemble replied, 'Fortunate for me—in my profession.'"

We find an echo of this pronouncement in Ellen Terry's "Story of her Life," where she exclaims, "Once more I reflect that a *face* is the chiefest equipment of the actor."

* "Reminiscences of a Very Old Man," John Sartain, 1808–1897. [D. Appleton & Co., N. Y.]

MEMOIRS OF THOMAS SULLY

Dr. Johnson, in speaking of David Garrick at Mrs. Thrale's house, is quoted as saying, " David, Madam, looks much older than he is ; for his *face* has had double the business of any other man's ; it is never at rest ; when he speaks one minute he has quite a different countenance to what he assumes the next ; I don't believe he ever kept the same look for half an hour together in the whole course of his life ; and such an eternal restless fatiguing play of the muscles must certainly wear out a man's face before its real time."

Charles Kemble spoke from a long experience, when making his semi-playful retort to Sully : " These ' counterfeit presentments ' of the Kembles, father and daughter, arrest the eye of the visitor to the gallery of portraits at the Philadelphia Academy of Fine Arts, and recall their early triumphs here in Philadelphia."

CHAPTER VIII

SECOND VISIT TO ENGLAND—COMMISSIONED BY ST. GEORGE'S SOCIETY TO PAINT A PORTRAIT OF QUEEN VICTORIA FROM LIFE SITTINGS—VOYAGE OVER—ARRIVAL IN LONDON—DELAY IN OBTAINING DESIRED SITTINGS —PAINTS OTHER PORTRAITS—QUEEN CONSENTS TO SIT—PORTRAIT BEGUN FROM LIFE ON MARCH 22ND, 1838.—SOME ACCOUNT OF SITTINGS —PICTURE COMPLETED MAY 15TH—PAINTS A "BISHOP'S HALF-LENGTH" OF THE QUEEN FOR HODGSON & GRAVES—VISITS PARIS, FRANCE— IMPRESSIONS AT LOUVRE AND LUXEMBOURG—RETURNS TO LONDON— SAILS FOR HOME.

IN the full plenitude of his powers, Sully determined to revisit England. Twenty-seven years had elapsed since his experiences as a student in London. Great changes had naturally come about in the English art world. Benjamin West had long since been laid to rest under the dome of St. Paul's Cathedral.* Raeburn, the great Scotch painter, was no more;† and only a few years preceding the time of which we write Sir Thomas Lawrence had been suddenly carried off,‡ when it was reasonable to suppose that a decade at least remained to him for the practice of his art. Sully may possibly have felt that the time was peculiarly propitious for an artist of established reputation to try his fortune at the English capital. Without scrutinizing closely the list of native English painters of that period, it can be safely advanced that beyond one or two names in the field of portraiture, that branch of painting lacked votaries of marked distinction.

On the eve of his proposed voyage, the reputation Sully had already acquired was significantly confirmed through his selection to paint a portrait of the young Queen Victoria, who had just succeeded to the English

* West died in 1820.

† Raeburn died in 1823.

‡ Lawrence died in 1830.

46

throne. The Society of the Sons of St. George in Philadelphia, learning of our artist's intended visit to England, adopted the resolution "to memorialize her Majesty to sit for her picture to Mr. Sully for the gratification and use of the Society." The memorial was couched in most flattering terms towards our artist, reciting as it did: "We have been induced thus to petition your Majesty in consequence of the contemplated departure of Thomas Sully, Esq., for England, whom we beg leave to recommend to your Majesty as the most finished artist in portraits in America, who would do ample justice to your picture, and who combines in himself the various recommendations of being an Englishman by birth, an accomplished artist and a gentleman."

The generally received opinion has been that Sully went to England for no other purpose than the painting of the Queen's portrait. It will be noticed that the trip had been determined upon previously to the commission from the St. George Society.

Our artist was not to travel alone, for after discussion in the home circle it was decided that his daughter Blanche should accompany him. It was a natural choice, for she had ever been his close companion, accompanying him in his walks and rambles about the city and its environs, and her father on that account facetiously used to call her his "walking-stick". We shall find Blanche playing an important part in Sully's English surroundings and contributing in no small degree towards the success of her father's mission abroad.

"Poulson's Advertiser" of October 5, 1837, alludes to our artist's approaching departure: "We understand that our distinguished fellow citizen, Mr. Sully, the artist, is about to visit Europe, having been called thither to paint several portraits of eminent men." We think our modern journalists would have been more alert in ascertaining and noting the commission for the Queen's portrait. On the eve of Sully's departure, friends and admirers in Philadelphia, opened a subscription paper "for the purchase of a memorial of respect and friendship to be presented to Mr. Sully." A sum approximating $300 was promptly raised, Mr. John

Vaughan * being appointed Treasurer of the fund. The names of the subscribers are so representative that we append the list, the original having been found among the papers of the late Nicholas Biddle. Just what form the Committee finally adopted for the memorial we have not been so fortunate as to trace. It may have been decided that the fund raised would be acceptable as a traveling purse, and so presented; but this is only conjecture.

"MEMORIAL TO MR. SULLY.

" The undersigned will pay to Mr. Vaughan as treasurer the sums set opposite their names, for the purchase by the Committee appointed this evening, of a memorial of respect and friendship to be presented to Mr. Sully.

4th Octr. 1837.

Committee :

John Vaughan, Esq.	Jn. Vaughan	$10
Dr. Chapman	R. M. Patterson	10
N. Biddle, Esq.	Wm. Kneass	10
James B. Longacre	Wm. E. Tucker	10
Wm. E. Tucker	J. K. Kane	10
J. K. Kane, Esq.	Willis G. Clark	10
Dr. Patterson	John Neagle	
Willis G. Clark, Esq.	Chas. Toppan	10
Isaac Elllot * $5	James B. Longacre	10
E. Carey	Lawrence Seckel	5
Isaac Lea	R. M. Bird	
C. Gobrecht	R. Maywood	10
W. E. Burton	Jos. Sill, by J. V.	10
Jos. Hirtz (Hirst?)	J. K. Mitchell	10 Pd.
J. Vanderkemp	N. Chapman, by J. V.	10
Dr. Emerson	Jno. Swift	10
D. Paul Brown	C. Chauncey, per J. K. K.	10
Thos. Underwood	Cadw. Evans	10
R. Bald	N. Biddle	10 Paid."

* A prominent citizen of Philadelphia, and Treasurer of the American Philosophical Society from 1791 to 1841, and its Librarian from 1804 down to his death in 1841. See short memoir in Simpson's " Lives of Eminent Philadelphians."

Just before the date fixed for sailing, our artist's younger son, Alfred, born in 1821,* received an appointment to West Point, and the father's pleasure is shown in the following letter, addressed to the then Secretary of War, with whom he was on particularly friendly terms:

" TO HONORABLE JOEL POINSETT : "
Dear Sir :

    I have taken passage with my daughter for London and am to sail on the 10th inst. from New York.

    I cannot leave home without the gratification of returning you my grateful thanks for your kindness in appointing my son on trial as a cadet at West Point. I hope his future good conduct will prove his gratitude for the privilege.

    I pray God bless and prosper you.

Very sincerely your friend and obliged
humble S'v't
THOS. SULLY.

Philada., Oct. 2, 1837."

With these fresh evidences of friendship and regard from his fellow townsmen, and the notification of his son's appointment as a cadet at West Point, it must have been in a happy frame of mind that Sully embarked with his daughter on his English pilgrimage.

Enroute to New York to embark, Blanche in a farewell note to her mother writes : "but before I close this epistle let me tell you we had the satisfaction of having a shake of Horace Binney's hand at the wharf in Burlington, and moreover of seeing Mr. Carey running down the Main Street after our boat had left the wharf."

In after letters written by Blanche Sully and her father, incidents of the voyage are related, and references made to some of the passengers on board the ship " Quebec," Captain Hebard.

---

* Was graduated at West Point in 1841, and served with much distinction. At the close of the Civil War, in which he fought, was brevetted Maj. Genl. of Volunteers and Brigadier Genl. in the regular army. " *Fort Sully*," established in Dakota Territory in 1866 was named for him.

They liked both the ship and the captain, so much so, that their minds were set upon returning in the same vessel if possible.*

Two days before entering the British Channel the ship encountered a heavy gale, but on Nov. 1st, Sully was able to write his wife: "We are at this moment gliding calmly by the Isle of Wight and the mainland—we have a noble vessel and a complete Captain; I wish we could return with him—Blanche is a noble and brave girl; but Oh! how she has suffered with seasickness (for the first week)—we have had pleasant passengers and many we hope to see again."

The next day (Nov. 2nd) Blanche writes: "This morning immediately after our breakfast we assembled our baggage, put it on board the Pilot-Boat and were off before 10 o'clock.—At twelve got into the Stage for London." She describes the beauty of the scenery, stopping at Guilford in the evening for dinner, falling asleep and then "I found myself rumbling over stones—'twas London!—think of it. I thought I was dreaming—but no, the noise and bustle soon convinced me to the contrary—at nine arrived at a splendid hotel called Hatchett's,—took us up stairs into a handsome drawing room—had a fire and by ten another waiter in full dress brought us our tea in great style."

They did not settle themselves at the later address in Marlborough Street until towards the end of the month, for through the medium of that invaluable record which Sully kept we find under date of Nov. 29th (1837) the following entry: "Bust, Miss E. Bates, painted in London at 46 G. Marlborough St." This lady, born June 25, 1820 and christened Elizabeth Anne, was the daughter of Mr. Joshua Bates and his wife Lucretia Sturgis.† Mr. Bates, the father, came from Wareham, Mass., and was for many years a partner in the banking house of Baring Bros. —this daughter Elizabeth was married in England to Sylvain van der

---

* March 24th. Sully notes (in letter) from London having engaged their State Rooms on the "Quebec" for return trip in *August*.

† For these particulars we are indebted to Mrs. Charles Edward Ingersoll (nee Sturgis) of Philadelphia.

Weyer, then Belgian Minister to England, in 1838. Blanche Sully writing from London to her family, communicates "In the evening dressed and went to Mrs. Bates' was introduced to the Belgian Minister, with his star and garter (?), by the way he has the handsomest legs I ever saw." (!) Other entries of portraits painted follow the one of Miss Bates showing that Sully was not idle but employing his time while awaiting the hoped-for opportunity to paint the Queen's portrait from life.

The Memorial drawn up by the St. George's Society had been sealed and delivered into Sully's hands; but when he made application to our Embassy in London for its presentation, he discovered that royal and diplomatic usages forbade the delivery of or receiving of a sealed communication into the hands of the Queen or her representative. Here was a dilemma! Fortunately, our artist had in some way provided himself with a copy of the sealed paper,* and this the American Minister, readily undertook to transmit. It was on Dec. 28th or almost two months following our traveler's arrival in England that notice of a favorable reply to the solicitation embodied in the Memorial of the St. George's Society came to hand. On that day Blanche wrote to her family: "(Thursday) Mr. Jaudon took his first sitting—soon after he went, in popped Mr. Stevenson (U. S. Minister to Court of St. James) to inform us of good news!!! The Queen consents to sit most willingly—think of that! The news came through Lord Melbourne. She is now at Windsor Castle passing the Christmas holidays . . . and as soon as she comes to town she sends word that she'll gratify Mr. Sully."

The intimation received through Lord Melbourne's note was that the first sitting would be granted "in the middle of February" (1838). We find Sully writing his daughter Jane (Mrs. Darley) under date of Feb. 14th: "I have kept this letter open in hope to tell you at its close, that I had begun the Queen's portrait but the day is not yet fixed until

* Sully writes his wife from London in November: "Tell Mr. Sill it was fortunate that he gave me a Copy of the Memorial as otherwise the one intended for the Queen could not have been received, as it was *sealed*."

J S C

after the 'Drawing-Room' but I am told it will be arranged this month" (*February*).

As will appear later, the first sitting actually did not take place until more than a month after this was written, i. e., on March 22nd (1838).

A glance at Victoria's occupations and correspondence at this period will show the demands upon her time, and at the very moment that our artist was endeavoring to obtain sittings, active preparations had begun for the grand ceremony of her coronation, which took place in the June following. But in this matter of obtaining sittings let the artist recount his own story.*

"After I had almost despaired of being able to obtain a sitting, my friend Lord Francis Egerton secured Lord Palmerston's † influence in my behalf. I called early one day on the latter; he had just turned out of his bed and was sipping his morning coffee. 'Everything is being arranged,' he said. 'The Queen will sit to-day at ten.' I found him a delightful person, who reminded me of Henry Clay in his manners. A painting room was arranged for my accommodation in Buckinghan Palace. . . . The Queen came to the sittings with her Secretary, Baroness Lehtzen. She (the Queen) was very affable, like a well-bred lady of Philadelphia or Boston and used to talk about different things. I told her I would get my daughter to sit with the Regalia, if there would be no impropriety, in order to save her the trouble. 'Oh, no, no impropriety,' replied Victoria, 'but don't spare me; if I can be of service, I will sit.' After that my daughter sat with the Regalia, which weighed thirty or forty pounds. The earrings had to be tied with a loop, as I had not allowed her ears to be pierced. One day the Queen sent word that she would come in if my daughter would remain where she was. But of course Blanche stepped down, and the two girls, who were almost the same age, chatted together quite familiarly. . . . Her mouth was always a little open—probably owing to a shortness of the upper lip—and thus I painted

* "Hours at Home," Vol. X [Nov., 1869 to April, 1870].

† We think Lord Melbourne is intended. He was very close to the young Queen, and she was guided by his advice and knowledge of her duties, in this early stage of her career. It was Lord Melbourne who signified Victoria's willingness to sit for her portrait to Sully; communicated through our Minister Mr. Stevenson.

it. But the upper part of her face was very fine, and her eyes, although pro-
tuberant, were beautiful. . . ."

The foregoing appeared when Thomas Sully was a very old man,
and while his memory seems to have served him well, we think our
readers will enjoy the account of two sittings described by our artist
himself in letters to his family, and written at the actual time when the
sittings were taking place:

" Monday (April) 2nd. One o'clock.
Have just returned from the Palace, and sit down to write you all about it.
. . . At nine I received a note from the Baroness Lehzen to say Her Majesty
had commanded her to acquaint me that she would give me a sitting at eleven
o'clock. I answered by the Page in a note that I should be there at ten to pre-
pare myself. Changed my dress and reached the Palace at ten, via cab. I found
my way without help to my quarters in the Palace, set my Palette and all in apple-
pie order long before the Queen entered with the Baroness and a pet dog—a Republican dog! so independent in his taste, that he turned a deaf ear to the Sover-
eign of England when she called the audacious animal to her, in the most endear-
ing terms—and when the whim took him would mount the throne and lay his
head in her lap to be fondled! Two ladies entered by request and that the conversation between them and the Queen might not divert her from the proper
position, they were seated according to my wish close to my right. " Am I seated
properly " said the Queen—" Yes "—I replied " but I am not "—so I removed
my easel. The Tiara that her Majesty had put on was of the most suitable shape
and proportions, and she seemed pleased with my approval and its reason.

" Pray Mr. Sully what have you on that other canvass? "—(the black canvass
I had brought to cover my sketch). The Baroness enquired how it was that Saturday had not been used: " Did I not say that we should expect you then? " I
reminded her that I was to wait until I heard from her the pleasure of the Queen.

" Oh! then I am quite in fault, but the Queen waited for you ever so long."
Her Majesty laughed playfully and good naturedly at the blunder—Thought I,
turn about is fair play—I too have been twice disappointed.* (!)

* Sully here alludes to two postponed sittings after appointments fixed and attendance
on his part at Buckingham Palace.

In her conversation with the ladies, I had a rare opportunity of seeing The Queen throw off all constraint and talk and laugh like a happy girl of thirteen, long! long! may she have that light and happy heart.

In speaking of some lady's personal beauty she used an odd application of term: "very clever eyes." She asked if they knew who was to be presented next Levee. . . . "I cannot give you more than three quarters of an hour this morning Mr. Sully—but on Wednesday I will give you a good long sitting." So I bowed and the Queen left her Chair to look at what I had done. So did the rest—I begged their candid remarks, and I must be allowed to say that they warmly approved my beginning; particularly the mouth which is a nice point to achieve in her portrait. When the Queen and the Baroness had left the Room the ladies remained to look at the picture, and at my earnest request said that the face was rather full and the shadow under the lip rather strong. Put away my things and after some difficulty reached the door of exit—walked directly home and after washing my pencils have written you this long yarn."

"Wednesday 4th (April).

4 o'clock—just returned from Buckingham Palace and I sit down to tell you how I got on.

On entering the Palace, I met the Baroness in going to my room; I told her I had come thus early to get ready—"Quite right" said she, and directed a Page to accompany me. The fire was not kindled nor the room in order, but all was done like magic. In fixing the throne I placed the curtain here and there until I had fixed on the best position for light and shade. Got everything ready and at near 12 Her Majesty entered, attended by the same company—ascended the steps—placed her feet in the foot-muff and observed that I had changed the position—so I explained. She is a good sitter, and continues the same affable and unrestrained manner. But altho she said much to the Ladies and her Secretary the Baroness, I don't remember any remarkable observation. If one might judge by the manner I should conclude that in governing, she will have much her own way. (!) A Page announced the visit of Sir D(avid) Wilkie with his picture of her Majesty's first Council—but he had to wait at least half an hour until my sitting was over. She descended the throne and came 'round and looked at the picture and seemed satisfied. As she approached the door I advanced and opened it, and the next; this I thought I might be allowed, altho' I would not presume to offer any aid in taking or leaving the chair—yet after all she is not a person to be offended with a well-timed and respectful courtesy tho' offered by one not privileged. The Baroness afterward brought me the Royal Crown to paint from, and it kept me busy until past three. She requested when I had done to ring for a Page and send (it) to her as it was her particular care to keep the jewels of the Crown and she would not have anyone meddle with it. . . . The Crown being disposed of, and an appointment made for next Saturday, I left the Palace."

The formal description and title of the painting is to this effect: "Portrait of Her Majesty The Queen in her robes of state ascending the throne in the House of Lords", and this attitude the Philadelphia picture most graphically and gracefully portrays. Sully's daughter Blanche, whose connection with the sittings has been described, related after her father's death that "in response to an inquiry from the Queen why Mr. Sully had painted her ascending the throne instead of seated upon it, he replied that she was too short of stature ; that had she been seated, the draperies would have spoiled the whole effect."

This was a brave statement of fact, as well as an artistic truth ; and the Queen appears to have had too much native good sense to be offended by the reference to her lack of inches.* In fact, Blanche Sully added that "it evidently pleased her, for she presented the artist with two of her autographs."

Of all the various portraits of The Queen painted at the period of this picture or within a few years of it, none, to the writer's mind, conveys an equal queenly grace. Sully's portrayal, without derogating from the dignity expected in the heiress of the British throne, invests the figure with a certain youthful charm of expression that at once enlists sympathy and admiration. Her letters at this time to her uncle, King

---

* That the Queen was not blind to her deficiency in height is made manifest by an entry in her Journal : " I lamented my being so short, which Lord M.—— smiled at, and thought no misfortune." ("Girlhood of Queen Victoria." Conversation with Lord Melbourne at about the date of Sully's visit.)

Leopold of Belgium, reveal a warm and affectionate nature. "My be-loved Uncle," "My dearest Uncle," are her invariable forms in address-ing him; and as showing the affection she inspired in him, he addressed her as "My dearest and most beloved Victoria". It is the reflection of such a nature that Sully has succeeded so admirably in getting on his canvas. What has been written of his art by Tuckerman is brought to mind. "His organization fits him to sympathize with the fair and lovely, rather than the grand and comic.—Sully's forte is the graceful."

Letters written from home exhibit the interest with which our artist's family followed his fortunes abroad. Thomas Sully, Jr.,* his eldest son, then painting portraits himself, writes his sister Blanche:

"I hope now you have both of you been long enough in London to feel less homesick, the first 3 months away is the worst part of it. I should like to know what father is doing. . . . I hope father will paint the Queen."

This was written from Philadelphia on February 1, 1838, and under this date young Sully adds, "and a very cold day."

In April he writes her again:

"Do not hurry home. I hope father will finish the Queen's picture com-pletely in London, to show it there; if living in London has cost him so much, one month more will not hurt him; when of course he is aware of the great bene-fit it will hereafter be to him, as I know that his picture will be the best of them. Robes again I say. Tell him to excuse my impertinence."

The question of costume (robes) here hinted at is emphasized in a letter addressed to his father in the same month:

*Thomas Wilcocks Sully, commonly called "Thomas Sully, Jr.," was born January 3rd, 1811, in Philadelphia and followed his father's profession. He painted with a good deal of ability and had as sitters a number of well-known actors: Wm. E. Burton as Bob Acres; Edwin S. Conner as Romeo; Edwin Forrest, and Robert C. Maywood as Tam O'Shanter were among these. His father was very much attached to him all through his life and did everything possible to encourage him. His health gave way, and he died when in his 36th year. Sully's "Boy with a Torn Hat" (in the Boston Museum) is a likeness of him when 10 years of age.

"I hope you will paint the Queen and in her *robes, of course*, for it will do for a portrait of anybody without them, and we are not used to seeing such things here."

These are the only intimations found that any consideration had ever been given to any different style of portrait than the one Sully actually painted. The subject might have been discussed *en famille*, but we doubt whether any other form of portrait than the one adopted and carried out had ever formed itself in our artist's mind. The head painted of the Queen and now hanging at the Metropolitan Museum in New York City, was begun on March 22nd and completed on May 15th. (From this portrait all the others were produced.) The length of time for its painting is explained by the difficulty encountered for sittings in regular sequence. A hurried note from the Queen's Secretary, given below, throws light on the situation :

"Monday.

"The Baroness Lehtzen presents her compliments to Mr. Sully and hastens to inform him that her Majesty will give Mr. Sully a sitting at ½ p. 12 to-day.

"The note she had written on Saturday was unfortunately not delivered."

The word "immediate" appears with the address of "Sully, Esq., 46 Gt. Marlborough St."

To a man of methodical habits, it must have proved something of a trial to receive but an hour or two's notice for so important an appointment. Social civilities were not wanting; we find among some Sully family papers an invitation addressed :

"Mr. Sully.
Lady Francis Egerton
At Home
Saturday, March 3rd.

Bridgewater House.   ½ past 10 o'clock.

Sully when writing to his wife describes this entertainment:

"At eleven I took a cab and was put down at Bridgewater House. You approach it as to Head's Hotel in 3rd Street—it recedes from the street with the same arrangement for carriages. Two servants assisted me out, and the pavement and portico were carpeted. I passed through a regiment of servants to the attiring room, and from thence up the grand stairway—my name traveling before me from attendant to attendant—Ushered into the Reception Room I soon selected the hostess Lady Egerton and made my bow—her reception of me was most cordial and polite. (Mrs. Rogers formerly Miss Fairman will give you some idea of her face, person and manner.) Lord E(gerton) came up and welcomed me, and I then strolled through the rooms to gaze upon the crowd of visitors; and soon discovered that I was rubbing elbows (with) against the nobles of the land! Princes of the blood, Dukes, Duchesses, and Lords in numbers. Now and then Lord E—— would join me and point out some remarkable personages—'That is the Duke of Wellington, those two ladies to your right the Duchess of Cambridge and of Cumberland—Sir Robert Peel, Lord Brougham—Dacres— Duke of Sussex, etc., etc.' During the evening I was frequently pressed close to Wellington and could follow his conversation—His portraits are generally like— but they make him appear too old. There were some beautiful women there, and as there were many, I think, I might venture to give an opinion on the comparative beauty of the females of the two countries and I should decide that in Phila. we surpass them in face, form and grace.

The immense gallery and five other rooms were thrown open and by twelve o'clock I should judge that there were three hundred persons there—I wish I were able to give you a description of the dresses—I thought them gorgeous and becoming, but those of black velvet pleased me most. Feathers, turbans and diamonds in profusion.

Lady E—— frequently engaged me in conversation about Fanny Butler to whom she seems much attached."

An invitation to dine at Bridgewater House followed the attendance at the Reception.

MEMOIRS OF THOMAS SULLY

" LORD AND LADY FRANCIS EGERTON
request the honor of
MR. SULLY'S
Company at Dinner
On Monday, March 12, ¼ past 7 o'clock."

Of this entertainment Sully writes to his family:

"When about to be seated at the dinner table Lady Egerton called me 'round to her side and I found myself installed between her Ladyship and another fine-looking woman, full of delightful conversation, so that between the two I quite neglected dining." A Mr. Babbage well known to science dined with us— At table Lady E. bent her head close to mine, and said in a mysterious manner: "Perhaps I know more of your movements in London than you dream of "—I thanked her for the honor done me—" I received a note from you addressed to Lady Dacre, and that Lady has received one intended for me—we compared *notes* and found all was right and I learn you are to dine with them next Saturday! "—One of my usual blunders you perceive in addressing a note to the wrong person.

The Garrick Club opened its doors to the visiting artist, electing him an Honorary Member in December, "for the ensuing three months." *

* On his return to the United States, Sully paid his acknowledgments by painting and presenting a portrait of Edwin Forrest to the Club. The following letter attests the Club's appreciation :

" Garrick Club, London,
14 April, 1840.

" *Sir:*
I am desired by the Committee of the Garrick Club to offer you their best acknowledgments for your very handsome present of a portrait of Mr. Edwin Forrest. They also desire me to express the great gratification you have afforded them of adding to their collection the work of so eminent an artist. I have the honour to be,

Sir,
Your very obedient servant,
W. WINSTON, Sec'y.

To THOS. SULLY, ESQ.

Apropos of the social side of life, young Sully, in a letter to his father, writes :

"It is a pity Fanny Butler was not in London when you got there, for Blanche's sake, however, she appears to be very well engaged visiting, but might have shared your treat with you amongst the nobility with Fanny's aid."

After completing the head of the Queen, Sully immediately began, and finished shortly, the very beautiful three-quarter or "Bishop's half-length" for Hodgson & Graves, from which a very charming engraving was produced. This portrait now hangs on the walls of Hertford House (Wallace Collection), having been purchased by Lord Hertford at Christie's Auction Rooms in June, 1855.* It bears the distinction of being the single example of the "American School" contained in this justly celebrated collection of pictures and art objects. A copy made from it is said to hang at Windsor Castle.

This three-quarter length portrait evidently came under notice of the Queen, for Richard Hodgson, of the engraving firm, writes from

"6 Pall Mall, Saturday.

" *My dear sir :*

The Queen was pleased with your picture, but said, 'She expected to have seen you again before you left England,' and if you like even now to postpone your departure, you could, I dare say, see her on Monday, as the picture is to remain at the Palace till Monday; this, however, you must do as you think best; *all I shall require* is to have the benefit of the autograph until your return, as she declined giving her name by stating that you had it already. . . . I enclose you a letter for Messrs. Goupil of Paris, but unfortunately Mr. Graves has gone home without writing the letter for Brussels, but if you have made up your mind to go there, just let me know, and I will send it to you in Paris, and I am

My dear Sir,

Very Truly Yours,

RICHARD HODGSON.

* Note from " Wallace Collection " Catalogue.

P. S.—As the Autograph is really of great importance, pray be so kind as to leave it out and Mr. F. Graves will call for it on Monday morning.

Yrs, R. H."

This refers to the autograph given Sully during the painting of the head portrait.

These two likenesses by Sully of the Queen, viz: the head on a canvas of "kit-cat" size, from life sittings, and the three-quarter length (Bishop's half-length), just described, were the only ones executed in England. The full-length for the St. George's Society was painted at his studio on Fifth Street, Philadelphia, where he began it following his return on September thirtieth, and finished it on January fourteenth, 1839.

Before the Queen's sittings had been arranged for, Sully, *en attendant*, painted four portraits in London. One of these was the likeness of Samuel Jaudon, at that time representing the United States Bank under its Pennsylvania state charter, in London. He also made copies of the celebrated "Strawberry Girl" and the "Girl and Bird", both after Reynolds, from the originals owned by the poet Rogers.

The three-quarter length portrait of Victoria, painted for Hodgson & Graves, was finished on June twenty-fourth. It is probable, therefore, that the Hodgson letter, referring to the portrait being at Buckingham Palace, was written a few days following that date, and on the eve of Sully's departure for Paris.

In the following month he has crossed over to France and guided by his "Notes" we find him in Paris at the Louvre on July 6th, and commenting as follows: "In my first superficial view of the Louvre I was much impressed with the advantage of good color. I could not avoid being most attracted by Rubens notwithstanding his grossness," and when at the Luxembourg—"The Luxembourg Palace has a gallery where specimens of the best French artists are placed. In these works I found great excellence and even when they fail to please it is not through their deficiency in Art, but too great anxiety to show their knowledge." (!)

(A shrewd piece of criticism on Sully's part.) "Horace Vernet however rises superior to all trammels. He is a great *painter* and cultivating as he does the highest walk of Art I consider him according to my experience unrivalled. De La Roche comes next to him but is not so good a colorist. The French artists are accomplished draughtsmen and as every touch of the brush is in a degree drawing, they might be good handlers of paint if they were not so rigid and harsh in their markings."

He is back in London by July 25th and visits Holland House where he notes a very fine portrait of Sterne by Reynolds, adding, "The portrait of Sterne is equal to any portrait I have ever seen by Sir Joshua."

He notes also seeing there the original of "Mrs. Siddons as the Tragic-Muse."

The time of his departure is at hand however and the Comte de Survilliers (Joseph Bonaparte) then in London writes his friend Joseph Hopkinson in Philadelphia under date of July 24th: "I do not want Mr. Sully to leave without telling you that he has had great success in this country" (England).* We think the word "success" means not only artistic success but refers as well to the recognition of his personal qualities. Letters of Blanche and her father to the home circle show the many doors that were opened to them, and the cordial relations invariably established between them and their new-found friends. There was a manly sincerity about Sully, accompanied as it was by great modesty, and a readiness to appreciate the labors of others, that could not fail to attract. We find him on most pleasant terms with the circle of British artists in London, visiting at their studios and interchanging calls.

He speaks in high terms of Sir M. A. Shee's art. Of David Wilkie he writes: "Wilkie charmed me; not more in his simple unaffected kindness of manner than in his noble and exquisite works." †

"Blanche Sully writes her family: "We have just had a visit from

---

* Joseph Bonaparte had visited and dined him in London.
† Letter to John Neagle dated "London, Nov. 22, 1837."

Sir David Wilkie, really he is a delightful man ; Jane, I can hardly describe him ; he is a mixture of Walter Scott and Mr. McMurtrie,* not so heavy as the former, nor quite so dignified as the latter—speaks quite Scotchy, has eyebrows shaped something like father's, but reddish, sandy hair—no beauty, yet that good quiet look of Scott."

A breakfast with the poet Rogers is mentioned in one of Sully's letters, and of whose house he writes: "a precious mansion every part of which seems stocked with valuable relics of Art, Science and Taste." He dines with John Murray the noted publisher, meeting at his table John Smith of the "Rejected Addresses," described as "an elderly, pale and large gentleman," Thos. Moore and Edward Landseer. . . . "Moore although unwell, showed himself to be that joyous, sparkling mortal, I have always thought him to be ; his wit, his short stories were so pat to the occasion, and the cause of wit in others, that he proved to be the soul of the company." . . . On a later occasion father and daughter dine and pass an evening with the same host, meeting Lockhart. Blanche writes of it : "Went to Mr. Murray's to dine, there we had the honor of meeting *the* Mr. Lockhart. It was some time before I could realize it for I had pictured Mr. L. rather an old man but he is youngish and somewhat handsome, very entertaining, and of course highly intellectual."

With these glimpses of the wide social intercourse enjoyed by Blanche and her father during their London sojourn, we bring this portion of our story to an end.

The homeward voyage was undertaken in the early part of August, and we shall find Sully returned and at work in his studio in Philadelphia at the end of September, where, from the life studies made of the Queen, he began his full-length portrait of her on September thirtieth, 1838. Before its completion, a misunderstanding arose between the Society and

*James McMurtrie (1784–1854), an early patron of Art residing in Philadelphia. On intimate terms with the artist Henry Inman.

Mr. Sully. The former took the ground that their ownership in the portrait of Queen Victoria was of such a nature that the artist was precluded from exhibiting it before delivery, or of painting any second picture of a similar character. To this view Mr. Sully strenuously objected. The question had been raised from the circumstance that, when visiting our artist's studio, the Committee from the St. George's Society had found there a replica of the full-length picture under way, and which Mr. Sully frankly stated was for his own use. The upshot of this state of things was the bringing of a bill by the Society, praying the Supreme Court to issue an injunction to restrain any exhibition of their portrait before its delivery, and to prevent any replica being made of it. Following the granting of a preliminary injunction, Mr. Sully's answer and motion for a dissolution of the injunction was duly filed. In his answer he maintained that he was not going beyond his rights, according to the received custom of artists, both in Philadelphia and elsewhere. Before the motion was argued, and by agreement of counsel, the question involved in the Bill and Answer were submitted for arbitration and settlement to three of the most distinguished members of the Bar of Philadelphia: the gentlemen chosen being Messrs. Horace Binney, William Rawle and Thomas I. Wharton.

After an examination of witnesses and argument by counsel on both sides, Messrs. Binney and Rawle signed an award, in which they found in favor of Mr. Sully on the question of his right to paint and retain a replica of the Queen's portrait.* The right to exhibit before delivery was not passed upon. That the artist was free from any mercenary motive is clearly shown by the fact that not long afterwards the replica he painted was presented by himself to the St. Andrew's Society of Charleston, S. C., in recognition of civilities, etc., shown him. Curiously

---

*Mr. Thomas I. Wharton filed a dissenting opinion, holding that while the artist had a right to retain his studies and sketches with freedom to use or dispose of them, he did not think that the said artist had the right " to combine them so as to assume exactly the same figure without infringing the rights of the owners of the original."

enough, while the valuation of the London three-quarter length portrait is put down in his Register at $1,000,* as also the one painted for the St. George's Society, these being the figures he obtained, the portrait forwarded to the Charleston Society is entered at a valuation of $2,000. It seems to us that Sully's revised valuation was much nearer the mark.

---

* The portrait painted for the St. George's Society was exhibited soon after by the Society in New York, Boston, Montreal, Quebec, New Orleans, etc., producing a considerable revenue for the charitable funds of the organization.

CHAPTER IX

IT has been hinted at by the writer of an earlier biographical notice that while Thomas Sully's career was not precisely meteoric in character, nevertheless that his genius suffered an eclipse after the lapse of something like twenty years. How so distorted a view could be adopted we are at a loss to understand. It is true that some of his best brush work was done following his return from England in 1810, but on the other hand he is found producing portraits of the highest merit, following his second visit in 1837–38. His prestige was probably as great in the years between 1830 and 1840 as in any period of his career; and that this fame was well deserved, the canvasses dating from that decade are eloquent proof. Our judgment is that for a period of thirty years at least his powers remained undiminished; and that after that length of time, the change was so gradual that portraits coming from his hand continued to possess a charm of coloring and a grace of outline, distinguishing them unmistakably from contemporaneous canvasses.

Portraits painted in 1857, when Sully was entering his 75th year, exhibit much of his former art—desirable portraits still—and five years later (!) he is sought to paint likenesses of childhood and youth. For an artist to be singled out at 80 years of age by people of culture and means to paint likenesses of their children is as remarkable as it is rare.

With advancing years it is evident that our artist sought to concentrate his energies on the single pursuit of his art. In 1831, after fifteen years' service as a Director of the Pennsylvania Academy of Fine Arts, he tenders his resignation. A very flattering request from its President to continue on the Board he feels constrained to decline.*

In 1834 we find his son-in-law, John Neagle, urging him very strongly to head a newly-formed association of artists, afterwards known as the "Artists' Fund Society." Neagle writes to Sully:

". . . The reputation which you have so deservedly acquired at the summit of professional excellence fully authorizes my solicitation, and I trust that it will not be denied. . . . I am aware of your disinclination to mingle with the business transactions of a society, but what we desire is the influence of your name and approbation, not undivided attention to the ordinary duties and drudgery of office."

Gratifying, doubtless, as were these evidences of confidence and regard, Sully is not swerved from his determination when once formed. The wording of his reply to his son-in-law we can only surmise, but that he was prompt (as usual) in acting on a decision arrived at an endorsement on the Neagle letter illustrates:

"J. Neagle, Esq., on subject of Association of Artists, Septr. 7th, 1834. Answered Septr. 7th."

It is possible that Sully in his reply may have suggested or even urged Neagle to take upon himself the reins of office. At any rate, that is what occurred, for in the following year at the establishment of the "Artists' Fund Society" we find John Neagle occupying the office of President. He remained at its head for eight years (1835–1843). That Sully was prudent in his resolve was justified by after events; for, less than two years following the formation of the Society there was a bitter

* See Appendix for letters passing between Jos. Hopkinson, Prest., and Thomas Sully, touching his resignation.

quarrel between a contentious member and the recently elected President.

Another invitation, however, to assume important official duties was still in store for Sully. In 1842, following the death of Joseph Hopkinson, who had long served the Pennsylvania Academy of Fine Arts as its distinguished President, that body proceeded to elect Thomas Sully to the vacant office. Sully, when declining the honor—expressed in very graceful terms—adverted to his resolution "to avoid all situations of official rank." *

A reference to Sully's supposed gains during his long career seems appropriate at this point.

Elsewhere it has been advanced that, based upon a supposed sum total received, he had enjoyed an average annual income of something over $3500, which the writer of the article concludes to have been "a very comfortable income for the greater part of his life, during the period he lived." A careful examination of Sully's entries in his "Account of Pictures" proves the foregoing calculation to have been founded upon the *valuations* placed by the artist himself upon his canvasses; and not, it is to be observed, on the actual receipts in payment therefor. An illustration or two will make this clear. In the year of his painting Queen Victoria, he enters a valuation of five hundred dollars ($500) for the portrait (head size) painted at Buckingham Palace, and of two thousand dollars ($2000) for the full-length replica of the picture painted for the St. George's Society. In neither instance did he receive any money for these paintings. The first mentioned portrait of the Queen he kept during his entire lifetime. It is the one inherited by his daughter, Mrs. Darley, and now hanging in the Metropolitan Museum of Art, New York City. As to the larger picture, valued at *two thousand dollars*, he *presented* this later to the St. Andrews' Society of Charleston, S. C. An earlier instance is the portrait of General Lafayette, which we have shown

* See Appendix for correspondence.

to have been valued at six hundred dollars ($600) by the artist (a most moderate valuation) and for which he never appears to have been paid more than two hundred and fifty ($250) dollars.

Sully kept a separate book to which he invariably referred, for " Cash received." Unfortunately this book has not been preserved ; at least we do not know of its whereabouts, if it is still intact. We are, however, fully convinced, from the system he followed, that a very considerable reduction should be made in the estimated grand total of his actual earnings. Following the *valuation* figures as has been done in the estimate made by the writer previously referred to, these amounted to nearly $247,000 (two hundred and forty-seven thousand dollars); a resultant average annual income of $3500. We believe this estimate much beyond the actual facts, when the method of calculation is looked into.

One thing, however, stands out clearly on the record, and that is our artist's indefatigable industry. Our catalogue numbers 2600 works of all kinds, or an average of 37 for each year that he painted. Had Thomas Sully in the United States received anything like the remuneration for his art which Sir Thomas Lawrence did at the same period in England,* he would beyond a doubt have accumulated a handsome competence for his declining years. As it was, even with all his industry and careful living there was little left to be set aside "for a rainy day." A letter written in 1843 to his son Alfred, then serving as Lieutenant (U. S. A.) and stationed at Sackett's Harbor, N. Y., reveals something of this :

"I will give you a general account of how I stand at present, from which you will perceive that with all my management, I shall only be able to save a small pittance for your sisters when I die ; but they will

* As early as 1806 Lawrence was paid 50 guineas—$250 for his small (head-size) portraits ; in 1810 his price was 100 guineas—$500. In 1820 (ten years previous to his death) this figure was advanced to 200 guineas—$1000. His price for larger portraits rose in proportion : £420 for a half-length, £630 for a full length. Lord Gower paid Lawrence 1500 guineas for his fine portrait of his wife and child, and 600 guineas was paid by Lord Durham for his portrait of Master Lambton.

have to depend chiefly on their own industry for support." He goes on to speak of certain losses through bank failures, amounting to five thousand ($5000) dollars, mentions having loaned out $6500 (sixty-five hundred dollars) through Henry Darley, "returnable next November with interest," and then follows: "I have an insurance on my life for one thousand dollars and property in paintings at least worth one more. Thus you are in possession of all my expectations." He is able to add, however, "In the meantime I *owe not one dollar*, and have a few hundred lying in the bank for any exigence. Add to these good things the blessings of excellent health and troops of friends, and I think I have no right to complain. At your time of life this statement is due. When I go, your sisters will depend on you and your brother (Thomas, Jr.) for advice and confidences, and I feel confident that they will not be disappointed."

What a charming picture of the affectionate relations existing between father and son! Sully's domestic circle was a never-failing source of affectionate concern to him, and its members always appear to have been bound together by ties of warmest sympathy.

During his long life he was to suffer many bereavements—at times following close upon each other. In 1845 died his step-daughter Mary Chester Sully, who had married John Neagle the artist in 1826. Sully was much attached to her, as also to her children. She is often mentioned under the pet-name of "Moggy." A harder blow followed in 1847 when both his son Thomas Wilcocks (usually spoken of as Thomas Sully, Jr.) and a daughter Rosalie Kemble passed away within a few months of each other.

The letter which follows was written the year following these mournful events, and there is a reference to them.* We are introducing it however more particularly as picturing the later period of Sully's life; it reflects his outlook on life at that time, and exhibits his amiability of

* For use of this letter we are indebted to Mr. Jos. T. Kinsley of Philadelphia.

character. There are touches of humor, and a very natural outburst of indignation at the close, for what he rated a mean performance. The letter is evidently written to his brother-in-law, Prof. Porcher of S. C., married to his sister Harriet, and who were living at Charleston, S. C.

Philada., March 11, 1848, Saturday.

I am now seated at our round table with the women-folk who are sewing and of course talking; so if I make some blunders in this letter you will make due allowance.

Sweep your chimnies.

I suppose you have insured your house? but are you aware that if your house was burnt by the chimney taking fire, and it was ascertained that you had not caused it to be cleaned at the lawful time you would forfeit your insurance? Your letter came to us yesterday. We should have been very anxious about you but that we occasionally heard of you by one of our neighbors, who corresponds with Miss Cheesborough of your city. I would have written but as Walter Scott says, "I am like a ghost who always waits to be spoken to first."

. . . You mention an unpleasant winter. We have had the warmest weather that has been known for 20 years, and it is feared that ice will be scarce next summer.*

* * * * * * * *

Pray don't plague yourself with the Harper money. I have long ago made up my mind to give it up. I wish it were all that I have lost. It sometimes vexes me to think that I have worked for every dollar that I claim and have been defrauded of upwards of Ten thousand Dollars.† I have been desirous of making enough for old age or infirmity, but that is out of the question now. My present hope is to earn enough to leave the female part of my family enough with care and a little industry on their part to "keep the wolf from the door," and one or two successful winters would enable me to do so. I could not leave home this last winter, the family were too depressed by our recent loss.‡ I am encouraged to visit Savannah next winter. But I will not determine until next summer is over.

* How familiar a prognostication to the Philadelphia consumer of a later day.

† This doubtless refers to some unfortunate investments.

‡ The death of Thomas Sully, Jr., in the previous year, as also his daughter Rosalie.

71

We will send you our copy of Capt. Henry's Mexico, by the first conveyance.

What a contrast the last winter must have been to Mrs. Chadwick when compared to the one previously passed in Europe! It must have deen dull, particularly so to Henry. Yet, notwithstanding all the fine things which books and travelers tell of foreign parts; there are pains, anxieties and inconveniences not put down in the account which would quite balance the pleasure. Henceforth, I shall be satisfied to hear, and read of travels.

Mr. and Mrs. Wake are delightful people, especially Mrs. Wake. Please give Blanch's and my sincere regards to them.

Mrs. Gilman * has dedicated the *second* volume of her late work to me, and an order to her bookseller in N. Y. to deliver it to me; but Felix Darley who presented the order, has brought me home the *first* volume. But I will soon have it changed.

You ask me my plans for the coming Summer. In June, I have promised to visit Providence for the purpose of varnishing the pictures I painted there last year. I will endeavor to take Blanch with me. If I am employed I may remain there during the warm weather. I have lately received a letter from Yale College of New Haven to know my prices, as they desire to have a portrait of one of their Professors. If they conclude to select me as the painter, I shall go there after a short visit to Providence. I must seek for business this coming summer, as [the] last year has been a very expensive one. By the way, I have paid all the debts of poor Tom that I could hear of.

Alfred is yet in Burlington recruiting Soldiers for the Army. But as we are to have peace † (thank God) he will perhaps be ordered to some garrison fort as he was fixed formerly, but in what part of the country I cannot guess. He is in good health and as his expenses are but light, he is enabled to save money, and has remitted to me from time to time $500, which I have invested for him. All this I believe is greatly owing to Jane, who has perseveringly prayed him to save money. If he continues in this practice he will eventually provide against a " rainy day."

* Mrs. Caroline Gilman, née Howard, of Boston, Mass., distinguished authoress, wrote " Recollections of a Southern Matron", " Poetry of Traveling," etc., etc. Married Rev. Saml. S. Gilman, D. D., pastor of Unitarian Church, Charleston, S. C.

† With Mexico.

Blanch is not so strong to take long walks as she used to be, but except for a touch of indigestion, her health is good. She is at present much taken up with a young friend of hers who is about to be married, Martha Berg, the only daughter of a most amiable woman, that we have long been acquainted with, who has all her life struggled with poverty. The gentleman whom she is engaged to is an excellent man, and very rich, so that at least one evil will be put away.

Sally as usual continues ministering to the wants of others and fidgeting at home. I think Sarah (Mrs. Sully) has become still more anxious for the comfort of animals. The notice that a dog or horse is ill-treated in the neighborhood will quite destroy her tranquility. Jane has lately been called upon to take some portraits. She is always ready to receive an order to paint. I think she paints better than she ever did, perhaps it may be because her health is firmer. Darley battles along but no doubt he has plenty of difficulty.

Chip has grown to 5 ft. 5½ inches (remember that 5 ft. 9 inches is the common height of personable men). He is but little over 12 years. . . . He seems to have much talent for music, no doubt will be a professional musician. . . .*

So Chester has removed to New Orleans! It will give him a better field for industry and adventure, but will the summer suit his family? We are pleased and surprised that Annita is about to be married. I hope it may be a proper match. . . . Has Fraser told you how Mr. Saunders, the miniature painter, has mended? . . .

We hear regularly from Wheeler,† and all things go on prosperously with them. We expect a visit from them next summer.

The lease of Mr. Earle's house has expired and he has determined to give up business and retire. Of course he will sell off his stock next April and I intend to sell all the pictures I have in his Gallery.

Dr. Hewson is dead. He has been our physician and good friend these thirty years.

* This paragraph must refer to the late Francis Thomas Sully Darley, the artist's grandson. As may be recalled, he was a man of large physique and became distinguished as an organist.

† Col. John Hill Wheeler, of North Carolina, married the artist's daughter Ellen.

73

The landlord of the property adjoining my painting-window had given leave to his tenant to build against me; which would have destroyed my light and would have obliged me to move. On my expostulating with him on the subject he has requested his tenant to construct the building a few feet to the left, it being a matter of perfect indifference to them where it should be constructed on the premises, but the landlord, Mr. Sheaf, bargained with me that I should for that accommodation paint his portrait.* I have long been persuaded from experience that the world in which we live is made up of a few just men, a portion also of Fools and the balance of knaves who prey upon the fools.

The usual quiet of our city has been broken in upon by the visit of Mr. Clay and the funeral of Adams.† Dr. Chapman, a notorious punster as well as an excellent physician, was deputed to be with Clay on the day of his reception of Ladies' visits. The Doctor observing that his hair was tumbled about insisted upon restoring it to order before the company came, and taking his comb from his side pocket, he adjusted the disordered hair of Mr. Clay, saying, " There, sir, now you look comb-ly." !

All round the table send their love to you and Harriet and the household.

Always Yr's

THOS. SULLY.

I am painting a large half-length of Prof. Chapman for the University.‡

* Sully painted a Mr. Sheaf in 1804 and Mrs. Sheaf in 1814—too early to be connected with this anecdote.

† John Quincy Adams died Feby. 23, 1848.

‡ Painted for Dr. Chapman's class of students in that year. Portrait now hangs in "Medical Hall," University of Pennsylvania.

CONCLUSION

WHEN beginning this biography, we expressed the view that the period lending itself best to description was from the outset of Sully's active career as a portrait painter, and for the next succeeding forty years. We have endeavored to trace as faithfully as possible (allowing for the distance of time) the events of those years. The reader, we feel convinced, will realize as we do, that it was through no adventitious aid that Thomas Sully achieved his high reputation. Writing to his son Alfred, who afterwards rose to prominent military rank, he remarks, "How true it is that we make our own fortunes ; talent, money, nothing will do without regular habits and industry ; these my dear boy you have and I have no fear on your account". When speaking of a fellow artist of acknowledged genius, he notes that he was "Capricious, and never would paint unless he was in the humor, although the way is to begin and the humor will come afterwards". The cardinal principles of industry and punctuality were so ingrained in Sully's nature that sitters coming to him were not put off or disappointed as so often happens, perhaps especially when the Artist has gained great celebrity. We read of Sir Thomas Lawrence's procrastinations and Gilbert Stuart's delays. Not so with Sully ; a promise made or an engagement entered into is to be fulfilled at all costs. The integrity of the man is on a level with his genius ; and as a consequence, he rings true at every stage of his career. While surviving to a great age, Sully was spared many of the bodily infirmities that usually accompany it. He had always been of an active habit and continued to take regular walks down to a very late period of his life. Tuckerman* describes a visit paid him at his Studio

---

* " Book of the Artists ", by Henry T. Tuckerman.

not many years previous to his decease: "The veteran was found working diligently at his Easel.* During a half-hour's conversation, Mr. Sully exhibited a wonderful richness of anecdote and observation, nor did his memory seem to be seriously impaired."

A gentleman,† still living in our midst, has recently put on record his recollections of the Artist, his home, and family circle. Naturally these recollections deal with Mr. Sully's later years. When referring to his painting room and the preparation of colors, for which the artist was noted, he remarks: "Now this implied labor, manual labor, involving the expenditure of considerable energy; and I remember that the work required in the preparation of *white* was especially arduous because Mr. Sully in his advanced years while preparing other colors gave up making *white* because of his failing strength". Continuing he narrates, "Mr. Sully always delightful in any society was especially charming in his Studio. To be with him in his Studio, when he was not at work and was in a talking mood was a rare privilege. He was full of recollections of the great men of the early days of our land." Here we find the capacity for social intercourse still happily preserved, following a full use of all the faculties. The same gentleman goes on to comment on Sully's tastes, and in passing notes his inability to appreciate Milton. "He simply could not enjoy Milton, and being one of the most honest men who ever lived he could not pretend to enjoy the sublime poet." Sully is in good company on this point. In a book describing "Some Aspects of Thackeray," by Lewis Melville, we read: "For instance while as a matter of course he (Thackeray) admitted that Milton was a great poet he added that 'he was such a bore that no one could read him' (!). What makes the comparison particularly applicable in this case is that the author of the book referred to exclaims as does Mr. Sully's biographer, "What-

---

* Now preserved in the Board Room at the Pennsylvania Academy of Fine Arts, having been presented to that institution by Garrett C. Neagle.

† Henry Budd, Esq. "Thomas Sully," a paper read before the Historical Society of Pennsylvania, January 14, 1918.

ever one may think of the discernment of a man who says that, it is impossible to doubt his honesty."

The writer of this memoir can very distinctly recall Mr. Sully accompanied by his ever faithful Blanche, walking about the streets of our city. This was about 1861–62—ten years before his decease, but he was even then almost an octogenarian (born in 1783). The description of his appearance at that time given by Mr. Budd in his very charming address already cited: "Wearing his well-known great coat with large fur cuffs and collar, and always wearing a high silk hat" fits precisely with the writer's recollection. Although but a boy at the time, there remains very vividly with him, the memory of a spare, slightly stooping yet dignified figure, costumed as just described, with a woman of sprightly mien (Blanche Sully) hovering protectingly by his side.

Mrs. Sully pre-deceased her husband by a little over five years, so that towards the last it was Blanche who ministered to her father. Any memorial of the Artist must include mention of that bright spirit who accompanied him so unfalteringly through life. Less endowed apparently than the other members of the family with a capacity for Art,* her interests and affections seem always to have centered on her father. Early in life we find her the companion of his accustomed rambles afoot. Afterwards she accompanied him to England and proved herself of the greatest service to the Artist in his new surroundings. Always at her father's side, she shares his sorrows and his joys, finally becoming the comfort and solace of his declining years. She was the apple of his eye and merited the affection he always felt for her. When the parting came, the separation must have meant much to gentle Blanche. She survived her father twenty-six years, living down to 1898, when at the age of eighty-four she also passed away.

We have already related how Sully was left in undisturbed posses-

* Allusion is to the capacity for execution. The other daughters, notably Jane (Mrs. Darley) all possessed this faculty.

sion of Girard's house in Fifth Street above Chestnut Street, and where he lived continuously for something like forty-five years. Here his death occurred on November 5th, 1872. The obsequies were conducted from the house, and a description of the closing scene is given by one who was present and entered an account of it in his diary : " November 9th—went to Mr. Sully's funeral. It had originally been intended that it should be strictly private, but it seems that it was not possible to keep it perfectly quiet and accordingly quite a number came to the house. Very few, however, went to the grounds, probably only the invited ones. The old Gentleman was laid out in his painting room. It seemed peculiarly fitting that he should be. From what other place should he start for his last earthly home? The suffering he had been through had left some marks upon his face, but, on the whole, he seemed calm as he lay there surrounded by his utensils, the picture half finished on the easel, where he had probably left it when he became unable to paint more. Dear old Man, he is gone, a perfect gentleman, a thorougly pure, good, noble man ".*

Not long ago the writer of this biography, on a summer's day, entered the main gates of the cemetery at Laurel Hill and made his way to where lie so many of the Sully name. A very simple head-stone marks the resting place of the Artist and his wife, while all about them are the graves of their children. The burial lot is situated at about the center of the main cemetery † on slightly rising ground, with open views on all sides. It is indeed a "beautiful resting place," as some one writing of it has remarked, and its unpretentious character throughout makes a strong appeal to the feelings. As the writer moved about among the simple headstones and read their inscriptions, the spirit of the united affections of those lying beneath seemed to hover about the place and make it doubly sacred.

* This mention is made in Mr. Budd's printed address on Thomas Sully. We are inclined to think from its sympathetic tone that Mr. Budd himself may have been the writer in the diary mentioned.

† Section A, Lot No. 41, in name of Thomas Sully.

MEMOIRS OF THOMAS SULLY

It is something of a reproach that here in Philadelphia no memorial to Thomas Sully's memory of a public character seems ever to have been proposed. Recently a tablet commemorating Gilbert Stuart's genius on the site of his former studio, has been placed on the Drexel Building at Fifth and Chestnut Streets. If eulogistic mention of Thomas Sully's name were to be similarly placed, close to the site of his former home and studio at Fifth and Ranstead Streets, it would seem highly appropriate. Boston has her " Copley Square," and we believe a street named after Gilbert Stuart, although where his ashes lie, alas! is veiled in doubt. In our own city there is nothing to commemorate in a public manner the name of an Artist, so justly celebrated, and so universally identified with Philadelphia, as that of Thomas Sully.

FOREWORD

The Historical Society of Pennsylvania owns the original autograph list of the paintings by Thomas Sully, written throughout in his minute, painstaking handwriting. It includes most of his portraits painted on canvas and panel, his miniatures on ivory, and numerous subject paintings and many sketches. This register is now for the first time fully published, together with the description of a number of his portraits hitherto unrecorded. Sully for some unexplainable reason failed to note a number of his portraits in his register, and these omissions have taken away to some extent the value of the original list as an authority, or as a means of identification of his work ; therefore a more complete catalogue of his work has been required by the student of American painting.

In describing the painting "head to left" or "right" it is meant that the head of the subject is turned to the left or right of the person viewing the picture. Wherever possible, the original paintings have been consulted for the description and measurements. The artist notes in his list of paintings the standard sizes of the canvases used. These sizes are in inches, Head 17″ by 20″; Bust 20″ by 24″ ; Half-length 25″ by 30″ ; Kit-Cat 20″ by 36″ ; Three-quarter length 40″ by 50″ ; Bishop's half length 44″ by 56″ ; Whole length 68″ by 94″. There are variations in the sizes of canvases and in the placing of the portrait upon the canvas, but the above are the standard sizes and descriptions of life-portraits. Sully signed his paintings with his monogram TS and the date, either in an inconspicuous manner on the face of his picture or on the back of the canvas.

Sully notes in his register of paintings the dates, and under each year he records the month and day he started the work, the words "Begun" and "Finished" showing the length of time occupied by the

FOREWORD

work. He also notes the price, date, and in some cases where the painting was a present or gift this represents the valuation he set at that time on his work. Where he introduced the hands of the sitter his price was often increased, and he notes it in the register, as well as some note or description of the sitter, family connection, or place of residence. As a means of identification and interest in the work, the authors have added wherever possible, biographical information of the sitter and the present ownership of the paintings. Owing to the Artist's high reputation and great industry he has left us many portraits of well-known people; in the City of Philadelphia his list of sitters might well be called "The Blue Book" of that day. It is gratifying to find at this time so many of the portraits he painted still in the hands of the families and descendants of the original owners, although the study of American painting has drawn many of the best portraits of Stuart and Sully into public galleries and collections.

At the conclusion of their labors, the authors desire to express their hearty appreciation of the aid and assistance rendered to them throughout the progress of their work by many eminent authorities on American painting, in addition to the invariable consideration and ready cooperation of the present owners of the paintings of Thomas Sully.

LIST OF PAINTINGS

1 ABERCROMBIE, DR. JAMES (1758–1841).

Graduated at College of Phila., 1776, merchant in Phila., afterwards Episcopal clergyman and minister of the United Churches of Christ Church and St. Peter's, Phila. Principal of Philadelphia Academy, 1800 to 1817.
Portrait begun Aug. 12th, 1810, finished Sept. 12th, 1810.
Size 29″ × 36″. Price, $30.00

2 ABERCROMBIE, DR. JAMES (1758–1841).

Painted for his son in Baltimore. Portrait begun Jan. 23rd, 1826, finished May 11th, 1826. Size 34″ × 42″. Price, $75.00

3 ABERT, JOHN JAMES (1788–1863).

Colonel of Topographical Engineers 1811, was painted at request of his corps, and presented to the Academy at West Point. Seated with elbow resting on desk and holds a pamphlet in hand, curtain in background. Portrait begun July 26th, 1839, finished Aug. 10th, 1839.
Size 40″ × 50″. Price, $500.00
Owned by the United States Military Academy at West Point.

4 ADAMS, JOHN QUINCY (1767–1848).

Sixth President of the United States. Full length seated at library table. Painted for W. H. Morgan, a print seller of Phila. Portrait begun Feb. 28th, 1825, finished May 7th, 1825; it was painted from life, and was engraved by A. B. Durand (S 551). Size 33″ × 25″. Price, $250.00
Owned by A. S. Cochran, Phillipse Manor, Yonkers, New York.

5 ADAMS, JOHN QUINCY (1767–1848).

Noted in the register as a study in chalk to finish the whole length portrait left unfinished by Gilbert Stuart. Begun Aug. 15th, 1829, finished August 17th, 1829. Price, $5.00

6 ADAMS, JOHN QUINCY (1767–1848).

Gilbert Stuart painted the head, and Sully completed the portrait a whole length standing figure entirely different from No. 4. Painting begun Dec. 1st, 1829. Price, $350.00
Owned by Harvard College, Cambridge, Mass. Now in the Harvard Union.

7 ADAMS, JOHN QUINCY (1767–1848).

Bust, head to right, white stock. Inscribed on back of canvas, " Painted from life in Washington City 1824." Size 20″ × 24″.
Owned by C. Harris, Esq., New York.

8 ADAMS, JOHN QUINCY (1767–1848).

Portrait painted by Sully when Adams was Secretary of State. Head three-quarter to right, left hand on a book on his knee, size 28″ × 36″.
Owned by Brooks Adams, Esq., Boston, Mass.

9 ADAMS, MISS MARY.

Portrait painted for Mrs. Adams, begun Oct. 27th, 1834, finished Nov. 12th, 1834. Bust. Price, $125.00

10 ADAMS, MRS.

Portrait painted for Mrs. Washington, Mount Vernon, begun May 16th, 1836, finished June 17th, 1836. Bust. Price, $150.00

11 ADAMS, MRS. CHRISTOPHER (1813–1898).

Miss H. J. McCall was the daughter of William McCall of Phila., and married Christopher Adams of New Orleans, La. She was a noted beauty. Portrait begun Sept. 22nd, 1840, finished Oct. 9th, 1840. Half length, in low-necked dress, fur-trimmed cloak over shoulder, and arms crossed. Vase of flowers in background. Size 29″ × 36″. Price, $300.00
Owned by Sitgraves Adams, Esq., Brighton, England.

12 ADAMS, MRS.

Was a Miss McCall, a daughter of a planter who lived on the river above New Orleans. The portrait shows a lady about 30 years old seated in an opera box, holding opera glasses. She is dressed in red velvet, low-necked with short sleeves, a black lace scarf falls over her bare arms. Canvas signed " TS "
Owned by Dr. Isaac M. Cline, New Orleans, La.

13 AITKIN, DR.

The register notes this portrait as being the first painted in the house built by Stephen Girard for Sully. It was on Fifth Street above Chestnut St., Phila. The picture was begun on Oct. 24, 1828, and was finished on Dec. 1st, 1828. Size 17″ × 20″, Price, $50.00

14 ALEXANDER, ELIZABETH.

Daughter of the surgeon Dr. Joseph Alexander. Head slightly to right, low-necked light buff dress, with pink scarf. Size 20″ × 30″.
Probably painted about 1851, owned in 1919 by Knoedler & Co., of New York.

NOTE.—Alexander Family Group. This group of five, representing members of four generations are gathered together around a table on which stands a vase of flowers. Four are busts of adults, and one a full length of a little girl about two years old. Painted about 1851 or 1852, size 50″ wide and 40″ high. Owned by Mrs. Kennedy Boone and exhibited at Maryland Institute, Sully Portraits, 1921.

LIST OF PAINTINGS

15 ALEXANDER, ELIZABETH.

Portrait painted when about two years old. Begun March 18th, 1851. and finished June 20th, 1851. Whole length.   Price, $200.00

16 ALEXANDER, MR. M.

(One of the group of five.) Painting begun March 22nd, 1851, finished June 20th, 1851. The register noted the portrait as a " bust, with hand introduced."   Price, $150.00

17 ALEXANDER, MRS.

(Deceased, copied from miniature.) Size 29″ × 36″. Painting begun March 24th, 1851, finished June 20th, 1851.   Price, $200.00

18 ALEXANDER, PAULINE.

Painted for Mrs. T. Biddle, begun Jan. 26th, 1828, finished Feb. 5th, 1818. Head.   Price, $50.00

19 ALIBONE, MRS. SARAH.

Mrs. Sarah Alibone, a widow, had a boarding house at No. 139 Walnut Street, Phila., in the year 1830. Portrait begun Aug. 14th, 1830, finished Sept. 7th, 1830. Bust.   Price, $75.00

20 ALLEN, GEORGE (1808–1876).

Professor of ancient languages at the University of Pennsylvania from 1845 until his death. He was a profound student, noted chess player and the author of the Life of Philidor. Portrait begun Dec. 26, 1855, finished Jan., 1856. Bust.   Price, $100.00

21 ALLEN, MRS. GEORGE.

Wife of Professor Allen of the University of Penna. Portrait begun Jan. 23rd, 1864, finished Feb. 3rd, 1864. Head.   Frice, $50.00

22 ALLEN, MRS. GEORGE.

Portrait begun Aug. 3rd, 1865, finished Aug. 15th, 1865. Head.
            Price, $50.00

23 ALLEN, HEMAN.

Portrait painted for his father Professor George Allen, begun Feb. 8th, 1864, finished Feb. 15th, 1864. Head.   Price, $30.00

24 ALLEN, HEMAN.

Copy of former portrait, painted for his father-in-law. Portrait begun Feb. 11th, 1866, finished Feb. 20th, 1866. Head.   Price, $30.00

25 ALLEN, MISS TOOLULA.

(Of Savannah.) Painted March 19th, 1846, finished March 31st, 1846. Head. Price, $150.00

26 ALLSTON, MRS.

Great-grandmother of R. W. Allston, portrait begun June 27th, 1842, finished July 14th, 1842. Head. Price, $150.00

27 ALLSTON, MRS. ROBERT FRANCIS WITHERS.

Of Georgetown, South Carolina, nee Adele Petigru. Was a sister of James Lewis Petigru of Charleston, and married Robert F. W. Allston, who was governor of the state, 1856–58. Portrait begun Feb. 18th, 1842, finished Feb. 25th, 1842. Head. Price, $150.00
Owned by her daughter Mrs. Arnoldus Vander Horst, and exhibited at Charleston, S. C., 1901.

28 ALLSTON, MRS.

(Copy from Morse of Mrs. Allston's portrait.) Portrait begun Jan. 28th, 1846, finished March 26th, 1864. Bust. Price, $200.00

29 ALLSTON, MR.

(Copy from Morse of Mr. Allston's portrait.) Portrait begun Feb. 21st, 1846, finished March 26th, 1846. Bust. Price, $200.00

30 ALLSTON, COL. J. A.

Of Georgetown, S. C. Portrait begun Sept. 6th, 1825, finished October 7th, 1825. Bust. Price, $60.00

31 ALLSTON, MRS.

From Georgetown, South Carolina. Portrait begun June 2nd, 1837, finished June 9th, 1837. Head. Price, $150.00

32 ALLSTON, THOMAS.

Portrait painted for his father Col. J. A. Allston of Georgetown, S. C. Begun Oct. 3rd, 1826, finished Dec. 3rd, 1826. Bust. Price, $60.00

33 ALLSTON, THOMAS.

Portrait painted for his father Col. J. A. Allston of Georgetown, begun Oct. 14th, 1826, finished Oct. 20th, 1826. Study for a whole length, size 17" × 20". Price, $10.00

34 ALLSTON, THOMAS.

Portrait painted for his father Col. J. A. Allston of Georgetown, begun Dec. 16th, 1826, finished April 15th, 1828. Whole length 63" × 44".
Price, $200.00

LIST OF PAINTINGS

35 ALLSTON, WILLIAM.

Portrait painted for his father Col. J. A. Allston of Georgetown, begun Oct. 3rd, 1826, finished Dec. 3rd, 1826. Bust.　　　Price, $60.00
Exhibited by G. T. Miller in 1896 at Portrait Exhibition, Cincinnati, Ohio.

36 ALLSTON, MRS. WILLIAM.

A portrait of Mrs. William Allston attributed to Thomas Sully, was exhibited by G. T. Miller in 1896 at the Portrait Exhibition at Cincinnati, Ohio. The painting is not noted in Sully's register.

37 ANABLE, MISS H. I.

Portrait painted for her relatives, begun Sept. 22nd, 1853, finished Oct. 13th, 1853. Head.　　　Price, $80.00

38 ANDERSON, MRS.

(Of New Orleans, La.) Painted in 1851, size small half-length, begun June 5th and finished July 12th.　　　Price, $300.00

39 ANDREWS, REV. JOHN (1746–1813).

Provost of the University of Penna., 1810–1813. Bust in robes, nearly full face. Engraved by David Edwin (Fielding, No. 15). Portrait begun Jan. 14th, 1813, finished March 4th, 1813. Head.　　　Price, $50.00
Owned by Rev. John Andrews Harris, D. D., Chestnut Hill, Phila.

40 ANDREWS, REV. JOHN (1746–1813).

Replica of the portrait painted in 1813. Panel 25″ × 30″.
Owned by the University of Penna., Philadelphia.

41 ANDREWS, JOHN (1783–1860).

Was cashier of the Bank of the United States, Chestnut St., Phila. Bust, head to right, with black stock. Panel, size 20″ × 24″. Signed "TS 1836."　　　Price, $100.00
Portrait begun April 2nd, 1836, finished April 20th, 1836.
Owned by Mrs. Benj. Chew Tilghman of Phila.

42 ANDREWS, THE MISSES.

Daughters of John Andrews (two heads). Anne Baynton Andrews (1811–1833), Elizabeth Callender Andrews (1783–1860). Heads, canvas 25″ × 30″ wide. Portraits begun Dec. 4, 1832, finished Dec. 22nd, 1832.　　　Price, $120.00
Owned by Mrs. Benj. Chew Tilghman, Philadelphia.

LIST OF PAINTINGS

43 ANNELY, MISS AMELIA.

Of Charleston, S. C.   Portrait begun Feb. 10th, 1842, finished Feb. 19th, 1842.   Head.   Price, $150.00
Portrait owned by Miss Blake of Charleston, S. C.

44 ANNELY, MISS MARIA.

Of Charleston, S. C.   Portrait begun April 14th, 1842, finished April 25th, 1842.   Head.   Price, $150.00
Portrait owned by Mrs. Blake of Charleston, S. C.

45 APPLETON, REV. EDWARD T.

Of Trenton, N. J.   Portrait begun July 18th, 1865, finished August 15th, 1865.   Head.   Price, $50.00

46 APPLETON, MRS. SAMUEL.

De Lancey St., Phila.   Wife of Rev. Saml. E. Appleton, rector of P. E. Church of the Mediator, Phila.   Portrait begun Sept. 21st, 1865, finished Oct. 6th, 1865.   Head.   Price, $30.00

47 ARFWEDSON, CARL DAVID.

Author of De Colonia Nova Svecia in Americam Borealem deducta historiola Upsaliae, 1825.   He was born in Stockholm and married Elizabeth Ashhurst of Phila.   Portrait painted for Richard Ashhurst, begun April 14th, 1834, finished June 19th, 1834.   Head.   Price, $80.00
Owned by R. H. Bayard Bowie, Esq., of Phila.

48 ARMISTEAD, WALTER KEITH (1785–1845).

Graduate of West Point and chief engineer in the War of 1812.   Bust in uniform.   Painted for Military Academy of West Point, begun Oct. 26th, 1829, finished Nov. 20th, 1829.   Size 20″ × 24″.   Price, $75.00
Owned by U. S. Military Academy, West Point, N. Y.

49 ARMSTEAD, WILLIAM.

Of Richmond, brother of Thomas.   This portrait was Sully's first attempt in oil colors.   Size 12″ × 10″.   Begun Nov. 23rd, 1802, and finished Dec. 1st, 1802.   Price, $10.00

50 ARROT, MR.

Portrait begun June 1st, 1819, finished June 17th, 1819.   Bust.
                                                          Price, $100.00

LIST OF PAINTINGS

51 ASHE, THOMAS.

He was an early New York cabinet maker who also made picture frames for the artists. Bust, head to left, high coat collar, white stock, hair curling on forehead. Portrait begun Nov. 1st, 1807, and finished Nov. 19th, 1807. Size 28″ × 22″. Price, $30.00

This portrait was owned by the Ehrich Galleries of New York.

52 ASHHURST, ELIZABETH (1777–1857).

Married Richard Ashhurst. Portrait begun May 26th, 1834, finished June 19th, 1834. Head. Price, $80.00

Owned by Mr. R. H. Bayard Bowie, of Phila.

53 ASHHURST, ELIZABETH (1812–1899).

Married Carl D. Arfwedson of Stockholm, she was the daughter of Richard Ashhurst of Phila. Portrait begun Jan. 31st, 1834, finished Feb. 12th, 1834. Head. Price, $80.00

54 ASHHURST, LEWIS RICHARD (1806–1874).

Eldest son of Mr. and Mrs. Richard Ashhurst of No. 263 Arch St., Phila. He was a member of the firm of Richard Ashhurst & Sons and First President of Phila. Tr. S. D. & Ins. Co. He married Miss Mary Hazlehurst. Portrait painted for his mother, begun May 28th, 1833, finished June 22nd, 1833. Bust. Price, $100.00

Owned by R. H. Bayard Bowie, Esq., of Phila.

55 ASHHURST, MRS. RICHARD (1777–1857).

She was Miss Elizabeth Crotto, widow of Captain Hughes, and lived at No. 263 Arch St., Phila. Half length, arm resting on table, nearly full face with lace head-dress. Portrait begun Dec. 10th, 1832, finished May 17th, 1833. Size 29″ × 36″. Price, $150.00

Owned by R. H. Bayard Bowie, Esq., of Phila.

56 ASHHURST, RICHARD (1784–1861).

Merchant, and lived at No. 263 Arch St., Phila. Portrait begun March 7th, 1826, finished April 13th, 1826. Size 29″ × 36″. Price, $120.00

This painting was destroyed, having been injured beyond repair.

57 ASHHURST, THE MISSES.

(Group of three.) Mary Beck Ashhurst (1811–1900), married Charles McEuen of Phila.; Elizabeth Ashhurst (1812–1899), married Carl David Arfwedson; Catherine H. Ashhurst (1814–1910), married Thos. L. Bowie. Painting begun Jan. 30th, 1830, finished April 22nd, 1830. Size 34″ × 44″. (See illustration.) Price, $250.00

Owner, Mrs. Bayard Bowie, of Phila.

58 ASTOR, MISS MARGARET.

Portrait painted for her father, begun Jan. 2nd, 1807, finished on Feb. 11th, 1807. Bust. Price, $30.00

NOTE.—Mr. John Jacob Astor had three daughters, Magdalen, Dorothea and Eliza.

59 AUSTIN, SAMUEL (1865–1867).

Son of Saml. Austin who was for a time a tutor in a lady's family who afterwards married a Mr. Fry (Sully notes the portrait as painted "for a friend of Mrs. Fry," and adds in pencil [Mrs. Austin]). Head of a child, begun Dec. 2nd, 1869, finished Dec. 20th, 1869. Size 14″ × 17″. Signed on back "TS, 1869, December."
Owned by Miss Caroline S. Austin, of St. Paul, Minn.

60 AYERS, MR.

Copied from an old picture for Mr. Savage, begun April 30th, 1850, finished May 30th, 1850. Size 51″ × 40″. Price, $200.00

61 BACH, JOHN SEBASTIAN (1685–1750).

After the painting by Hansemann. Painted for the Musician Series, begun Oct. 16th, 1862, finished Oct. 27th, 1862. Size 17″ × 12″.
Price, $30.00

62 BACHE, CAPT. HARTMAN (1797–1872).

Great grandson of Benjamin Franklin, graduated in 1817 from West Point, and served in the engineer corps of the U. S. Army. Portrait begun July 19th, 1824, finished Sept. 16th, 1826. Head. Size 17″ × 20″.
Price, $30.00
Owned by Mrs. Albert D. Bache, Phila.

63 BACHE, CAPT. HARTMAN (1797–1872).

Replica painted for his mother, begun June 7th, 1828, and finished June 14th, 1828. Head. Size 17″ × 20″. Price, $50.00
Owned by Mrs. R. Meade Bache, Phila.

64 BACHE, SARAH (1744–1808).

Daughter of Benjamin Franklin. The original portrait by John Hoppner is in the Metropolitan Museum of Art, N. Y., from which painting Sully made his copy. Painting begun May 19th, 1834, finished June 8th, 1834. Painted for the Artist's collection. Bust. Size 25″ × 30″. Price, $125.00
Owned by Mrs. Albert D. Bache, Phila.

LIST OF PAINTINGS

65 BACHE, SARAH (1744–1808).

Painted for her grandson, and copied from the portrait by John Hoppner, begun March 15th, finished March 22nd, 1865. Size 30″ × 20″.

Price, $100.00

66 BACHE, MISS LIZZIE.

(Brooklyn, N. Y.) Portrait begun Nov. 11th, 1864, finished Nov. 13th, 1864. Head. Price, $80.00

67 BACKER, J.

Portrait begun April, 1805, and finished May, 1805. Size 25″ × 30″.

Price, $25.00

68 BLACKWELL, REV. ROBERT, D. D. (1748–1831).

Painted from a miniature for Mr. Wallace. Dr. Blackwell was one of the ministers of the United Churches, whose only daughter Rebecca married George Willing, and whose daughter Dorothea Frances married John William Wallace. Painting begun July 6th, 1853, finished July 20th, 1853. Bust. Size of canvas 25″ × 30″. Signed TS 1853. Price, $100.00 Owned by Willing Spencer, Esq., Philadelphia.

69 BACON, MRS.

(Formerly Miss Fry.) Portrait begun Dec. 17th, 1850, finished Dec. 31st, 1850. Head. Price, $100.00

70 BACON, MR.

Portrait begun Feb. 28th, 1851, finished March 8th, 1851. Painted as a companion to his wife's portrait No. 69. Head. Price, $100.00

71 BACON, MRS.

The artist's register of paintings notes that this portrait was painted in 1808, and retouched in 1835. It was a bust, and as the price is set at only $50 it is evidently for the retouching, begun on Sept. 16th, 1835, and finished Sept. 28th, 1835.

72 BADGER, MRS.

Daughter of Dr. Bradley (No. 194). Portrait painted for her husband, Alderman Badger, begun March 9th, 1835, finished March 25th, 1835. Head. Price, $80.00 Owned by William H. Badger of Wayne, Penna.

73 BAIRD, CAROLINE AND FANNY LEA.

Were the nieces of Edward L. Carey of Phila. Sully started this painting Oct. 14th, 1836, and finished it Nov. 28th, 1845. Bust. Price, $250.00

74 BAIRD, CAROLINE CAREY (1831–).

Daughter of Thomas and Eliza Baird and granddaughter of Mathew Carey. Portrait begun Dec. 19th, 1842, and finished Jan. 26th, 1843. Signed on back of canvas " TS." Size 16″ × 19½″. Price, $50.00

Painted for Edward L. Carey. Owned by Mrs. Henry C. Scott, Pottsville, Pa.

NOTE.—The register records the " Head as painted for a subscription at the low price of $50.00."

75 BALDWIN, HENRY (1780–1844).

Justice of the Supreme Court of the United States, 1830. Painted for his son, begun Aug. 28th, 1833, finished Sept. 18th, 1833. Bust.
Price, $100.00

76 BALDWIN, JUDGE HENRY (1780–1844).

Portrait begun July 15th, 1834, finished Sept. 3rd, 1834. Bust.
Price, $125.00

77 BALL, MR.

Portrait copied from a painting by Joshua Cantir, a Dane who was painting in Charleston, S. C., about 1800. This portrait was painted for Mrs. Simmons, begun April 4th, 1846, finished April 16, 1846. Bust.
Price, $200.00

78 BALTIMORE, LORD.

Sir Charles Calvert, 5th Lord Baltimore. Copy of the painting by Kneller, begun Aug. 6th, 1853, finished Aug. 30th, 1853. Price, $800.00
Full length, standing in court costume, holding baton in his hand.
This portrait was presented by the artist to the Maryland Historical Society who elected him an Honorary Member of the Society.
Owned by the Maryland Historical Society, Baltimore, Md.

79 BANCKER, CHARLES N. (1776–1869).

For many years the President of the Franklin Insurance Co. of Philadelphia. Portrait begun Dec. 7th, 1812, finished Feb. 1st, 1813. Head. Size 25″ × 30″. Price, $70.00
Owned by Miss Anna Bancker Beasley, Phila.

80 BANCKER, CHARLES N. (1776–1869).

Painted for his son James Bancker, begun July 14th, finished July 24th. 1846. Size 18″ × 14″. Price, $50.00

81 BANCKER, CHARLES (1776–1869).

> Painted in place of a former portrait, begun Oct. 23rd, 1830, finished Dec. 1st, 1830. Bust. Size 25″ × 30″. ⊤S Decm., 1830. Price, $75.00
> Owned by John Cadwalader, Esq., Phila.

82 BANCKER, CHAS., SR.

> Painting begun April 5th, 1855, finished April 17th, 1855. Portrait given in place of condemned painting. Head. Size 20″ × 24″. Price, $80.00
> Signed " ⊤S 1855."
> Owned by Mrs. Henry J. Rowland, Phila.

83 BANKS, J.

> Portrait begun Dec., 1805, finished the same month, size 25″ × 30″.
> Bust. Price, $30.00

84 BARBER, MR.

> Of Georgetown, D. C., painted from a daguerreotype of the deceased. Portrait begun Nov. 26th, 1853, finished December 10th, 1853. Bust.
> Price, $100.00

85 BARBER, MRS.

> Of Georgetown, D. C. Portrait painted Nov. 21st, 1853, and finished Dec. 6th, 1853. Bust. Price, $100.00

86 BARBER, MRS.

> For her sister in Georgetown, D. C., painted from a daguerreotype. Begun Aug. 29th, 1855, finished Sept. 8th, 1855. Head. Price, $100.00

87 BARCLAY, MRS.

> Portrait begun April 29th, 1828, finished May 19th, 1828. Bust.
> Price, $75.00

88 BARKER, MRS. ABRAHAM (1780–1845).

> (Née Priscilla Hopkins.) Portrait seated in Quaker costume, begun Nov. 24th, 1817, and finished on Dec. 4th, 1817. Bust, canvas size 24½″ × 30″. Price, $100.00
> Owned by Mr. Robt. W. Johnson, Baltimore, Md.

89 BARKER, MRS.

> Painted for Major Barker, begun Dec. 12th, 1829, finished Dec. 23rd, 1829. Size 17″ × 20″. Price, $50.00

90 BARKSDALE, MR.

> Of Virginia. Portrait begun June 15th, 1830, finished June 22nd, 1830.
> Bust. Price, $75.00

91 BARKSDALE, MR. (JUNR.).

Deceased, painted in Washington for his father, portrait begun May 1st, 1840, finished May 7th, 1840.　Head.　Price, $150.00

92 BARKSDALE, MR. (JUNR.).

Portrait painted for his father, begun Sept. 18th, 1851, finished Oct. 2nd, 1851.　Size 17″ × 20″.　Price, $80.00

93 BARKSDALE, MRS.

Copied from portrait by James Worrell of Va., painting begun Oct. 7th, 1853, finished Nov. 1st, 1853.　Head.　Price, $80.00

94 BARKSDALE, MRS.

Portrait copied from painting by James Worrell.　Begun Aug. 30, 1860, finished Sept. 14th, 1860.　Bust.　Price, $100.00

95 BARKSDALE, MISS HANNAH.

(Infant of about eight months.)　Painting begun Dec. 17th, 1850, finished Jan. 5th, 1851.　Bust.　Price, $200.00

96 BARNES, MISS ANNE (1826–　　).

Portrait painted for Dr. J. Rush of Phila., begun July, 1849, finished on July 25th, 1849.　Size 17″ × 20″.　Price, $80.00
Head, nearly full face, dark hair parted in the middle with curls showing on both sides of her face.　Signed on back " TS 1849."
Owned by John Hampton Barnes, Esq., of Philadelphia.

97 BARROW, ROBERT L. W.

Of New Orleans.　Portrait begun Sept. 16th, 1844, finished Dec. 19th, 1844.　Size 29″ × 36″.　Price, $200.00

98 BARROW, MRS.

Of New Orleans, La.　Portrait begun Sept. 14th, 1844, finished Dec. 19th, 1844.　Size 29″ × 36″.　Price, $200.00

99 BARTON, DR. WILLIAM P. C. (1786–1856).

Studied medicine under his uncle Dr. Benj. Smith Barton at the University of Penna.　He was appointed surgeon in the U. S. Navy.　Bust in uniform, blue coat and gold braid, head to left, arm resting on end of divan, buff gloves.　Portrait begun April 16th, 1809, finished May 12th, 1809.　Size 25″ × 30″.　Price, $50.00
Owned by Wiltstach Collection Memorial Hall, Fairmount Park, Phila. Gift of Wm. Barton Brewster.

100 BATES, MISS ELIZABETH ANNE (1820–1878).

This portrait was the first painted by Sully in London at his second visit. Miss Bates married Sylvain van der Weyer, Belgian Minister to England in 1838. The portrait was begun on Nov. 29th, 1837, and finished Dec. 26th, 1837. Bust.   Price, $250.00

Continues in possession of descendants in England.

101 BAYARD, ANDREW (1761–1832).

First President of the Commercial Bank 1814, also of Philadelphia Saving Fund Society. One of the founders of the Academy of Fine Arts. He married Sarah daughter of Chas. Pettit.

Bust, head to left, copied by Sully from portrait by Jacob Eicholtz. Size 25″ × 30″, begun Nov. 12th, 1832, finished Dec. 13th, 1832.   Price, $100.00

Owned by the Philadelphia Saving Fund Society.

102 BAYARD, MR.

Of Wilmington, Del. Portrait begun May 15th, 1822, finished July 6th, 1822. Bust.   Price, $100.00

Owned by Richard Bayard, Esq., Baltimore, Md.

103 BAYARD, MRS. RICHARD HENRY.

Of Wilmington, Delaware. Portrait begun May 15th, 1822, finished July 2nd, 1822. Bust.   Price, $100.00

Owned by Mrs. Oswald Jackson of New York, who exhibited it at Loan Collection, N. Y., 1895.

104 BAYLEY, MR.

Of Maryland. Portrait begun Aug. 8th, 1815, and finished Aug. 18th, 1815. Bust.   Price, $80.00

105 BAYRARD, WILLIAM.

Of Edisto Island, S. C. Portrait begun Aug. 30th, 1825, finished Sept. 20th, 1825. The artist's register notes that the hand was introduced in the painting. Bust.   Price, $75.00

106 BECK, PAUL, JR. (1757–1844).

Prominent Philadelphia merchant, active in many city institutions of philanthropy. Three-quarter length, seated, facing right. Portrait begun April 2nd, 1813, finished Sept. 6th, 1813. Size 28″ × 36″.   Price, $100.00

Engraved by Saml. Sartain, in " Eminent Philadelphians."

Owned by Henry Dwight Beck, and Exhibited by him in 1887 in Loan Exhibition at the Penna. Acad. of Fine Arts.

107 BECK, PAUL, JR. (1757–1844).
   Copied from a portrait painted in 1813, replica begun Jan. 10th, 1860, finished Jan. 23rd, 1860.   Bust.   Price, $100.00

108 BECK, MRS. PAUL, JR.
   Was Mary Harvey, the second wife of Paul Beck, Jr.   Three-quarter length, facing right, seated.   Size 28″ × 36″.   Portrait was begun April 23rd, 1813, and finished June 8th, 1813.   Price, $100.00
   It was exhibited in the Loan Collection of 1887 at the Penna. Academy of Fine Arts, and was owned by Henry Dwight Beck.

109 BEEKMAN, MISS ANN.
   Married George Hoffman.   Portrait begun Feb. 20th, 1807, finished March 24th, 1807.   Bust.   Price, $40.00
   The register notes hand introduced, the artist makes a slight increase over his usual rate for a bust in this case.
   Owned by George Hoffman of New York.

110 BEEKMAN, JOHN KOCK.
   Portrait painted for Benj. Chew Wilcocks of Phila., whose portrait was also painted for his friend Beekman, begun June 20th, 1807, finished July 4th, 1807.   Bust.   Price, $50.00
   Bust with head to right, white stock and ruffle.   Son of James and Sara Beekman.   Sold by Ehrich Gallery, New York.

111 BEEKMAN, MISS SARAH.
   Of New York.   Painting begun Dec. 10th, 1806, finished July 20th, 1808. Size 12″ × 10″.   Price, $30.00

112 BEERMAN, MISS SARAH.
   Portrait begun March 10th, 1807, and finished March 24th, 1807.   Bust.
                                                      Price, $30.00

113 BEETHOVEN, LUDWIG VAN (1772–1827).
   Copied from a painting by a German artist, for the " Musician series," begun Oct. 31st, 1862, finished Nov. 3rd, 1862.   Size 17″ × 12″.
                                                      Price, $30.00

114 BEETHOVEN, LUDWIG VAN (1772–1827).
   Painted for the Musician series, the former being erased.   Begun March 17th, 1863, finished March 31st, 1863.   Head.   Price, $30.00

LIST OF PAINTINGS

115 BELL, JOHN, M. D. (1796–1872).

Physician and medical writer, lecturer for several years in the Philadelphia Medical Institute. Bust facing left. Portrait begun Nov. 2nd, 1860, and finished Nov. 19th, 1860. Size 20″ × 24″. Price, $80.00
Deposited by the Colonization Society at the Historical Society, Locust St., Phila.

116 BELL, MR. S.

Portrait begun Sept. 9th, 1816, finished Oct. 10th, 1816. Bust.
Price, $100.00

117 BELLOWS, MR.

Of Northumberland. Portrait begun Dec. 18th, 1830, finished Dec. 31st, 1830. Bust. Price, $75.00

118 BENDER, MAJ. GEORGE (b. ——, d. 1865).

Entered the army in 1812 and was made Major of 5th Infantry, April 23, 1830. Portrait begun Feb. 8th, 1830, finished March 4th, 1830. Bust.
Price, $75.00

119 BERNARD, MRS.

Copy from Vanderlyn's portrait for Tennent, portrait painted in Baltimore, begun Nov. 18th, 1852, finished Dec. 8th, 1852. Head. Price, $100.00

120 BETTON, MRS. SAMUEL.

" Of Germantown (Deceased)." Wife of Dr. Saml. Betton, née Mary Forrest, whose son Dr. Thos. Forrest Betton, married Sarah Elizabeth Logan. Price, $100.00
Portrait begun Sept. 1st, 1815, finished Sept. 1815. Size 29″ × 36″. Half length seated, nearly full face, wearing a low-necked black dress with arm resting on a red cushion. Deposited at " Stenton " by the Logan family.

121 BEYLARD, MR.

Portrait begun Jan. 8th, 1827, finished Feb. 2nd, 1827. Head.
Price, $50.00

122 BEYLARD, MRS.

(Was Miss Du Barry.) Portrait begun June 1st, 1825, finished August 1st, 1825. Size 29″ × 36″. Price, $100.00

123 BEYLARD, MRS.

Portrait painted for her relatives in Bordeaux, France. Begun Jan. 30th, 1826, finished Dec. 1st, 1826. Size 23″ × 18″. Price, $40.00

LIST OF PAINTINGS

124 BIDDLE, ALEXANDER WILLIAMS (1856–   ).

Master Alexander Biddle was painted for his mother; he was the eldest son of Colonel Alexander and Julia Williams Biddle. Portrait begun Feb. 23rd, 1861, finished March 5th, 1861. Head. Size 25″ × 30″.

Price, $80.00

Owned by Estate of Alexander Biddle, Phila., Pa.

125 BIDDLE, ANNIE E. (1822–1908).

Portrait painted for her mother who was Mrs. Mary Biddle, a sister of Nicholas Biddle. Painting begun April 3rd, 1827, finished April 23rd, 1827. Head.   Price, $50.00

Owned by Mrs. P. S. Van Rensselaer of Phila., now residing in Paris.

126 BIDDLE, THE MISSES.

Miss Annie E. Biddle, 1822–1908, and her cousin Miss Meta C. Biddle, 1825–1913, who married James Stokes Biddle of the U. S. Navy. The portrait, two busts, was begun March 25th, 1836, finished June 18th, 1836. Bust.   Price, $300.00

Owned by Misses Jane C. and Meta C. Biddle, Phila.

127 BIDDLE, MRS. CLEMENT (–1831).

Was Rebecca Cornell. Painted for her son Thomas Biddle who was the founder of the banking house of Thomas A. Biddle & Co. Bust. Portrait begun July 12th, 1824, finished Aug. 13th, 1824.   Price, $60.00

Owned by Henry W. Biddle, Esq., Philada.

128 BIDDLE, MRS. CLEMENT (–1831).

Replica painted for James Biddle, begun July 26th, 1824, finished August 23rd, 1824. Size 10″ × 8″.   Price, $30.00

Owned by Henry W. Biddle.

129 BIDDLE, HENRY RUSH (1858–1877).

Master Henry Biddle was painted for his mother, he was the younger brother of Alexander Williams Biddle, and son of Colonel Alexander and Julia Williams Biddle. Portrait begun Feb. 20th, 1861, finished March 5th, 1861. Head. Size 35″ × 30″.   Price, $80.00

Owned by estate of Alexander Biddle, Phila.

130 BIDDLE, JAMES CORNELL (1795–1838).

(Deceased, was copied by Sully from the portrait painted by Inman.) Begun July 8th, 1841, finished July 16th, 1841. Size 29″ × 36″.

Price, $300.00

Owned by the Misses Catharine M. C. and Sarah Biddle, Phila.

131 BIDDLE, JAMES STOKES (1819–1900).

Entered the navy in 1833 and resigned in 1856. In 1846 he married his cousin Miss Meta Craig Biddle for whom this portrait was painted. Begun Dec. 21st, 1846, finished Dec. 29th, 1846. Bust. Price, $100.00
Owned by the Misses Biddle, Phila. (Daughters.)

132 BIDDLE, JAMES, U. S. N., (1783–1848).

Entered the navy in 1800, was on board the frigate Philadelphia when wrecked in 1803. Congress voted him a gold medal in 1815. Portrait painted for his brother Nicholas, begun Oct. 28th, 1839, finished Nov. 18th, 1839. Bust. Price, $200.00
Owned by Mrs. Thos. F. Dixon, Chestnut Hill, Phila.

NOTE.—An excellent copy by Leopold Seyffert hangs at the Philadelphia Club. Another copy made under same artist's supervision belongs to *Genl. John Biddle, U. S. A.*

133 BIDDLE, CAPT. JAMES (1783–1848).

Commodore Biddle entered the navy in 1800, he gained distinction and was awarded a medal by Congress. Begun April 15th, 1826, finished on April 21st, 1826. Head facing left in uniform, size 17″ × 20″. Signed "TS 1826." Price, $40.00
Owned by Mrs. Saml. H. Thomas, Philadelphia.

134 BIDDLE, CRAIG (1823–1910).

Master John Craig Biddle, at the age of 16 years, painted for his mother. Begun Oct. 8th, 1839, finished Oct. 15, 1839. Head. Price, $150.00
Judge Craig Biddle was member of Legislature of Penna., aide-de-camp of Genl. Patterson and military aide to Gov. Curtin. Elected Judge in 1875 and twice re-elected.
Owned by the Misses Biddle, Phila. (Nieces.)

135 BIDDLE, JOHN (1792–1859).

Major in the United States army which he entered in 1812. He afterwards settled in Detroit, Michigan, and was the delegate in Congress 1829–31. He married Eliza Bradish. Portrait begun April 13th, 1818, and finished April 22nd, 1818. Bust. Price, $100.00
Was owned by Miss Susan D. Biddle of Detroit, and now in the National Gallery of Art, Washington, D. C.

136 BIDDLE, MRS. JOHN (1892–1859).

(Née Eliza Bradish of New York.) Portrait begun Dec. 1st, 1821, finished Dec. 24th, 1821. Bust. Price, $100.00
Now loaned to the National Gallery of Fine Arts, Washington, D. C. An excellent copy by Alvah Bradish has often been confused with the original by Sully.

137 BIDDLE, JULIA RUSH (1859–1885).

Head and shoulders of a child about four years of age, nearly full face with golden curls. Portrait painted for her mother Mrs. Julia Williams Biddle, begun April 22nd, 1863, finished May 30th, 1863. Size 17″ × 12″.

Price, $40.00

Owned by Estate of Alexander Biddle, Phila.

138 BIDDLE, MRS. LYDIA (1766–1858).

Daughter of the Rev. Elihu Spencer who married William Macfunn Biddle and removed to Carlisle, Pa. Portrait painted for her son William, begun Sept. 11th, 1826, finished Nov. 1st, 1826. Head.   Price, $50.00

Owned by Mrs. Herbert G. Ponting, Berkeley, California.

139 BIDDLE, NICHOLAS (1786–1844).

Son of Charles Biddle, graduated at Princeton, 1801, and passed several years in Europe, returning to Phila. he edited "The Port Folio". Elected President of the United States Bank in 1823.

Bust facing left, portrait begun July 26th, 1826, finished Oct. 31st, 1826. Size 25″ × 30″.   Price, $75.00

Engraved by S. Cousins in London.

Owned by Charles Biddle, Esq., Andalusia, Penna.

140 BIDDLE, NICHOLAS (1786–1844).

Entirely different from the former portrait. Painting begun Dec. 20th, 1830, finished June 9th, 1831. Bust.   Price, $75.00

Portrait was engraved by John Sartain. Painting was destroyed by fire in Marquard's storage house New York. Had belonged to Mrs. Edward Biddle, Phila.

141 BIDDLE, NICHOLAS (1786–1844).

Replica painted for Mr. Coperthwait from portrait painted in 1826. Copy begun Feb. 4th, 1839, finished Feb. 13th, 1839. Head.

Price, $200.00

Owned by the Misses Biddle, Phila.

142 BIDDLE, NICHOLAS (1786–1844).

Copy of portrait painted in 1826, copy begun on June 17th, 1837, and finished on June 26th, 1837. Head.   Price, $150.00

NOTE.—Sully's register of paintings notes that the portrait of Nicholas Biddle, painted in 1826, was retouched and the hand introduced in 1828, for which painting he notes the price as $100, the original portrait was noted as $75. The canvas was signed and dated at the time the additional work was added to the original. No. 139.

LIST OF PAINTINGS

143 BIDDLE, MRS. NICHOLAS (1793–1856).

She was Jane M. Craig. Bust, head to left with large hat and feathers, low-necked gown with cloak over left shoulder. Portrait begun April 22nd, 1826, finished Feb. 27th, 1827. (See illustration.) Bust.   Price, $75.00
Owned by Charles Biddle, Andalusia, Penna.

144 BIDDLE, MRS. NICHOLAS (1793–1856).

Portrait painted for her brother J. Craig, begun April 27th, 1827, finished June 4th, 1827. Head.   Price, $40.00
Owned by the Misses Biddle, Phila. (Granddaughters.)

145 BIDDLE, RICHARD (1796–1847).

Bust, head to right, wearing spectacles and holding a letter in his hand. Painted in 1821 but not noted in Sully's register of painting. Canvas signed " TS." Reproduced in " Memoir of Sebastian Cabot." By Richard Biddle. (Reprinted, 1915.)
Portrait owned by Mrs. Heard (née McIlvaine) of Pittsburgh, Pa.

146 BIDDLE, THOMAS (1790–1831).

Major Biddle served with distinction in the United States army. He fell in a duel in 1831 with Spencer Pettis, member of Congress. Portrait half length standing, in uniform, head to left, begun March 5th, 1818, finished April 22nd, 1818. Size 29″ × 36″.   Price, $150.00
Engraved by Saml. Sartain, in " Eminent Philadelphians."
Owned by Mrs. P. S. Van Rensselaer of Paris, France.

147 BIDDLE, THOMAS (1790–1831).

Copy by Thomas Wilcocks Sully of Major Biddle (No. 146), retouched by his father. The work of retouching must have been considerable as it was begun Jan. 10th, 1832, and the price or value of the work was $70. Size 28″ × 36″.
Owned by Thomas B. Clarke, Esq., New York.

148 BIDDLE, THOMAS (1776–1857).

Eminent banker and founder of the firm of Thos. A. Biddle & Co. of Phila. He married the daughter of Genl. Jonathan Williams, U. S. A., first commander of West Point. Portrait begun March 3rd, 1828, finished April 1st, 1828. Size 19″ × 15″.   Price, $50.00
Owned by Mrs. Arthur Biddle, Phila.

149 BIDDLE, MRS. THOMAS.

(Née Christine Williams, daughter of General Jonathan Williams, U. S. A.) Portrait begun Jan. 21st, 1828, finished Feb. 5th, 1828. Head.
    Price, $50.00
Owned by Mrs. Arthur Biddle, Phila.

LIST OF PAINTINGS

150 BINNEY, ELIZABETH.
Grandchild of Mrs. Horace Binney. Portrait begun Feb. 2nd, 1835, finished March 6th, 1835. Signed and dated " IS 1835." Head.
Price, $80.00
Owned by Archibald R. Montgomery, Esq., Bryn Mawr, Pa.

151 BINNEY, ESTHER COXE (1817–   ).
Daughter of Hon. Horace Binney and wife of Judge J. I. Clark Hare (1816–1905). Bust, head to left, low-necked dress, hands clasped on musical instrument. Portrait begun June 27th, 1836, finished March 16th, 1836. (See illustration.)
Price, $150.00
Owned by Mrs. Horace Binney Hare, Radnor, Pa.

152 BINNEY, HORACE (1780–1875).
Eminent Phila. lawyer admitted to the bar 1800, son of Dr. Barnabas Binney. Half length standing, facing right. Portrait painted for Law Association, begun Sept. 11th, 1833, finished Oct. 23rd, 1833. Signed " IS. 1833." Painting owned by Law Association and Engraved by John Sartain. Size 29" × 36".
Price, $150.00
Illustrated in " Life of Horace Binney."

153 BINNEY, HORACE (1780–1875).
Head to left, white stock and high collar to coat. Portrait painted for Genl. Cadwalader, begun Nov. 2nd, 1833, and finished Nov. 15th, 1833. Bust.
Price, $125.00

154 BIRCH, DR.
Portrait begun June 10th, 1807, finished in July, 1807. Bust.
Price, $50.00

155 BISPHAM, MRS. MARTHA LAURIE.
Wife of John B. Bispham and daughter of Mrs. Isaac Collins. Portrait painted for her husband, begun Jan. 29th, 1834, finished Feb. 14, 1834. Head.
Price, $80.00
Owned by David Bispham, Esq., of Phila. and New York.

156 BLACK, JUDGE JAMES R. (1785–1839).
Of New Castle, Delaware. Deceased, his portrait by Bass Otis, was copied by Sully, begun June 2nd, 1847, and finished June 10th, 1847. Signed on back of canvas "After Otis IS 1847." Bust, head to left, white stock, brown background. Size 20" × 24".
Price, $80.00
Owned by Mrs. James Young, Germantown, Pa.

157 BLACK, MRS. JAMES R. (1785–1872).

(Née Maria Stokes.) Portrait painted for her grandson Mr. Young, begun March 14th, 1850, finished April 1st, 1850. Bust, nearly full face, with lace cap, breast pin holding lace at neck. Size 20″× 24″, signed on back of canvas " TS. 1850." Price, $80.00

Owned by Mrs. James Young, Germantown, Pa.

158 BLACK, MRS.

(Deceased, a copy from a photograph.) Begun March 11th, 1862, finished April 15th, 1862. Size 25″ × 30″. Price, $50.00

159 BLACKBURNE, WILLIAM.

Philadelphia merchant. Portrait begun Jan. 23rd, 1829, finished Feb. 20th, 1829. Head. Price, $50.00

160 BLAIR, MISS E.

Of Washington, married Lieut. Saml. P. Lee of the U. S. Navy. Painting begun June 15th, 1840, finished June 27th, 1840. Head. Price, $50.00

161 BLAIR, FRANCIS P. (1791–1876).

He was the editor of "The Globe," Washington, D. C., and a prominent statesman and politician. Portrait begun May 1st, 1845, finished May 14th, 1845. Bust, head to left, rather bald, wearing high black stock and a cloak or overcoat. Picture was engraved by John Sartain. Bust. Price, $100.00

162 BLAIR, MONTGOMERY (1813–1883).

Statesman, son of Francis P. Blair, Sr., was graduated at West Point 1835. He was district attorney for Missouri, and mayor of St. Louis. Portrait begun May 1st, 1845, finished May 17th, 1845. Head. Price, $80.00

163 BLAIR, JUDGE MONTGOMERY (1813–1883).

Same as above. Painting begun May 15th, 1845, and finished May 24th, 1845. Second portrait. Head. Price, $80.00

164 BLAIR, MR. JAMES.

Painted for his father in Washington, begun Oct. 14th, 1843, finished Oct. 25th, 1843. Head. Price, $80.00

165 BLAIR, MRS.

Painted at Washington, begun April 20th, 1840, finished May 25th, 1840. Bust. Price, $200.00

166 BLAIR, MRS.

Was formerly Miss Woodbury, portrait begun Aug. 26th, 1846, finished Sept. 1st, 1846. Head. Price, $80.00

167 BLAIR, MRS.
>Copy by Sully from former picture, begun Oct. 5th, 1846, finished Oct. 22nd, 1846. Head. Price, $80.00

168 BLAKELEY, MISS UDNEY.
>Painted for Mrs. Abbot of St. Croix, begun Oct. 15th, 1830, finished Nov. 3rd, 1830. Bust. Price, $75.00

169 BLAMYER, MISS.
>Of Charleston, S. C. Painted for Mrs. P. Smith, begun Oct. 2nd, 1754, finished Oct. 17th, 1854. Head. Price, $80.00

170 BLODGET, MRS. SAMUEL (1772–1837).
>Copied by Sully from the painting by Gilbert Stuart for H. Smith. Painting begun Nov. 19th, 1855, and finished Nov. 30th, 1855. Head.
>Price, $80.00
>Original canvas about 10″ × 12″ is inlaid into a canvas 25″ × 30″.
>Owned by Albert Rosenthal, Phila.

171 BLOOMFIELD, MRS. JOSEPH.
>Of Burlington, New Jersey, wife of Governor Joseph Bloomfield. Portrait begun Feb. 10th, 1822, finished March 13th, 1822. Size 29″ × 36″.
>Price, $150.00

172 BOGGS, MR.
>Merchant, portrait begun Jan. 2nd, 1815, finished April 2nd, 1815. Bust.
>Price, $80.00

173 BOGGS, MRS.
>Portrait begun Jan. 9th, 1815, finished April 27th, 1815. Bust.
>Price, $100.00

174 BOILEAU, NATHANIEL B.
>Secretary of state under Governor Snyder. Portrait begun Jan. 8th, 1809, finished Jan. 22nd, 1809. Bust. Price, $50.00

175 BOLLING, ROBT.
>Of Petersburg, Va. Portrait begun May 26th, 1825, finished May 28th, 1825. Head. Price, $30.00

176 BOLLING, ROBERT.
>Of Petersburg, Va. Portrait begun May 22nd, 1832, finished July 12th, 1832. Bust. Price, $100.00

177 BOLLING, MRS.
>Wife of Robert Bolling of Petersburg, Virginia. Portrait begun June 22nd, 1832, finished July 14th, 1832. Bust. Price, $100.00

LIST OF PAINTINGS

178 BOONE, DANIEL (1735–1820).

Bust, facing front, one hand rests on a book. Engraved in the Century Magazine illustrating Life of Lincoln.

Not noted in artist's register, was exhibited in Loan Collection, Penna. Acad. of Fine Arts in 1887. Sold at auction in 1916. Size 22″ × 27″. Owned by Mr. John Braun in 1920.

179 BOONE, MRS.

Portrait painted for her son in Baltimore, begun April 27th, 1818, finished May 10th, 1868. Size 25″ × 30″. Price, $100.00

180 BORIE, JOHN J. (–1832)

Portrait begun by John Robinson, an English miniature painter who came to Phila. in 1817 with letters of introduction from Benjamin West. Thomas Sully began the painting Sept. 14th, 1825, and finished the portrait Nov. 26th, 1825. Bust. Price, $60.00

181 BORKEL, MRS.

Daughter of Dr. McCauley. Portrait painted at Baltimore, begun April 11th, 1853, finished May 10th, 1853. Head. Price, $100.00

182 BORDLEY, ELIZABETH.

See Mrs. James Gibson.

183 BOSLEY, COL. NICHOLAS.

Of Hayfields, Maryland. Portrait begun May 3rd, 1823, finished July 2nd, 1823. Bust. Price, $100.00

184 BOSLEY, MRS. NICHOLAS.

Of Hayfields, Maryland. Portrait begun Jan. 13th, 1823, finished Feb. 13th, 1823. Bust. Price, $100.00

Loaned by Wm. B. P. Closson of Newton, Mass., to National Gallery of Art, Washington, D. C.

185 BOUDINOT, DR. ELIAS (1740–1821).

Of Bordentown, N. J., was a patriot and philanthropist. Director Phila. Mint, President of American Bible Society. Portrait painted as a study for a whole length, begun Aug. 20th, 1816, finished Feb., 1818. Size 20″ × 24″. Price, $100.00

The head of this portrait has been engraved by Boyd (S–247).

NOTE.—The whole length portrait of Boudinot owned by the American Bible Soc. of New York is by Waldo & Jewett and not by Sully.

186 BOUDINOT, DR. ELIAS (1740–1821).
Whole length, portrait begun July 8th, 1817, finished Oct. 9th, 1817.
Size 58″ × 94″.   Price, $400.00

187 BOWEN, MR.
(Of Virginia.) Portrait begun Sept. 25th, 1816, finished Dec. 6th, 1816.
Bust.   Price, $100.00

188 BOYCE, MISS.
Portrait begun May 3rd, 1835, finished May 13th, 1835.   Head.
                                                                Price, $80.00

189 BOYER, MRS.
Painted for Dr. De Wees.   Portrait begun Jan. 2nd, 1811, finished Feb.
13th, 1811.   Bust.   Price, $60.00

190 BOYLAND, LILIE.
Painted for her father, portrait begun April 8th, 1857, finished May 8th,
1857.   Group.   Price, $200.00

191 BOYLAND, LOUISA.
Painted for her father, portrait begun April 8th, 1857, finished May 8th,
1857.   Group.   Price, $200.00

192 BOYLAND, WALTER.
Painted for his father, portrait begun March 11th, 1857, finished March
18th, 1857.   Head.   Price, $80.00

193 BRACKENBRIDGE, MR.
Painted from a miniature, portrait begun Sept. 23rd, 1814, finished Sept.
30th, 1814.   Bust.   Price, $50.00
Owned by Mrs. James H. Hutchinson, Phila.

194 BRADFORD, MR.
Portrait begun March 15th, 1807, and finished March 24th, 1807.   Bust.
                                                                Price, $50.00

195 BRADLEY, DR.
Painted for his daughter who married Alderman Badger.   Portrait begun
March 19th, 1835, finished March 24th, 1835.   Head.
Owned by Mr. John H. Braun, Phila.

196 BRADY, AMELIA E. (1832–1847).

Portraits of a young girl of about seventeen. Two heads, one to right the other to left with blond or golden hair, black dresses and bonnets tied under chins with black ribbons. Size 20″ h, 24″ w.
Owned by Mrs. Emily Drayton Taylor, Philadelphia, Pa.

197 BRATTLE, MR.

Deceased, painted from a daguerreotype, portrait begun Feb. 23rd, 1855. finished March 3rd, 1855. Bust. Price, $100.00

198 BRAZER, P.

" Alderman." Portrait begun March 12th, 1807, finished March 16th, 1807. Size 29″ × 36″. Price, $40.00

199 BREWSTER, MRS. MARIA HAMPTON.

Mother of Miss Anne M. Hampton Brewster. Head, nearly full face, hair smooth and parted in middle, wearing a red hood. Size of canvas 17″ × 20″.

NOTE.—This painting was in Italy for over twenty years, now owned by " The Library Company of Phila."

200 BRINTON, MRS.

Portrait begun Dec. 25th, 1808, finished March 27th, 1809. Bust.

201 BRINTON, MISS AND MASTER BRINTON.

Portrait begun Nov. 19th, 1808, finished Jan. 23rd, 1809. Size 20″ × 24″. Price, $60.00

202 BRODBENT, MR.

Painted for his father, portrait begun Feb. 15th, 1864, finished March 3rd, 1864. Head. Price, $50.00

203 BROOKS, MRS. GORHAM.

(Was Miss Shepard.) Portrait begun Aug. 26th, 1831, finished Nov. 4th, 1831. Bust. Price, $120.00
Owned by Shepard Brooks, Boston, Mass.

204 BROWN, ALBERT GALLATIN (1813–1880).

He was Governor of Mississippi, 1843–48, and U. S. Senate, 1854–61, when he resigned to take part in the rebellion. Portrait begun Dec. 27th, 1849, finished Jan. 7th, 1850. Bust. Price, $150.00

205 BROWN, MRS. ALBERT GALLATIN.

Wife of Governor of Mississippi. Portrait begun Sept. 13th, 1848, finished Sept. 23rd, 1848. Bust. Price, $100.00

LIST OF PAINTINGS

206 BROWN, MRS. ALEXANDER.
Portrait painted for Mr. Hunter, begun March 15th, 1839, finished May 4th, 1839.   Size 29″ × 36″.   Price, $300.00
Owned by Mrs. Howard Potter, New York.

207 BROWN, DIXON.
Portrait begun April 4th, 1804, finished April 16th, 1804.   Price, $12.00

208 BROWN, GENL. JACOB (1775–1828).
Commander-in-chief of the Army of the United States, awarded a gold medal by Congress for services in the War of 1812.   Portrait begun April 3rd, 1815, finished April 4th, 1815.   Head.   Price, $50.00

209 BROWN, JACOB (1775–1828).
Distinguished commander of the War of 1812.   Congress awarded him a gold medal.   Drawing made for the design Sept., 1817.   Size 6″ × 6″.
Price, $50.00

210 BROWN, JAMES.
Portrait begun Aug., 1805, finished Sept., 1805.   Size 12″ × 10″.
Price, $15.00

211 BROWN, NICOLAS (1769–1841).
He was of the well-known Rhode Island family and gave his name to Brown University as well as founding the Butler Hospital of Providence. Portrait painted at Providence, begun Aug. 12th, 1847, finished Aug. 23rd, 1847, for the Insane Hospital.   Full length, standing by table with arm extended to left.   Canvas 58″ × 84″.   Price, $800.00
Owned by the Butler Insane Asylum of Providence, R. I.

212 BROWN, O.
Painted from a portrait by King, as a present to Wheeler, begun Aug. 8th, 1848, finished Aug. 18th, 1848.   Bust.   Price, $150.00

213 BROWN, MR. WILLIAM.
Chestnut Street, Phila., this portrait was begun May 22nd, 1833, finished June 6th, 1833.   Bust.   Price, $100.00

214 BROWN, MRS. WILLIAM.
Bust, portrait was begun on June 11th, 1833.   The register notes it as "Condemned," and the price as $100.

215 BROWN, MRS. WILLIAM.
(Miss Norris.)   Portrait begun Dec. 16th, 1833, finished Dec. 31st, 1833.
Bust.   Price, $100.00

216 BROWN, GENERAL.

Of Tennessee (Deceased). He was a relative of Charles Ingersoll of Philadelphia. Portrait begun Jan. 2nd, 1844, and finished April 25th, 1844. Head. Price, $80.00

217 BROWNE, JOHN COATS (1838–1918).

Child seated on floor, low-necked and short-sleeved dress, playing with nine-pins. Painting begun Aug. 13th, 1842, and finished Sept. 5th, 1842. Size 25″ × 30″. Signed JS 1842. Price, $150.00
Owned by Mrs. John C. Brown, Clinton St., Phila.

218 BRUCE, MRS. CHARLES.

(Née Sarah Seddon, of Charlotte Co., Va.) Portrait begun April 28th, 1849, finished May 22nd, 1849. Bust, size 16″ × 20″. Price, $150.00
Sold by Macbeth Gallery, New York.

219 BRUCE, MRS. CHARLES.

Copy of my former painting, begun May 6th, 1849, finished June 6th, 1849. Bust. Price, $150.00

220 BRUCE, MR. CHARLES.

This portrait was painted at Richmond, Virginia, begun April 18th, 1849, finished April 30th, 1849. Bust. Price, $150.00
Owned by William Cabell Bruce, Staunton Hill, Charlotte Co., Virginia.

221 BRUCE, MR. CHARLES.

This portrait was painted in Virginia, was begun April 18th, 1849, finished April 30th, 1849. Head, 17″ × 20″. Price, $100.00
Owned by William Cabell Bruce, Staunton Hill, Charlotte Co., Virginia.

222 BRUJERE, MADAME.

Dunlap mentions that the Brujere portraits were painted as New Year presents for Madame and Monsieur Brujere, who were then living in Phila. Portrait begun Dec. 13th, 1814, finished Dec. 28th, 1814. Bust.
Price, $100.00

223 BRUJERE, MONSIEUR.

A French gentleman living in Philadelphia. Portrait begun April 20th, 1815, finished May 24th, 1815. Bust. Price, $80.00

224 BRUJERE, MADAME AND CHILD.

Portrait begun Jan. 3rd, 1815, finished May 12, 1815. Bust.
Price, $150.00

225 BRYAN, GUY (1755–1829).

Half length, seated in a red color chair, one hand holding a paper, full face, arm resting on book on table, dark coat, white neck-piece, florid complexion, thin white hair curled over ears. Portrait begun March 21st, 1825, finished May 31st, 1825. Bust. Price, $60.00

226 BRYAN, GUY.

Copy of my former painting, begun by Jane Sully, portrait finished by Thomas Sully, begun Jan. 7th, 1826, finished Jan. 7th, 1826. Price, $50.00

227 BRYAN, GUY.

The second copy of my former painting (introducing hand), begun Feb. 4th, 1826, finished Feb. 16th, 1826. Painted for his son. Bust. Price, $60.00

228 BRYAN, GUY.

The third copy of my former painting, begun Feb. 5th, 1826, finished Feb. 17th, 1826. Bust. Price, $50.00

229 BRYAN, GUY.

The fourth copy of my former painting, begun Feb. 6th, 1826, finished April, 1826. Bust. Price, $50.00

230 BRYAN, GUY.

There was evidently a fifth copy made but it is not noted in the register.

231 BRYAN, GUY.

The sixth copy of my former painting (for his son Timothy), was begun Feb. 12th, 1830, finished April 11th, 1830. Bust. Price, $75.00

232 BRYAN, GUY.

The seventh copy of my former painting (for his son Guy Bryan, Jr.), was begun March 20th, 1830), finished April 10th, 1830. Bust. Price, $75.00

233 BRYAN, GUY.

The eighth copy of my former portrait painted for his son Thomas Jefferson Bryan (1800–1870), was begun Sept. 21st, 1832, finished Nov. 3rd, 1832. Size 36½″ × 28″. Price, $100.00
Is among the collection of paintings in the New York Historical Society left by Thos. J. Bryan.

234 BRYAN, MRS. J.

With her son Francis, painting begun March 18th, 1839, finished April 27th, 1839. Portraits grouped. Size 29″ × 36″. Price, $500.00

LIST OF PAINTINGS

235 BRYAN, MRS.

(Deceased, of Texas, painted from a daguerreotype.) Portrait begun Sept. 17th, 1831, finished Oct. 2nd, 1851. Head. Price, $80.00

236 BRYAN, THOS. JEFFERSON (1800–1870).

Son of Guy Bryan. Portrait begun Dec. 14th, 1829, finished Jan. 4th, 1836. Head. Price, $50.00

237 BRYAN, THOMAS JEFFERSON.

The copy being begun by Jane Sully on June 9th was finished by Thos. Sully on June 11th, 1831. Head. Price, $50.00

238 BRYAN, MISS.

See portrait painted with Miss Swann.

239 BUCK, MRS.

The artist's register notes this portrait as painted "from a photograph, she being ill." The picture was begun Sept. 1st, 1857, and is noted as "Relinquished." Size 29" × 36". Price, $200.00

240 BUCKLER, DR. JOHN.

A prominent physician of Baltimore. The portrait was painted in Baltimore, begun Aug. 4th, 1840, finished Aug. 15, 1840. Bust.

Price, $200.00

Owned by Thomas H. Buckler of Baltimore.

241 BUCKLEY, MRS.

Painted for her son Edward, portrait begun Jan. 13th, 1854, finished Jan. 26th, 1854. Bust. Price, $100.00
Owned by Mrs. Edward S. Buckley, Chestnut Hill, Phila.

242 BUCKLEY, MR. (SENIOR).

Painted for his son, portrait begun Feb. 16th, 1854, finished March 16th, 1854. Bust. Price, $100.00

243 BUDD, HENRY (1849–1921).

Philadelphia lawyer, he read a paper on Thomas Sully before the Pennsylvania Historical Society, Jan., 1918. Portrait of Master Harry Budd, painted for his grandmother, Mrs. Burgh, begun Oct. 4th, 1856, finished April 25th, 1857. Head. Price, $80.00
Owned by Miss Ida Budd, Philadelphia.

244 BUDD, IDA.

Painted for her grandmother, Mrs. Burgh, portrait begun Oct. 3rd, 1857, finished May 2nd, 1857. Sister of No. 243. Head. Price, $80.00
Owned by Miss Ida Budd, Philadelphia.

245 BUDD, MRS. MATTIE.

Portrait painted for the artist's daughter, Blanch Sully, begun April 2nd, 1870, finished April 19th, 1870. Size 16″ × 20″. Price, $100.00
Owned by Mr. Johnson, Uniontown, Penna.

246 BUERTON, MISS MARY.

Portrait painted at Baltimore, begun December 7th, 1852, finished Dec. 30th, 1852. Head. Price, $100.00

247 BULLOCK, MR.

Portrait begun Aug. 30th, 1816, finished Sept. 6th, 1816. Bust.
Price, $100.00

248 BURD, EDWARD.

Painted for his stepson, Mr. Cox, portrait begun May 20th, 1828, finished on July 2nd, 1828. Bust. Price, $75.00

249 BURGESS, MRS. SOPHIA KIP.

This portrait was exhibited as painted by Thomas Sully in the Exhibition of Portraits of Women. Boston, Mass., 1895. This picture has not been seen by the authors.
Owned by Miss Storrs.

250 BURK, MRS.

Half length, head to left, low-necked dress and resting on chair, hands crossed. The painter's register notes " of the Gothic Mansion." This building was built by John Dorsey and stood on the north side of Chestnut St., between 12th and 13th Sts., Phila. Portrait begun May 25th, 1827, finished July 28th, 1827. Size 36″ × 28″. Signed " TS 1827." Price, $120.00
Sold by Ehrich Galleries of New York.

251 BURK, MRS.

Ordered by Miss North, and copied from the former portrait. Begun April 22th, 1862, finished May 14th, 1862. Size 29″ × 36″.
Price, $60.00

NOTE.—Portraits of the Misses Burk (group, Miss Elinor and Louisa Burk at about sixteen years of age) are attributed to Sully by the owner, Mrs. Catherine F. Lord of Rosemont, Phila.

252 BURK, MISS CAROLINE.

Painted for Miss North, portrait begun Jan. 10th, 1864, finished Feb. 4th, 1864. Head. Price, $40.00

253 BURK, MR.

Portrait begun July 6th, 1835, finished July 30th, 1835. Size 29" × 36".
Price, $200.00

254 BURKE, MRS.

(Née Miss Sally Carneal, of Cincinnati. Portrait begun Aug. 5th, 1844, finished Oct. 29th, 1844. Size 29" × 36". Price, $200.00
Owned by B. B. Howard, New Orleans, La.

255 BURK, MRS.

Of New Orleans, La., was Miss Rogers. Portrait begun July 6th, 1835, finished July 30th, 1835. Size 29" × 36". Price, $200.00

256 BURKHEAD, MR. (SENIOR).

Of Baltimore. Painted for his son. Portrait begun June 27, 1853, finished July 5th, 1853. Head. Price, $100.00

257 BURNETT, MRS.

Of Philadelphia. Bust, head to right, hair parted in middle with ringlets, gown open at neck. Portrait begun June 9th, 1844, and was finished June 18th, 1844. Signed "TS 1844." Size 20" × 24". Price, $80.00
Owned by Toledo Museum of Art, Toledo, Ohio.

258 BURR, DAVID.

Of Richmond, Va. Portrait begun Sept. 13th, 1834, finished Sept. 30th, 1834. Bust. Price, $125.00

259 BURR, MRS. DAVID.

Of Richmond, Va. Portrait begun Sept. 15th, 1834, finished Sept. 30th, 1834. Bust. Price, $125.00

260 BURROUGH, MRS. HORATIO NELSON.

Painted for her father, Samuel Augustus Mitchell, the publisher of Mitchell's School Atlas. Begun May 8th, 1863, finished May 26th, 1863. Size 24" × 30". Price, $40.00

261 BUTLER, CYRUS (1767–1849).

He was a prominent merchant of Providence, R. I., who gave his name and forty thousand dollars to founding the Butler Insane Hospital of Providence, R. I. This portrait was painted at Providence, R. I., begun July 22nd, 1847, finished Aug. 3rd, 1847. Full length, standing by table, figure to right. Canvas 58" × 94". Price, $800.00
Owned by the Butler Insane Hospital, Providence, R. I.

262 BYRON, LORD (1788–1824).

The English poet, after the original portrait painted by Richard Westall. Bust facing to left, chin resting on hand. Painted for J. R. Murray of New York, begun in 1826 and finished in 1828. Acquired by Jacob Eichholtz, the portait painter of Lancaster, Pa., in payment of a debt, who gave it to Geo. H. Munday, of Phila., in 1833. Size 29" × 23¾". Price, $50.00
Owned by Mr. Arthur Meeker, Chicago, Ill.

263 CABBEL, MRS.

Wife of Dr. Cabbel of Virginia. Portrait painted for her father, Mr. Caskie, of Richmond, Va., begun June 4th, 1849, finished June 15th, 1849. Head. Price, $100.00

264 CABEL, MRS. COLTER.

Formerly of South Carolina. Portrait begun Dec. 7th, 1850, finished Aug. 4th, 1851. Head. Price, $100.00

265 CABOT, MRS.

Deceased, painted from a sketch by Jarvis, begun Jan. 11th, 1819, finished Jan. 24th, 1819. Bust. Price, $100.00

266 CADWALADER, DR.

Deceased, copy for Mr. Read, of Albany, N. Y. Portrait begun Dec. 9th, 1864, finished Dec. 23rd, 1864. Bust. Price, $100.00

267 CADWALADER, GENL. JOHN (1742–1786).

General of the Revolution, and fought the duel with Conway. Copied from the portrait by Chas. Willson Peale. Copy begun July 7th, 1818, finished July 13th, 1818. Bust. Price, $100.00

268 CADWALADER, GENL. JOHN (1742–1786).

Copied from Sully's first picture after Peale's portrait. Portrait begun Dec. 4th, 1818, finished Dec. 31st, 1818. Bust. Price, $100.00

269 CADWALADER, GEORGE (1804–1879).

Soldier, and son of Genl. John Cadwalader; he served throughout the Mexican War and was brevetted major-general for gallantry; in 1862 he was commissioned a major-general of volunteers. He was later placed on the military board of the United States. Portrait painted about 1850 in uniform. Panel 18" × 20".
Owned by George H. Story, of New York City.

270 CADWALADER, THOMAS (1779–1841).

Eldest son of Genl. John Cadwalader of the Revolutionary War. He served with the Phila. City Troop in the Whiskey Insurrection of 1799, and was admitted to the bar in 1801. He was agent for the Penn estate for more than 25 years. Bust facing left, size 25" × 30". Portrait was begun Nov. 9th, 1833, finished Nov. 15th, 1833, painted for Horace Binney.
Reproduced in lithography. Price, $125.00

271 CADWALADER, FRANCIS.

See Lady Erskine.

272 CAGE, MR.

Of Cincinnati. Portrait begun July 8th, 1828, finished July 23rd, 1828. Size 29" × 36". Price, $120.00

273 CALDWELL, ELIAS BOUDINOT (1776–1825).

Clerk of the Supreme Court of the United States, 1801 to 1825. Portrait painted from a miniature, begun March 9th, 1839, finished April 3rd, 1849. Head. Size 20" × 24". Price, $80.00
Owned by the Penna. Historical Soc., Phila., Pa.

274 CALMADY CHILDREN.

Painted by Sir Thomas Lawrence, copy begun Sept. 23rd, 1867, finished Sept. 29th, 1867. Size 17" × 14". Price, $50.00

275 CALVERT, MRS.

Of Bladensburg, Md. The register notes that the hand of the sitter was introduced in the portrait, begun March 22nd, 1843, finished March 30th, 1843. Head. Price, $100.00

276 CALVERT, MR.

Of Bladensburg, Md. Portrait begun April 14th, 1824, finished Aug. 5th, 1824. Bust. Price, $60.00

277 CAMAC, MRS.

Painted for her mother Mrs. Markoe. Portrait begun April 8th, 1839, finished April 29th, 1839. Head. Price, $150.00

278 CAMPBELL, MRS. EMMA (1821–1843).

Daughter of Dr. Patterson. Portrait begun Jan. 7th, 1843, and noted in register of paintings as " Expunged." It was bust-size and the price entered was $100.00

LIST OF PAINTINGS

279 CAMPBELL, MRS. EMMA (1821–1843).

Daughter of Dr. Patterson. The register notes the portrait as the second attempt painted for Dr. Patterson, begun Feb. 25th, 1843, finished April 7th, 1843. Bust.   Price, $100.00

Owned by Mrs. Mary Stanley Liddell, of Lafayette, Indiana.

280 CAMPBELL, GEORGE.

President of the Musical Fund Society of Phila., 1827–1856. Bust, head to left. Portrait painted for the Musical Fund Society and hanging in their building on Locust St., Phila. Portrait begun May 16th, 1856, finished June 17th, 1856. Size 29″ × 36″. Signed on back "TS 1856."

Price, $100.00

281 CAMPBELL, MRS. JAMES H.

Of Pottsville, Pa. (Née Miss Juliet H. Lewis, daughter of Judge Ellis Lewis, of Phila., and wife of Hon. James H. Campbell the United States Minister to Sweden.) Bust, nearly full face with ringlets and blue ribbon in hair and at throat. Portrait begun Dec. 29th, 1862, finished Jan. 31st, 1863. Size 24″ × 20″. Signed on back of canvas "TS 1863."   Price, $40.00

Owned by Penna. Historical Soc., Phila.

282 CAMPBELL, MISS SUSAN.

Of Charleston, S. C. She was the daughter of Colin and Susan Wharton Campbell. Head, full to front, with brown ringlets. Painted in Phila. Signed "TS 1842," on millboard, size 20″ × 24″. Begun on Sept. 27th, 1842, finished Oct. 11th, 1842.   Price, $100.00

Purchased at sale of Mrs. Benj. Thaw, New York, by John F. Lewis, Phila.

283 CANIETOR, SIGNORA.

Portrait painted for her mother, begun Nov. 30th, finished Dec. 26th, 1831. Bust.   Price, $80.00

284 CANIETOR, SIGNOR.

Portrait begun Nov. 29th, 1831, finished Jan. 10th, 1832. Bust.

Price, $80.00

Nothing further than the entry in the register of paintings is known of the "Canietor" portraits.

285 CAPERTON, MRS. HUGH.

Of Georgetown, D. C. Painted for her mother, Mrs. Mosher, at Baltimore. Portrait begun Feb. 1st, 1853, finished Feb. 8th, 1853. Head to left, hair parted in middle.   Price, $100.00

Owned by Mrs. Hugh Carpenter, Jr., Baltimore, Md.

286 CAREY, EDWARD L. (1806-1845).

Philadelphia publisher and art collector; he was a son of Matthew Carey. At the time of his death he was President of the Penna. Academy of Fine Arts. This portrait was painted by Sully from a water color by Hoppner Meyer, a nephew of John Hoppner, begun Aug. 8th, 1856, finished Sept. 6th, 1856. Head. Price, $100.00
Owned by the Penna. Acad. of Fine Arts.

287 CAREY, EDWARD L. (1806-1845).

Portrait painted for Henry Carey, from former portrait. Begun May 2nd, 1857, finished May 26th, 1857. Bust. Price, $100.00

288 CAREY, EDWARD L. (1806-1845).

(Deceased.) Copy of former portrait painted for Henry Carey, begun Jan. 31st, finished Feb. 12th, 1859. Bust, facing front. Signed on back "TS." Size 25" × 30". Price, $100.00
Owned by the Penna. Academy of Fine Arts.

289 CAREY, VIRGINIA.

Portrait painted in a group with Miss Adelaide and Emma Leslie, for her father, Henry Carey. See Leslie.

290 CARROLL, HENRY.

Portrait painted at Baltimore for Mr. Winchester, begun Jan. 20th, 1853, finished March 5th, 1853. Bust. Price, $150.00

291 CARROL, MRS. CHARLES (1775-1861).

Portrait begun May 16th, 1822, finished July 6th, 1822. Bust. Signed "TS 1822." Price, $100.00
Owned by Mrs. G. Woolsey Hodge, Philadelphia.

292 CARROLL, CHARLES (1737-1830).

Of Carrollton. American patriot and signer of the Declaration of Independence. Painted as a study for the whole length for the Marquis of of Wellesley, begun May 22nd, 1826, finished May 25th, 1826. Bust.
Price, $40.00

293 CARROLL, CHARLES (1737-1830).

Full-length portrait painted for the Marquis of Wellesley, begun June 29th, 1827, finished Aug. 21st, 1827. Size 58" × 94". Price, $500.00

294 CARROLL, CHARLES.

(Of Carrollton.) Portrait painted for Mrs. Carroll, begun Sept. 29th, 1827, finished Nov. 18th, 1827. Bust. Price, $75.00

295 CARROLL, CHARLES.

(Of Carrollton.) Full length seated by table, head slightly to right. Painted for the State of Maryland, begun Oct. 22nd, 1833, finished Jan. 27th, 1834, Signed " TS 1834." Deposited in the Senate Chamber of the Capitol at Annapolis, Md. Size 58" × 94".   Price, $1000.00

Exhibited at Maryland Institute, Baltimore, at Exhibition of Sully Portraits, 1921.

296 CARROLL, CHARLES.

A copy of the head painted in 1826 and 1827 is signed " E. S. 1836," hangs in the Penna. Historical Society. It is recorded as " Painted and presented by the Sully family to the Penna. Colonization Society." It has been attributed to Thomas Sully but is probably largely the work of his daughter Ellen, who is mentioned in family letters about this time as " copying in a most creditable way a number of portraits " of her father.

NOTE.—A half-length portrait of Charles Carroll, seated, nearly full face, holding a book in his hand. Size 29" × 36". Is attributed to Sully; it was loaned by Peabody Institute to Sully Exhibition at Maryland Institute in 1921. A study or unfinished bust portrait (canvas 20" × 24") is attributed to Sully and is owned by the Massachusetts Historical Society of Boston.

297 CARTER, MISS MILDRED LEE.

Of Virginia, was the daughter of Bernard Moore Carter, and married Louis de Potesdad. Portrait painted for Mr. Hopkinson of Phila., begun Feb. 5th, 1812, finished April 27th, 1812. Size 29" × 36". Price, $100.00

298 CARTER, MISS MILDRED LEE.

Of Virginia. Portrait begun May 3rd, 1844, and noted in the register of the artist as " given up." It was a head, price $80 and was evidently a copy of the former painting made in 1812.

299 CASKIE, MR.

Of Richmond, Va. Portrait begun Sept., 1835, finished Oct. 20, 1835. Bust.   Price, $125.00

300 CASKIE, MRS.

Of Richmond, Va. Portrait begun in Sept., 1835, finished Oct. 22nd, 1835. Bust.   Price, $125.00

301 CASSIDY, MRS. LEWIS C.

(Née Truman.) Portrait painted for her husband the well-known Philadelphia lawyer, painting begun May 19th, 1864, and finished June 1st, 1864. Head.   Price, $50.00

Owned by her son, Judge Gilbert H. Cassidy, of Phila.

302 CHAFFER, MRS.

Portrait begun Jan. 28th, 1846, finished Feb. 16th, 1846. Bust.

Price, $200.00

303 CHAMBERLAIN, CAPT. WILLIAM.

Was a Philadelphian. The portrait was begun Nov. 10th, 1810, finished Dec. 14th, 1810. Bust, seated, head three-quarters to right. Arm over back of chair, wears a double-breasted great coat open at the neck showing under coat and white stock. Canvas 31½" × 26". See illustration.

Portrait owned by Herbert L. Pratt, of New York.

304 CHAMBERLAIN, MRS. WILLIAM.

(Was Miss Cornelia Mitchell of Virginia.) Head to left, low-necked dress with cloak over shoulder. Portrait begun June 1st, 1810, finished Aug. 2nd, 1810. Canvas 31" × 26".

Owned by Herbert L. Pratt, of New York.

305 CHAMBERS, MRS.

Portrait begun March 19th, 1862, finished April 17th, 1862, Size 30" × 25". Price, $50.00

306 CHAPMAN, EMILY (1810–1852).

Eldest child of Dr. Nathaniel Chapman, of Philadelphia, married John Montgomery Gordon, of Virginia. Head to left, dark hair parted in the middle with curls at side. Portrait begun Feb. 11th, 1828, finished March 6th, 1828. Size of canvas 17½" × 15", signed "TS 1828." Price, $50.00

Owned by Mrs. Arthur Poultney and exhibited at Maryland Institute, 1921.

307 CHAPMAN, EMILY (1810–1852).

Replica of portrait No. 306. Size 18" × 15".

Owned by the estate of Alexander Biddle, Esq., Chestnut Hill, Phila.

308 CHAPMAN, GABRIELLA.

Granddaughter of Dr. Chapman, married Louis de Potesdad. Portrait begun March 30th, 1837, finished April 11th, 1837. Head. Price, $150.00

309 CHAPMAN, GEORGE WILLIAMS (1816–1853).

Painted as a youth of seventeen in the uniform of the U. S. Naval Academy. He married Emily, daughter of John Markoe. Head to left, size 17" × 20". Signed on back " TS Feb., 1833." Portrait painted for his father, Dr. Nathaniel Chapman. Begun Feb. 13th, 1833, and finished Feb. 19th, 1833. Price, $60.00

Owned by George C. Thayer, Villanova, Penna.

310 CHAPMAN, JOHN BIDDLE (1812–1845).

Son of Dr. Nathaniel Chapman. Portrait painted for Miss Brocken-borough, begun Dec. 2nd, 1833, finished Dec. 12th, 1833. Head.

Price, $80.00

311 CHAPMAN, MRS. JOHN BIDDLE.

(Was Mary Randolph, of Virginia.) Portrait painted for her mother, begun June 17th, 1833, finished July 1st, 1833. Head. Price, $60.00

312 CHAPMAN, MASTER.

Portrait painted for Dr. Chapman, begun July 4th, 1829, finished July 20th, 1829. Head. Price, $50.00

313 CHAPMAN, NATHANIEL (1780–1853).

Born in Virginia, graduated at medical department of University of Penna. in 1801, studied in Edinburgh and England. In 1808 married Rebecca Biddle, daughter of Col. Clement Biddle. Portrait painted for his class of students, three-quarter length standing, as if speaking, begun Feb. 19th, 1848, finished March 15th, 1848. Size 45″ × 57″. Price, $300.00
Owned by University of Penna.

314 CHAPMAN, NATHANIEL (1780–1853).

Half length seated, high-collared black coat, hands appear as making a gesture to emphasize his speech. Portrait begun April 14th, 1817, finished July 1st, 1817. Size 43″ × 33″. Price, $200.00
Portrait engraved by Goodman & Piggot (Stauffer No. 1128).
Presented to the College of Physicians, Phila., by his grandson's widow, Mrs. Henry C. Chapman.

NOTE.—The American Philosophical Society own a copy by S. B. Waugh of the portrait painted by Thomas Sully of Dr. Nathaniel Chapman.

315 CHASE, MRS. PHILIP.

Miss Guilielma Maria Collins, married Philip Brown Chase, and this portrait was painted for her sister, Mrs. Bispham, No. 155. Begun Feb. 26th, 1840, finished March 7th, 1840. Head. Price, $150.00

316 CHAUNCEY, CHARLES (1777–1849).

Member of Philadelphia Bar. Half length, seated in chair with hands clasped in lap, elbow resting on table with book. Head to left. Portrait begun Aug. 23rd, 1833, finished Dec. 31st, 1833. Size 29″ × 36″.

Price, $150.00
Engraved by John Sartain. Portrait belongs to Law Association of Phila.

317 CHAUNCEY, ELIHU (1779–1847).

Brother of Charles Chauncey, No. 316, he was admitted to the Philadelphia Bar, and was a leader in the management of the Philadelphia and Reading Railroad. The portrait was painted for Mr. Dillingham, and the register notes it as begun Jan. 30th, 1834, and that it was not finished. Bust.
Owned by Elihu Chauncey, Esq., New York.

318 CHAUNCEY, NATHANIEL (1789–   ).

Graduated at Yale College 1806, and was admitted to the Philadelphia Bar. Portrait painted for Mr. Dillingham. Begun March 22nd, 1834, finished April 25th, 1834. Bust.   Price, $125.00

319 CHAUNCEY, MRS. NATHANIEL (–1850).

(Née Elizabeth Sewall.) She married Nathaniel Chauncey, June 8th, 1836. Portrait begun on Feb. 19th, 1837, finished Feb. 28th, 1837. Head.
                                                        Price, $100.00

320 CHAUNCEY, MISS.

Daughter of Charles Chauncey the Phila. lawyer. Portrait begun Sept. 25th, 1836, finished Oct. 13th, 1836.   Head.   Price, $100.00

321 CHAUNCEY, MISS.

(Deceased, copy from portrait by Bass Ottis.) Begun Dec. 8th, 1836, finished Dec. 23rd, 1836.   Head.   Price, $100.00

322 CHEVALIER, PETER.

Of Richmond, Virginia. Father of Sally Chevalier, a famous Richmond belle. Portrait begun Jan. 1st, 1804, finished Jan. 14th, 1804. Size 10″ × 12″.   Price, $12.00

323 CHEVALIER, MISS SARAH.

Daughter of Peter Chevalier, of Richmond, Va. She married Abram Warwick, was a famous belle, and was one of the trio called the " Richmond Graces." Portrait begun May 29th, 1832, finished July 24th, 1832. Bust. Head to left, with hair parted in middle and curls at sides of face, low-necked dress. Reproduced in Peacock's Famous American Belles of the 19th Century.   Price, $100.00
Owned by Col. Thos. A. Ellis, Richmond, Va.

324 CHEVALIER, MISS SARAH.

Of Richmond, Va. Copy made for Mr. Barksdale, begun Sept. 24th, 1860, finished Sept. 30th, 1860. Bust.   Price, $100.00

325 CHEVALIER, MISS SARAH.

Of Richmond, Va. Second copy made for Mrs. Warwick, begun Sept. 24th, 1860, finished Sept. 30th, 1860. Bust.   Price, $100.00

326 CHISOLM, MISS SUSAN.

Of Charlestown, South Carolina. She married Mr. Oliver H. Middleton. Portrait painted for her mother, begun Sept. 30th, 1826, finished Oct. 31st, 1826. Size 29" × 36".   Price, $120.00
Owned by Miss Eliza Blake, Arden, N. C.

327 CIMABUE, GIOVANNI (1240–1302).

A celebrated Florentine painter. Copy, portrait begun Oct. 29th, 1871, finished Dec. 8th, 1871. Size, 9" × 7".   Price, $30.00
Sold at executor's sale, Dec. 20th, 1872, by Thomas & Sons., 4th St., Phila.

328 CLARK, COL. I.

(Of the Armory.) Portrait begun March, 1806, finished same month, size 12" × 10".   Price, $15.00

329 CLARK, MRS.

(Mother of Mrs. Alexander.) Portrait begun March 25th, 1851, finished June 20th, 1851. Head.   Price, $100.00

330 CLARK, MISS.

Of Baltimore. Portrait begun July 15th, 1834, finished July 21st, 1834. Head.   Price, $80.00

331 CLAY, HENRY.

NOTE.—A portrait of Henry Clay attributed to Thomas Sully has been exhibited for many years. The authors do not agree in the attribution, but note it for reference. Bust seated, head to right, size 27" × 36".

332 CLEMENT, CHARLES W.

Of New Orleans, La. Portrait begun Sept. 23rd, 1825, finished Nov. 3rd, 1825. Bust.   Price, $60.00

333 CLIFFORD, MISS.

Portrait begun Sept. 16th, 1810, finished Sept. 20th, 1810. The register notes that " both hands were introduced " in the portrait, which accounts for the price of $70 for a bust size at that time.

334 CLOPPER, MR.

Portrait begun Nov. 20th, 1810, finished Dec. 20th, 1810. Bust. The register notes that the " hand was introduced " in the painting, and the price as $70.

335 COALE, MARY (1789–1831).

Daughter of Dr. Samuel Coale, she married William Town Proud, of New Bedford, Mass. Portrait begun March 22nd, 1809, finished April 13th, 1809. Bust. Subscribers' Price, $30.00

336 COATES, BENJAMIN (1808–1887).

A prominent Abolitionist and worker for the African race. Presented by the artist to the Penna. Colonization Society. Begun April 2nd, 1863, finished April 19th, 1863. Bust, head to right, with black stock. Size 24" × 20". Price, $40.00
Owned by the Penna. Historical Society, Phila., Pa.

337 COATES, SAMUEL (1748–1830).

Philadelphia merchant, was Treasurer of the Library Company and Manager and President of the Pennsylvania Hospital. Full length standing, writing desk and window in background. Size 64" × 94". Portrait begun Aug. 25th, 1812, finished Aug. 29th, 1812. Presented by the artist to the Hospital. Price, $400.00
Owned by Penna. Hospital, Philadelphia.

338 COCHRAN, MR.

Of Baltimore, Md. Portrait begun Nov. 4th, 1815, finished Nov. 30th, 1815. Bust. Price, $100.00

339 COCHRAN, MRS.

Of Baltimore, Md. Portrait painted for Mrs. Brady, begun Nov. 10th, 1815, finished Dec. 5th, 1815. Size 10" × 8". Price, $50.00

340 COGNIET, LEON (1794–1880).

French painter, this portrait copied from " Arts Union." Begun March 22nd, 1849, finished March 26th, 1849. Size 18" × 14". Price, $50.00

341 COLEMAN, MR.

Father of Mrs. Alexander (Deceased). Portrait begun March 20th, 1851, finished June 20th, 1851. The register notes the portrait as a " bust with hand " introduced. Price, $150.00

342 COLEMAN, MR.

Of Lancaster. Portrait begun Dec. 2nd, 1821, copied from Peale's portrait. Bust. Price, $100.00

343 COLEMAN, MISS.
Of Lancaster (Deceased). Portrait begun Jan. 11th, 1820, finished Jan. 28th, 1820. Bust. Price, $100.00

344 COLEMAN, ANNA AND HARRIET.
Half-length portrait, begun Nov. 2nd, 1846, finished Dec. 18th, 1846. Price, $300.00

345 COLEMAN, MISS MARY.
Sketch for painting a whole-length portrait, begun July 4th, 1828, finished July 6th, 1828. Size 10" × 8". Price, $10.00

346 COLEMAN, MISS MARY.
Full length, painted for James Ross, begun Nov. 11th, 1828, finished Dec. 20th, 1828. Size 29" × 36". Price, $230.00

347 COLEMAN, MARY.
Portrait painted for Mrs. J. Coleman. Whole-length portrait, 50" × 37". Painting begun March 27th, 1833, finished May 18th, 1833. Price, $250.00

348 COLEMAN, MISS MARY.
Copied from former portrait for the artist. Size 29" × 36". Portrait begun Nov. 15th, 1828, finished April, 1835. Price, $200.00

349 COLEMAN, GROUP OF THE MISSES MARGARET, ISABELLA AND SARAH.
Begun March 6th, 1844, finished April 13th, 1844. Size 28" × 36". Price, $300.00

350 COLEMAN, MISS.
Sketch for a whole length, begun Jan. 25th, 1833, finished Jan. 26th, 1833. Size 12" × 8". Price, $50.00

351 COLES, MRS. EDWARD.
She was Sally Logan Roberts, and married Edward Coles, Governor of Illinois. Portrait begun April 4th, 1836, finished May 2nd, 1836. Head. Price, $100.00
Owned by the Penna. Historical Society.

352 COLES, GEORGE.
Bust, head to left, high coat collar and white stock. Size 25" × 30".
Exhibited at Metropolitan Museum, New York, 1892.
Owned by Knoedler & Co., of New York, in 1919.

LIST OF PAINTINGS

353 COLES, TUCKER.

Of "Tallwood," Albemarle Co., Virginia. Brother of Edward Coles, Governor of Illinois. Bust, seated, stock and black coat. Portrait begun June 7th, 1835, and finished June 27th, 1835. Bust, size of canvas 25″ × 30″.   Price, $125.00

Owned by Dr. J. Hall Pleasants, and exhibited at Maryland Institute, Baltimore, 1921.

354 COLES, MRS. TUCKER (1790–1865).

Of "Tallwood," Albemarle Co., Virginia. (Née Helen Skipwith, daughter of Sir Peyton Skipwith, Bart.) Portrait bust, head to left, with large black hat and white ostrich plumes, black dress. Begun June 7th, 1835, and finished June 27th, 1835. Signed "℔ 1835." Bust, size of canvas 24½″ × 29½″.   Price, $125.00

Owned by Dr. J. Hall Pleasants, and exhibited at Maryland Institute, Baltimore, 1921.

355 COLLET, MRS.

Of Patterson, N. J. Formerly Miss Wallace. Portrait begun Oct. 22nd, 1836, finished Nov. 4th, 1836. Bust.   Price, $150.00

356 COLLINS, MARGARET MORRIS (1792–1852).

Wife of Isaac Collins, whose daughter Martha married John B. Bispham. Portrait begun March 5th, 1834, finished March 28th, 1834. Head.   Price, $80.00

357 COLLINS, MRS.

Of Pittsburgh. Copy. Painting begun Jan. 19th, 1837, finished Feb. 2nd, 1837. Bust, 25″ × 30″.   Price, $150.00

358 COLLINS, MASTER.

(Deceased.) Portrait painted for Mrs. Wm. Biddle, of 4th St., Phila., begun July 22nd, 1826, finished Sept. 6th, 1826. Size 24″ × 16″. (Lydia Biddle married James Collins.)   Price, $50.00

359 COLT, ROSWELL J.

Of Baltimore, Md. Head, full face, with high stock and collar, hair curly. Bust.   Price, $80.00

Lithographed by Albert Newsam, Phila.

Owned by Lyman Roswell Colt, Seattle, Washington.

360 CONNELLY, H.

Cabinet maker. Portrait begun July 15th, 1808, finished August 19th, 1808. Bust. Price, $50.00

361 CONNELLY, JOHN (1752–1827).

An auctioneer of Philadelphia. Portrait painted for Mrs. Eyre, begun April 3rd, 1813, finished Sept. 5th, 1813. Size 28″ × 36″. Half length, seated, head to right. Price, $100.00

Owned by Manuel Eyre Griffith, of Philadelphia.

362 COOK, ELIZABETH.

(Afterwards Mrs. Benjamin Franklin Bache, of Phila.) An intimate friend of the artist's daughters, and painted and sketched as ideal or fancied subjects. Half length, standing with large sun-bonnet and shawl over shoulders, arm through handle of basket. Engraved by John Cheney for the "Gift of 1842" as "Country Girl" or "Maidenhood." Signed "TS 1839." Canvas 30″ × 24¾″. Price, $300.00

Owned by John Hill Morgan, New York.

363 COOK, ELIZABETH.

Study or sketch for portrait as "Country Girl." (Noted in the register as for Kane.) Painting begun Oct. 18th, 1839, finished Nov. 6th, 1839. Size 17″ × 20″. Price, $150.00

364 COOK, MRS. WILLIAM.

Of Richmond, Va. Portrait begun Feb. 13th, 1813, finished March 4th, 1813. Head. Price, $70.00

365 COOK, MRS. WILLIAM.

Of Richmond, Va. Deceased, painted from a miniature, begun March 1st, 1813, finished March 7th, 1813. Head. Price, $70.00

366 COOKE, GEORGE FREDERICK (1755–1812).

A well-known English actor of very dissipated habits who played in this country in 1810 and died in New York City in 1812. See "Life of Cooke," by Wm. Dunlap, for account of Sully's portraits of Cooke. Bust, head to right seen in half view, fur-trimmed cloak thrown back from the shoulders, showing a buff vest, his left hand rests upon a book. Portrait begun April 8th, 1811, finished May 7th, 1811. Size 24½″ × 29½″. Price, $60.00

Was in collection of Edw. Bierstadt. Sold at Anderson's Auction, April 27th, 1905, New York.

LIST OF PAINTINGS

367 COOKE, GEORGE FREDERICK (1755–1812).

In character as Richard III. Full length, life size facing right. This portrait was begun on April 13th, 1811, and finished June 13th, 1812; it was purchased for $300, raised by subscription from Cooke's friends and admirers, and presented to the Penna. Academy of Fine Arts. Canvas size 60″ × 94″. Signed on front with monogram " $\mathbb{TS}$ 1811."
Owned by Penna. Academy of Fine Arts, Phila.

368 COOKE, GEORGE FREDERICK (1755–1812).

In costume facing left, with red cloak and broad lace collar with points. Portrait painted for Benj. Chew Wilcocks, of Phila., begun April 20th, 1811, and finished June 4th, 1811. Bust, size 25″ × 30″.   Price, $60.00
Engraved by David Edwin. (See Fielding No. 41.)
Owned by Mrs. Alexander Campbell (née Wilcocks), of Phila.

369 COOKE, GEORGE FREDERICK (1755–1812).

In costume, facing left, with cloak, broad lace collar with points. Portrait copied from first painting, it was engraved by David Edwin. (See Fielding No. 41.) Painting begun Feb. 4th, 1819, finished Feb. 20th, 1819. Bust.
    Price, $100.00

370 COOKE, GEORGE FREDERICK (1755–1812).

Portrait painted from Sully's first picture, begun June 29th, 1816, finished Sept. 17th, 1816. Head.   Price, $50.00

371 COOLIDGE, MRS.

(Deceased.) Portrait painted for her daughter. Begun June 2nd, 1845, finished June 10th, 1845. Head.   Price, $80.00

372 COOLIDGE, MISS A. S.

Of Boston. Portrait begun June 2nd, 1845, finished June 9th, 1845. Head.   Price, $80.00

373 COOPER, THOMAS ABTHORPE (1776–1849).

An English actor, appearing in Phila., 1796; in 1804 he became lessee of the Park Theatre, New York. Portrait painted for Miss Nichols, begun August, 1805, finished September, 1805. Size 10″ × 12″.   Price, $15.00

374 COOPER, THOMAS ABTHORPE (1776–1849)

Portrait begun in Richmond, Va.. Feb. 4th, 1807, and finished in New York, June 5th, 1807. Size 10″ × 12″.   Price, $15.00

127

375 COOPER, MRS. THOMAS A.

Was Mary Fairlie. Their daughter Priscilla married Robert Tyler, a son of President Tyler, and for a time presided over the White House. Portrait painted for the actor Cooper, begun May 4th, 1807, and finished May 27th, 1807. Size 29″ × 36″. Price, $60.00

376 COPE, CALEB (1797-1888).

Portrait painted for the Horticultural Society of Phila. He was the seventh President of the Academy of Fine Arts (1859-1871) and President of the Phila. Saving Fund from 1863 until his death. Portrait begun March 12th, 1852, finished March 22nd, 1852. Bust. Price, $100.00
Owned by Horticultural Society of Phila.

NOTE.—A replica of the portrait of Caleb Cope is said to be in the possession of a relative of the Cope family in Ohio.

377 COPE, MISS ABBIE ANN (1804-1845).

She married her cousin Caleb Cope in 1838, for whom this portrait was painted, begun May 15th, 1837, and finished May 31st, 1837. Size 29″ × 36″. Price, $300.00
Owned by Mrs. Yarnall, Phila.

378 CORNISH, CAPT.

Of the English East India Service. Portrait begun May 11th, 1817, finished June 7th, 1817. Size 29″ × 36″. Price, $150.00

379 CORTES, HERNANDO (1485-1547).

Painting a copy of painting of Rosalie Sully's, begun Sept. 21st, 1871, finished Oct. 2nd, 1871. Size 16″ × 16″. Price, $50.00

380 COX, JOHN (1788-1864).

Merchant of Philadelphia and President of Lehigh Coal and Navigation Co. Portrait begun Feb. 12th, 1829, finished March 18th, 1829. Size 25″ × 30″. Price, $75.00
Owned by his grandson John Lyman Cox, of Chestnut Hill, Phila.

381 COX, MRS. JOHN (1792-1831).

Was Miss Martha Lyman, daughter of Genl. Wm. Lyman, of Mass. Portrait begun Feb. 11th, 1829, finished March 11th, 1829. This was the second portrait painted, the first being condemned. Bust, wearing hat, and ermine cape. Size 25″ × 30″. Price, $75.00
Owned by her grandson, John Lyman Cox, of Chestnut Hill, Phila.

LIST OF PAINTINGS

382 COXE, MRS. JOHN REDMAN.

Sarah, daughter of Col. John Cox, of New Jersey, married Dr. Coxe, of Phila. Bust, head to left, resting on hand. Portrait begun Sept. 5th, 1813, finished Oct. 12th, 1813. Size 29" × 36". Price, $100.00
Owned by Mrs. Edward Parke Custis Lewis, of Hoboken, N. J.

383 CRAIG, MRS. JOHN.

Was the beautiful Jane Josephine Sarmiento, whose first husband Mr. Craig was a brother of Mrs. Nicholas Biddle, and whose second husband, Edward Biddle, was a son of her first husband's sister. Portrait begun June 12th, 1836, finished March 26th, 1837. Bust. Price, $150.00
Painting destroyed by fire of Marquard's Storage House, New York.

384 CRAIG, JOHN.

Infant son of Mrs. John Craig (née Sarmiento). Portrait was painted for Mrs. John Craig, begun Nov. 19th, 1839, and finished Dec. 2nd, 1839. Head. Price, $150.00
Painting destroyed by fire at Marquard's Storage House, New York.

385 CRAWFORD, MRS. JUDGE.

Of Mobile. Painting begun May 29th, 1837, finished June 16th, 1837. Size 29" × 36". Price, $300.00

386 CRESSON, CALEB.

(Copied from a portrait by Leslie, for his nephew.) Portrait begun Oct. 26th, 1824, finished Nov. 5th, 1824. Size 17" × 20". Price, $30.00

387 CRESSON, CALEB.

Portrait copied from a painting by Charles Robert Leslie. Painting begun October 26th, 1824, and finished November 5th, 1824. Copied for his nephew. Head. Price, $30.00

388 CRESSON, ELLIOT (1796–1854).

An American philanthropist who became interested in the Pennsylvania Colonization Society. Bust, facing right. Size 20" × 24". Portrait begun on Oct. 14th, 1849, and finished Oct. 25th, 1849. Price, $80.00
Deposited with the Historical Society of Penna. by the Colonization Society of Penna.

389 CRESSON, ELLIOT (1796–1854).

American philanthropist. Portrait begun July 5th, 1824, finished July 10th, 1824. Head. Price, $30.00

390 CRESSON, ELLIOT (1796–1854).

Copy from the former portrait. Begun March 12th, 1855, finished March 29th, 1855. Head. Price, $50.00

391 CRESSON, MARY EMLEN (1809–1890).

She married Joseph P. Smith, by whose order this portrait was painted, begun May 20th, 1828, and finished June 4th, 1828. Head. Price, $50.00

392 CRESSON, SARAH.

For her brother Caleb. Portrait begun April 4th, 1826, finished April 14th, 1826. Head. Size 17″ × 20″. Price, $30.00

393 CRESSON, MASTER.

Copied from painting by Sir Joshua Reynolds. Painting begun Dec. 9th, 1815, finished Dec. 19th, 1815. Size 17″ × 20″. Price, $50.00

394 CREW, MASTER.

Copied from painting by Sir Joshua Reynolds. Painting begun Dec. 9th, 1815, finished Dec. 19th, 1815. Size 17″ × 20″. Price, $50.00

NOTE.—Crosier. See Crozer.

395 CROSS, BENJAMIN (1786–1857).

Half length, seated, with hand resting on table, head slightly to left. Director of music and a well-known organist of Phila. Portrait painted from a daguerreotype for the Musical Fund Society of Phila., begun Jan. 22nd, 1861, finished Jan. 31st, 1861. Signed on back of canvas " TS 1861," size 29″ × 36″. Price, $100.00
Owned by Musical Fund Society of Philadelphia.

396 CROSS, BENJAMIN (1786–1857).

Copy of former portrait, painted for his son Edward, begun Feb. 26th, 1866, finished March 12th, 1866. Size 30″ × 25″. Price, $100.00

397 CROSSMAN, GENL. GEO. H. (1798–1882).

General Crossman was for many years Chief Quartermaster for the Department of the East, with his headquarters in Philadelphia where he died. He was the father of the actress Henrietta Crossman. Portrait begun Dec. 2nd, 1861, finished Dec. 22nd, 1861. Size 25″ × 30″. Price, $50.00

398 CROSSMAN, MRS. GEORGE H.

Portrait painted for Mr. Fitzgerald, begun Nov. 1st, 1861, finished Nov. 20th, 1861. Size 25″ × 30″. Price, $50.00

399 CROZER, JOHN PRICE (1793–1866).

President of the Colonization Society in 1860.

NOTE.—Sully has been credited with painting the portraits of both 400 and 399, but the only record in his register is " Mr. Crozer, begun March 20th, 1862, finished April 25th, 1862. Price, $50." Pres. of Colonization Soc. Size 25" × 30".

400 CROZER, DR. SAMUEL A. (1796–   ).

A younger brother of John Price Crozer; he was the first physician and agent appointed by the Society to proceed to Africa. He was President of the Penna. Colonization Society from 1860 until his death.

401 CRUGER, MRS. H. D.

Portrait copied from one by Sir Wm. Beechey. Begun Jan. 19th, 1844, finished Feb. 6th, 1844. Size 29" × 36". Price, $200.00

402 CUMMINGS, MRS. WILLIAM (1805–1847).

Emily Richardet, daughter of Richard Alexander, married William Cummings, a well-known merchant of Philadelphia. Half length, seated, head turned to right. Wears a white, low-necked dress with necklace and pendant cross. Portrait begun March 11th, 1847, finished April 3rd, 1847. Bust, size 25" × 30". Signed on back " TS 1847."
Owned by Hon. Norris S. Barratt, Phila.

NOTE.—Wm. Cummings' portrait was painted by John Neagle.

403 CUNNINGHAM, MR.

Portrait begun Oct. 31st, 1807, finished Dec. 2nd, 1807. Bust.
Price, $60.00

404 CUSHMAN, CHARLOTTE (1816–1876).

Distinguished American actress. Born in Boston, in 1845 she went to England where she acted with success for several years. The register notes " Of the Walnut St. Theatre, Phila." The portrait was begun March 1st, 1843, finished April 27th, 1843. Head. Price, $80.00

405 CUSHMAN, CHARLOTTE.

Portrait painted for Mrs. Gardette. Painting begun June 28th, 1843, the register notes this portrait as " Expunged " and the price $80. Head.

406 CUSHMAN, CHARLOTTE.

Portrait painted for Mrs. Gardette in lieu of the one expunged, begun July 21st, 1843, finished July 29th, 1843. Head. Price, $80.00

407 CUTHBERT, MR.

Of Beaufort, South Carolina. Portrait begun Sept. 20th, 1825, finished Nov. 26th, 1825. Bust. Price, $75.00

408 CUTHBERT, MRS.

(Née Rush.) Painted from a miniature. Portrait painted for Mrs. Julia Williams Biddle, begun April 23rd, 1862, finished May 31st, 1862. Half length, seated in red chair, nearly full face, white dress with blue ribbons around waist. Size 30″ × 25″. Price, $50.00
Owned by estate of Alexander Biddle, Philadelphia, Pa.

409 CUTHBERT, MRS.

Deceased, painted from a miniature, begun June 19th, 1826, finished Sept. 2nd, 1826. Bust. Price, $75.00

410 DACLAY, MISS.

Portrait begun July 2nd, 1810, finished August 1st, 1810. Head.
Price, $30.00

411 DALE, LIEUT. JOHN MONTGOMERY (1797–1852).

Son of Com. Richard Dale, he attained the rank of commander in the United States Navy. Portrait begun Sept. 18th, 1818, finished Oct. 7th, 1818. Bust. Price, $100.00

412 DALE, RICHARD (1756–1826).

Commodore Dale was Paul Jones' lieutenant at the time of the fight between the Bonhomme Richard and the Serapis. Bust, nearly full face, black coat and buff vest. Portrait copied from painting by Eicholtz. Sully began the painting Jan. 31st, 1833, and finished it April 23rd, 1833. Canvas size 25″ × 30″. Signed " TS 1833 after Eicholtz."
Owned by Edward C. Dale, Philadelphia.

413 DALL, MRS. AUSTIN.

Portrait painted at Baltimore, begun Jan. 12th, 1853, finished April 25th, 1853. Head. Price, $100.00

414 DALLAS, ALEXANDER JAMES (1759–1817).

Copied from the original portrait by Gilbert Stuart, for Mr. Dallas' son, begun April 28th, 1834, finished May 7th, 1834. Head. Price, $80.00

415 DALLAS, ALEXANDER JAMES (1759–1817).

Copy from portrait by Gilbert Stuart. Painting begun Aug. 28th, 1835, finished Sept. 18th, 1835. Copied for Alexander Dallas. Head.
Price, $80.00

LIST OF PAINTINGS

416 DALLAS, ALEXANDER JAMES (1791–1844).

Son of No. 415. Entered the U. S. Navy in 1805, and attained the rank of commodore. Half length, standing, facing left. Size 28″ × 34″. Portrait begun April 12th, 1811, and finished on June 7th, 1811. Portrait has been lithographed. Price, $80.00

Owned by Mrs. J. Curtis Patterson, of Phila., in 1887, and exhibited in Loan Collection at the Penna. Academy of Fine Arts.

417 DALLAS, ALEXANDER JAMES, JR.

Eldest child of Hon. George Mifflin Dallas. Died Sept. 30th, 1826. Boy standing, half length to left. Portrait begun Sept. 8th, 1810, finished Sept. 20th, 1810. Size 29″ × 24″. Price, $50.00

Was owned by Miss Sophia Dallas, of Philadelphia, and exhibited in Loan Collection Penna. Academy of Fine Arts, 1887.

418 DALLAS, GEORGE MIFFLIN (1792–1864).

Philadelphia lawyer and statesman, he was admitted to the Bar in 1813, to the U. S. Senate 1831–33, and was Vice-President of the United States 1844–48. Bust, head facing left. Size 15″ × 19″. Painted about 1830. Engraved for the "Century Magazine," June, 1891.

Owned by Miss Elizabeth Dallas Tucker, of Philadelphia.

419 DALLAS, GEORGE MIFFLIN (1792–1864).

Portrait begun May 1st, 1844, finished May 13th, 1844. Bust, facing front, size 25″ × 30″. "May, 1844." Price, $100.00

When exhibited in Philadelphia in 1887 was owned by Mrs. J. Curtis Patterson.

420 DALLAS, MRS. GEO. MIFFLIN (1798–1869).

(She was Sophia Ann, daughter of Philip and Juliana Chew Nicklin.) Bust, facing front. Painted June, 1830. Size 15″ × 19″. Price, $50.00

Owned by Miss Elizabeth Dallas Tucker and exhibited in Loan Collection 1887 Penna. Academy Fine Arts.

421 DALLAS, MRS. GEORGE MIFFLIN (1798–1869).

Noted in Sully's register as being the second attempt, begun Sept. 28th, 1830, finished Oct. 7th, 1830. Head. Price, $50.00

422 DALLAS, MRS. GEORGE MIFFLIN (1788–1869).

Bust, facing right, 25″ × 28″. Portrait begun May 27th, 1844, finished June 20th, 1844. Price, $100.00

When exhibited in Philadelphia in 1887 was owned by Mrs. J. Curtis Patterson.

133

LIST OF PAINTINGS

423 DALLAS, J.

Secretary to Russian Legation. Portrait begun April 4th, 1813, finished May 13th, 1813. Size 29″ × 36″. Price, $100.00

424 DALMATIA, MR.

Portrait begun April 10th, 1810, and finished May 30th, 1810. Bust.
Price, $60.00

NOTE.—Thomas Sully records in his register of paintings that this was the first portrait painted after his return from England.

425 DALMATIA, MRS.

Portrait begun June 5th, 1810, and finished June 21st, 1810. Bust.
Price, $60.00

426 DANIEL, PETER VIVIAN (1784–1860).

Of Virginia, was made Justice of the Supreme Court of the United States in March, 1841. Portrait begun June 11th, 1858, finished July 7th, 1858. Size 33½″ × 25″. Price, $100.00

427 DANIEL, MRS. PETER V.

(Deceased.) (Née Miss Lucy Nelson Randolph, daughter of Edmund Randolph, of Washington's cabinet.) Portrait painted for Judge Daniel, begun Feb. 13th, 1858, finished July 6th, 1858. Size 32½″ × 26″.
Price, $150.00

428 DANNENBERG, MRS.

Portrait begun Oct. 4th, 1815, finished Nov. 14th, 1815. Head.
Price, $50.00

429 DANNENBERG, MR.

Portrait begun Oct. 16th, 1815, finished Nov. 30th, 1815. Head.
Price, $50.00

430 DARLEY, MR. JOHN (1765–1853).

An English actor who first appeared on the American stage about 1794. He afterwards entered the U. S. Marines but returned to the stage. Portrait painted for Thos. A. Cooper when Darley was playing at the New York Theatre, begun April 1, 1807, and finished the same month. Head.
Price, $30.00

431 DARLEY, ELEANOR WESTRAY (1780–18).

Actress, wife of John Darley the English actor. Mother of F. O. C. Darley the illustrator, and of William Henry Westray Darley who married Jane Cooper, daughter of Thomas Sully. Portrait begun Dec. 8th, 1806, and finished the same month. Bust. Price, $30.00

134

432 DARLEY, JANE, AND HER SON FRANCIS.

Jane Sully (1807–1877) married Wm. Henry W. Darley in 1833; her son was Francis Thomas Sully Darley, the organist. Portrait begun on April 13th, 1839, finished Dec. 31, 1839. Size 57″ × 45″. Full length seated, with boy standing; wears white satin shirt, brown bodice, rests her elbow on red shawl thrown over stone wall. Spaniel lies at their feet and a large urn to the right. Price, $1000.00

Bequest of F. T. S. Darley to Metropolitan Museum of New York.

433 DARLEY, JANE, AND HER SON FRANCIS.

Small copy of portrait No. 432. Painted for Stanfield, begun on May 31st, 1866, finished June 7th, 1866. Size 18″ × 14″. Price, $30.00

434 DARLEY, JANE (1807–1877).

Daughter of the artist Thomas Sully. Portrait painted in 1840.

NOTE.—For other portraits see Jane Sully.

435 DARLEY, FRANCIS THOMAS SULLY.

Son of Jane Sully Darley, and well known in Philadelphia as an organist. Portrait painted 1866. Size 18″ × 14″.

436 DAVID, JEAN TERFORD (1792–1838).

He was a Frenchman who came to this country with his parents, he married Mary Sicard, and served as paymaster in the War of 1812. Half length in uniform with red sash and white trousers, begun Feb. 13th, 1813, finished March 3rd, 1813. Size 27½″ × 35¼″. Signed " TS 1813." See illustration.

Owned by Cleveland Museum of Fine Arts, Cleveland, Ohio.

437 DAVID, MRS. JEAN TERFORD (1792–   ).

(Née Mary Sicard, of Philadelphia, whose father came to Philadelphia during the political troubles in France. Half length in low-necked white gown with red shawl, begun Nov. 4th, 1813, finished Dec. 4th, 1813. Size 27½″ × 35″. Signed " TS 1813." See illustration. Price, $100.00

Owned by Cleveland Museum of Fine Arts, Cleveland, Ohio.

438 DAVID, JULIA, FERDINAND AMD STEPHEN.

A group of three children of Jean Terford David and Mary Sicard David. Painting begun April 26th, 1826, and finished May 16th, 1826. Size 38″ × 44″. Signed " TS 1826." Price, $250.00

Was lithographed by Albert Newsam. Owned by Albert Rosenthal, Philadelphia.

439 DAVID, FERDINAND (1822–   ).

 At the age of four years, study for a group painted for J. David. Begun Feb. 27th, 1826, finished March 1st, 1826. Head.   Price, $10.00
 Owned by J. Foster Jenkins, Yonkers, New York.

440 DAVID, JULIA (1820–   ).

 At the age of six years, study for a group painted for J. David. Begun March 4th, 1826, finished in April, 1826. Head.   Price, $10.00
 Owned by J. Foster Jenkins, Yonkers, New York.

441 DAVIDGE, MRS. F. AND CHILD.

 Painted for Mrs. Scot, begun Dec. 16th, 1822, finished Feb. 5th, 1823. Bust.   Price, $130.00

442 DAVIS, ISAAC P. (1771–1855).

 Of Boston, was an early patron of American artists, he met Sully at Gilbert Stuart's when Sully made his first call and sat to Sully for his portrait as a specimen for Stuart to judge of his ability. Portrait begun Aug. 4th, 1807, finished Aug. 9th, 1807. Head.   Price, $30.00

443 DAVIS, MASTER.

 Grandson of Mrs. Florence. Portrait begun June 2nd, 1853, finished June 8th, 1853. Head.   Price, $80.00

444 DAVIS, COL. SAMUEL B. (1776–1854).

 Was in command of the coast defences in the War of 1812. Full length standing in uniform, facing left with hat in hand. Portrait painted for State of Delaware, begun June 19th, 1819, finished July 15th, 1819. Size 86″ × 60″. Signed " 𝕋𝕊 1819."   Price, $500.00
 Bust lithographed by Newsam.
 Owned by Sussex D. Davis, Esq., of Philadelphia.

 NOTE.—This portrait has been exhibited as a replica, but is the original, as the State of Delaware does not own a portrait of Davis.

445 DAVIS, SAMUEL.

 Of 256 Chestnut Street, Philadelphia. Portrait begun Dec. 9th, 1839, finished Dec. 30th, 1839. Bust.   Price, $200.00

446 DAVY, MRS. ELIZABETH.

 Of Dover, Delaware. Portrait begun Nov. 22nd, 1862, finished June 29th, 1863. Bust, seated, facing front. Size 30″ × 25″.   Price, $80.00
 Owned by the Penna. Academy of Fine Arts, Philadelphia.

447 DAWSON, ANNE (1798–1866).

See Mrs. Anne Morrison.

448 DAY, MRS.

Of New London, Conn. Portrait painted for her son Thomas, begun Jan. 1st, 1849, finished Jan. 9th, 1849. Bust.   Price, $100.00

Owned by Mr. Newton Helm Day, of Long Island.

449 DAYTON, MR.

Of New York. Painted for M. Levy. Portrait begun Nov. 3rd, 1813, finished Dec. 14th, 1813. Bust.   Price, $100.00

450 DECATUR, STEPHEN (1779–1820).

Commodore Decatur, celebrated commander of the United States Navy, fell in a duel with Commodore Barron. Portrait begun July 12th, 1814, finished Sept., 1814. Size 94″ ×66″. Painted for the City of New York and now hanging in City Hall, N. Y. Full length in Colonial uniform, with one foot advanced, right hand on hilt of sword. In front of him are seen Castle William and New York Bay.   Price, $500.00

451 DECATUR, STEPHEN (1779–1820).

This portrait of Commodore Decatur was painted for Mr. S. Price, begun Aug. 20th, 1814, finished Sept., 1814. Bust.   Price, $100.00

452 DECATUR, STEPHEN (1779–1820).

Small whole length, being a study painted before the start on the large portrait ordered by the City of New York. The register notes the date it was begun as Aug. 10th, 1814, the size 24″ × 30″, and the price as $150.00

453 DECATUR, STEPHEN (1779–1820).

This portrait was painted for a medal awarded him by Congress. Bust in full uniform, high coat collar, head to right in profile. Painting begun April 25th, 1816, finished April 28th, 1816. Size 20″ × 24″. Painted in sepia. Bust.   Price, $50.00

Owned by United States Naval Academy, Annapolis, Md.

454 DECATUR, STEPHEN (1779–1820).

Small bust in uniform, head to right in profile. Painted on a panel 9″ × 7″. Presented to the Penna. Historical Society in 1861 by Samuel Breck.

NOTE.—This picture may be No. 451, or an entirely different portrait from those listed by the artist.

455 DE CUESTA, SIGNORA E.

Portrait painted for her daughter, begun Nov. 28th, 1831, finished Dec. 28th, 1831. Bust.   Price, $80.00

456 DELAPLAINE, BROCKHOLST L.

Portrait begun Feb. 25th, 1817, finished March 20th, 1817. Head.
Price, $50.00

457 DENNIE, JOSEPH (1768–1812).

Editor of the " Portfolio Magazine," and head of the literary circle that made Philadelphia famous at that time. Copied from the original portrait by Rembrandt Peale. Copy begun March 7th, 1835, finished March 14th, 1835. Head. Price, $80.00

NOTE.—A copy of Sully's portrait of Dennie made by J. E. Wartel in 1848 is owned by the Penna. Historical Society, Philadelphia.

458 DE SILVER, ANTOINETTE (1805–1820).

Daughter of Robert and Margaret De Silver, buried in St. Paul's Church-yard, 3rd St., Philadelphia. Deceased, painted from a mask, begun Sept. 13th, 1837, finished Sept. 27th, 1837. Head. Price, $150.00

459 DEWEES, WILLIAM POTTS, M. D. (1768–1841).

Distinguished Philadelphia physician and first President of the Musical Fund Society (1820–1838). Portrait begun Dec. 1st, 1811, finished April 12th, 1812. Size 29" × 36". Price, $100.00

460 DEWEES, WILLIAM POTTS, M. D.

Painted for Benj. Carr, begun Feb. 1st, 1814, finished March, 1814. Head. Price, $50.00

461 DEWEES, DR. WILLIAM POTTS.

Copy of portrait by John Neagle at the University of Pennsylvania. Painting begun March 18th, 1856, finished April 8th, 1856. Size 29" × 36". Bust, head to right. Signed on back " TS 1856." Price, $100.00
Painted for the Musical Fund Society and hanging in their building on Locust St., Philadelphia.

462 DEWEES, MRS. WM.

Wife of Dr. William Potts Dewees. Portrait begun Dec. 5th, 1808, finished June 30th, 1809. Size 29" × 36". Price, $60.00
Owned by Mrs. H. M. Dewees, of New York.

463 DEWEES, MISS ADELINE.

Daughter of Dr. William Potts Dewees, portrait painted for her father, begun Jan. 12th, 1824, finished Nov. 18th, 1825. Half length seated, white satin dress, dark hair, nearly full face to right. Size 29" × 36".
Price, $100.00
Owned by Mrs. John Muckle, of Philadelphia.

464 DEWEY, CAPTAIN SAMUEL.

The Boston sea captain, who saved the carved figure-head of Andrew Jackson from the U. S. frigate "Constitution" by sawing it off the vessel during a storm. Portrait begun Oct. 4th, 1834, finished on Oct. 18th, 1834. Signed "℔S 1834." Bust, wearing brown overcoat. Size 23" × 30".

Price, $125.00

Owned by Mrs. Paul L. Tiers, of Germantown, Philadelphia.

465 DIBBLEE, MR.

(Lawyer.) Portrait begun Feb. 9th, 1807, finished March 24th, 1807. Bust. Price, $30.00

466 DILLARD, DR. THOMAS.

Portrait painted for his wife, who was a daughter of Henry Kuhl. Begun Feb. 21st, 1839, finished March 2nd, 1839. Head. Price, $150.00

467 DOBBIN, MISS.

Portrait painted for her father and copied from a daguerreotype, painting begun March 4th, and finished March 27th, 1854. Head. Price, $100.00

468 DODSON, MR. (SR.).

A copy painted for his son. Begun March 4th, 1862, finished March 14th, 1862. Size 20" × 24". Price, $40.00

469 DONALDSON, MRS. JAMES LAURY.

Of Baltimore, Md. Portrait begun April 6th, 1816, finished June 4th, 1816. Bust, seated, wearing a red velvet garment over an ivory white dress, brown hair dressed high on her head. Price, $100.00

Owned by Mrs. Robert M. Cushing, Baltimore, Md.

470 DONNELLY, MRS.

(Née Miss Slevin.) Painted for her father, begun Oct. 21st, 1856, finished Oct. 28th, 1856. Head. Price, $80.00

471 DONNELLY, MRS.

(Copy of former portrait.) Begun Nov. 9th, 1856, finished Nov. 21st, 1856. Head. Price, $80.00

472 DORSEN, MR. AND SON.

Copy begun by Tom, March 1st, 1839, finished March 20th, 1839. Half length. Price, $400.00

139

LIST OF PAINTINGS

473 DORSEY, JOHN SYNG (1783–1819).

He received the degree of Doctor of Medicine from the University of Pennsylvania at the early age of 18. Engraved for the Portfolio Magazine, 1819. (Stauffer, No. 1132.) The register notes the price as $100, and that the hands were introduced in the painting, begun May 1812, finished May 22nd, 1812. Size 20″ × 24″.

Owned by Mrs. Elizabeth Gardner Du Pont, Wilmington, Del., copy made by O. H. Perry, for University of Penna.

474 DORSEY, MRS. JOHN SYNG (1787–1833).

Née Marie Ralston, daughter of the Philadelphia merchant Robert Ralston, married Dr. Dorsey April 30th, 1807. Portrait begun Aug. 24th, 1812, finished Sept. 17th, 1812. Bust, head to right, with dress open at the neck. The register notes "hands painted" and the price as $100.

Owned by Miss Elizabeth Gardner Du Pont, Wilmington, Delaware.

475 DORSEY, MRS.

Of Baltimore, Md. Portrait begun Oct. 6th, 1808, finished Oct. 20th, 1808. Bust.   Price, $50.00

476 DOUGLASS, MISS.

Deceased, painted for Mrs. Cruger, of New York. Portrait begun May 4th, 1836, finished May 12th, 1836. Head.   Price, $100.00

477 DOUGLAS, MISS M.

Painted after death; Sully records painting two pictures. Begun Feb. 1st, 1844, finished Feb. 7th, 1844. Bust.   Price, $150.00

478 DOUGLASS, SAML.

Of Mississippi. (Uncle of Mrs. Cruger of New York). Portrait begun May 9th, 1843, finished May 17th, 1843. Bust.   Price, $100.00

479 DOWNING, MISS MARY.

Of Downingtown, Penna. Portrait begun Sept. 27th, 1837, finished Oct. 3rd, 1837. Head.   Price, $150.00

480 DOWNING, MRS. JOHN W. (1800–1826).

(Née Eliza Bartleson.) Half length, facing front, seated. Portrait begun March 3rd, 1825, finished July 7th, 1825. Size 30″ × 40″. Price, $100.00
Owned by Mrs. Hartman Kuhn, of Philadelphia.

481 DRAYTON, MR.

Of Georgia. Portrait painted for his father, Col. Drayton, begun Oct. 7th, 1843, finished Nov. 2nd, 1843. Size 29″ × 36″.   Price, $200.00

482 DRAYTON (JR.), MR.

(Of the United States Navy.)   Begun Jan. 31st, 1835, finished March 6th, 1835.   Bust.   Price, $125.00

483 DRAYTON, PERCIVAL (1812–1865).

Of South Carolina; he entered the United States Navy at 15 years of age, and was commander of Admiral Farragut's flagship at Mobile Bay, 1864. Begun Nov. 27th, 1827, finished Dec. 30th, 1827.   Bust, facing left in uniform.   Size 30″ × 24″.   Price, $75.00
Owned by Mrs. Morris Lewis, of Philadelphia.

484 DRAYTON, CAPTAIN PERCIVAL (1812–1865).

Portrait painted for R. Rush, begun Jan. 6th, 1857, finished Jan. 15th, 1857.   Head.   Price, $80.00

NOTE.—Captain Drayton saved the life of the son of Mr. Rush of Philadelphia, who ordered the portrait painted.

485 DREW, MRS. JOHN (1820–1897).

Louisa Lane, married Henry Hunt, 2nd Geo. Mossop, and 3rd John Drew. She was a finished comedy actress and was playing at the Arch Street Theatre when the portrait was painted, begun Oct. 20th, 1864, finished Nov. 3rd, 1864.   Bust, head to right, low-necked dress with shawl over shoulder.
                                          Price, $100.00
Owned by John Drew, of New York.

486 DRINKER, MISS ANNA (b. 1828–   ).

Poet, writer and publisher of poems and stories.   She assumed the name of Edith May, and resided in Philadelphia.   Portrait begun April 15th, 1850, finished May 10th, 1850.   Signed " TS 1850."   Head in profile to left.   Size 21″ × 17″.   Price, $80.00
Owned by Faris C. Pitt, Baltimore, Md.

487 DUANE, WILLIAM JOHN (1780–1865).

Secretary of the Treasury under Jackson until his removal for refusing to order the transfer of the deposits from the United States Bank.   Portrait painted for his daughter Ellen, begun May 4th, 1841, finished June 12th, 1841.   Bust.   Price, $200.00

488 DUANE, MRS. DEBORAH.

Granddaughter of Benjamin Franklin and wife of William John Duane. Portrait begun June 23rd, 1841, finished July 5th, 1841.   Bust.
                                          Price, $200.00

LIST OF PAINTINGS

489 DUFFIELD, MISS.
   Portrait begun Nov., 1805, finished the same month, size 12" × 10".
                                                          Price, $15.00

490 DUGAN, MISS.
   Of Philadelphia. Portrait begun Nov. 17th, 1810, finished Feb. 5th, 1811.
   Size 29" × 36".   Price, $80.00

491 DUGAN, MR. CUMBERLAND.
   Portrait begun Jan. 4th, 1821, finished Feb. 9th, 1821. Size 29" × 36".
                                                          Price, $130.00

492 DUGAN, JOSEPH A.
   Philadelphia merchant and President of the Penna. Academy of Fine Arts,
   1842–45. Three-quarters, seated in arm-chair with left arm over back of
   chair, head to left. Portrait begun Nov. 17th, 1810, finished Dec. 18th,
   1810. Size 29" × 36".   Price, $80.00
   (In the artist's register he misspells the name and enters it as Dougan.)
   Owned by Herbert L. Pratt, New York.

   NOTE.—The Pennsylvania Academy of Fine Arts own a copy of No. 492 painted
   by Albert Rosenthal.

493 DUGAN, MRS.
   (Née Miss Gilliams.) Portrait begun June 22nd, 1864, finished July 2nd,
   1864. Head.   Price, $50.00

494 DUMOUNT, MR.
   Portrait begun Feb. 16th, 1807, finished March 6th, 1807, Bust.
                                                          Price, $30.00

495 DUNANT, SARAH BRINGHURST (1793–1831).
   She married John Stull Williams. Three-quarter length, seated, hands
   crossed resting on arm or end of sofa, head to left, low-necked dress. Size
   29" × 36". Signed " TS 1812."   Price, $100.00
   Reproduced in " History of Arts of Design," by Wm. Dunlap, published
   by Goodspeed & Co., 1918, Vol. II.
   Owned by Miss Sarah D. Williams, Boston, Mass.

496 DUNANT, REBECCA.
   Portrait begun June 8th, 1812, finished Sept. 17th, 1812. Size 29" × 36".
                                                          Price, $100.00

497 DUNCAN, MR.
   Copied from another painting, begun March 31st, 1827, finished April
   14th, 1827. Bust.   Price, $75.00

498 DUNGLISON, ROBLEY (1798–1869).

An eminent physician, teacher and writer. He was Vice-President and President of the Musical Fund Society. Bust, arm resting on table supporting head, he has a gray beard and mustache. Size 29″ × 36″. Signed on back " ℡ 1868." Begun Feb. 4th, 1868, finished Feb. 21st, 1868.

Price, $100.00

Owned by the Musical Fund Society, Philadelphia.

499 DUNLAP, MRS. (SR.).

Portrait begun April 17th, 1809, finished May 4th, 1809. Bust.

Price, $50.00

500 DUNLOP, ANNE.

Portrait painted for her parents, begun May 5th, 1849, finished June 1st, 1849. Head. Price, $100.00

501 DUNSMORE, I.

Merchant of Richmond, Virginia. Portrait begun Jan., 1805, and finished the same month. Bust. Price, $25.00

502 DUNSMORE, I.

Of Richmond, Va. Portrait begun June 26th, 1808, finished July 10th, 1808. Bust. Price, $50.00

503 DU PONCEAU, PETER STEPHEN (1760–1844).

Came to this country in 1777 as secretary to Baron Steuben, and became second President of the Penna. Historical Society. Bust to left, wearing spectacles, brown coat. Painted for the American Philosophical Society, begun March 1st, 1830, finished March 27th, 1830. Engraved by John Sartain. Size 25″ × 30″. Price, $75.00

Owned by American Philosophical Society; The Penna. Historical Society have a copy by W. S. Mason of the above portrait.

504 DUPONT, MR.

Portrait painted for Mrs. R. Smith, begun March 30th, 1827. Expunged. Bust. Price, $75.00

505 DUPONT, CHARLES (1797–1869).

Of "Brandywine," Wilmington, Del. He married Miss Dorcas M. Van Dyke, of New Castle, Del., in 1824; his second wife was Miss Ann Ridgely, of Dover, Del. Portrait begun Nov. 30th, 1831, finished Dec. 4th, 1832. Bust. Price, $80.00

Owned by Mr. Alexis I. Dupont, of Wilmington, Delaware.

506 DUPONT, MRS. CHARLES IRENÉE (1806–1838).

The portrait was painted for Miss Van Dyke at Philadelphia, begun Oct. 6th, 1831, finished Dec. 10th, 1832. Bust, head to left, wearing ear-rings and a broad lace collar. (Was Dorcas M. Van Dyke.) Bust. Price, $80.00
Reproduced in Wharton's " Salons Colonial and Republican."
Owned by Mr. Alexis I. Dupont, of Wilmington, Delaware.

507 DUVAL, MR.

Partly copied from a portrait by Rembrandt Peale, for his son L. Duval, begun Jan. 24th, 1822, and finished March 16th, 1822. Bust.
Price, $100.00

508 DUVAL (SENR.), MRS.

Painted for her son, begun Jan. 14th, 1822, finished Feb. 20th, 1822. Bust. Price, $100.00

509 DWIGHT, MR.

Painted as a specimen of portraiture, begun Aug. 13th, 1807, finished Sept. 13th, 1807. Bust. Price, $50.00

510 DWYER, JOHN H. (–1843).

Irish actor who came to America and acted at the Park Theatre, New York, in 1810. Portrait begun April 26th, 1810, and finished June 8th, 1810. Bust. Price, $60.00

511 EARLEY, MR.

Philadelphia merchant living at Market St. and Water St., Philadeiphia. Portrait begun Jan. 24th, 1862, finished Feb. 26th, 1862. Size 30" × 29".
Price, $50.00

512 EARLEY, MRS.

Portrait begun May 11th, 1863, finished May 25th, 1863. Size 25" × 30". Price, $50.00

513 EARP, MISS.

Portrait painted for her mother, begun Feb. 24th, 1859, finished March 16th, 1859. Size 25" × 30". Price, $100.00

514 EASTMAN, MISS.

Portrait painted from a daguerreotype, begun March 19th, 1869, finished March 29th, 1869. Size 20" × 24". Price, $100.00

515 EDDS, MRS.

(Mother of Mrs. Carson.) Portrait painted at Baltimore, begun Nov. 30th, 1852, finished Feb. 4th, 1853. Bust. Price, $150.00

516 EDGE.

A child of Mr. Edge. Portrait begun Jan. 4th, 1870, finished Jan. 14th, 1870. Size 20″ × 24″. Price, $50.00

517 OLFRITH, MRS. AND HER DAUGHTER.

Portrait begun April 16th, 1836, finished June 3rd, 1836. Size 24″ × 20″. Price, $200.00

518 ELLIOTT, MISS.

Of Beaufort, South Carolina. Portrait begun Nov. 1st, 1821, finished Dec. 1st, 1821. Leans back in a blue and white striped arm-chair with a red shawl over arm; she wears a white dress. Her sister married Chas. Cotesworth Pinckney. Size 29″ × 36″. Price, $150.00

519 ELLIOTT, MISS ANN.

Of Beaufort, S. C. Daughter of William Elliott, portrait begun Sept. 31st, 1839, finished Nov. 16th, 1839. Size 29″ × 36″. Price, $300.00

520 ELLIOTT, MISS MARY.

Daughter of William Elliott, portrait begun Sept. 31st, 1839, finished Nov. 18th, 1839. Size 29″ × 36″. Price, $300.00
Owned by Miss M. E. Pinckney, Blowing Rock, N. C.

521 ELLIOTT, WILLIAM (1788–1863).

Author, born in Beaufort, S. C. He was prominent in state politics and devoted to agriculture and rural sports. Bust portrait with head to right, white stock and collar, hand thrust in front of waistcoat. Painting begun Oct. 14th, 1823, finished Nov. 21st, 1823. Size 29″ × 36″. Price, $150.00
Reproduced in " Carolina Sports," by William Elliott (1918 Edition).
Portrait owned by Ambrose Elliott Gonzales, of Columbia, S. C.

522 ELLIS, MRS. JOHN W.

Of Salisbury, Va. Portrait painted for her husband, begun Sept. 23rd, 1846, finished Sept. 30th, 1846. Bust. Price, $100.00

523 ELLIS, POWHATAN (1794–1844).

Virginia jurist and politician. Portrait begun Aug. 22nd, 1846, and finished Sept. 7th, 1846. Bust. Price, $100.00

524 ELLIS, THOMAS HARDING.

Of Richmond, Va. Portrait painted in Richmond, begun Oct. 22nd, 1850, finished Nov. 6th, 1850. Head. Price, $100.00

525 ELLIS, MRS. THOS. H.

Of Richmond, Va. Portrait painted in Richmond, begun Oct. 23rd, 1850, finished Nov. 6th, 1850. Head.   Price, $100.00

526 ELLISON, MRS.

Portrait begun Oct. 2nd, 1860, finished October 15th, 1860. Bust.
                                                              Price, $50.00

527 ELLISON, MRS.

In lieu of the first portrait, begun Dec. 28th, 1861, finished Jan. 4th, 1862. Head.   Price, $80.00

528 ELLSLER, FANNY (1810–1844).

Dancer, who came to this country in 1840, first appearing in the Park Theatre, New York. Portrait full length in ballet costume, seated in dressing room of theatre. Signed " IS after Inman, Philadelphia, 1842." Size 22″ × 28″.

Painted for Sully's friend Benj. Chew Wilcocks and now owned by Mrs. Alexander Campbell (née Wilcocks), of Philadelphia.

529 ELWYN, REV. ALFRED LANGDON (born 1832).

When a child of five years old with long curls, head to right, nearly full face. Engraved by John Cheney for the "Gift," of 1840. Was owned by Edw. L. Carey and for many years hung at the Academy of Fine Arts, Philadelphia. Portrait begun April 13th, 1837, finished May 13th, 1837. Bust.
                                                              Price, $235.00
Owned by Mr. Elwyn's daughter, Mrs. Gordon Wendell, of New York.

530 ELWYN, REV. ALFRED LANGDON.

A replica or copy of No. 529. Probably largely the work of the artist's daughter. Mill-board panel, size 28 × 23½″.
Owned by Mr. Albert Rosenthal, Philadelphia.

531 EMLEN, DR. SAML. (1789–1828).

Physician of the Pennsylvania Hospital. Portrait painted from a cast for Dr. Meigs, begun May 5th, 1828, finished Sept. 8th, 1828. Head.
                                                              Price, $50.00

532 ERSKINE, LADY (1781–1843).

Was Francis Cadwalader and married David Montague Erskine, afterwards Lord Erskine. She was a sister of Genl. Thomas Cadwalader, for whom it was painted. Portrait begun July 10th, 1830, finished Aug. 2nd, 1830. Head.   Price, $50.00
Owned by John Cadwalader, Esq., Phila.

533 ERSKINE, LORD (1776–1855).

David Montague married Frances Cadwalader. This portrait was a copy of the painting by Gilbert Stuart, and was made for the Cadwalader family of Philadelphia, begun June 16th, 1830, finished July 10th, 1830. Head.

Price, $50.00

Owned by John Cadwalader, Esq., Phila.

NOTE.—In Sully register Lord Erskine's portrait is placed under Sterling.

534 ESPY, JAMES POLLARD (1785–1860).

Celebrated meteorologist and a founder of the weather department at Washington. He was a member of the American Philosophical Society and received their gold medal in 1836. He was elected a member of the Smithsonian Institution, where his portrait now hangs; painting begun March 27th, 1849, finished March 31st, 1849. Bust. Size 25" × 30". Price, $100.00

535 ETHERAGE, MISS CAROLINE.

Of Boston, Mass. Portrait begun Sept. 17th, 1835, and finished Oct. 15th, 1835. Head. Price, $80.00

536 ETTING, MISS.

Of Baltimore, Md. Portrait begun May 18th, 1808, finished May 25th, 1808. Bust. Price, $50.00

537 ETTING, MRS. SOLOMON.

(Sister of Miss Rebecca Gratz.) Portrait begun April 20th, 1835, finished April 28th, 1835. Head. Price, $80.00

538 ETTING, MISS SALLY.

Of Baltimore, Md. Half-length portrait seated, facing right, begun May 16th, 1808, finished May 25th, 1808. Size, 25" × 30". Price, $50.00
Owned by Frank M. Etting, Philadelphia.

539 EUGENIE, EMPRESS (1826–1920).

Portrait painted from a photograph. Begun Oct. 14th, 1863, finished Oct. 20th, 1863. Head. Price, $30.00

540 EWING, ROBERT.

Merchant, Third St., Philadelphia, and Democratic sheriff for that city under Governor Curtin. Portrait begun April 22nd, 1831, finished May 21st, 1831. Bust. Price, $75.00

541 EWING, MRS. ROBERT.

Of No. 7 South 4th St., Philadelphia. Portrait begun Feb. 20th, 1831, finished May 13th, 1831. Bust. Price, $75.00

LIST OF PAINTINGS

542 FREY, MR.

Of Virginia. Portrait begun Aug. 3rd, 1830, and finished Sept. 30, 1830. Bust. Price, $75.00

543 FAIRLIE, MRS. JAMES.

Was Maria Yates, daughter of Robert Yates, Chief Justice of New York, and wife of Major Fairlie, member of the staff of Baron Steuben and Secretary of the Society of Cincinnati. Mrs. Fairlie is painted as a Madonna portrait, begun June 16th, 1807, finished July 10th, 1807. Size 35″ × 28⅞″.
Price, $80.00
Owned by Mrs. Emily Fairlie Ogden Nelson, Astoria, L. I.

544 FAIRMAN, GEORGE.

Son of Col. Gideon Fairman (No. 546). Head to left, holding a scroll in his hand supporting his chin; a marble bust is in the background and a dog's head is shown to the left. Portrait begun Jan. 27th, 1816, finished September, 1816. Size 18¼″ × 22¼″. Price, $50.00
Owned by H. H. Furness, Esq., Philadelphia.

545 FAIRMAN, GEORGE AND CAROLINE.

Children of Col. Gideon Fairman (No. 546). Busts of two children, the little girl having her arms around the neck of her brother. Portrait begun March 29th, 1819, finished July 22nd, 1819. Signed " $\mathbb{TS}$ 1819." Size 23″ × 25″. Price, $150.00
Owned by H. H. Furness, Esq., Philadelphia.

546 FAIRMAN, COL. GIDEON (1774–1827).

Philadelphia engraver, he was colonel of militia and volunteers in the War of 1812. Bust facing right, portrait painted on a panel, size 8″ × 10″, begun Feb. 24th, 1824, finished March 9th, 1824. $30.00
Owned by the Penna. Academy of Fine Arts.

547 FAIRMAN, COL. GIDEON (1774–1827).

Bust, head to right, with coat having a red collar, he holds a high hat in his hand. Portrait painted on a panel, 9½″ × 7⅞″.
Exhibited in New York Portrait Exhibit of 1890, by Mrs. James S. Warren.
Owned by H. H. Furness, Esq., of Philadelphia.

548 FARR, MISS.

Portrait painted for her mother, begun June 10th, 1850, finished June 24th, 1850. Head. Price, $80.00

148

LIST OF PAINTINGS

549 FARREN, ELIZABETH (1759–1829).

English actress, afterwards Countess of Derby, from the celebrated painting by Sir Thomas Lawrence. Copy begun Jan. 11th, 1867, finished Jan. 16th, 1867. Size 21″ × 17″.　　　　　　　Price, $50.00

550 FARREN, ELIZABETH (1759–1829).

Copied from painting after Sir Thomas Lawrence, begun Feb. 24th, 1870, finished April 2nd, 1870. Size 10″ × 8″.　　　　Price, $25.00

551 FINLEY, JOHN.

Head, dark curly hair, and wears a black coat and full white neck-cloth. Canvas size 18⅛″ × 14⅛″. Signed "TS 1821." Portrait painted for H. Robinson, begun June 14th, 1821, and finished June 22nd, 1821.

　　　　　　　　　　　　　　　　　Price, $50.00

Owned by the Metropolitan Museum of New York.

552 FIRTH, MR.

Portrait begun Nov. 20th, 1814, finished Dec. 20th, 1814. Bust.

　　　　　　　　　　　　　　　　　Price, $80.00

553 FISHER, CHARLES HENRY (　　–1862).

Painted for his brother Sidney. He was President of the Western Saving Fund. Portrait begun Dec. 10th, 1833, finished Dec. 18th, 1833. Head size.

　　　　　　　　　　　　　　　　　Price, $80.00

554 FISHER, GEORGE SIDNEY (　　–1871).

Member of the Philadelphia Bar, married the daughter of Charles Ingersoll, and was the father of Sidney George Fisher, the historian. Portrait begun Dec. 9th, 1833, finished Dec. 19th, 1833. Head.　　Price, $80.00

555 FISHER, JAMES.

Merchant. Portrait begun May 26th, 1804, finished July 30th, 1804, size 12″ × 10″.　　　　　　　　　　Price, $15.00

556 FISHER, MRS. JAMES.

Portrait begun Jan., 1805, and finished in February of same year. Size 10″ × 12″.　　　　　　　　　　Price, $15.00

557 FISHER, JAMES C.

Merchant of Philadelphia, and a trustee with Stephen Girard and others in the building of the Merchants Exchange on Third St. and Dock, Philadelphia, in 1831. Portrait begun Jan. 19th, 1811, and finished Feb. 6th, 1811. Bust.　　　　　　　　　　　Price, $80.00

558 FISHER, JAMES C.

Corner Ninth and Chestnut Streets, Philadelphia. Painted for his son; begun May 2nd, 1827, finished June 6th, 1827. Bust.   Price, $75.00

559 FISHER, MRS. JAMES C.

Corner Ninth and Chestnut Streets, Philadelphia. Painted for her son, begun April 30th, 1827, finished June 8th, 1827. Bust.   Price, $75.00

560 FISHER, JAMES LOGAN (–1833).

Brother of Sidney Fisher, died in Paris. Portrait begun Dec. 21, 1833, finished March, 1834. Head.   Price, $80.00

561 FISHER, JOSEPH (b. —–, d. 1864).

An optician of Philadelphia. Bust, nearly full face to right, wearing spectacles, with white stock and collar. Signed on back " TS." Size 30″ × 24″.   Price, $75.00
Owned by Library Company of Philadelphia.

562 FISHER, ELIZABETH AND SOPHY.

Daughters of Joshua Fisher. Elizabeth married Robert Patterson Kane, and Sophy married Eckley Brinton Coxe. Portrait begun Feb. 19th, 1847, finished March 20th, 1847. Busts.   Price, $200.00
Owned by Eliza Kane Cope, of Germantown, Philadelphia.

563 FISHER, REDWOOD (1782–1856).

Of Philadelphia; when quite a young man he entered the counting house of Thomas, Samuel, and Miers Fisher. Portrait begun May 30th, 1808, finished July 10th, 1808. Bust.   Price, $50.00
In 1847 Sully notes retouching this portrait, beginning Dec. 15th, and finishing Dec. 17th, 1847.   Price, $20.00

564 FISHER, WILLIAM.

Portrait begun May 30th, 1808, and finished June 16th, 1808. Bust.
    Price, $50.00

565 FITZGERALD, MRS.

Of Norfolk, Va. Portrait begun May 2nd, 1853, finished May 9th, 1853, at Baltimore. Head.   Price, $100.00

566 FITZGERALD, COL. THOMAS (1819–1891).

Journalist, he established the Philadelphia " Item." He was a director of the Musical Fund Society. Portrait begun June 28th, 1860, finished July 19th, 1860. Bust.   Price, $100.00
Owned by the estate of Col. Thos. Fitzgerald.

J S C

567 FITZGERALD, COL. THOMAS (1819–1891).
Portrait begun Feb. 10th, 1865, finished Feb. 25th, 1865. Size 30" × 25". Price, $100.00

568 FITZGERALD, COL. THOMAS (1819–1891).
Portrait painted in place of one condemned, begun Sept. 17th, 1866, finished Sept. 30th, 1866. Size 25" × 30". Price, $100.00

569 FITZGERALD, MRS. THOMAS.
(Née Sarah Levering Riter.) Daughter of Dr. George Riter, of Philadelphia. Portrait begun March 11th, 1858, finished March 29th, 1858. Bust. Price, $100.00
Owned by estate of Col. Thomas Fitzgerald.

570 FITZGERALD, MRS. THOMAS.
Portrait begun March 11th, 1858, finished March 29th, 1858. Bust. Price, $100.00

571 FITZGERALD, MRS. THOMAS.
Painted for her son Riter Fitzgerald. Portrait begun Dec. 23rd, 1861, finished May 2nd, 1862. Size 25" × 30". Price, $30.00

572 FITZGERALD, MRS. THOMAS.
Portrait begun Sept. 18th, 1862, finished Oct. 2nd, 1862. Size 34" × 25". Price, $30.00

573 FITZGERALD, MRS. THOMAS.
Portrait begun Feb. 26th, 1864, finished March 29th, 1864. Bust. Price, $30.00

574 FITZGERALD, MRS. THOMAS.
As a peasant, painted for her son. Begun Nov. 22nd, 1864, finished Dec. 12th, 1864. Bust. Price, $100.00

575 FITZGERALD, MRS. THOMAS.
Portrait painted for her son Riter, begun April 2nd, 1866, finished May 23rd, 1866. Bust. Price, $50.00

576 FITZGERALD, MRS. AND HER DAUGHTER MATILDA.
Portrait begun April 8th, 1861, finished June 27th, 1861. Size 30" × 25". Price, $60.00

577 FITZGERALD, MRS. AND SON HILDEBRAND.
Painting begun Aug. 3rd, 1863, finished Sept. 8th, 1863. Size 29" × 36". Price, $60.00
Owned by Mrs. Hildebrand Fitzgerald, Philadelphia.

578 FITZGERALD, HARRINGTON (1847–   ).

Portrait painted for his father, begun Nov. 30th, 1863, finished Dec. 17th, 1863.   Size 30″ × 25″.   Price, $30.00

Owned by Mrs. R. M. Brookfield, Philadelphia.

579 FITZGERALD, MISS MAUD.

Daughter of Col. Thomas Fitzgerald, married Mr. Hubbard of Philadelphia.   Portrait begun Oct. 3rd, 1864, and finished Nov. 3rd, 1864.   Size 29″ × 36″·   Price, $60.00

Owned by Mrs. A. Hallam Hubbard, Philadelphia.

580 FITZGERALD, RITER.

(Son of Col. Thomas Fitzgerald.)   Portrait painted for his mother, begun July 23rd, 1860, finished Aug. 13th, 1860.   Bust.   Price, $100.00

581 FITZGERALD, ROBERT AND GILBERT.

Portrait painted for their mother, begun May 11th, 1867, finished May 28th, 1867.   Size 30″ × 25″.   Price, $60.00

582 FITZHUGH, WILLIAM HENRY (1792–1830).

Of Virginia, was graduated from Princeton in 1808.   He became Vice-President of the American Colonization Society, and was an active opponent to slavery.   The portrait was painted at Princeton College, being begun Oct. 1st, 1808, and finished Oct. 6th, 1808.   Price, $50.00

Portrait at " Ravensworth," Fairfax Co., Va.

583 FITZHUGH, MR. (1792–1830).

Portrait begun Feb. 15th, 1816, finished March 16th, 1816.   Bust.
Price, $100.00

NOTE.—Bust, full face, bald head, high white stock ; portrait of gentleman presumably between 50 and 60 years old.   Said to be William Henry Fitzhugh (1792–1830) and owned by the Rhode Island School of Design.   (Sully does not record painting William Henry Fitzhugh later than 1816.)

584 FITZHUGH, MRS. WILLIAM HENRY.

Was the daughter of Gov. Goldsborough, of Dorset, Maryland, and married William Henry Fitzhugh, of Virginia, on Jan. 10th, 1814.   The portrait was begun Feb. 15th, 1816, finished March 10th, 1816.   Bust.
Price, $200.00

Portrait at " Ravensworth," Fairfax Co., Va.

585 FITZWHYSONN, W.

Of Richmond, Va.   Portrait begun Aug. 25th, 1824, finished Oct. 11th, 1824.   Bust.   Price, $60.00

586 FITZWHYSONN, W.

Of Richmond, Va. Portrait copied from the first picture, begun Sept. 24th, 1824, finished Oct. 29th, 1824. Bust.　　Price, $20.00

587 FLEEMING, MRS. CHARLES.

(Née Miss Mary Rotch, and afterwards Mrs. Geo. B. Emmerson.) Bust. head to right, wearing a pink, low-necked dress, with wide sleeves. Portrait begun Aug. 25th, 1831, finished Dec. 9th, 1831. Size 25″ × 20″. Owned by Mrs. George B. McClellan, Philadelphia.

588 FLEMING, MR.

Portrait begun May 25th, 1851, finished June 6th, 1851.　Head.
　　　　　　　　　　　　　　　　　　　　　　　　　　Price, $80.00

589 FLEMING, MRS.

Portrait begun April 17th, 1844, finished April 29th, 1834. Bust.
　　　　　　　　　　　　　　　　　　　　　　　　　　Price, $100.00

590 FLETCHER, LEVI.

Painted for his mother, begun June 3rd, 1830, finished June 26th, 1830. Bust.　　　　　　　　　　　　　　　　　　　　　Price, $75.00

591 FLINN, REV. ANDREW (1773–1820).

He was the first pastor of the Second Presbyterian Church of Charleston, S. C. Portrait begun June 1st, 1812, finished June 20th, 1812. Bust.
　　　　　　　　　　　　　　　　　　　　　　　　　　Price, $70.00
The portrait has been engraved. It is owned at Charlotte, N. C.

592 FLURSLY, MASTER KETLAND.

The name is badly blotted in the register and might be intended for "Hursly." The portrait was begun July 2nd, 1811, and finished Sept. 4th, 1811. Size 29″× 36 ″.　　　　　　　　　　　　Price, $100.00

593 FONSHEE, DR. I.

Portrait begun Jan., 1805, and finished the same month. Size 10″ × 12″.
　　　　　　　　　　　　　　　　　　　　　　　　　　Price, $20.00

594 FORD, MR.

The register notes it " as a sketch to cancel Jane's." Painting begun Nov. 30th, 1831, finished Dec. 7th, 1831. Head.　　　　Price, $30.00

595 FORD, MRS. C.

Portrait painted for Thos. Bryan, begun Oct. 30th, 1829, finished Nov. 20th, 1829. Head.　　　　　　　　　　　　　　Price, $50.00

596 FORD, MRS. C.

Head, nearly full face, lace cap and blue ribbon. Signed " TS 1830." Size 14" X 20". Second portrait, begun Jan. 30th, 1830, finished Feb. 1st, 1830. Price, $50.00

Owned by Miss Mary W. Schott, Phila.

597 FORNEY, JOHN WEISS (1817–1881).

Journalist and politician, clerk of the House of Representatives and then of the Senate of the United States. Editor of the " Press " and other Philadelphia publications. Portrait begun Dec. 29th, 1863, finished Feb. 4th, 1864. Size 25" X 30". Price, $50.00

598 FORNEY, MRS. JOHN W.

Portrait begun Dec. 20th, 1862, finished Jan. 27th, 1863. Size 30" X 25". Price, $50.00

Owned by Brigadier-General James Forney, U. S. M. C., Philadelphia.

599 FORREST, EDWIN (1806–1872).

Popular actor, and founder of the Forrest Home for Actors; portrait painted for the Garrick Club, begun Sept. 19th, 1836, finished Oct. 26th, 1839. Bust. Price, $200.00

600 FORREST, REV. J.

Of Charleston, S. C. The register notes the portrait as a present, begun March 17th, 1846, finished April 8th, 1846. Bust. Price, $200.00

601 FOX, GILBERT (1776–   ).

An English engraver who came to Philadelphia in 1795. He was also an actor and singer, and it was for Fox that Joseph Hopkinson wrote " Hail Columbia," which he sang for the first time at his benefit in 1798. Portrait begun June 21st, 1824, finished on June 28th, 1824. Bust, size 17" X 20". Price, $30.00

602 FRANKLIN, BENJAMIN (1706–1790).

This painting was begun by Jane Sully, it was a copy and was finished by Thomas Sully. Begun July 19th, 1834, finished July 23rd, 1834. Half length. Price, $200.00

603 FRANKLIN, BENJAMIN (1706–1790).

Portrait painted as a bas-relief and presented to the Franklin Institute of Philadelphia. Painting begun June 17th, 1825, finished June 28th, 1825. Head. Price, $20.00

LIST OF PAINTINGS

604 FRANKLIN, BENJAMIN (1706–1790).

Painted as a present to his great-grandson, William Duane (1807–1882). Portrait begun July 10th, 1860, finished July 19th, 1860. Bust.

Price, $100.00

Owned by Mrs. Louise Bodine Wallace, Philadelphia.

605 FRANKLIN, JUDGE WALTER (1773–1838).

Was Attorney-General of Pennsylvania in 1809. Bust, seated in red chair with book in hand, hair powdered, dark eyes and wears spectacles, portrait begun May 8th, 1810, finished May 29th, 1810. Size 25″ × 30″.

Price, $60.00

Owned by his great-grandson, Rev. Dr. Edw. D. Johnson, of Annapolis, Md.

606 FRANKLIN, ANNE EMLEN (1784–1852).

Wife of Judge Walter Franklin, she has brown hair, blue eyes, and is dressed in white with a white head-dress with bow in front. Portrait was begun June 11th, 1810, and finished June 12th, 1810. Size 25″ × 30″.

Price, $60.00

Owned by her great-grandson, Rev. Dr. Edward D. Johnson, Annapolis, Md.

607 FRELAND, MR.

Portrait painted from a daguerreotype, begun Oct. 7th, 1856, finished Oct. 15th, 1856. Head.

Price, $80.00

608 FRELAND, MR.

Portrait painted from a daguerreotype, begun Oct. 7th, 1856, finished Oct. 29th, 1856. Painted for Mr. Daniels, of Mississippi. Bust. Price, $100.00

609 FRELAND, MR.

From Mississippi. Portrait begun July 27th, 1857, finished Aug. 17th, 1857. Size 29″ × 36″.

Price, $200.00

610 FRELAND, MRS.

From Mississippi. Portrait begun July 27th, 1857, finished Aug. 17th, 1857. Size 29″ × 36″.

Price, $200.00

Note.—Frieland or Freland (607 to 610). Correct spelling not known.

611 FRELINGHUYSEN, THEO. (1787–1862).

· (Deceased.) Portrait painted from a photograph, begun Jan. 6th, 1865, finished May 1st, 1865. Size 44 × 34″. Price, $300.00

LIST OF PAINTINGS

612 FRELINGHUYSEN, THEO. (1787–1862).

Copy of former portrait for the Colonization Society, begun May 9th, 1865, finished May 15th, 1865. Head. Size 20″ × 24″. Price, $80.00

Deposited by Colonization Society at the Historical Society of Penna., Philadelphia.

613 FRENCH, MRS.

Portrait painted in Baltimore, begun Nov. 24th, 1820, finished Dec. 2nd, 1820. Bust. Price, $75.00

614 FRENCH, MRS.

(Née Miss Read.) Portrait begun April 17th, 1847, finished April 29th, 1847. Size 17″ × 14″. Price, $80.00

615 FRY, MR.

Printer. Portrait begun May 25th, 1809, finished June 4th, 1809. Bust. Price, $50.00

616 FRY, MR.

Father of, painted from a bust, portrait begun May 11th, 1870, finished June 14th, 1870. Size 25″ × 30″. Price, $100.00

617 FRY, MRS.

Mother of, painted from a sketch. Begun June 9th, 1870, finished June 27th, 1870. Size 14″ × 17″. Price, $50.00

618 FRY.

Mrs. Fry's father, painted from a photograph, begun Dec. 7th, 1870, finished Jan. 7th, 1871. Size 17″ × 14″. Price, $50.00

619 FRY.

Mrs. Fry's father, copied from a photograph, begun Feb. 7th, 1871, finished Feb. 9th, 1871. Size 17″ × 14″. Price, $50.00

620 FRY, MRS.

Of Green Hill. Portrait begun April 25th, 1868, finished June 8th, 1868. Size 25″ × 30″. Price, $100.00

621 FRY.

Portrait of Mrs. Fry's father, begun July 12th, 1870, finished July 30th, 1870. Size 17″ × 14″. Price, $50.00

622 FRY.

Son of Mr. and Mrs. Fry. Portrait begun May 19th, 1869, finished May 29th, 1869. Size 20″ × 24″. Price, $80.00

623 FRY.

Grandfather of Mrs. Fry. A copy begun Dec. 6th, 1869, finished Dec. 26th, 1869. Size 14″ × 17″. Price, $50.00

624 FRY.

Infant of Mrs. Fry. Painted with figure of an angel, begun Feb. 25th, 1870, finished March 7, 1870. Size 24″ × 20″. Price, $100.00

625 FRY, GROSS.

Painted from a photograph. Copy begun April 27th, 1870, finished May 19th, 1870. Size 25″ × 30″. Price, $100.00

626 FRY, GROSS.

Portrait painted 1870. Size 30″ × 25″.

627 FULLER, MRS.

(Miss Montellius.). Portrait begun March 9th, 1837, finished March 25th, 1837. Bust. Price, $150.00

628 FURNESS, REV. WM. HENRY (1802–1896).

Distinguished Unitarian Minister of Philadelphia. Bust, nearly full face, wearing spectacles and white stock. Size 25″ × 31″. Portrait begun Sept. 27th, 1830, finished Oct., 1830, painted for Mrs. Hughes. Engraved by John Sartain.
Owned by F. R. Furness, Esq., of Philadelphia.

629 FURNESS, MRS. WM.

Painted for her husband, begun Oct. 24th, 1829, finished Dec. 31st, 1829. Bust, seated with elbow on arm of chair, black dress, head to left. Size 25″ × 30″. Price, $75.00
Owned by Mr. Horace Howard Furness, Philadelphia.

630 GAINES, EDWARD PENDLETON (1777–1849).

General Gaines served with distinction in the War of 1812, and defended Fort Erie with success in 1814. He was awarded a gold medal by Congress. Drawing made for design of medal Sept., 1817. Size 6″ × 6″.
Price, $50.00

631 GALES, JOSEPH (1786–1860).

In conjunction with W. W. Seton he published the "National Intelligencer" in Washington, D. C. They were also the exclusive reporters of the proceeding of the United States Congress. Portrait begun Oct. 20th, 1843, finished Nov. 10th, 1843. Bust. Price, $100.00

LIST OF PAINTINGS

632 GALLEGO, MR.
Painted from a drawing by Robert Field, begun Nov. 23rd, 1803, finished Nov. 30th, 1803. Size 12″ × 10″. Price, $12.00

633 GAMBLE, ROBERT.
Portrait begun June 6th, 1804, finished July 17th, 1804. Size 10″ × 12″. Price, $15.00

634 GANNET, MR.
Painted for his partner, Mr. Johnston. Begun July 18th, 1810, finished Aug. 4th, 1810. Bust. Price, $50.00

635 GARDETTE, MRS.
(Was Miss Badger.) Portrait begun Jan. 21st, 1829, finished Feb. 13th, 1829. Head. Price, $50.00

636 GEE, MISS MARTHA.
Of Virginia. The register notes that the hands were introduced in the painting, and that the portrait was begun on Sept. 14th, 1835, and finished Oct. 26th, 1835, for Dr. Mutter. Bust. Price, $150.00

637 GEORGE, CAPTAIN EDWARD.
Portrait begun July 27th, 1826, finished August 7th, 1826. Head. Price, $50.00
Owned by Mrs. H. E. George, Mobile, Alabama.

638 GEORGE, MRS. M.
(Was Miss Potter.) Portrait begun July 31st, 1826, finished August 15th, 1826. Head. Price, $50.00
Owned by Mrs. H. E. George, Mobile, Alabama.

639 GETTY, MR.
President of the Corn Exchange Bank, Philadelphia. Portrait begun Sept. 16th, finished Oct. 8, 1863. Size 29″ × 36″. Price, $100.00

640 GETTY, MR.
Same subject as No. 639. Begun Dec. 21st, 1863, finished April 1st, 1864. Size 29″ × 36″. Price, $150.00

641 GIBBON, MR. AND MRS.
Portrait begun June, 1805, finished July, 1805, size 25″ × 30″. Price, $60.00

642 GIBBON, MRS.
Of Richmond, Virginia. Portrait begun May 22nd, 1810, finished August 2nd, 1810. Bust. Price, $60.00

643 GIBSON, MRS. JAMES (1773–1863).

Was Elizabeth Bordley, daughter of John Beale Bordley. Portrait begun Nov. 10th, 1821, finished Jan. 20th, 1822. Size 25″ × 30″. Price, $200.00

This portrait was the property of the late Edw. Shippen, of Philadelphia, and appeared in the Loan Collection, 1887, Academy of Fine Arts.

644 GIBSON, MRS. DR. WILLIAM.

Painted for her mother in Baltimore, begun July 10th, 1820, finished July 25th, 1820. Bust. Price, $75.00

645 GIBSON, DR. WILLIAM (1788–1868).

Distinguished surgeon and professor of surgery at University of Pennsylvania. Painted for Sir Charles Bell, the famous London surgeon, begun June 1st, 1820, finished June 8th, 1820, size 14″ × 17½″. Price, $50.00

646 GIGER, GEORGE MUSGRAVE (1822–1865).

Professor of Greek and Latin at Princeton College, New Jersey, from 1846 until the year of his death. Portrait begun Oct. 18th, 1859, finished Nov. 23rd, 1859. Bust. Price, $100.00

Owned by Princeton College, New Jersey.

647 GILESPIE, MR.

Of Nashville, Tenn. Portrait begun June 22nd, 1841, finished July 2nd, 1841. Bust. Price, $200.00

648 GILL, MRS.

Portrait painted for her sister, Mrs. Lockwood, begun Jan. 4th, 1850, finished Jan. 15th, 1850. Bust. Price, $80.00

649 GILLIOT, ALFRED.

(And his dog.) Painted for Mr. Gallego, begun Dec. 21st, 1803, finished Dec. 29th, 1803. Size 12″ × 10″. Price, $30.00

650 GILMAN, REV. SAMUEL (1791–1858).

Unitarian Minister of Charleston, S. C. He had charge of the Unitarian Church there from 1819 until his death. The register notes the portrait as painted as a present, begun Dec. 23rd, 1845, finished Jan. 13th, 1846. Size 25″ × 30″. Price, $200.00

651 GILMOR, ROBERT, JR. (1774–1848).

Of Baltimore, was an early American collector of paintings and autographs. Copied from his portrait by Sir Thomas Lawrence, which was also engraved by John Sartain. Begun June 3rd, 1823, finished June 20th, 1823. Bust. Price, $100.00

652 GILMOR, ROBERT, JR. (1774–1848).

 Copy of the first portrait after Lawrence. Begun June 3rd, 1823, finished June 22nd, 1823. Size 29″ × 36″.   Price, $100.00

Mr. Gilmor refused to sit a second time for his portrait and directed Mr. Sully to paint from his picture painted by Sir Thomas Lawrence.

653 GILMOR, MRS. ROBERT.

 (Was Miss Sarah Reeves Ladson.) Half length, seated, head to left, Roman scarf, head-dress or turban, white dress short-waisted with green cloak lined with fur over shoulders. Portrait begun April 27th, 1823, finished July 2nd, 1823. Size 29″ × 36″.   Price, $100.00

Owned by Mrs. William Henry Ladson, of Charleston, S. C.

654 GILMORE, MRS. WILLIAM.

 Painted in Baltimore, portrait begun Dec. 11th, 1820, finished February, 1821. Bust.   Price, $100.00

655 GIRAULDTS, MR.

 Of Natchez. Portrait begun March 11th, 1816, finished March 15, 1816. Bust.   Price, $100.00

656 GLENE, MISS.

 Copy for Mr. Thompson. Portrait begun April 29th, 1846, finished May 14th, 1846. Head.   Price, $150.00

657 GLENN, JOHN (1795–1853).

 Of Baltimore, Md. (Deceased.) He was a lawyer, and at the time of his death was Judge of the United States District Court of Maryland. Portrait painted for his son, William W. Glenn, begun May 15th, 1857, finished Aug. 29th, 1857. Signed "TS 1857." Size 24″ × 20″. Price, $80.00

Owned by his grandson, John M. Glenn, of New York, N. Y.

658 GLENTWORTH, PLUNKETT F. (1760–1833).

 A well-known Philadelphia physician. Portrait begun Dec. 10th, 1812, finished March 3rd, 1813. Bust.   Price, $70.00

 NOTE.—Glynn, William. (See Gwynn.) An error of Sully's in transcribing the name in the register.

659 GODEY, CHARLOTTE.

 (Deceased.) Portrait painted from a daguerreotype, begun April 5th, 1847, finished April 24th, 1847. Size 24″ × 20″.   Price, $100.00

LIST OF PAINTINGS

660 GODEY.

(Group of three children.)   Louis A. Godey, whose three children were painted in a group by Sully, was a Philadelphia publisher and owner of Godey's Lady's Book.   Begun April 16, 1844, finished Aug. 1st, 1844. Size 26″ × 36″.   Price, $250.00

661 GODEY, MRS.

Wife of Louis A. Godey, publisher of Godey's Lady's Book, Philadelphia. Portrait begun April 6th, 1843, finished April 26th, 1843.   Head.
                                                                       Price, $80.00

662 GORDON, MR.

Son of John Montgomery Gordon, of Virginia; his mother was Emily, eldest daughter of Dr. Nathaniel Chapman, of Philadelphia.   Portrait begun Oct. 7th, 1846, finished Oct. 17th, 1846.   Head.   Price, $80.00

663 GOURDIN, THEODORE (–1826).

He was a planter of Pineville, South Carolina, and a member of Congress from Charleston, 1813–1815.   Half length, head to right.   Size 29″ × 24½″.   Portrait begun March 18, 1815, finished April 1st, 1815.
                                                                       Price, $80.00
Owned by Herbert L. Pratt, Long Island, N. Y.

664 GRAHAM, MISS ELIZABETH.

(Wife of Dr. George Graham, publisher of Graham's Magazine, Philadelphia.)   Bust.   Begun Dec. 27th, 1842, finished Jan. 10th, 1843.
                                                   Subscriber's price, $100.00
Owned by Mrs. Hannah E. Wilson, Jenkintown, Philadelphia.

665 GRATIOT, GENERAL CHARLES (1788–1855).

Served in the War of 1812 with distinction.   Painted for United States Military Academy at West Point, begun June 26th, 1830, finished July 5th, 1830.   Bust.   Price, $75.00
Bust in uniform, unbuttoned military coat showing a buff waistcoat. Heavy cloud background.
Owned by the United States Military Academy, West Point, N. Y.

666 GRATIOT, GENERAL CHARLES.

Portrait painted for West Point Academy, begun Oct. 15th, 1832, finished Nov. 5th, 1832.   Bust.   Price, $80.00

667 GRATIOT, GENERAL CHARLES.
Copied at West Point for Col. North, begun July 8th, 1833, finished on July 15th, 1833. Bust. Price, $100.00

668 GRATIOT, MRS. CHARLES.
Wife of General Charles Gratiot. Portrait begun June 30th, 1829, finished August 5th, 1829. Size 29″ × 36″. Price, $120.00

669 GRATZ, BENJAMIN (1792–1884).
Was a son of Michael Gratz, of Philadelphia. Portrait begun April 1st, 1831, finished April 9th, 1831. Head, 17″ × 20″. Signed " TS 1831." Owned by Mrs. Thomas Clay, Lexington, Ky.

670 GRATZ, MRS. BENJAMIN (d. 1841).
(Was Maria Cecil Gist.) Head size. Price, $50.00
Owned by Mrs. Thomas Clay, Lexington, Ky.

671 GRATZ, MICHAEL (1740–1811).
A well-known Hebrew merchant of Philadelphia. Bust, head to left with long hair, high stock, curtain in background. Portrait begun April 18th, 1808, finished June 26th, 1808. (Subscriber.) Price, $30.00
Owned by Mr. Henry Joseph, Montreal, Canada.

672 GRATZ, REBECCA (1781–1869).
Beautiful and brilliant Jewess of Philadelphia who identified herself with Hebrew benevolent work. Bust, head to right, wearing hat with wide brim, hand rests on neck. Painted for her brother, portrait begun Oct. 25th, 1830, finished June 8th, 1831. Size 25″ × 30″. Price, $75.00
Reproduced in " Reminiscences of a Very Old Man." By John Sartain, 1899. Owned by Henry Joseph, Montreal, Canada.

673 GRATZ, REBECCA.
Portrait copied from a miniature by Edward G. Malbone, for Thomas A. Cooper, begun Feb. 16th, 1807, finished June 6th, 1807. Bust.
Price, $30.00

674 GRATZ, REBECCA (1781–1869).
A second portrait painted for Hyman Gratz and noted in register as " erased." Bust. Size 16″ × 19″, begun Nov. 15th, 1830. This painting was probably finished; there is a tradition in the Gratz family that it was not accepted on account of a turban or head-dress painted in the portrait by the artist. The finished picture shows a turban which emphasizes the oriental beauty of her features. Price, $75.00
Owned by John Gribbel, of Philadelphia.

LIST OF PAINTINGS

675 GRATZ, REBECCA.

Portrait painted for Mrs. Benjamin Gratz, begun May 16th, 1831, finished June 11th, 1831. Head, panel 17" × 20". Price, $50.00
Owned by Mrs. Thomas Clay, Lexington, Ky.

NOTE.—A copy by a Kentucky artist hangs in the Jewish Foster Home, Germantown, Philadelphia.

676 GRAY, MR.

A well-known and wealthy brewer. Portrait begun Feb. 18th, 1811, finished March 10th, 1811. Size 29" × 36". Price, $80.00

677 GRAY, MR.

Of New Orleans, La. Portrait begun July 15th, 1808, finished October 1st, 1808. Bust. Price, $50.00

678 GRAY, MISS MARTHA.

Portrait painted in Baltimore for her father, Edward Gray. Picture begun May 12th, 1853, finished May 20th, 1853. Head. Price, $100.00

679 GREEN, EDMUND.

Portrait begun Dec. 16th, 1819, finished Dec. 20th, 1819. Bust. Price, $100.00

680 GREEN, MRS.

Of Natchez. Portrait begun Aug. 2nd, 1816, finished Sept. 21st, 1816. Bust. Price, $100.00

681 GREEN, MRS.

(Was Miss Ritchie.) Bust. Portrait begun Sept. 25th, 1833, finished Oct. 9th, 1833. Price, $125.00

682 GREENE, GENERAL NATHANIEL (1742–1786).

A distinguished officer of the Revolution. Deceased, copied from Peale's picture. Portrait begun May 10th, 1816, finished May 12th, 1816. Head. Price, $80.00

683 GREINOBAUM, MR.

Father-in-law to Mrs. Greinobaum. Portrait begun April 15th, 1863, finished April 29th, 1863. Size 25" × 30". Price, $50.00

684 GREINOBAUM, MRS.

Portrait begun April 10th, 1863, finished May 17th, 1863. Size 25" × 30". Price, $50.00

685 GRIFFIN, MR.
Portrait begun Oct. 27th, 1830, finished Nov. 27th, 1830. Bust.
Price, $75.00

686 GRIFFIN, MRS.
Of Cincinnati. Portrait begun Oct. 27th, 1830, finished Nov. 27th, 1830.
Bust. Price, $75.00

687 GRIFFIN, MRS.
Of Wilmington, Del. Begun April 19th, 1866, finished May 26th, 1866.
Head. Price, $80.00

688 GRIFFITH, ROBERT EGLESFELD (1756–1833).
Merchant of Philadelphia. Copied from the portrait painted by Gilbert
Stuart. Copy begun on March 28th, 1825, finished May 12th, 1825, for
Mr. Pollock. Size 29″ × 36″. Price, $60.00

689 GRIFFITH, MRS.
She was the mother of Mrs. Thomas I. Wharton. Portrait painted for
Mrs. Hughes, begun Sept. 24th, 1829, finished Dec. 21st, 1829. Bust.
Price, $75.00
Owned by Mrs. Charles B. Coxe, of Philadelphia.

690 GRIFFITHS, DR. E.
Portrait begun Feb. 22nd, 1808, finished **March** 20th, 1808. Bust.
(Subscriber.) Price, $30.00

NOTE.—Thirty subscribers for portraits at $30 each; this was the first painted and
is so noted in the register.

691 GRIGG, MISS EMILY.
Daughter of John Grigg, of Philadelphia. Portrait begun June 9th, 1856,
finished June 27th, 1856. (The youngest sister.) Head. Price, $80.00

692 GRIGG, MISS FANNY.
Daughter of John Grigg, of Philadelphia. Portrait begun May 19th,
1856, finished May 26th, 1856. Head. Price, $80.00

693 GRIGG, MISS FANNY.
Portrait copy of the former painting, begun June 18th, 1856, finished
June 30th, 1856. Head. Price, $80.00

694 GRIGG, MISS NANNY.
Daughter of John Grigg, of Philadelphia. Portrait begun May 20th,
1856, finished June 28th, 1856. Head. Price, $80.00

LIST OF PAINTINGS

695 GRIGG, MISS NANNY.

Painted in lieu of former portrait, begun May 9th, 1857, finished May 25th, 1857. Size 24″ × 20″. Price, $80.00

696 GRILLET, MADAME.

Portrait begun March 27th, 1807, and finished May 2nd, 1807. Size 58″ × 94″. Price, $100.00

697 GROOME, COL. JOHN C. (1800–1866).

Of Elkton, Md. Lawyer, and the father of John Black Groome. Portrait begun Aug. 28th, 1856, and finished Aug. 30th, 1856. " TS 1856." Bust, size 25″ × 30″. Price, $100.00

Owned by Mrs. Caroline Van Syckel, of Columbus, Ohio.

698 GROOME, JAMES BLACK (1838–1893).

Eminent lawyer and Governor of Maryland in 1874, and United States Senator in 1879 to 1885. Portrait begun May 21st, 1855, finished June 17th, 1855. Bust. Price, $100.00

699 GROSVENOR, LADY ELIZABETH.

Copy of the portrait painted by Sir Thomas Lawrence, begun Sept. 10th, 1861, finished Sept. 20th, 1861. Size 13″ × 9½″. Price, $20.00

700 GRUBB, MR.

Copied from St. Memin's portrait. Portrait begun Sept. 29th, 1824, finished March 3rd, 1825. Bust. Price, $60.00

701 GRUBB, MR. EDWARD.

Head to left, curly black hair and side whiskers. Painted for his mother, Mrs. Henry Bates Grubb. Portrait begun Feb. 7th, 1833, and finished Feb. 22nd, 1833. Size of canvas 16¾″ × 20″. Price, $60.00

Owned by Mrs. Joseph Sailer, Philadelphia.

702 GRUBB, MRS. HENRY BATES.

Of "Mount Hope," Lancaster Co., Pa. Bust, nearly full face. Lace cap, low-necked black dress with ermine cape. Portrait begun Sept. 18th, 1824, finished Feb. 27th, 1825. Size of canvas 25″ × 30″. Price, $60.00

Owned by Miss Strawbridge, of Philadelphia.

703 GRUBB, MR.

Of Burlington, N. J. Portrait begun March 4th, 1868, finished April 18th, 1868. Size 20″ × 24″. Price, $80.00

LIST OF PAINTINGS

704 GRUNDY, MR.

Of Baltimore, Md. Portrait begun May 4th, 1814, finished May 8th, 1814. The register states that the hands were introduced in the portrait. Bust.   Price, $80.00

705 GUERARD, MISS SOPHIA.

Portrait painted for Mrs. Crawford, begun March 14th, 1864, finished April 6th, 1864. Bust, wears a white satin dress with transparent gauze drawn over her shoulders and caught by a rose-bud.   Price, $200.00
Owned by Miss A. B. Rose, Charleston, S. C.

706 GUERIN, MONSIEUR.

Of Savannah, Ga. Portrait begun June 7th, 1816, finished July, 1816. Bust.   Price, $100.00

707 GUMBES, MRS. WILLIAM HENRY (1789–   ).

Rebecca Wetherill Gumbes was the daughter of John Price Wetherill for whom this portrait was painted, begun July 17th, 1822, finished Aug. 7th, 1822. Signed on the belt of her dress " TS 1822." Bust. Size 25" × 30".   Price, $100.00
Owned by Mrs. T. Ridgway Barker.

708 GWATHONEY, MRS.

In place of Hubbard's portrait, begun March 15th, 1851, finished April 8th, 1851. Head.   Price, $100.00

709 GWINN, CAPT. JOHN, U. S. N. (d. 1849).

He entered the navy in 1809. Portrait begun Sept. 18th, 1837, finished Sept. 22nd, 1837. Head.   Price, $150.00

710 GWYNN, WILLIAM (1779–1846).

A lawyer of Baltimore. Life-size, dark curly hair, wears black coat and vest. Portrait begun May 8th, 1821, finished May 15th, 1821. Canvas 24" × 20". Painted for H. Robinson.   Price, $100.00
Owned by the Metropolitan Museum of New York.

711 GWYNN, MRS.

Formerly Miss Lynch. Portrait begun March 23rd, 1839, finished April 29th, 1839. Head.   Price, $150.00

712 HACKLEY, MRS.

Portrait painted for Mrs. Talcot, begun Dec. 29th, 1835, finished March 1st, 1836. Bust.   Price, $100.00
Owned by Mrs. Richard D. Cutts, Washington, D. C.

LIST OF PAINTINGS

713 HACKLEY, MISS FANNY.

Portrait painted for her mother. Begun Oct. 17th, 1836, finished Oct. 27th, 1836. Head.   Price, $100.00

714 HALBERSTADT, GEORGE (1805–1860).

Portrait painted when he was a student at the University of Pennsylvania. Signed on back of canvas "TS." Head.
Owned by his granddaughter, Mrs. Harriet Grant, of Pottsville, Pa.

715 HALDERMAN, SARAH JACOBS.

Married William J. Haly. Portrait painted for Miss Fox, begun July 12th, 1829, finished July 21st, 1829. Head, facing front. Size 15″ × 20″.
Owned by Mrs. Edwin Longnecker, Wernersville, Penna.   Price, $50.00

716 HALDEMAN, MISS.

Of Harrisburg, Penna. Portrait begun Feb. 28th, 1860, finished March 20th, 1860. Bust.   Price, $100.00

717 HALE, MR. R. C.

Of Harrisburg, Penna. Portrait begun Feb. 4th, 1863, finished Sept. 28th, 1864. Size 20″ × 24″.   Price, $100.00

718 HALE, MRS.

Portrait begun Oct. 1st, 1810, finished Oct. 13th, 1810. The register notes "both hands introduced" in the portrait. Bust, size 20″ × 24″.
     Price, $70.00

719 HALE, MRS. JAMES TRACY.

(Née Jane Walker Huston.) Of Philipsburg, Penna. Portrait begun June 7th, 1865, finished June 17th, 1865. Bust.   Price, $100.00

720 HALE, THOMAS (–1840).

Second President of Philadelphia Saving Fund Society, he was in the continuous service of the Society for nearly twenty-four years. Portrait painted about 183–. Bust, seated, head to right.
Portrait owned by Mrs. John Lowell, of Chestnut Hill, Boston, Mass.

NOTE.—The original painting was not seen by the authors. Reproduced in " History of Philadelphia Saving Fund Society," by J. M. Willcox. This portrait has been attributed to Sully for many years, but the authors are doubtful of the attribution.

721 HALL, MRS. WILLIAM (1806–1830).

(Née Christianna Guilielma Penn-Gaskell.) Bust, facing right, red hat and feathers, yellow low-neck gown, with fur-trimmed cloak, vase in background.   Size 25″ × 30″.   Price, $75.00
Owned by Mrs. James Hancock and Miss Guilielma Hall.

722 HAMILTON, MR.

Of Williamsborough, N. C.   Portrait begun Oct. 2nd, 1851, finished April 9th, 1851.   Head.   Price, $100.00

723 HAMILTON, MR.

Of Kentucky.   Portrait begun April 16th, 1850, finished May 10th, 1850. Bust.   Price, $100.00

724 HAMILTON, MRS.

Of Kentucky.   Portrait begun April 16th, 1850, finished May 10th, 1850. Bust.   Price, $100.00

725 HAMILTON, ESTELLE.

Portrait painted for her mother, begun Jan. 13th, 1855, finished Jan. 22nd, 1855.   Head.   Price, $80.00

726 HAMILTON, J.

Painted in Van Dyke costume.   Portrait begun May 12th, 1810, and finished Dec. 2nd, 1810.   Bust.   Price, $80.00

727 HAMILTON, JAMES.

Portrait begun Dec. 10th, 1810, finished Dec. 29th, 1810.   Bust.
                                                                  Price, $60.00

728 HAMILTON, JAMES.

Of Philadelphia.   Portrait begun March 10th, 1807, finished March 17th, 1807.   Bust.   Price, $30.00

729 HAMILTON, JAMES.

Of Philadelphia.   Portrait begun Dec. 15th, 1808, finished Jan. 24th, 1809.   Size 17″ × 20″.   Price, $30.00

730 HAMILTON, WILLIAM (1745–1813).

Of the "Woodlands."   Deceased, painted from a miniature, begun June 1st, 1814, finished July 6th, 1814.   Bust.   Price, $80.00

NOTE.—Benjamin West's full-length portrait of William Hamilton is in the Historical Society of Pennsylvania.

731 HAMMOND, MR. JOHN.

Painted for H. V. Newman, begun May 28th, 1821, finished June 20th, 1821. Size 25" × 30". Bust. Price, $100.00
Owned by Mrs. James R. Fitzgerald, and loaned to the Boston Museum of Fine Arts.

732 HANDEL, GEORGE FREDERICK (1685–1759).

Portrait copied from a painting by a German artist for the Musician Series of Pictures, begun Oct. 23rd, 1862, finished Nov. 3rd, 1862. Size 17" × 12". Price, $30.00

733 HANDY, MISS.

Deceased, painted from a miniature, portrait begun June 28th, 1842, finished July 9th, 1842. Bust. Price, $150.00

734 HANKEY, MRS.

Head, to left, dark hair. The Hankey's were relatives of Col. Alexander Biddle. Size 17" × 20".
Owned by the estate of Alexander Biddle, Philadelphia.

735 HARDING, MISS CAROLYN T.

Bust, with hand introduced, low-necked pink gown. Portrait painted about 1849. Signed " TS." Size 25" × 30".
Owned by Ehrich Galleries, New York.

736 HARE, CHARLES WILLING (1787–1827).

An eminent Philadelphia lawyer. Portrait begun May 20th, 1814, finished July 5th, 1814. Bust. Price, $80.00

737 HARE, HORACE BINNEY.

He was the only child of Judge John Innes Clark Hare and Esther Binney Hare, and grandson of the Hon. Horace Binney. Sketch made on Nov. 13th, 1847, for painting portrait No. 738. Size 13" × 8". Price, $10.00

738 HARE, HORACE BINNEY.

Of Philadelphia. Painted as a child of four years old. Bust, wearing a large hat with feather and resting his hand on the arm of a chair. Portrait begun Dec. 22nd, 1847, finished Jan. 10th, 1848. Bust. Price, $125.00
Owned by Mrs. Horace Binney Hare, of Radnor, Penna.

739 HARE, ROBERT (1781–1858).

Professor of Chemistry at the University of Pennsylvania in 1847. He was one of the early advocates of Spiritualism. Portrait begun on April 2nd, 1827, finished May 7th, 1827. Bust. Price, $75.00

LIST OF PAINTINGS

740 HARPER, MISS EMILY.

Portrait painted at Baltimore, begun Feb. 15th, 1853, finished April 24th, 1853. Head. Price, $100.00

741 HARPER, WILLIAM (1790–1847).

Senator from South Carolina in 1826, Chancellor 1828, Judge of the Court of Appeals 1830. The portrait was painted for the college at Columbia, begun Feb. 17th, 1864, finished March 5th, 1864. Bust.
Price, $200.00

742 HARPER, WILLIAM (1790–1847).

Copy of former portrait, begun March 7th, 1864, finished April 8th, 1864. Bust. Price, $200.00

743 HARRIS, MR.

Portrait begun Dec. 26th, 1836, finished Jan. 5th, 1837. Bust.
Price, $150.00

744 HARRISON, MRS. GEORGE (b. ——, d. 1851).

Of Philadelphia. Portrait painted for her nephew, Joshua Francis Fisher, begun Jan. 2nd, 1852, finished Feb. 1st, 1854. Head. Price, $100.00

745 HARRISON, GENL. WILLIAM HENRY (1773–1841).

Design for medal awarded by Congress to Genl. Harrison. Size 10″ × 12″. Begun Oct. 3rd, 1822, finished October 5th, 1822. Price, $50.00

746 HARWOOD, JOHN E. (1771–1809).

An English actor noted for his handsome face and fine figure, he married Miss Bache, a granddaughter of Benjamin Franklin, and was the father of Admiral Andrew A. Harwood, U. S. Navy. Portrait begun Nov. 3rd, 1806, and was finished the same month. Bust. Painted for Thomas A. Cooper when Harwood was connected with the New York Theatre. Price, $30.00

747 HASELTON, MRS.

Portrait begun March 18th, 1834, finished April 26th, 1834. Bust.
Price, $125.00

748 HASLAM, MRS.

Portrait painted for Anna Peale, begun Jan. 17th, 1839, finished Feb. 22nd, 1839. Bust. Price, $200.00

749 HATCH, MR.

Of Vicksburg, Tenn. Portrait begun Sept. 4th, 1843, finished Sept. 12th, 1843. Head. Price, $80.00

750 HAVEN, GROUP OF LESLIE, EMMA AND GEORGE.
Painting begun Nov. 4th, 1848, finished Dec. 13th, 1848. Size 29" × 36". Price, $150.00

751 HAVILAND, MRS.
Portrait begun March 8th, 1837, finished March 15th, 1837. Bust. Price, $150.00

752 HAXALL, ANNE T. (1820–1892).
Daughter of Richard Triplett and wife of Bolling W. Haxall, of Richmond, Va. Portrait painted for her son, begun June 19th, 1849, finished June 30th, 1849. Head. Size 17" × 20". Price, $100.00
Owned by Anne T. Harrison Jackson, Garrison, Maryland.

753 HAXALL, ANNE T. (1820–1892).
Portrait begun Nov. 11th, 1850, and finished Dec. 1st, 1850. Head. Size 17" × 20". Price, $100.00

754 HAYDEN, JOSEPH (1732–1809).
Painted for the Musician Series. Begun April 1st, 1863, finished May 29th, 1863. Head. Price, $30.00

755 HAYNE, MISS.
Of Charleston, S. C. Portrait begun Sept. 12th, 1840, finished Sept. 21st, 1840. Head. Price, $150.00

756 HAYNE, MRS. PAUL.
Portrait painted for Miss Hayne, begun April 4th, 1842, finished April 14th, 1842. Head. Price, $150.00

757 HAYNES, MRS. AND HER GRANDDAUGHTER.
Portrait begun April 4th, 1803, finished June 4th, 1803. Size 29" × 36". Price, $25.00

758 HAYNES, MACAULAY.
Portrait begun March 1st, 1803, finished March 10th, 1803. Bust. Price, $20.00

759 HAZELHURST, MRS.
Portrait painted for her son, begun March 28th, 1831, noted in register as condemned. Bust. Price, $75.00

760 HAZELHURST, MRS.

The second attempt, begun May 21st, 1831, finished June 8th, 1831. Bust. Price, $75.00

761 HAZELHURST, MRS.

Deceased, replica of the former portrait, begun June 9th, 1842, finished June 24th, 1842. Bust. Price, $150.00

762 HAZELHURST, MR. ISAAC.

Portrait begun March 30th, 1835, finished Nov. 10th, 1835. Bust. Price, $125.00

763 HAZELHURST, MRS. ISAAC.

Portrait begun May 6th, 1839, finished May 20th, 1839. Head. Price, $150.00

764 HAZELHURST, MISS MARY (1806–1890).

Daughter of Samuel Hazelhurst, married Lewis Richard Ashhurst. Portrait begun Oct. 27th, 1831, finished Nov. 27th, 1831. Bust. Price, $80.00

765 HEAD, JOSEPH.

Portrait begun, Dec. 20th, 1807, finished Jan. 10th, 1808. Bust. Price, $50.00

766 HENDERSON, MR.

(Near Norristown.) Portrait begun Oct. 1st, 1833, finished Nov. 27th, 1833. Price, $200.00

767 HENDREE, MRS. G.

Portrait begun May 30th, 1815, finished July 9th, 1815. The register notes that the "hands were introduced." Size 20″ × 24″. Price, $100.00

768 HENDY, MRS.

Of Boston. Portrait begun May 25th, 1844, finished June 19th, 1844. Bust. Price, $100.00

769 HENRY, MRS. BERNARD (1789–1876).

Half length, facing right, as if in motion. Size 24″ × 29″. She was Mary Miller, daughter of Dr. Samuel Jackson, and one of the "three pocket Venuses" mentioned in Salmagundi. This portrait was begun July 4th, 1811, and finished Oct. 5th, 1811, it did belong to Morton P. Henry, of Philadelphia, and was exhibited by him at the Loan Collection of 1887 at the Pennsylvania Academy of Fine Arts. The register notes the price paid as $70.

172

LIST OF PAINTINGS

770 HENRY, PATRICK (1736–1799).

Statesman and lawyer, he was a delegate to the first Continental Congress. Painted from a miniature by a French artist (from life) and copied by Sully for the Hon. Wm. Wirt. Engraved by Leney (S. 1776) and by Wellmore for National Portrait Gallery. Portrait begun Nov. 11th, 1815, finished Nov. 20th, 1815. Bust. Size 20″ × 24″. Price, $100.00
Owned by Charles Hamilton, Esq., Philadelphia.

771 HENRY, PATRICK (1736–1779).

Presented to the Historical Society of Virginia. Portrait begun June 6th, 1851, finished June 28th, 1851. Size 20″ × 24″. Bust. Price, $150.00
Owned by the Historical Society of Virginia.

772 HENRY, MRS. WILLIAM HAMILTON.

The authors have not been able to see this portrait, it was exhibited at the "Portrait Exhibition of Women," New York, 1894. It was owned at that time by Mr. William Hamilton Henry, of New York.

773 HERRING, MAJOR.

Of New Orleans, La., formerly of the United States army. Portrait begun Sept. 9th, 1846, finished Sept. 17th, 1846. Bust. Price, $100.00

774 HEWIT, MRS.

Sister of C. Hupfield. Portrait begun Jan. 30th, 1824, finished Feb. 9th, 1824. Size 8″ × 16″. Price, $30.00

775 HEWSON, DR. THOMAS TICKELL (1773–1848).

He was the son of Dr. Franklin's friend, Mary Stevenson, who married William Hewson, a celebrated English anatomist. He became one of the most eminent of Philadelphia physicians. Portrait painted after Dr. Hewson's death, from a daguerreotype, begun Feb. 25th, 1848, finished June 3rd, 1848. Bust. Price, $100.00
Owned by Dr. Addinell Hewson.

776 HEWSON, MRS. THOMAS T.

Was Emily Banks, of Washington, D. C., and married Dr. Thomas T. Hewson, of Philadelphia, for whom the portrait was painted. Begun May 2nd, 1825, finished April 15th, 1826. Bust. Price, $60.00

777 HEWSON, MRS. THOMAS T.

Painted for Mrs. Biddle, begun May 31st, 1826, finished June 6th, 1826. Size 17″ × 20″. Price, $40.00
Now owned by the Hewson family.

778 HEWSON, MRS. THOMAS T.

Portrait painted for Dr. Thomas T. Hewson, begun Jan. 31st, 1839, finished Feb. 22nd, 1839. Head. Price, $150.00

779 HEYWARD, THOMAS, JR. (1746–1809).

He was a signer of the Declaration of Independence from South Carolina. Portrait painted for Charles Manigault, of South Carolina, begun July 5th, 1837, finished on Sept. 12th, 1837. Bust. Price, $200.00

780 HEYWARD, THOMAS, JR. (1746–1809).

Portrait copied for his grandson, painting begun March 20th, 1854, finished March 25th, 1854. Head. Price, $80.00

781 HINDSMAN, MISS.

Portrait painted at about four years of age, begun Nov. 22nd, 1831, finished April 4th, 1832. Whole length. Price, $150.00

782 HINDMAN, MISS SARAH E.

(Red Ridinghood.) Portrait of a young fair-haired girl, full length, in a white dress, red hood, resting her basket on a rock. Portrait begun Sept. 26th, 1832, and finished Jan. 19th, 1833. Size 36″ × 48″.
Owned by Peabody Institute, Baltimore, Md.

783 HINDMAN, MRS.

Portrait begun Nov. 6th, 1832, finished Jan. 14th, 1833. Bust. Price, $100.00

784 HISLOP, MR.

Portrait begun Feb. 5th, 1807, finished May 9th, 1807. Bust. Price, $30.00

785 HOBAN, MRS. JAMES.

(Née Marian Blackwell French.) Bust, to left, black hair and brown eyes, she wears a low-necked white dress, with red shawl over right shoulder. Portrait begun Sept. 24th, 1844, finished Sept. 30th, 1844. Size 20″ × 24″. Price, $80.00
Owned by Mrs. E. R. Alexander, of Cleveland, Ohio.

786 HODGKIN, DR. THOMAS (1798–1866).

This portrait was painted from a photograph for the Colonization Society, begun Dec. 2nd, 1858, finished Dec. 9th, 1858. Head. Price, $80.00
Deposited at the Pennsylvania Historical Society, Philadelphia.

LIST OF PAINTINGS

787 HODSON, JOHN.
Painting begun June 5th, 1804, finished July 13, 1804. Size 10″ × 12″.

788 HOFFMAN, MRS.
Painted for the Female Asylum, begun July 20th, 1814, finished Aug., 1814. Size 29″ × 36″.   Price, $150.00

789 HOFFMAN, MRS.
Portrait begun Feb. 5th, 1807, finished March 9th, 1807. Size 29″ × 36″.
Price, $40.00

790 HOFFMAN, MRS. DAVID (1797–1882).
Née Mary McKean, married David Hoffman, lawyer, in 1816. Portrait begun May 2nd, 1821, finished June 22nd, 1821. Bust, head turned to right, open-necked dress, wearing a cloak.   Price, $100.00
Owned by Mrs. Kerr, of West Chester, Penna.

791 HOFFMAN, GEORGE (1770–1834).
Painted in Baltimore, begun March 30th, 1820, finished April 21st, 1820. Half length, seated, head to right; one hand in front of coat, the other rests on end of sofa. Size 25″ × 30″.   Price, $150.00
Owned by R. C. Hoffman, Baltimore, Md.

792 HOFFMAN, MRS. GEORGE AND CHILD.
Portrait begun Jan. 1st, 1821, finished Feb. 9th, 1821. Size 29″ × 36″.
Price, $150.00

793 HOFFMAN, PETER.
Painted in Baltimore, begun Dec. 8th, 1820, finished February, 1821. Bust, head to right, holding his hand on breast.   Price, $130.00
Owned by Richard Curzon Hoffman, of Baltimore, Md.

794 HOFFMAN, MRS. PETER (1777–1856).
A smaller painting as a study for portrait painted a few months later. Begun Feb. 19th, 1821, finished Dec., 1822. Bust.   Price, $30.00

795 HOFFMAN, MRS. PETER (1777–1856).
(Née Deborah Owings.) Half length, seated, dark blue velvet dress with lace neck frill, over shoulders a yellow cloak trimmed with swansdown. Portrait begun April 9th, 1821, finished Dec., 1821. Size 29″ × 38″.
Price, $130.00
Owned by her great-granddaughter, Miss Frances H. Hoffman, of Baltimore, Md.

796 HOFFMAN, MASTER WILLIAM HENRY.

Son of George Hoffman, died in 1865. Portrait of a boy wearing a battered old torn hat. Painting begun on April 29th, 1821, finished May 11th, 1821. Size 17″ × 21″. Price, $30.00
Owned by Richard C. Hoffman, of Baltimore, Md.

NOTE.—Similar composition to portrait of the artist's son, " The Torn Hat."

797 HOGG, JOHN (1770–1813).

("Formerly of the Theatre.") Bust, head to right, white stock, the upper buttons of the waistcoat being unbuttoned. Painting begun June 2nd, 1807, and finished June 14th, 1807. Canvas 26½″ × 22″. Price, $30.00
Sold in auction of Mrs. Benjamin Thaw, New York.

798 HOLBROOK, MRS.

Of Charleston, S. C., was the wife of the celebrated naturalist John Edward Holbrook. Portrait begun July 30th, 1860, and finished Sept. 14th, 1860. Bust, wearing black gown and transparent white cap. Price, $100.00
Owned by her niece, Miss Rutlege, and exhibited at Charleston, S. C., 1901.

799 HOLLIDAY, MR.

Portrait begun Oct. 16th, 1858, finished Oct. 28th, 1858. Bust.
Price, $100.00

800 HOLLIDAY, MRS.

(Née Miss Gamble.) Portrait begun Oct. 15th, 1858, finished Oct. 28th, 1858. Bust. Price, $100.00

801 HOLLINGSWORTH (SENR.), SAMUEL.

Portrait begun Jan. 28th, 1823, finished Feb. 8th, 1823. Bust.
Price, $100.00

802 HOLLINGSWORTH, MISS LYDIA.

Painted for T. B. Morris, of Philadelphia, begun Jan. 14th, 1823, finished March 6th, 1823. Bust. Price, $100.00

803 HONQUA.

Chinese merchant. Painted for Mr. Cabot in 1819. Bust.

804 HONQUA.

Small full-length portrait, painted for Mr. Wilcocks, begun August 29th, 1828, finished Sept. 13th, 1828. Size 26″ × 19″. Price, $200.00

LIST OF PAINTINGS

805 HOOD, MR.

Of Missouri. Portrait begun July 2nd, 1824, finished July 14th, 1824. Painted for Edinburgh. Head. Price, $30.00

806 HOOPER, MISS.

Painted for Mrs. Mallon. Portrait begun May 1st, 1816, finished June 4th, 1816. Bust. Price, $100.00

807 HOPKINS, JOHN HENRY (1792–1868).

First Protestant Episcopal Bishop of Vermont, Oct. 31st, 1832. Portrait begun Aug. 17th, 1835, finished Aug. 28th, 1835. Size 29¾" × 25". Head. Price, $80.00
Owner, Mrs. Frank Hinckley, portrait loaned to Boston Museum of Fine Arts.

808 HOPKINS, NICHOLAS.

Half length, seated, with arm resting on back of chair, hand thrust under coat, the other gloved, white stock, head to right. Portrait begun May 11th, 1813, finished July 1st, 1813. Size 29" × 36". Price, $100.00
Owned by William Hopkins, Esq., Philadelphia.

809 HOPKINSON, FRANCIS (1796–1870).

Portrait begun May 19th, 1834, finished June 9th, 1834. Size 16" × 21". Head. Price, $80.00
Owned by Charles Harris, Esq., New York.

810 HOPKINSON, MRS. FRANCIS (1800–1863).

(Née Miss Ann Biddle.) Head to left, with large hat and drooping feather, fur-trimmed cloak. Portrait begun May 12th, 1834, finished May 24th, 1834. Head. Engraved by J. B. Forrest. Size 16" × 20".
Price, $80.00
Owned by Charles Harris, Esq., New York.

811 HOPKINSON, JUDGE JOSEPH (1770–1842).

Author of "Hail Columbia" and United States Judge for the Eastern District of Pennsylvania. He was president of the Academy of Fine Arts of Pennsylvania. Head looking left. Size 17" × 20". Portrait begun May 25th, 1832, finished July 6th, 1832. Engraved by John Sartain.
Price, $60.00
Owned by Edward Hopkinson, Esq., Philadelphia, Pa.

812 HOPKINSON, JUDGE JOSEPH (1770–1842).

Portrait painted for Dartmouth College, begun March 23rd, 1835, finished April 20th, 1835. Bust, seated before a desk, holding a quill pen in his hand, which rests on a sheet of paper.   Price, $125.00
Owned by Dartmouth College, New Hampshire.

813 HOPKINSON, MRS. JOSEPH (17— –1850).

Was Emily Mifflin, daughter of Genl. Thomas Mifflin, who was Governor of Pennsylvania. She married Joseph Hopkinson, author of "Hail Columbia," and President for years of Pennsylvania Academy of Fine Arts. Portrait begun July 1st, 1808, finished July 5th, 1808. Half length, standing with arm resting on pedestal, white low-necked gown, drapery over head. Signed " TS." Canvas 25″ × 30″.   Subscriber's price $30.00
Sold in Thomas B. Clarke's sale, American Art Association, New York, 1919, and now owned by Senator Brandegee.

814 HORNER, DR. WILLIAM E. (1793–1853).

Professor of Anatomy at University of Pennsylvania. Portrait begun May 28th, 1836, finished July 8th, 1836. Head.   Price, $100.00

815 HOSACK, DAVID, M. D. (1769–1835).

An eminent scientist and practitioner of medicine in New York, and a pioneer in the study of botany in America. Portrait begun Aug. 8th, 1815, and finished Sept. 17th, 1815. Size 29″ × 36″. Half length, seated at table, one hand rests on a book, head to left, black coat, high white stock. Engraved by Durand (S-597) in National Portrait Gallery of Distinguished Americans, Vol. II.   Price, $100.00
Portrait owned by Mrs. George Biddle, of Philadelphia.

NOTE.—The New York Historical Society own a copy of the portrait of Dr. David Hosack, by Sully, painted by Augustus G. Heaton.

816 HOSACK, DAVID, M. D. (1769–1835).

An entirely different portrait from No. 815. Half length, seated, in robes with both hands resting on lap, column and buildings in background. Engraved by Charles Heath, and published by Joseph Delaplaine from the portrait painted by Thomas Sully.

817 HOSACK, MRS. DAVID, AND CHILD.

Dr. Hosack married Mary Eddy. The portrait shows her seated with their son David Hosack, Jr. standing at her knees holding her watch to his ear. Portrait begun August 1st, 1815, and finished Sept. 15th, 1815. Size 29″ × 36″.   Price, $150.00
Owned by Mrs. George Biddle, of Philadelphia.

178

818 HOUSTON, LADY.

At Oakville, Trenton, N. J. Portrait begun Aug. 15th, 1819, finished Oct. 3rd, 1819. Bust.

819 HOWARD, COL. JOHN EAGER (1752–1827).

Governor of Maryland, and United States senator. He married Peggy Chew, who was much admired by Major Andre. Copied from the portrait by Peale for the Maryland Historical Society. Begun April 28th, 1834, finished May 14th, 1834. Bust, head to right, black coat, buff waistcoat. Size 20″ × 24″. Price, $125.00
Owned by the Maryland Historical Society of Baltimore, Md.

820 HOWARD, MRS. BENJAMIN CHEW.

(Was Jane Grant Gilmore, sister of Robert Gilmore, of Baltimore.) Painted in Baltimore, begun April 5th, 1820, finished April 21st, 1820. Bust. Price, $100.00

821 HOWARD, MRS. BENJAMIN CHEW.

(Was Jane Grant Gilmore.) This portrait would appear from the register to be the same picture as No. 820, and was afterwards changed and retouched. The alterations must have been considerable as the work was begun Nov. 8th, 1834, and finished Nov. 15, 1834, the price noted as "$50." Bust.

822 HOWARD, MISS JULIET.

Portrait painted for Mrs. Rawle, begun March 20, 1837, finished April 6th, 1837. Head. Price, $100.00

823 HOWELL, MRS. ANNA BLACKWOOD (1764–1855).

Wife of Colonel Howell, of New Jersey. Portrait copied from a daguerreotype for her mother. Painting begun July 4th, 1855, finished July 17th, 1855. Bust. Price, $80.00
Owned by Mrs. James Findlay, Hagerstown, Maryland.

824 HOWELL, MRS. BENJAMIN (1764–1855).

Wife of Colonel Howell, and mother of Benjamin Howell and Anna B. Howell. Bust. Painted in 1813.
Owned by W. D. Jessup, Woodbury, N. J.

825 HOWELL, MRS. BENJAMIN, AND HER TWO CHILDREN.

Portrait begun Jan. 21st, 1814, finished May 2nd, 1814. Size 29″ × 36″. Price, $300.00
Owned by Mrs. Edmund H. Rippert, Uniontown, Penna.

826 HOWELL, MISS ANNA B. (1836–1904).

Daughter of Joshua B. Howell, married D. Shiver Stewart.   Portrait begun
July 5th, 1856, finished July 16th, 1856.   Head.   Price, $80.00
Owned by Andrew Stewart, Esq., Washington, D. C.

827 HOWELL, MISS FRANCES (1791–1829).

Daughter of Col. Joshua L. Howell, of New Jersey, she married her cousin
Benjamin Betterton Howell.   Portrait begun Oct. 27th, 1808, finished May
2nd, 1809.   Bust.   Price, $50.00
Owned by Benjamin Howell Campbell, Elizabeth, New Jersey.

828 HOWELL, COL. JOSHUA LADD (1762–1818).

Colonel of the 2nd Regiment, New Jersey Militia.   Portrait begun March
12th, 1813.   Size 29″ × 36″.   Price, $100.00
Owned by Henry W. Howell, of New York.

829 HOWELL, COL. JOSHUA LADD (1762–1818).

Portrait copied from a sketch of Col. Howell painted in 1812 for his son.
This portrait begun Jan. 21st, 1818, finished February, 1818.   Size 20″ ×
24″.   Price, $100.00
Owned by Mrs. Joshua L. Howell, Chestnut Hill, Philadelphia, Pa.

830 HOWELL, GROUP OF THREE BOYS.

Sons of Asher Howell and Harriet K. Howell.   The three boys are seated
on a sofa, the one in center having his arm around his younger brother to
the left, the youngest on the right leans his head on his brother's shoulder.
Size 35″ × 30″.   Painted about 1834.

Joseph Kirkbride Howell, 1819–1887 ⎫
Arthur William Howell,   1821–1840 ⎬ Group.
Francis Kirkbride Howell, 1823–1865 ⎭

Portrait owned by Mrs. Arthur W. Howell, of Philadelphia.

831 HOWELL, MRS. (SR.).

Portrait painted for Mrs. Jones.   Copy 2 begun July 24th, 1855, finished
Aug. 27th, 1855.   Bust.   Price, $80.00
Owned by Mrs. Malcolm Lloyd, Philadelphia.

832 HOWELL, MRS. (SR.).

Deceased.   Painted for her son Joshua.   Copy No. 3 begun Aug. 9th,
1855, finished Aug. 28th, 1855.   Bust.   Price, $80.00

833 HOWELL, MRS. (SR.).

Deceased.   Painted for B. P. How.   Copy No. 4, begun Aug. 18th, 1855,
finished Aug. 28th, 1855.   Bust.   Price, $80.00

834 HOWELL, MRS. (SR.).

Portrait painted for her daughter of Kingston. Copy No. 5. **Begun Aug.** 29th, 1855, finished Sept. 8th, 1855. Bust. **Price, $80.00**

Owned by Mrs. Malcolm Lloyd, Philadelphia.

835 HUBBELL, FERDINAND WAKEMAN (1800–1852).

Deceased, was a prominent lawyer. This portrait copied from the painting by Geo. W. Conarroe, is owned by the Law Association of Philadelphia. Painting begun March 2nd, 1858, finished May 1st, 1858. Bust.

Price, $100.00

836 HUDSON, DR. HENRY EDWARD (1772–1833).

A prominent dentist of Philadelphia. Bust, head to right, wearing a brown cape coat with fur collar. Portrait begun April 29th, 1810, finished June 4th, 1810. Size 25″ × 30″. Price, $50.00

Owned by Mrs. Rich, of Burlington, New Jersey.

837 HUDSON, HENRY EDWARD (1772–1833).

Head to left, with high white stock. This portrait was painted after the death of Dr. Hudson for Chinnery. Signed in lower, right corner, " TS 1841." Begun March 24th, 1841, finished May 1st, 1841. Panel. Size 17″ × 20″. Price, $150.00

Owned by Mrs. Rich, of Burlington, New Jersey.

838 HUDSON, HENRY EDWARD.

Portrait begun May 25th, 1828, finished Aug. 24th, 1828. Size 17″ × 20″. Price, $50.00

Portrait was painted " for Chinnery " and is now owned by Mrs. T. Hudson Rich, of Philadelphia.

839 HUDSON, HENRY EDWARD.

Portrait painted for Mr. Strainer, begun Feb. 29th, 1824, finished March 31st, 1824. Bust. Price, $60.00

840 HUDSON, MRS. H. E. (1795–1862).

(She was Maria Mackie.) Bust, seated, nearly full face with lace cap. Wears a light peach-color coat with fur collar over a white dress. Landscape in background. Portrait painted for Mr. Trainer, of New York, begun March 12th, 1824, finished April 17th, 1824. Size 25″ × 30″.

Price, $50.00

Owned by Mrs. Rich, of Burlington, New Jersey.

841 HUDSON, MRS. H. E.

Portrait begun May 21st, 1814, finished July 5th, 1814. Bust.

Price, $80.00

842 HUGHS, MARGARET (1820–1899).

Margaret Kay was adopted by Mrs. Hughs; she married George Taylor, of Philadelphia. Painted for Mrs. Hughs as a child of seven on her way to school, with slate. She wears a long red dress and large hat, and is playing with a kitten. Full length, 36″ × 54″, begun Jan. 13th, 1827, finished Feb. 14th, 1827. Signed " IS 1827." Price, $200.00
Owned by Miss Elizabeth Taylor, of Germantown, Philadelphia.

843 HUGHS, MARGARET (1820–1899).

Sketch painted for the large full-length portrait. Panel 8¾″ × 5¾″. (Little girl in red dress.)
Owned by the Ehrich Gallery, New York.

844 HUGHS, MASTER MACY.

Son of Captain Hughs. Portrait begun Oct. 19th, 1844, finished Oct. 26th, 1844. Head. Price, $80.00

845 HUGHS, MRS. MARY.

Portrait painted for her sister in England, begun March 10th, 1831, finished June 12th, 1831. Bust. Price, $75.00

846 HUGHS?

(Mother of Mrs. Hughs.) Portrait begun June 10th, 1824, finished June 23rd, 1824. Size 10″ × 8″. Price, $30.00

847 HUNDIGE, MRS. E.

Deceased, painted from a miniature, begun June 28th, 1842, finished July 9th, 1842. Bust. Price, $150.00

NOTE.—The register has a memorandum of " Handy " after noting the portrait.

848 HUNT, MRS. S. W.

Portrait copied from a miniature for her father. Painting begun Feb. 19th, 1852, finished Feb. 27th, 1852. Size 23″ × 27″. Price, $100.00

849 HUNTER, JOHN (1728–1793).

The celebrated London anatomist. Painted by Sir Joshua Reynolds. A copy by Leslie was recopied by Sully for Dr. Henry C. Chapman, of Philadelphia. Copy begun June 20th, 1863, finished July 1st, 1863. Size 20″ × 24″. Price, $30.00
Sold at executor's sale of artist's paintings in 1872 and later at Henkel's Auction Rooms, Philadelphia, 1917.

LIST OF PAINTINGS

850 HURLEY, REV. MICHAEL.

Roman Catholic divine, painted for St. Augustine's Church, Philadelphia. Half length, seated in chair, head to left, hands resting on book. Portrait begun March 1st, 1813, finished May 10th, 1813. Size 29" × 36".

Price, $100.00

Owned by St. Augustine's Church, Philadelphia.

851 HUSTICK, MRS.

Portrait painted for Mr. Harris, begun April 15th, 1828, finished April 30th, 1828. Size 20" × 24". Price, $75.00

852 HUTCHINSON, MRS. PEMBERTON (1810–1849).

Miss Margaretta Hare, daughter of Charles Willing Hare, married Israel Pemberton Hutchinson, April 28th, 1831. This portrait did belong to Charles Hare Hutchinson. Painting begun Nov. 3rd, 1840, finished Dec. 11th, 1840. Size 25" × 30". Bust, seated, facing front. Price, $200.00

853 INGERSOLL, CHARLES JARED (1782–1863).

Bust, facing left. Size 25" × 30". Son of Jared Ingersoll, born in Philadelphia. Elected to Congress, 1812, 1840–1844; appointed United States District Attorney for Pennsylvania by President Madison, 1815. Published "Inchiquin's Letters," 1810, and "A Historical Sketch of the Second War between the United States of America and Great Britain." Portrait signed and dated, " TS 1838."

Portrait owned in 1887 by Mrs. Henry Ingersoll.

854 INGERSOLL, CHARLES JARED (1782–1863).

Painted for his son, portrait begun Sept. 16th, 1839, finished Sept. 28th, 1839. Bust, size 25" × 30". Price, $200.00

855 INGERSOLL, MRS. CHARLES JARED (1784–1862).

(Née Mary Wilcocks, and sister of Benjamin Chew Wilcocks, married Charles J. Ingersoll in 1804.) Portrait begun Jan. 20th, 1808, finished Feb. 3rd, 1808. Bust. Price, $50.00

856 INGERSOLL, MRS. CHARLES JARED (1784–1862).

Replica of former portrait, copy begun Jan. 22nd, 1808, finished Feb. 8th, 1808. Bust. Price, $50.00

857 INGERSOLL, MRS. CHARLES JARED (1784–1862).

Bust, head to left with curls on forehead. Replica from original portrait painted in 1808 and inscribed on back, "Copied from a portrait painted by me in 1808. TS 1843." Size 20" × 24". Mrs. Ingersoll was Mary Wilcocks, sister of Benjamin C. Wilcox. Replica begun Dec. 24th, 1842, and finished Feb. 7th, 1843. Subscriber's price, $50.00

Owned by Miss Ann Ingersoll Meigs, of Philadelphia.

858 INGERSOLL, CHARLES, JR. (1805–1882).

Son of Mrs. Charles Ingersoll, No. 855. Half length, seated, head to left, holds a book upright on table. Portrait painted for Benjamin C. Wilcocks, of Philadelphia, begun Oct. 6th, 1841, finished Oct. 29th, 1841. Size 28″ × 36″. Price, $300.00

Owned by the Misses Hutchinson, of Philadelphia.

859 INGERSOLL, MRS. CHARLES.

(She was Susan Catherine Brown, daughter of General Brown, of Tenn.) Portrait begun Oct. 24th, 1841, finished Nov. 8th, 1841. Size 29″ × 36″. Price, $300.00

Owned by Mrs. J. Moylan Thomas, Philadelphia.

860 INGERSOLL, MRS. EDWARD.

Was Miss Brinton. Portrait begun June 14th, 1816, finished July, 1816, Bust. Price, $100.00

861 INGERSOLL, MRS. HARRY.

(She was Sarah Roberts.) Portrait painted for Benjamin Chew Wilcocks, of Philadelphia. Begun Oct. 14th, 1841, and finished Nov. 8th, 1841. Half length, in black low-necked dress. Size 28″ × 56″. Price, $300.00

Owned by Historical Society of Pennsylvania, from estate of S. R. Smith.

862 INGERSOLL, JOSEPH REED (1786–1868).

Bust, facing right, seated. 25″ × 30″. On stone by A. Newsam. Son of Jared Ingersoll, was born in Philadelphia; graduated at Princeton; admitted to the Bar, 1807; eminent in his profession; Member of Congress, 1835–37, 1842–49; Minister to England, 1852; President of Pennsylvania Academy of Fine Arts, 1846–1852, and of Historical Society of Pennsylvania, 1860–1868. Portrait painted by Sully for the students of Ingersoll and presented to the Law Association of Philadelphia. Signed " TS 1832," and wrongly attributed to Inman on lithograph by Newsam.

Owned by Law Association of Philadelphia.

863 INGRAHAM, MRS. EDWARD DUFFIELD.

Wife of the noted wit and book collector of Philadelphia. Painted for Mrs. Barney. Portrait begun Sept. 20th, 1836, finished Oct. 1st, 1836. Head. Price, $100.00

864 INGRAHAM, MRS. EDWARD DUFFIELD.

Portrait painted for Lawyer Ingraham, begun March 31st, 1830, finished Dec. 27th, 1830. Head. Price, $50.00

865 INMAN, HENRY (1801–1846).

Artist and pupil of Jarvis, painted portraits and miniatures. The register notes, "In exchange for one painted of me." Begun Feb. 21st, 1837, finished Feb. 24th, 1837. Size 20″ × 24″. Price, $100.00

866 INSKEEP, JOHN (1757–1834).

Was Mayor of Philadelphia, 1800–1801, and 1805–1806, and President of the Insurance Company of North America, 1806–1836. Portrait begun Sept. 8th, 1810, finished Nov. 3rd, 1810. Bust. Size 30″ × 25″.
Price, $60.00
Owned by Mrs. Louise Bodine Wallace, Philadelphia.

867 IRVING, WASHINGTON (1783–1859).

American author, portrait painted partly from memory and from illustration in Harper's Weekly. Begun May 25th, 1871, finished June 5th, 1871. Size 25″ × 30″. Price, $100.00

868 ISRAEL, MRS.

Portrait painted for her son, begun May 22nd, 1808, finished June 8th, 1808. Bust. Price, $50.00

NOTE.—Also written in register as Israil and Isrial.

869 ISRAEL, MR.

Portrait begun Oct. 4th, 1810, finished Oct. 13th, 1810. The register notes "hands introduced" in the portrait. Bust. Price, $70.00

NOTE.—Also written in register as Israil and Isrial.

870 ISRAEL, MR.

(Also written as Isrial and Israil.) Portrait painted by the artist's daughter Ellen, afterwards Mrs. Wheeler, and retouched by Thomas Sully, painting begun Sept. 29th, 1836, finished Oct. 6th, 1836. Bust.
Price, $80.00

871 IVES, MRS. HOPE.

Portrait painted for her son, R. Ives, begun June 24th, 1847, finished July 21st, 1847. Size 29″ × 36″. Price, $250.00

872 IVES, MRS. R.

Portrait painted at Providence, R. I. Begun June 24th, 1847, and finished July 27th, 1847. Size 29″ × 36″. Price, $250.00

LIST OF PAINTINGS

873 IZARD, RALPH (1742–1804).

Father of General George Izard of the United States Army. Copied from West's painting now in the Brook Club of New York. Whole length, size 29″ × 36″. Portrait begun Nov. 2nd, 1818, finished Dec. 2nd, 1818.

Price, $200.00

874 IZARD, MRS. ROSA.

Portrait painted for Mrs. Pinckney, begun Feb. 25th, 1842, finished March 7th, 1842. Head. Price, $150.00

875 JACKSON, GENERAL ANDREW (1767–1845).

The seventh President of the United States. Design for a medal awarded by Congress to General Jackson after the battle of New Orleans, 1815. Drawing made September, 1817. Size 6″ × 6″. Price, $50.00

876 JACKSON, ANDREW (1767–1845).

The second design made for the congressional medal awarded to General Jackson. Begun Aug. 24th, 1822, and finished Sept. 27th, 1822, size 10″ × 12″. Price, $50.00

Engraved by J. W. Steel. (See No. 1494 of American Engravers by Fielding, 1817.)

877 JACKSON, ANDREW (1767–1845).

Portrait begun Feb. 17th, 1819, finished Feb. 24th, 1819. Bust.

Price, $100.00

878 JACKSON, ANDREW (1767–1845).

Three-quarter length, in uniform, face front, right hand on hilt of sword, left hand on holster holding reins of a horse. Portrait painted for the Association of American Artists, begun March 26th, 1819, finished April 15th, 1819. Size 25″ × 30″. Price, $200.00

Engraved by J. B. Longacre (Stauffer, No. 2012). Published Nov., 1820.

879 JACKSON, ANDREW (1767–1845).

Bust, in uniform, facing front. On canvas 24″ × 20″. Exhibited by L. Taylor Dickson, in 1887, at Loan Exhibition, Pennsylvania Academy of Fine Arts.

Property of the Ehrich Galleries, New York City (1921).

880 JACKSON, ANDREW (1767–1845).

Bust, in uniform, high military coat, collar with cloak over shoulder with red cape. Portrait painted for Mr. Loyd, begun July 4th, 1829, finished Aug. 6th, 1829. On a panel 7″ × 9″. Price, $30.00

Presented in 1861 to the Pennsylvania Historical Society, by Samuel Breck.

LIST OF PAINTINGS

881 JACKSON, ANDREW, GENERAL.

Portrait noted in register as painted from a study of him made in 1824. Begun June 20th, 1845, finished June 28th, 1845. Head, to right. Oval canvas 20″ × 24″. Inscribed on back "From a study made in 1824 from Genl. Jackson. TS 1845."
Owned by Francis Fisher Kane, Philadelphia.

882 JACKSON, ANDREW.

Full length, standing in long military cloak, one hand gloved holding hat and papers, the other glove lying at his feet. Portrait begun July 8th, 1845, finished on July 31st, 1845. Size 97″ × 60″. Price, $800.00
Owned by the Corcoran Art Gallery, Washington, D. C.

883 JACKSON, ANDREW.

Study for the full-length portrait painted 1845, and owned by the Corcoran Art Gallery of Washington. Size 8″ × 14″.
Owned by the artist, Albert Rosenthal, of Philadelphia.

884 JACKSON, GENERAL ANDREW.

Portrait begun April 9th, 1845, finished April 18th, 1845. Copied from Sully's former painting. Head. Price, $50.00

NOTE.—Engraved by Thomas B. Welch from the portrait by Thomas Sully, then in the possession of Francis Preston Blair. (Reproduced in "The True Andrew Jackson." By Cyrus T. Brady.)

885 JACKSON, ANDREW.

Portrait painted from a study painted in 1819, begun Jan. 16th, 1857, finished Jan. 24th, 1857. Bust. Price, $100.00

886 JACKSON, ANDREW.

Copy of former portrait, begun July 1st, 1858, finished July 20th, 1858. Painted for Edwin Forrest. Bust. Price, $100.00
Owned by the Forrest Home, at Holmesburg, Philadelphia, Penna.

887 JACKSON, ANDREW, GENERAL.

Small whole length painted from a sketch, begun June 3rd, 1870, finished June 18th, 1870. Size 25″ × 16½″. Inscribed on back, "General Jackson after the Battle of New Orleans, from a former sketch TS 1870."
Price, $70.00

Owned by Mrs. Albert Sully, Brooklyn, N. Y.

NOTE.—The original pencil drawing of the head of Andrew Jackson, drawn from life, and inscribed "General Andrew Jackson, taken immediately after the Battle of New Orleans. T. Sully." Is also owned by Mrs. Albert Sully.

187

LIST OF PAINTINGS

888 JACKSON, MR.

Portrait begun Sept. 18th, 1818, finished Oct. 7th, 1818. Bust.
Price, $100.00

889 JACKSON, MRS.

Was Miss Grant, of Baltimore, Md. Portrait begun Sept. 18th, 1818, finished Oct. 2nd, 1818. Bust. Price, $100.00

890 JACKSON, MRS.

Portrait painted for Dr. Jackson, begun Sept. 28th, 1830, finished Oct. 21st, 1830. Bust. Price, $75.00

891 JACKSON, MISS ELIZABETH WILLING (1803–1821).

At the age of 18 years (deceased, portrait painted from a pencil sketch), begun March 1st, 1822, finished March 19th, 1822. Half length, seated, with hand on arm of chair, white low-necked gown with red shawl over shoulders. Size 30″ × 25″. Daughter of Major and Mrs. William Jackson.
Price, $100.00
Gift of her sister, Anna Willing Jackson, to the Penna. Academy of Fine Arts, Philadelphia.

892 JACKSON, MRS. ISAAC R.

Exhibited at the Loan Exhibition of Portraits, New York, November, 1895. It was owned at the time by Mrs. Oswald Jackson, of New York.

893 JACKSON, JOHN.

Painted for Mrs. Kirkman, begun Jan. 25th, 1819, finished Feb. 10th, 1819. Bust. Price, $100.00
Owned by Miss Ellen R. Hunt, Louisville, Kentucky.

894 JACKSON, MRS. JOHN LEE.

NOTE.—The authors have not been able to see Nos. 892 and 894; they were exhibited in 1895 at the Loan Exhibition of Portraits in New York, and were owned by Mrs. Oswald Jackson, of New York.

895 JACKSON, MISS MARY.

A celebrated belle of Philadelphia, married Mr. Bernard Henry. Portrait begun Nov. 18th, 1808, finished March 27th, 1809. Bust.
Subscriber's price, $30.00
Noted as engraved by John Sartain in his "Reminiscences of a very old man."

896 JACKSON, MR. P.

From New Orleans, La. Portrait begun Feb. 15th, 1818, finished Sept. 19th, 1818. Bust. Price, $100.00

LIST OF PAINTINGS

897 JACKSON, DR. SAMUEL (1787–1872).

Graduated from medical department of the University of Pennsylvania in 1808; assistant to Professor Nathaniel Chapman. He was the author of many medical works. This portrait was painted for his wife on the order of Dr. Gibbes, of Columbia, S. C., begun June 5th, 1845, finished June 21st, 1845. Signed " TS 1845." Size 17″ × 20″. Head. Price, $80.00
Owned by the Pennsylvania Historical Society, Philadelphia.

898 JACKSON, DR. SAMUEL.

Portrait painted on order of Dr. Gibbes, begun June 18th, 1844, finished June 18th, 1845. Head. Price, $80.00

899 JACKSON, WASHINGTON.

(Brother of Mrs. Kirkman.) Portrait begun Nov. 11th, 1818, finished Dec. 3rd, 1818. Bust. Price, $100.00

900 JACOBS, MR. S.

Of Richmond, Va. Bust, head to left, wearing masonic collar and regalia. He was a Grand Master of Masons in Virginia, 1810. Portrait engraved by J. A. O'Neill. Portrait begun Aug. 25th, 1812, finished Aug. 29th, 1812.
Price, $70.00

901 JACOBS, MRS. S.

Of Richmond, Virginia. Portrait begun Aug. 11th, 1815; the register notes that the hand was introduced in the portrait, the price being $100.00. Bust.

902 JANEWAY, MISS MARIA LAWRENCE.

(Deceased.) Bust of a child wearing a red dress. Portrait painted for her parents, begun Nov. 10th, 1851, finished April 24th, 1852. Head, size 20″ × 24″, oval. Price, $80.00
Owned by Miss Maria Janeway, Walnut Hill, Montgomery Co., Pa.

903 JANEWAY, REV. JACOB JONES (1774–1858).

A prominent Presbyterian minister connected with Rutgers and Princeton Colleges in New Jersey. He married Martha Gray Leiper, for whom this portrait was painted, begun June 4th, 1839, finished June 12th, 1839. Bust.
Price, $200.00
A portrait of Rev. Jacob J. Janeway by Sully is owned by J. J. Janeway, of Greensburg, Penna.

904 JANEWAY, REV. DR.

Copy of portrait painted in 1839, begun July 23rd, 1853, finished Aug. 2nd, 1853. Bust. Price, $80.00

905 JANEWAY, REV. DR.

Second copy of portrait, begun Oct. 19th, 1853, finished Dec. 3, 1853. Bust.   Price, $80.00

906 JANEWAY, REV. DR.

Third copy of portrait, begun Oct. 20th, 1853, finished Dec. 10th, 1853. Bust.   Price, $80.00

907 JANEWAY, REV. DR.

Fourth copy of portrait, begun Oct. 21st, 1853, finished March 21st, 1854. Bust.   Price, $80.00

908 JANEWAY, REV. DR.

Fifth copy of portrait, begun Oct. 22nd, 1853, finished March 16th, 1854. Painted for his son. Bust.   Price, $80.00

909 JANEWAY, MRS. JOHN LIVINGSTON.

Painted for a group of five heads. Painting begun April 11th, 1854, finished June 28th, 1854. Head.   Price, $60.00
The group consists of John Price Wetherill, Mrs. J. P. Wetherill, Rachel Wetherill, John Price Wetherill, Jr., and Mrs. John L. Livingston.
Owned by Albert L. Wetherill, Jamestown, R. I.

910 JANNEY, ELIZABETH (1823–1849).

Daughter of Joseph Janney and his wife, née Hannah Howell Hopkins. The latter was born in 1791 at the Hopkins estate in Anne Arundel County, Maryland, known as "Whitehall", and died in 1838. Her mother was a Miss Howell, of Philadelphia. Joseph Janney's mother was also a Hopkins, and a sister of Johns Hopkins, founder of the Johns Hopkins Institute. Portrait painted for Mr. Heath, begun on March 6th, 1844, finished March 27th, 1844. Nearly full face, long ringlets, low-necked dress, hands clasped. Signed " TS 1844." Size 28" × 36".   Price, $200.00
Owned by Martin C. Schwab, Esq., Chicago, Ill.

NOTE.—A copy of this portrait was made by Albert Rosenthal, of Philadelphia, and is in the hands of descendants.

911 JANNEY, MRS. JOSEPH (1791–1838).

(Née Hannah Howell Hopkins.) Of Baltimore, daughter of Gerard Hopkins. Portrait painted for her daughter, Mrs. Joseph Merrefield, begun Feb. 3rd, 1849, finished March 7th, 1849. Bust, nearly full face, she wears a white headdress tied under the chin, black dress and holds a buff glove. Size 29" × 36".   Price, $200.00
Owned by Mrs. Benedict H. Hanson, and exhibited at Maryland Institute 1921.

912 JAUDON, SAMUEL.

Portrait painted for Cowperthwait Jaudon, was cashier of the Bank of the United States, and Cowperthwait was assistant cashier. Portrait begun Dec. 28th, 1837, finished Feb. 13th, 1838. Bust.   Price, $200.00

Owned by Peyton J. Van Rensselaer, Esq.

913 JAUDON, SAMUEL.

Copy begun by Tom on Jan. 7th, 1839, and finished by the artist on Jan. 11th, 1839. Size 30″ × 25″.   Price, $120.00

Owned by Mrs. A. Cortlandt Van Rensselaer.

914 JEFFERSON, THOMAS (1743–1826).

Third President of the United States, 1801–1809. Bust, facing left, fur collar to coat. Portrait begun March, 1821, but was not finished until June 1st, 1830. Inscribed by Sully "From Jefferson, 1821." Canvas, size 25″ × 30″. Portrait painted at his residence of "Monticello," Virginia.

      Price, $75.00

Owned by American Philosophical Society, Philadelphia.

915 JEFFERSON, THOMAS.

Small full length, as a study for the large portrait painted for West Point. Begun March 27th, 1822, finished April 10th, 1822. Size 29″ × 18″.

      Price, $150.00

916 JEFFERSON, THOMAS.

Full length, standing on portico, holding roll in hand. Size 103″ × 67″. The head a copy from the portrait painted from life at Monticello, begun in 1821, dressed in black, wearing a plum-colored top coat trimmed with fur. Portrait begun April 12th, 1822, finished May 7th, 1822. For the Military Academy at West Point.   Price, $500.00

917 JEFFERSON, THOMAS.

Bust, facing left, copy of former portrait, begun Dec. 6th, 1856, finished Dec. 11th, 1856. Painted for the actor Edwin Forrest. Bust.

      Price, $100.00

Owned by the Forrest Home at Holmesburg, Pa.

918 JEFFERSON, THOMAS.

Bust facing left, copy of former portrait, painting begun Dec. 11th, 1856, finished Dec. 29th, 1856, for the artist's own collection. Bust.

      Price, $100.00

NOTE.—Probably the painting at the capitol, Washington, D. C. The Jefferson Society in the University of Virginia also own a bust portrait of Jefferson by Sully that was formerly owned by President Monroe.

919 JENKS, JOSEPH R.

Painted for Dr. Kirkbride. Portrait begun Sept. 15th, 1843, finished Sept. 21st, 1843. Bust.   Price, $100.00
Owned by Dr. Stacy B. Collins, of New York.

920 JOHNSON, MRS. REVERDY.

This portrait of the wife of the celebrated Maryland statesman was painted in Baltimore, begun June 22nd, 1840, finished Sept. 8th, 1840. Size 58″ × 94″. Full length, standing on stone steps, with balustrade; white satin dress and red shawl.   Price, $1000.00
Owned by Mrs. Alfred Hodder, Princeton, N. J.

921 JOHNSTON, WILLIAM ROYAL.

Portrait begun April 19th, 1808, finished June 25th, 1808. Bust.
Price, $50.00

922 JOHNSTON, WILLIAM ROYAL.

Copy of my first portrait, begun June 1st, 1808, finished June 27th, 1808. Head.   Price, $20.00
Owned by Stitson Hutchins, of New York.

923 JOHNSTON, MR.

The register notes that he was a member of the firm of " Ganet & Johnston." Portrait begun Feb. 1st, 1913, finished in May, 1913. Size 29″ × 36″.   Price, $100.00

924 JOHNSTON, MRS.

Of Savannah, Ga. (Deceased.) Painted from a profile likeness, begun Aug. 9th, 1819, finished Oct. 1st, 1819. Bust.   Price, $100.00

925 JOHNSTON, ROBERT.

Of " Rosedale," near Richmond, Va. Half length, seated, head to right, with arm resting on back of chair. Portrait begun June 6th, 1804, finished July 19th, 1804. Size 12″ × 14″.   Price, $20.00
Owned by Ehrich Galleries, New York.

926 JOHNSTON, MRS. ROBERT.

Of " Rosedale," near Richmond, Va. Half length, seated, head to left, with hands crossed in lap. Portrait begun January, 1805, and finished in February, 1805. Size 12″ × 14″.   Price, $50.00
Owned by Ehrich Galleries, New York.

LIST OF PAINTINGS

927 JOHNSON, WILLIAM S.

Painted when nineteen months old, and grandson of Mrs. Henry D. Gilpin, who was first Mrs. Josiah Stoddard Johnson. Portrait begun Aug. 10th, 1841, finished Aug. 23rd, 1841. Size 25″ × 30″. Price, $200.00

928 JONES, MRS. CALEB (1809–1883).

Of Philadelphia (formerly Mrs. Minturn, of New York, of Grinnel and Minturn). Portrait begun May 30th, 1853, finished June 13th, 1853. Signed " TS 1853." Head. Price, $80.00
Owned by Mr. J. Howell Jones, Philadelphia.

929 JONES, DAVID S. (1777–1848).

Celebrated lawyer, graduated from Columbia College, 1796, and was secretary to Governor Jay. Portrait begun June 24th, 1807, and finished July 5th, 1807, for Washington Morton, Esq. Bust. Price, $50.00
Owned by the Brook Club, New York City.

930 JONES, DAVID S. (1777–1848).

Portrait begun June 8th, 1807, finished June 30th, 1807. Bust.
Price, $50.00

931 JONES, MRS. DAVID.

Portrait begun Feb. 16th, 1807, finished March 10th, 1807. Bust.
Price, $30.00

932 JONES, ISAAC.

Painted for his son, B. Jones. Portrait begun March 4th, 1829, finished March 23rd, 1829. Head. Price, $50.00

933 JONES, JACOB.

Celebrated naval commander, was a native of the State of Delaware. In the War of 1812 he commanded the "Wasp" which captured the "Frolic," for which Congress awarded him a medal. Portrait painted on order of the State of Delaware, begun May 16th, 1817, finished Aug. 6th, 1817. Bust.
Price, $1000.00
Owned by State of Delaware and deposited at the capitol, Dover, Del.

934 JONES, JACOB (1768–1850).

This portrait was painted for a medal, awarded him by Congress. It shows a bust in full naval uniform, head to right, in profile, painting begun April 15th, 1816, finished April 18th, 1816. Head. Painted in olive gray. Size 20″ × 24″. Price, $50.00
Owned by United States Naval Academy, Annapolis, Md.

935 JONES, W. W.

He was a boarder at the " Powhattan " during Sully's stay there. Portrait begun Jan. 13th, 1851, finished Jan. 25th, 1851. Head. Price, $100.00

936 JONES, MRS.

(Deceased.) Portrait painted for Mrs. Fitzgerald, begun Dec. 1st, 1860, finished Dec. 12th, 1860. Head. Price, $30.00

937 JONES, MRS.

(Mr. Irvine's sister-in-law.) Portrait begun Aug. 16th, 1858, finished Aug. 29th, 1858. Head. Price, $80.00

938 JORDAN, MISS MARY.

Deceased. Portrait painted from a photograph, begun Sept. 20th, 1855, finished Oct. 6th, 1855. Head. Price, $80.00

939 JORDAN, G. N.

Of Tabula, Yazoo Co., Miss. Portrait begun Sept. 5th, 1855, finished Sept. 18th, 1855. Head. Price, $80.00

940 JOYNE, MISS.

Granddaughter of Miss May. Portrait begun April 28th, 1858, finished July 12th, 1858. Head. Price, $80.00

941 JUNKIN, MRS.

Of Richmond, Va. Portrait begun Nov. 19th, 1855, finished Nov. 26th, 1855. Head. Price, $80.00

942 KANE, JOHN KINTZING (1795–1858).

He was Judge of the United States District Court of Philadelphia. President of the Musical Fund Society of Philadelphia, and father of Elisha Kent Kane, Arctic Explorer. Bust, head slightly to right, coat with fur collar, arms crossed. Portrait begun Nov. 2nd, 1836, finished Nov. 16th, 1836. Bust. Reproduced in Century Magazine, Vol. 34, page 489.

Price, $150.00

Owned by Dr. Evan O'Neill Kane. of Kane, Penna.

943 KANE, JOHN KINTZING (1795–1858).

Half length, seated with elbow on table, head supported on hand, full face. Portrait painted for the Musical Fund Society of Philadelphia, of which he was President from 1854 to 1856. Signed on back of canvas " TS 1861. Copied from a portrait painted by J. Hicks, of New York, in 1858." Size 29″ × 36″. Portrait begun Jan. 10th, 1861, finished Jan. 20th, 1861.

Price, $100.00

Owned by Musical Fund Society, of Philadelphia.

944 KANE, MRS. JOHN KINTZING (b. —— d. 1866).

(In costume of Mary Queen of Scots.) Bust, head to left, lace headdress and lace ruff to dress. Portrait begun Jan. 20th, 1832, finished April 3rd, 1832. She was Jane Duval Leiper, her portrait was reproduced in the Century Magazine, Vol. 34, page 489. Price, $80.00

Owned by Dr. Evan O'Neill Kane, of Kane, Pa. A copy by Schreyer is owned by Francis Fisher Kane, of Philadelphia.

945 KEIM, MISS.

Portrait painted for her fiancé, Dr. Wetherill, painting begun June 22nd, 1855, finished June 25th, 1855. Head. Price, $80.00

946 KEMBLE, CHARLES (1775–1854).

Actor, and brother of John Philip Kemble and Mrs. Sarah Siddons. He was the father of Fanny Kemble who married Pierce Butler. Bust, facing left, in hat and cloak. Size 25″ × 30″. Signed on front with monogram "IS 1833." In character as "Fazio." Head, portrait begun Feb. 27th, 1833, finished April 23rd, 1833. Price, $60.00

Presented by Mrs. John Ford to Pennsylvania Academy of Fine Arts.

947 KEMBLE, CHARLES.

In character as "Fazio." Head painted for the artist's own collection, begun Dec. 11th, 1832, finished Dec. 22nd, 1832. Size 25″ × 30″.
Price, $60.00

Sold in Henkel's Auction Rooms, Philadelphia, 1917.

948 KEMBLE, CHARLES.

In character as "Fazio." Copied from a former portrait. Begun Nov. 17th, 1865, finished Dec. 1st, 1865. Bust. Price, $100.00

949 KEMBLE, FRANCES ANNE (1809–1893).

An English actress and authoress, popularly known as Fanny Kemble, born in London, 1809; daughter of Charles Kemble; performed both tragedy and comedy with eminent success; in 1832 accompanied her father to the United States, where she married Pierce Butler, from whom she was divorced in 1849. Published "Journal of a Residence on a Georgia Plantation," and other works. Head facing front. Sketched from recollection for Mr. Childs. Portrait begun on Nov. 8th, 1832, finished Nov. 10th, 1832. Size 24″ × 29″. Price, $60.00

Lithographed by Childs and Inman, Philadelphia, 1833.

950 KEMBLE, FRANCES ANNE.

Portrait painted from recollection, begun Oct. 30th, 1832, finished Nov. 1st, 1832. Bust. In the character of "Juliet." Price, $60.00

951 KEMBLE, FRANCES ANNE.

Bust, facing right, canvas 25" × 30", signed on front with monogram " TS 1833." In character as "Bianca." Head, portrait begun Feb. 26th, 1833, finished April 23rd, 1833. Price, $60.00

Presented by Mrs. John Ford to the Pennsylvania Academy of Fine Arts.

952 KEMBLE, FRANCES ANNE.

In the character of "Bianca." Copied from a former portrait. Begun Nov. 16th, 1865, finished Nov. 30th, 1865. Bust. Price, $100.00

953 KEMBLE, FRANCES ANNE.

Head, in character as "Julia." Painted for Miss North, begun Feb. 23rd, 1833, finished March 21st, 1833. Signed " TS 1833." Size 30" × 25" (canvas). Price, $100.00

Lithograph by Albert Newsam in 1833, and published by Childs and Inman, Philadelphia.

Owned by Mrs. Shober, Spruce St., Philadelphia, who had it from Miss North.

954 KEMBLE, FRANCES ANNE.

Bust, in character as "Lady Macbeth." Painted for the artist, begun Feb. 25th, 1833, finished and noted in register as "Erased." Price, $150.00

955 KEMBLE, FRANCES ANNE.

In character as "Beatrice." Bust, facing left. Signed " TS 1833." Painted for E. Carey, begun Sept. 22nd, 1833, finished Oct. 7, 1833. Size 25" × 30". Engraved by John Cheney for the "Gift, 1836." (See illustration.) Price, $100.00

Owned by the Pennsylvania Academy of Fine Arts, Philadelphia.

956 KEMBLE, FRANCES ANNE.

Head, portrait painted for the artist, begun March 10th, 1833, finished March 14th, 1833. Size 25" × 30". Price, $60.00

NOTE.—The Boston Museum of Fine Arts owns a portrait signed on back "Miss F. A. Kemble, March 10th, 1832. TS."

957 KEMBLE, FRANCES ANNE.

Portrait painted for Pierce Butler, begun May 26th, 1834, finished June 18th, 1834. Size 29" × 36". Price, $200.00

958 KEMBLE, FRANCES ANNE.

Portrait painted to accompany her to England, begun May 26th, 1834, finished June 17th, 1834. Size 29" × 36". Price, $200.00

959 KEMBLE, FRANCES ANNE.

Entered in artist's register of painting as " Beatrice," copy of former painting. Begun Dec. 19th, 1860, finished Dec. 31st, 1860. For Joseph Harrison. Bust. Copy of No. 955. Price, $100.00
Sold in the Harrison Sale of Paintings at Auction Rooms of Philadelphia
Art Galleries for about $1600.

960 KEMELE, FRANCES ANNE.

Second copy from former painting. Begun Jan. 30th, 1860, finished Feb.
18th, 1860. " Beatrice." Head. Copy of No. 955. Price, $50.00

961 KEMBLE, FRANCES ANNE.

Third copy from former painting. Begun Feb. 24th, 1862, finished
March 3rd, 1862. " Beatrice." Size 25" × 30". Copy of No. 955.
Price, $100.00

962 KEMBLE, GOUVERNEUR (1786–1875).

He was an intimate friend of the author Washington Irving, and brother-
in-law of James K. Paulding and General Scott. Copied from a miniature,
begun Jan. 31st, 1839, finished March 22nd, 1839. Head. Price, $150.00

963 KEMBLE, JOHN PHILIP (1757–1823).

In the character of Richard III, a copy of the painting by Gilbert Stuart.
Bust, head to left, one hand holding cloak around shoulders. Copy begun
Jan. 1st, 1867, finished Jan. 9th, 1867. Size 21" × 16". Signed " TS
Jan., 1867." Price, $30.00
Owned by A. T. Bay, Esq., of New York.

964 KENNEDY, MRS. J. P.

Portrait painted in Baltimore for Mrs. Kennedy's father, Mr. Edw. Gray.
Begun May 5th, 1853, finished May 26th, 1853. Head. Price, $100.00

965 KEPPELE, MRS. MICHAEL (1774–1862).

(Was Catherine Caldwell, of Philadelphia.) The portrait was painted by
Gilbert Stuart, the original drapery in the picture was damaged by a young
artist and Sully was prevailed upon to repaint the damaged work, begun July
19th, 1824, finished Aug. 20th, 1824. Bust. Price, $30.00
Formerly owned by Mrs. Wm. P. Tatham, of Philadelphia.

966 KERBY, PETER.

(And his pet dog.) Painting 10" × 12", begun April 10th, 1804, finished
June 8th, 1804. Price, $30.00

967 KERR, CAPTAIN.

Portrait begun Sept. 20th, 1810, finished Oct. 15th, 1810. Bust.
Price, $60.00

968 KERR, MRS.

Portrait begun on Oct. 2nd, 1810. Bust.   Price, $60.00

969 KERSEY, JESSE (1768–1845).

A prominent Quaker minister and author, died in his 78th year. Painted
for Elliot Cresson, begun Jan. 11th, 1825, finished May 31st, 1825. Head.
Price, $30.00

970 KERSEY, JESSE.

Sketch painted from first portrait. Begun June 8th, 1825, finished Sept.·
1826. Head.   Price, $20.00

971 KID, R.

Portrait begun June 15th, 1811, finished July 24th, 1811. Head.
Price, $70.00

972 KID, MRS. R.

Portrait begun March 12th, 1811, finished July 22nd, 1811. Head.
Price, $50.00

973 KIEPS, MISS.

In the record of painting, kept by the artist it is noted that " Dr. Morton
employed him to copy Miss Kieps M" (miniature). Painting begun Sept.
1st, 1863, finished Sept. 12th, 1863.   Price, $50.00

974 KING, CHARLES B. (1785–1862).

Charles B. King was an American artist living in London at the time of
Sully's visit. He was engaged in the study of the fine arts. Painted in
London as a specimen to show to Benjamin West. Portrait begun July 25th,
1809, and finished August 2nd, 1809. Head.   Price, $40.00

975 KING, MRS. J.

The wife of J. King the gold-beater. Portrait begun Dec. 1st, 1830, finished Jan. 12th, 1831. Bust.   Price, $75.00

976 KINGSBURY, MAJOR.

Portrait painted for Mrs. Buckner, begun March 25th, 1859, finished April
18th, 1859. Bust.   Price, $100.00

977 KINGSBURY, MRS.

Portrait painted for Mrs. Buckner from a daguerreotype, begun March 26th, 1859, finished June 23rd, 1859.   Bust.   Price, $100.00

978 KINGSTON, MISS HARRIOTT.

Portrait begun Feb. 11th, 1812, finished April 3rd, 1812.   Size 29" × 36".
                                                            Price, $100.00

979 KINGSTON, MISS HARRIOTT.

(The second attempt.)   Portrait begun Jan. 1st, 1813, finished March 7th, 1813.   Size 20" × 24".   Price, $100.00

980 KINGSTON, STEPHEN.

Distinguished diplomat, whose commission in the diplomatic service was signed by President Adams.   Portrait begun Sept. 8th, 1812, finished Nov. 17th, 1812.   It is signed on back " JS 1812."   Seated in green chair, three-quarters length, head to left, he wears a brown coat, white stock and waistcoat, and holds a miniature in his hands.   Size 29" × 36".
                                                            Price, $100.00

Owned by Mrs. Hoffman, of Philadelphia.

981 KINTZING, ABRAHAM (1763–1835).

Merchant of Philadelphia.   Portrait begun Sept. 6th, 1815, finished October 3rd, 1815.   Bust.   Price, $100.00
Owned by the Pennsylvania Academy of Fine Arts.

982 KINTZING, ABRAHAM (1763–1835).

Copy of first portrait painted (No. 981), begun Dec. 12th, 1815, finished Dec. 18th, 1815.   Bust.   Price, $100.00

983 KINTZING, ABRAHAM (1763–1835).

Second copy of the first portrait (No. 981), begun Dec. 12th, 1815, finished Dec. 18th, 1815.   Bust.   Size 30" × 25".   Price, $100.00
Owned by A. T. Bay, Esq., New York.

984 KINTZING, MRS. ABRAHAM.   Of Philadelphia.   (Margaret Harbeson.)
Portrait begun Aug. 19th, 1812, finished Sept., 1812.   Bust.   Size 29" × 26".   The register notes " painted in wax " and the price as $100.
Owned by the Pennsylvania Academy of Fine Arts.

985 KINTZING, MRS. ABRAHAM.

(Second portrait.)   Painting begun Sept. 23rd, 1812, finished Nov. 16th, 1812.   Size 26" × 36".   Price, $100.00
Owned by Mrs. John Willing, Philadelphia.

LIST OF PAINTINGS

986 KIP, WILLIAM INGRAHAM (1811–1893).

The first Protestant Episcopal Bishop of California. He was an art lover and had a fine collection of paintings which were acquired by the Mark Hopkins Gallery, and were destroyed by the San Francisco earthquake of 1906. Portrait begun Oct. 24th, 1863, finished Nov. 29th, 1863. Size 24 × 20″.
Price, $50.00

987 KIRKMAN, MR.

Portrait begun Jan. 2nd, 1818, finished Jan. 19th, 1818. Bust.
Price, $100.00

988 KIRKMAN, MRS.

Was Miss Jackson. Portrait begun Nov. 25th, 1817, finished Dec. 4th, 1817. Bust.
Price, $100.00
Owned by Mrs. A. D. Hunt, Louisville, Ky.

989 KIRKMAN, MISS.

Of Nashville, Tenn. Portrait begun Aug. 19th, 1826, finished Sept. 27th, 1826. Size 29″ × 36″.
Price, $120.00

990 KITTERA, THOMAS (1789–1839).

Graduate of the University of Pennsylvania in 1805, was Attorney-General of Pennsylvania 1817 and member of Congress 1826. Prominent Mason and Grand Master. Portrait, half length, seated with arm over back of chair, head to left, white stock. Begun March 23rd, 1825, finished Nov. 5th, 1825. Size 29″ × 36″.
Price, $100.00
Owned by Masonic Hall, Philadelphia, Pa.

991 KLAPP, DR. JOSEPH (1783–1843).

Graduated from the University of Pennsylvania in 1805. Portrait begun June 3rd, 1814, finished July 6th, 1814. Size 29″ × 38″. Price, $100.00
Owned by Dr. William H. Klapp, Philadelphia.

992 KLAPP, MRS. DR. JOSEPH (1783–1841).

Was Miss Anna B. Milnor. Portrait begun June 3rd, 1814, finished July 6th, 1814. Size 29″ × 38″. Price, $100.00
Owned by Dr. William H. Klapp, Philadelphia.

993 KNEASS, WILLIAM HONEYMAN (1781–1840).

An engraver, was appointed engraver and die-sinker at the United States Mint. This portrait was painted for his son a year after his death. Painting begun Feb. 22nd, 1841, finished April 5th, 1841. Head, 17″ × 20″.
Price, $150.00
Owned by Strickland L. Kneass, Esq., Philadelphia.

200

LIST OF PAINTINGS

994 KNEASS, MRS.

Wife of Strickland Kneass, née Margaretta Sybilla, granddaughter of Judge George Bryan, of the Supreme Court of Pennsylvania. Portrait begun April 11th, 1839, finished April 29th, 1839. Bust. Price, $200.00

995 KNECHT, MR.

For the Corn Exchange, painting begun Nov. 29th, 1862, finished Dec. 18th, 1862. Size 29″ × 36″. Price, $100.00

996 KNECHT, MRS.

Portrait painted as companion to the picture of Mr. Knecht. Begun Jan. 19th, 1863, finished March 23rd, 1863. Size 29″ × 36″. Price, $100.00

997 KNOOR, MRS.

Portrait painted for her aunt, Mrs. Gilbert, begun Nov. 9th, 1859, finished Dec. 1st, 1859. Bust. Price, $100.00

998 KNOX, GENERAL HENRY (1750–1806).

Major-General of Artillery in the Revolutionary War, and Secretary of War in Washington's cabinet. Portrait painted from a miniature, begun April 29th, 1824, finished June, 1824. Head. Price, $25.00

999 KOCH, GERARD.

The register notes that it was drawn in outline from the portrait painted by Peale for his son Tom to finish, the price is recorded as $125, and it appears that Tom received $50 for his work. Portrait begun Dec. 27th, 1833, finished Feb. 9th, 1834. Size 29″ × 36″.

1000 KOCH, MRS.

Portrait copied from painting by Rembrandt Peale for Mr. Meschert, begun Nov. 4th, 1834, finished Nov. 26th, 1834. Size 29″ × 36″.
Price, $150.00

1001 KOECKER, LEONARD, M. D., D. D. S.

Born in Germany, lived in England and became dentist to King William IV. He resided in Philadelphia for many years. Portrait begun Nov. 1st, 1818, finished Feb. 11th, 1818. Half length, seated, black coat, gold buttons, white stock, nearly full face, holds papers in his hands before him. Size 29″ × 36″. Price, $150.00

Owned by Miss Koecker, Chestnut Hill, Philadelphia.

201

J S C

LIST OF PAINTINGS

1002 KOECKER, MRS. LEONARD.

(Née Maria Donath.) Half length, gray dress with red shawl over her shoulders. Blond hair arranged in curls at the sides of her face, landscape in background. Portrait begun Nov. 18th, 1820, finished Dec. 19th, 1820. Size 29″ × 36″.   Price, $150.00
Owned by Miss Koecker, Chestnut Hill, Philadelphia.

1003 KOECKER, MRS. LEONARD.

(Née Maria Donath.) Head, nearly full face, blond hair arranged in curls. Portrait begun Feb. 25th, 1822, finished March 7th. 1822. Head. Size 17″ × 20″.   Price, $50.00
Owned by Miss Koecker, Chestnut Hill, Philadelphia.

1004 KOECKER, LOUISE MELIZET (1822–1912).

Wife of Dr. Leonard R. Koecker, a dentist of Philadelphia. Portrait begun Feb. 11th, 1850, finished Feb. 20th, 1850. Head, nearly full face, with dark hair parted in the middle. Head, 18″ × 20″. (Presented.)
                                                                     Price, $80.00
Owned by Miss Koecker, Chestnut Hill, Philadelphia.

NOTE.—A portrait of Dr. Leonard R. Koecker and his brother as youths about 16 and 18 years old. Two heads on canvas 17″ × 20″, painted by Thomas Sully's daughter, Mrs. Darley; is owned by Miss Koecker, of Chestnut Hill, Philadelphia.

1005 KORN, WILLIAM HENRY (1814–1842).

Son of Henry Korn, of Philadelphia, was a lieutenant in 1840 in army during Seminole War. Half length, head to right, black stock and high-collared coat. The portrait is still in the possession of the family who were friends of the artist. On canvas H. 30 inches, W. 25 inches.
Owned by William Henry Fox, Esq.

1006 KRUMBHAAR, MR.

Copied from a painting by R. Peale, begun Sept. 19th, 1854, finished Oct. 5th, 1854. Bust.   Price, $100.00

1007 KRUMBHAAR, MR.

Portrait begun June 11th, 1813, finished July 17th, 1813.   Head.
                                                                     Price, $70.00

1008 KRUMBHAAR, MRS.

Portrait begun June 11th, 1813, finished July 17th, 1813.   Head.
                                                                     Price, $70.00

1009 KUHL, HENRY (1764–1856).

Assistant cashier of the Bank of United States. Portrait begun April 6th, 1829, finished May 18th, 1829. Bust.   Price, $75.00

LIST OF PAINTINGS

1010 KUHL, MRS. HENRY (1772–1853).

(Was Deborah Hillegas, daughter of Michael Hillegas, first Treasurer of the United States.) Portrait begun April 20th, 1829, finished May 18th, 1829. Bust. Price, $75.00

1011 KUHN, ELIZABETH.

Daughter of Hartman Kuhn. Portrait begun March 18th, 1829, finished April 8th, 1829. Head. Price, $50.00
Owned by Mrs. Alfred T. Mahan, of New York.

1012 KUHN, HARTMAN (1784–1860).

Member of the American Philosophical Society, and a trustee of the University of Pennsylvania from 1836 till his death. Portrait begun Oct. 22nd, 1829, finished Jan. 20th, 1830. Bust. Price, $75.00
Owned by C. Hartman Kuhn, of Philadelphia.

1013 KUSENBERG, MR.

Portrait begun Aug. 27th, 1866, finished Sept. 15th, 1866. Size 29″ × 36″. Price, $150.00

1014 KUSENBERG, MRS.

This portrait was painted to be sent to Mrs. Kusenberg's relatives in Germany, begun June 6th, 1866, finished June 26th, 1866. Size 29″ × 36″.
Price, $200.00

1015 LA BRUCE, MRS.

Portrait begun May 11th, 1846, finished May 20th, 1846. Head.
Price, $150.00

1016 LA COMB (INFANT).

Sketch made Jan. 10th, 1828. Head. Price, $10.00

1017 LAFAYETTE, MARQUIS DE (1757–1834).

Arrived in this country in 1777 and was appointed a Major General in the American Army. He again visited the United States in 1784 and in 1824. Portrait painted in Washington for the City of Philadelphia. Full length, high hat and cane in hand, wearing long cloak, the figures in the background are the Philadelphia City Troop, who acted as special escort for the General on his visit to Philadelphia in 1824–25. Painted by subscription, size 58″ × 94″. (For description see chapter VI.)
Owned by the City of Philadelphia, and hanging at Independence Hall.

1018 LAFAYETTE, MARQUIS DE (1857–1834).

Small full length, as a study for the large picture, begun Jan. 16th, 1826, finished. Size 29½″ × 19″. Price, $100.00
Owned by Arthur Church, of Philadelphia.

1019 LAFAYETTE, MARQUIS DE (1757–1834).

Head. Portrait painted in 1824. Signed and dated. Size 19″ × 22″.
Owned by Herbert Welsh, Philadelphia.

1020 LAFAYETTE, MARQUIS DE (1757–1834).

Bust, head to right, white stock. Portrait painted for the Pennsylvania Colonization Society, begun Nov. 20th, 1845, finished Dec. 1st, 1845. Size 22½″ × 19½″. Price, $80.00
Deposited with Pennsylvania Historical Society, Locust St., Philadelphia.

1021 LA FEVRE.

A child of Dr. La Fevre, painted with a pet dog, painting begun Sept. 9th, 1852, finished Sept. 20th, 1852. Size 24″ × 20″. Price, $100.00

1022 LAMB, THOMAS.

Portrait painted for his mother, begun July 28th, 1831, finished Sept. 13th, 1831. Bust. Price, $120.00
Owned by H. A. Lamb, of New York.

1023 LAMBDIN, JAMES READ (1807–1869).

He was a well-known Philadelphia portrait painter, and a pupil of Sully's for three years. Bust, to right, holding brushes and painter's palette in hand. Portrait begun May 26th, 1824, finished May 31st, 1824. Size 25″ × 30″. Price, $30.00
Owned by his grandson, Mr. Lambdin, of Baltimore, Md.

1024 LAMBERT, MISS.

Of New York. Portrait begun July 30th, 1814, finished Sept., 1814. Bust. Price, $100.00

1025 LA MOTTE, MR.

Portrait begun May 25th, 1812, finished Jan., 1813. Size 29″ × 36″.
Price, $100.00

1026 LANDMAN, MRS.

Deceased, copied from a daguerreotype, portrait begun June 16th, 1853, finished June 27th, 1853. Head. Price, $80.00

LIST OF PAINTINGS

1027 LARDNER, MRS. ALEXANDER (1819–1905).

She was Miss Esther Hoppin. Portrait begun Oct. 19th, 1840, finished Dec. 3rd, 1840. Size 20″ × 24″. Price, $150.00
Owned by Mrs. Isaac Starr, of Philadelphia.

1028 LATROBE, JOHN H. B. (1803–1891).

Eminent lawyer of Baltimore, Md., and President of the Maryland Historical Society. Bust, with arms crossed on breast, standing and wearing a black frock coat. Painted for and presented to the Pennsylvania Colonization Society. Size 25″ × 30″. Begun Jan. 17th, 1862, finished Feb. 20th, 1862. Price, $50.00
Painting at the Pennsylvania Historical Society, Locust St., Philadelphia.

NOTE.—In the book by John E. Semmes on " John H. B. Latrobe and His Times," there is reproduced a portrait said to be of John H. B. Latrobe and ascribed to Sully, that is entirely different from the painting for the Colonization Society.

1029 LATROBE, MRS. JOHN H. B. (1815–   ).

(Was Charlotte Virginia Claiborne, married Dec. 6th, 1832.) Bust, seated, head to right, in yellow gown with wide lace collar, arm resting on red arm of chair or sofa, with hand on neck.
Reproduced in " John H. B. Latrobe and His Times," by John E. Semmes.

1030 LAWRENCE, MRS. OTHO.

(Née Katharine Murdock Nelson.) Bust, nearly full face, black dress, lace cap. Portrait begun Jan. 23rd, 1850, finished Feb. 1st, 1850, painted for her son (Maryland). Bust, size 25″ × 30″. Price, $100.00
Owned by Miss L. M. Lawrence and exhibited in 1921 at Maryland Institute, Baltimore, Md.

1031 LAWRENCE, MISS ANN.

Daughter of Hon. John Lawrence, of New York, who was judge advocate general at the trial of Major Andre. She married George Wright Hawkes. Bust, seen to the waist. Canvas, size 26″ × 22¼″. Painting begun March 15th, and finished March 29th, 1807. Price, $30.00
Owned by Hon. McDougall Hawkes, of New York.

1032 LAWRENCE, MISS ANN.

Copy of former portrait, painting begun April 4th, 1807, finished on April 29th, 1807. Bust. Price, $50.00

1033 LAWRENCE, DR. JOHN (1747–1830).

Princeton A. B. 1764; Philadelphia M. D. 1768. Bust, facing left. Portrait begun Jan. 16th, 1813, finished March 4th, 1813. Size 27″ × 33″.
Price, $70.00
Owned by Miss Mary H. Penington, Philadelphia.

1034 LAWRENCE, SIR THOMAS (1769–1830).

Celebrated English portrait painter. The register notes "Copy for my-self," begun Dec. 11th, 1830, finished April 13th, 1831. Head, 17″ × 10″.
Price, $50.00

1035 LEALAND, DR.

Of Charleston, S. C. Portrait begun May 13th, 1814, finished May 30th, 1814. Bust. Price, $80.00

1036 LEAMING, THOMAS FISHER (1786–1839).

Brother of Miss Lydia Leaming and the second child and eldest son of Rebecca (Fisher) Leaming. Half length, seated with arm on back of chair, hand clasped, high collar and white stock. Portrait begun Feb. 14th, 1809, finished March 17th, 1809. Size 20″ × 24″. (Subscriber.) Price, $30.00
Owned by J. Somers Smith, Philadelphia.

1037 LEAMING, MRS. THOMAS (1757–1833).

Was Rebecca Fisher. Portrait painted for her daughter, Lydia Leaming, who married James S. Smith, begun March 6th, 1832, finished April 5th, 1832. Bust, seated, with lace cap and ruff, white lambs'-wool boa over shoulders. Signed "TS 1832." Size 25″ × 30″. Price, $100.00
Owned by J. Somers Smith, Philadelphia.

1038 LEAMING, MISS LYDIA (1789–1869).

Married James S. Smith. Half length, elbow resting on table, hand supporting head, low-neck gown with long hair and ringlets. Painted in 1806, though noted in register as 1808. Price, $50.00
Owned by J. Somers Smith, Philadelphia.

NOTE.—Family records state that Miss Leaming in removing her bonnet loosened her hair and that the artist requested her to let him paint her in this manner.

1039 LEBEID.

Arabian poet. Full length, standing in Turkish costume with landscape in background. This picture was engraved for the "Portfolio" of 1819, by W. S. Leney (see American Engravers, by Fielding, No. 965), after the painting by Thomas Sully.

1040 LEDYARD, MISS.

Painted for Mrs. Vanderkemp. Portrait begun Jan. 1st, 1834, finished Jan. 13th, 1834. Head. Price, $80.00

1041 LEE, MRS.

(Née Shapleigh.) Portrait was painted for her brother, Captain Boyce, begun Oct. 10th, 1828, finished Dec. 12th, 1828. Bust. Price, $50.00

LIST OF PAINTINGS

1042 LEE, MRS.

Copied from former portrait painted in 1828. Copy begun Feb. 11th, 1835, finished April 3rd, 1835. Head. Price, $80.00

This painting was owned by Albert Rosenthal, of Philadelphia.

1043 LEE, REV.

Deceased, painted for Mrs. Lee, begun April 26th, 1848, finished June 22nd, 1848. Size 20" × 24". Price, $80.00

1044 LEE, MRS.

Wife of the clergyman. Portrait begun May 18th, 1848, finished May 29th, 1848. Size 20" × 24". Head. Price, $80.00

1045 LEE, FANNY.

Niece of Edward L. Carey, of Philadelphia. Painted with Caroline Baird. See No. 73.

1046 LEE, MRS. JOSIAH.

Portrait painted in Baltimore, begun March 28th, 1853, finished April 22nd, 1853. Size 29" × 36". Price, $250.00

1047 LEE, SAMUEL PHILIPS (1812–1897).

Of the United States Navy, was born in Virginia, grandson of Richard Henry Lee. He entered the navy in 1825 and served during the Rebellion on the Union side. He married a daughter of Francis P. Blair, for whom this portrait was painted. Begun June 11th, 1845, and finished June 17th, 1845. Head. Price, $80.00

1048 LEGARÉ, HUGH SWINTON (1789–1843).

Attorney General of South Carolina, and Attorney General of the United States in President Tyler's cabinet. Portrait painted from a miniature, begun April 17th, 1846, finished April 21st, 1846. Size 20" × 24", painted in oval. Bust, head to left, black cravat and black coat. Price, $200.00

Owned by Mr. H. L. Le Compte, of Baltimore.

1049 LEIPER, ANN GRAY (1798–1881).

Daughter of Thomas Leiper and Elizabeth C. Gray, she married George Gray Thomas in 1839. Portrait painted for her brother-in-law, John K. Kane, begun Dec. 13th, 1836, finished Jan. 17th, 1837. Bust. Price, $150.00

Owned by Mary S. Liddell, Lafayette, Indiana.

1050 LENCLOS, NINON DE (1615–1705).

Celebrated French woman, noted for her social prominence and gaieties. Copy of portrait; sketched on Feb. 8th, 1834. Head. Price, $20.00

LIST OF PAINTINGS

1051 LE ROY, J. B.

Brother-in-law of the artist. Portrait begun Aug. 13th, 1807, finished Sept. 10th, 1807. Size 29″ × 36″. Price, $80.00

1052 LE ROY, J. B.

He married Thomas Sully's sister Jane. Portrait begun June 5th, 1814, finished July, 1814. Bust. Price, $70.00

1053 LE ROY, MRS. J. B.

Sister of the artist. Portrait begun Aug. 20th, 1807, finished Sept. 13th, 1807. Size 29″ × 36″. Price, $80.00

1054 LE ROY, JANE.

Sister of the artist, married J. B. Le Roy. Portrait painted for the artist's sister Betsy, begun May 6th, 1815, finished May 20th, 1815. Bust.

Price, $80.00

1055 LE ROY, MRS.

Formerly Miss Gardette. Portrait begun March 24th, 1817, finished June 29th, 1817. Bust. Price, $100.00

1056 LESLIE, ELIZA (1787–1858).

American authoress, sister of the artist, Charles Robert Leslie. Portrait begun Feb. 27th, 1844, finished April 17th, 1844. Bust, facing right, seated. Signed "TS 1844," size 28″ × 36″. Picture was engraved by John Cheney.

Price, $100.00

Owned by Pennsylvania Academy of Fine Arts, Philadelphia.

1057 LESLIE, MISS EMMA AND ADELAIDE.

Edward L. Carey married a sister of Captain Thomas J. Leslie, the brother of the artist, Charles Robert Leslie, and Adelaide and Emma Leslie were children of Captain Leslie. Portrait painted for Edward Carey's brother, Henry Charles Carey, begun July 18th, 1855, finished Aug. 25th, 1855. Busts of two children, the one on the left holding a rose. Size 20″ × 24″.

Price, $100.00

Owned by Pennsylvania Academy of Fine Arts, Philadelphia.

1058 LESLIE, GROUP.

Miss Adelaide and Miss Virginia Carey. Group was painted for Henry Carey. The Misses Leslie were daughters of Captain Thomas Jefferson Leslie. Portrait begun April 21st, finished May 15th, 1825. Size 29″ × 36″. Price, $130.00

LIST OF PAINTINGS

1059 LESLIE, MISS.

Of Alabama. Painted for Miss Greland, begun Jan. 27th, 1824, finished Feb. 20th, 1824. Bust. Price, $100.00

1060 LESLIE, MRS. ROBERT.

Mother of the artist and a present to him from Thomas Sully. (See letter of Aug. 9th, 1816, from Charles Robert Leslie, thanking Sully for the gift.)

1061 LESLIE, CAPTAIN THOMAS JEFFERSON (1796–1874).

Was a brother of the artist, Charles Robert Leslie; he graduated from West Point in 1815. Portrait painted at West Point, begun Sept. 5th, 1829, finished Sept. 17th, 1829. Head. Size 17″ × 20″. Price, $50.00
Owned by United States Military Academy, West Point, N. Y.

1062 LESLIE, CAPTAIN THOMAS J.

Copy made for Charles Robert Leslie, the artist, begun Sept. 8th, 1829, finished Sept. 18th, 1829. Head. Price, $50.00

1063 LESLIE, MRS. THOMAS J.

Wife of Captain Leslie, painted at West Point, portrait begun Sept. 7th, 1829, finished Sept. 19th, 1829. Head. Price, $50.00

1064 LEUTZE, MRS.

This portrait was painted for her son the artist, Emanuel Levtze (1816–1868). He was the historical painter, and was born in Württemberg and came to this country with his parents at an early age. He showed a talent for painting and was sent to Dusseldorf in 1841 to study under Lessing. His picture of "Washington Crossing the Delaware" is in the Metropolitan Museum, New York.
Owned by her granddaughter, Mrs. Carl Looss, Munich.

1065 LEVY, MRS.

Formerly Miss Yates, of Liverpool, portrait begun March 29th, 1842, finished April 11th, 1842. Head. Price, $150.00

1066 LEVY, MISS HENRIETTA (1792–1860).

Portrait begun Oct. 4th, 1810, finished Oct. 27th, 1810. (Sister of No. 1063.) Sitting under a spreading tree and holds a book in her hand, she is dressed in pale apricot. Portrait begun on Oct. 4th, 1810, finished Oct. 27th, 1810. Panel 20″ × 24″. Price, $60.00
Owned by Mr. J. J. Milligan, of Baltimore, Md.

1067 LEVY, MISS MARTHA (1798–   ).

Aged twelve, daughter of Judge Levy and wife of Judge Milligan. Portrait three-quarter length, standing by a spinnet, and turning the leaves of a music book. Panel 19″ × 23″. Begun Nov. 11th, 1810, and finished on Dec. 16th, 1810.   Price, $60.00

Owned by her granddaughter, Mrs. Bancroft, of Boston, and loaned to the Boston Museum of Fine Arts (1920).

1068 LEVY, SANSOM.

Brother of Judge Levy. Portrait begun March 1st, 1808, and finished May 24th, 1808. (A subscriber.) Size 24¼″ × 29½″. Bust. Half length, three-quarter view to left, head full front, holding a large book upright before him.   Price, $30.00

Owned by Mrs. Bancroft, of Boston, and loaned to Boston Museum of Fine Arts (1920).

1069 LEVY, MRS. SANSOM.

(Née Sarah Coates.) Portrait was begun May 31, 1808, finished July 10th, 1808. (A subscriber.) Bust. Size 24¼″ × 29½″. Seated, half length to right.   Price, $30.00

Owned by Mrs. Bancroft, of Boston, and loaned to Boston Museum of Fine Arts (1920).

1070 LEWIS, MISS ANN.

(Study for a large picture.) Painting begun Nov. 21st, 1810, finished Dec. 4th, 1810. Head.   Price, $30.00

1071 LEWIS, MRS. EDW. PARKE CUSTIS.

Of Hoboken, N. J. Painted for her mother, Mrs. Dr. Coxe, portrait begun March 19th, 1833, finished April 4th, 1833. Head.   Price, $60.00

1072 LEWIS, JOHN DELAWARE.

Private secretary to Henry Clay. Brother of William David Lewis. Portrait copied from one painted in Russia. Sully's copy begun Oct. 29th, 1820, finished Nov. 8th, 1820. Bust.   Price, $50.00

1073 LEWIS, J.

Painted in Charleston, S. C., for the Misses Anally, begun Jan. 6th, 1846, finished Jan. 30th, 1846. Size 25″ × 30″.   Price, $200.00

1074 LEWIS, J. R.

Portrait begun Feb. 15th, 1809, and finished March 5th, 1809. Bust.
                    Price, $50.00

LIST OF PAINTINGS

1075 LEWIS, J. W.

The register of paintings notes it was given "in exchange for the first painting." Portrait begun March 11th, 1829, finished April 2nd, 1829. Head. Price, $20.00

1076 LEWIS, MRS. JOHN W.

This picture was not seen by the authors; it is owned by Dr. Francis Porcher Lewis, and was exhibited in South Carolina Exposition, Charleston, 1901–02.

1077 LEWIS, MRS. MORDECAI.

Portrait begun Oct. 5th, 1843, finished Oct. 19th, 1843. Painted for her daughter, Mrs. Fisher. Head. Price, $80.00

1078 LEWIS, REEVE (1781–1820).

Portrait begun March 18th, 1808, and finished April 18th, 1808. Bust. (Subscriber.) Price, $30.00

Owned by Mr. W. W. Jessup, of Woodbury, N. J.

1079 LEWIS, MRS. REEVE.

(Née Rachel Waln Thomas.) Portrait begun April 25th, 1808, and finished May 19th, 1808. Bust. (Subscriber.) Price, $30.00

Owned by W. D. Jessup, of Woodbury, N. J.

1080 LEWIS, R.

Third child, study for a large picture. Begun Nov. 5th, 1810, finished Dec. 8th, 1810. Head. Price, $30.00

1081 LEWIS, MRS. R.

(Infant.) Whole length painting, size 20″ × 24″. Painting begun Oct. 26th, 1810, finished Nov 12th, 1810. Price, $50.00

1082 LEWIS, SAMUEL.

Copied from Rembrandt Peale. Portrait begun May 12th, 1809, finished May 26th, 1809. Bust. Price, $50.00

1083 LEWIS, MRS. S.

Mother of Reeve Lewis. Portrait begun May 5th, 1813, finished June 10th, 1813. Size 29″ × 36″. Price, $100.00

Owned by Mr. W. D. Jessup, of Woodbury, N. J.

1084 LEWIS, MRS. SAMUEL.
Portrait begun Oct. 20th, 1810, finished Dec. 9th, 1810. Bust.
Price, $60.00

1085 LEWIS, MRS. SAMUEL.
(Née Rebecca Thompson.) Holding her infant daughter (Martha Lewis). Half length, seated with her child standing in her lap with her arms about her. Portrait begun March 3rd, 1811, and finished Sept. 26th, 1811. Size 29″ × 36″. Price, $100.00
Owned by Mr. Jacob Waln, Haverford, Penna.

1086 LEWIS, MISS SUSANNAH.
Daughter of R. Lewis. Portrait begun Oct. 8th, 1810, finished Oct. 28th, 1810. Head. Price, $30.00

1087 LEWIS, THOMAS (1755–1801).
Massachusetts merchant, was the father of Commodore Jacob Lewis, of the United States Navy, serving in the War of 1812. Original portrait painted by Copley and copied by Sully, begun March 27th, 1807, finished April 25th, 1807. Full length, seated, with hand to head. Size 58″ × 94″.
Price, $100.00

NOTE.—The Copley portrait is owned by Lewis Johnson, Esq., of Plainfield, N. J. The ownership of the copy by Sully is unknown to the authors.

1088 LEWIS, WILLIAM (U. S. N.).
Commodore William Lewis entered the United States Navy in 1802, he was a lieutenant in 1807, and was lost on the "Epervier" in 1815. Portrait was begun Jan. 6th, 1807, and finished June 6th, 1807. Size 29″ × 36″.
Price, $70.00

1089 LEWIS, WILLIAM DAVID (1792–1881).
Collector of the Port of Philadelphia. Portrait begun Oct. 28th, 1820, finished Nov. 7th, 1820. Bust. Price, $75.00

1090 LEWIS, WILLIAM DAVID.
Copy of first portrait. Begun Oct. 29th, 1820, finished Nov. 7th, 1820. Bust. Price, $50.00

1091 LEWIS, MRS. WILLIAM D. (1801–1870).
(Was Miss Sarah Claypoole.) Portrait begun Feb. 9th, 1829, finished March 6th, 1829. Head. Size 17″ × 20″. Price, $50.00
Owned by her grandson, Lewis Neilson, St. Davids, Penna.

LIST OF PAINTINGS

1092 LEWIS, MRS.

Portrait painted for her husband, begun Jan. 26th, 1842, finished Feb. 18th, 1842. Bust. Price, $200.00

1093 LIGHTNER, ISAAC NEWTON.

Half length, seated, facing front. Size 24″ × 29″.
Owned by Mrs. George Nauman, and exhibited in the Lancaster Loan Collection, 1912.

1094 LINCOLN, ABRAHAM (1809–1865).

President of the United States. (Deceased.) Portrait painted from a photograph, begun April 28th, 1865, finished April 29th, 1865. Head. Price, $80.00

1095 LINCOLN, ABRAHAM.

President Lincoln. (Deceased.) Painted from a photograph, begun Sept. 8th, 1868, finished Feb. 28th, 1869. Size 25″ × 30″. Price, $150.00

1096 LINCOLN, ABRAHAM AND SON.

Portrait painted from a photograph. Painting begun May 30th, 1865, finished June 24th, 1865. Size 29″ × 36″. Price, $100.00

1097 LINDSAY, ROBERT M.

Picture dealer of Philadelphia; this was the last portrait painted by Thomas Sully, it was begun Oct. 18th, 1871, and finished Oct. 31st, 1871. Size 20″ × 24″. Price, $80.00
Owned by estate of Gilbert S. Parker, Philadelphia.

1098 LINGEN, MRS. GEORGE.

(Née Maria Oldmixon, wife of Dr. George Lingen.) Bust, head to right, wearing large hat. Size of canvas 28″ × 24″. The portrait was " painted for professional services," begun Sept. 29th, 1842, finished Nov. 10th, 1842. Price, $100.00
This portrait was owned by Mrs. Alfred C. Lambdin, of Philadelphia, and was acquired by the Art Institute of Chicago, through the Ehrich Galleries, New York.

1099 LINK, MISS.

Bust, head to left, black hair parted in the middle with pearls arranged in hair over ears. Low-necked white dress. Portrait painted for her mother, begun June 28th, 1858, finished July 7th, 1858. Signed on back " TS 1858, July." Size 20″ × 24″. Price, $80.00
Owned by Rosenbach & Co., Philadelphia.

1100 LINK, MISS.

Bust, head to right, light-brown hair parted in the middle and arranged in braids over ears, low-necked white gown with red shawl over left shoulder. Signed " ₮S 1856, Oct." Portrait painted from a daguerreotype for her mother, begun Oct. 9th, 1856, finished Oct. 18th, 1859. Size 20″ × 24″.
Price, $80.00

Owned by Rosenbach & Co., Philadelphia.

1101 LINTICUM, MISS.

Of Georgetown, D. C. Portrait begun May 7th, 1855, finished May 15th, 1855. Head.
Price, $80.00

1102 LIVEZEY, MR.

Who had his mill on the Wissahickon Creek at the foot of Livezey's Lane. The founder of the grist-mill also had a vineyard and Robert Wharton sent his wine to Franklin. Portrait begun June 7th, 1826, finished June 22nd, 1826. Head.
Price, $40.00

1103 LIVINGSTON, MISS.

Of New York. Portrait begun Feb. 10th, 1815, finished March 4th, 1815, Bust.
Price, $100.00

1104 LIVINGSTON, MISS ANGELICA.

Of New York. Portrait begun Sept. 6th, 1815, finished Dec. 19th, 1815. Bust.
Price, $100.00

1105 LIVINGSTON, EDWARD (1764–1836).

Statesman, graduated in 1781 from the College of New Jersey, studied law with his brother, Robert R. Livingston, in New York. Portrait copied of deceased for Mrs. Potter, begun Oct. 14th, 1848, finished Oct. 23rd, 1848. Head to left, high white stock and collar. Head.
Price, $80.00

1106 LIVINGSTON, MRS. MONTG.

Deceased, portrait painted from a daguerreotype, begun Aug. 8th, 1848, finished Aug. 25th, 1848. Head.
Price, $80.00

1107 LIVINGSTON, PETER VAN BRUGH (1710–1792).

Copied from painting by Sir Henry Raeburn. Begun Aug. 19th, 1828, finished Dec. 7th, 1828. Bust.
Price, $75.00

NOTE.—A portrait of Peter Van Brugh Livingston, painted by Sir Henry Raeburn, is owned by the Wadsworth Athenaeum at Hartford, Conn.

LIST OF PAINTINGS

1108 LOCKWOOD, MR.

Portrait painted from a daguerreotype, begun Jan. 2nd, 1850, finished Jan. 22nd, 1850. Size 24" × 30". Price, $80.00

1109 LOGAN, JAMES (1664–1751).

He came to this country in 1699 as William Penn's secretary, and died at his country place " Stenton " in Germantown, where the portrait that Sully copied hung for many years; it was believed to have been painted from life. Sully's copy belongs to the Library Company of Philadelphia, and was paid for by issuing a share of stock. Painted in 1831. Bust.

1110 LORTON, RICHARD.

An artist of Petersburg, Virginia. Painting 10" × 12", begun April 11th, 1804, finished June 4th, 1804. Price, $12.00

1111 LOWBER, JOHN C. (1789–1834).

(Deceased.) Painted for the Philadelphia Saving Fund, begun July 24th, 1834, finished July 30th, 1834. Size 25" × 30". Bust, head to left, seated with arm over the back of chair, hand rests on book. Price, $125.00
Reproduced in History of Philadelphia Saving Fund Society, by J. M. Willcox. Owned by the Philadelphia Saving Fund Society.

1112 LOWBER, MR. JOHN C. (1789–1834).

Lawyer of Philadelphia. Portrait begun May 11th, 1822, finished June 1st, 1822. Head. Price, $50.00

1113 LOWBER, MRS. JOHN C.

(Was Miss F. Sergeant.) Portrait begun June 5th, 1822, finished June 15th, 1822. Head. Price, $50.00

1114 LUCAS, MISS ELIZABETH.

Of New York. Painted for Mrs. Berg, portrait begun April 4th, 1836, finished April 26th, 1836. Head. Price, $100.00

1115 LUCAS, FIELDING (JR.) (1781–1854).

Prominent citizen of Baltimore and a well-known publisher and book dealer. Standing with hand on head of marble lion, he wears a brown coat, white stock or cravat with head to left. Portrait begun March 8th, 1808, finished April 19th, 1808. The size is now 23" × 28½", having been slightly cut down. It was painted for the " subscriber " price of $30.00
Owned by his great-grandson, Edward L. White, of Baltimore, Md.

1116 LUCAS, MRS. FIELDING (1788–1863).

She was Eliza Carrell, of Philadelphia, and married Fielding Lucas, Jr., of Baltimore, in 1810. Half length, holding book in hands. Portrait begun Oct. 15th, 1810, finished Dec. 24th, 1810. Size 29″ × 36″. Price, $70.00
Reproduced in "Ivy Mills," by Joseph Willcox.
Owned by William Fielding Lucas, Jr., of Baltimore, Md.

1117 LUDLOW, MARY.

Of Baltimore, Md. Portrait painted for Mr. Towne, begun Jan. 18th, 1847, finished Jan. 25th, 1847. Head. Price, $80.00

1118 LUGENBEEL, DR. JAMES WASHINGTON (1819–1857).

Appointed by the African Colonization Society physician to Liberia, where he served for many years. Head, nearly full face with black side whiskers and black stock. Portrait begun April 13th, 1864, finished April 26th, 1864. Size 20″ × 24″. Price, $50.00
Presented to the Colonization Society and now in Pennsylvania Historical Society.

1119 LYMAN, GENERAL.

Background and drapery. Painting begun Aug. 25th, 1828, finished August 27th, 1828. Size 18″ × 21″. Price, $20.00

1120 LYMAN, MISS.

Of Boston. Portrait begun May 11th, 1855, finished May 17th, 1855. Head. Price, $80.00

1121 LYMAN, MISS SUSAN.

Of Northampton. Portrait begun Sept. 16th, 1844, finished Sept. 23rd, 1844. Size 24″ × 30″. Price, $80.00

1122 LYONS.

The register notes "Mr. Lyons' two children, separately." The size 12″ × 10″, and the price as $30, so there were probably two paintings. Begun May 25th, 1804, finished July 4th, 1804.

1123 LYONS, JUDGE.

Portrait begun Jan., 1806, finished the same month. Bust. Price, $30.00

1124 MCALLISTER, JOHN JR. (1786–1877).

Optician, 48 Chestnut St., Philadelphia; was a well-known local antiquary and collector of art and historical objects; at the time of his death was the oldest living graduate of the University of Pennsylvania. Bust, portrait begun Dec. 16th, 1830, finished Jan. 22nd, 1831. Price, $75.00
Owned by W. H. McAllister, of Philadelphia.

1125 McALLISTER, MRS. JOHN JR.

(Was Eliza Melville Young.) Wife of the optician, Chestnut St., Philadelphia. Bust, portrait begun Dec. 13th, 1830, finished Jan. 12th, 1831.

Price, $75.00

Owned by W. H. McAllister, Philadelphia, Pa.

1126 McCALL, JUDITH KEMBLE (1743–1829).

Widow of Archibald McCall, of 308 Chestnut St., Philadelphia. Her sister married the British General, Thomas Gage. Portrait begun Jan. 27th, 1829, finished May 4th, 1829. Bust, head to right, black dress and wears a cap.

Price, $50.00

Owned by Miss McCall and Mrs. Keating.

1127 McCALL, JUDITH KEMBLE (1743–1829).

Copy from the first portrait. Bust, head to right, black dress and wears a cap, begun Aug. 27th, 1830, finished Sept. 7th, 1830.

Price, $75.00

1128 McCALL, JUDITH KEMBLE (1743–1829).

Copy from the first portrait. Bust, head to right, black dress and wears a cap, begun Aug. 28th, 1830, and finished Sept. 18th, 1830. Signed on face of canvas " TS 1830."

Price, $50.00

Owned by Miss Sally W. Fisher, Philadelphia.

1129 McCALL, MISS CATHERINE (1782–1859).

Daughter of Archibald McCall, of Philadelphia. Portrait begun Feb. 28th, 1809, finished March 13th, 1809, half length with arms resting on a red cushion, low-necked gown. Signed on back of panel " TS 1809." Panel 25" × 30".

Subscriber's price, $30.00

Owned by Mr. George McCall, of Philadelphia.

1130 McCALL, MRS. (1773–1858).

Née Miss Gibson. Portrait painted for her son Peter, begun May 6th, 1839, finished May 31st, 1839. Bust, to left, black dress, lace cap. Signed " TS 1839."

Price, $200.00

Owned by Miss G. K. McCall and Mrs. Keating, of Wawa, Delaware County, Pa.

1131 McCALL, MRS. PETER.

Portrait painted for her husband, begun May 1st, 1848, finished May 20th, 1848. Head.

Price, $80.00

Owned by R. Radcliffe Whitehead, Esq., Woodstock, Ulster Co., N. Y.

1132 McCALLASTER, Miss.

Portrait painted for Mr. Bacon, Jr., begun May 17th, 1808, finished July 14th, 1808. Bust. (See also Nos. 69, 70, 71.) Price, $50.00

1133 McCALLASTER, Miss.

Portrait begun Sept. 29th, 1812, finished Dec. 14th, 1812. Size 29″ × 36″. Price, $100.00

1134 McCALLESTER, Miss.

Portrait begun March 1st, 1817, finished March 20th, 1817. Size 29″ × 36″. Price, $150.00

1135 McCALLMONT, Mr.

Portrait begun Feb. 6th, 1812, finished March 14th, 1812. Size 29″ × 36″. Price, $100.00

1136 McCANDLESS, Mrs.

Portrait, with hands introduced, begun July 12th, 1837, finished July 31st, 1837. Bust. Price, $250.00

1137 McCAULEY, Senr.

Painted for Mr. Cooper Smith, begun July 25th, 1817, finished Sept. 19th, 1817. Bust. Price, $100.00

1138 McCAW, Dr.

The register notes a portrait of "Dr. McCaw and Lady, separately," so it is probable that two pictures were painted. The size was 12″ × 10″, and the pictures were begun on April 11th, 1804, and finished on June 4th, 1804. The price was $24.00

1139 McCLURE, Mrs.

Of Pittsburgh, Penna. Formerly Miss Collins. Portrait begun April 12th, 1841, finished April 24th, 1841. Head. Price, $150.00

1140 McCLURE, Mr.

Of Pittsburgh, Penna. A prominent attorney. Portrait begun April 13th, 1841, finished April 26th, 1841. Head. Price, $150.00

1141 McCONNELL, Mrs. Henry L. and child.

She was the daughter of John Savage, of Jamaica, W. I. Born 1820, died in Philadelphia 1911. The "child" was Henry L. McConnell, Jr. (1841–1881). Portrait begun Aug. 14th, 1843, finished Aug. 31st, 1843. Size. 25″ × 30″· Price, $160.00
Owned by Miss Graff, of Philadelphia.

LIST OF PAINTINGS

1142 McCoy, Mr.

Of New Orleans, La. Portrait begun Aug. 8th, 1818, finished Aug. 20th, 1818. Bust. Price, $100.00

1143 McCrea, Master.

Full-length portrait, begun Nov. 14th, 1816, finished Dec. 22nd, 1816. Size 29″ × 36″. Price, $250.00

1144 McCrea, Mrs.

Of Camden. Portrait painted for her sister, begun March 17th, 1842, finished April 2nd, 1842. Head. Price, $150.00

1145 McDonald, Mrs.

Portrait begun March 4th, 1803, and finished May 5th, 1803. Bust.
Price, $20.00

1146 McDonald, Mrs.

Painted from a daguerreotype, begun Sept. 16th, 1854, finished Dec. 30th, 1854. Size 29″ × 36″. Price, $300.00

1147 McDougal, General.

Painted from memory, begun Oct. 1st, 1811, finished Nov. 26th, 1811. Head. Price, $15.00

1148 McDougal, Gordon.

Painted for his sister. Portrait begun Feb. 23rd, 1829, finished Feb. 27th, 1829. Head. Price, $50.00

1149 McEuen, Charles (1801–1857).

Graduated at the University of Pennsylvania in 1821. Portrait begun March 11th, 1826, finished April 16th, 1826. Head. Price, $30.00

1150 McEuen, Mary.

Married William M. Boyce, U. S. A. Portrait painted for Mrs. Emily Smith, begun March 6th, 1826, finished April 10th, 1826. Head.
Price, $30.00
Owned by Oliver Boyce Judson, of Philadelphia.

1151 McEuen, Miss Mary and Emily.

Daughters of Charles McEuen, of Philadelphia. Portrait begun Nov. 3rd, 1823, finished Dec. 18th, 1823. Size 45″ × 35″. Price, $150.00
Mary married William M. Boyce, and Emily married a Mr. Smith.
Owned by Oliver Boyce Judson, of Philadelphia.

1152 McILVAINE, B. R.

Of Kentucky. Portrait begun Sept. 2nd, 1833, finished Sept. 30th, 1833. Bust. Price, $60.00

1153 McILVAINE, MRS. B. R.

Of Kentucky. Portrait begun Sept. 3rd, 1833, finished Sept. 24th, 1833. Bust. Price, $60.00

1154 McILVAINE, HENRY.

Portrait begun April 22nd, 1836, finished May 5th, 1836. Bust. Price, $150.00

1155 McILVAINE, MRS. H.

Portrait begun by Inman and finished by Sully. She was the daughter of Lady Mary Oldmixon, who died in Philadelphia and was buried in Old St. Andrew's Churchyard. Sully began painting Jan. 9th, 1835, finished Jan. 19th, 1835. Head to right, dark hair with a white rose, blue background. Panel 15″ × 19″. Price, $50.00
Portrait formerly owned by John Oldmixon Lambdin, of Baltimore " Sun." At Knoedler's Galleries, New York, in 1919.

1156 McILVAINE, MRS. H.

Deceased, portrait copied from picture by Inman. Copy begun Oct. 29th, 1834, finished Nov. 29th, 1834. Bust. Price, $125.00

1157 McILVAINE, JOSEPH (1768–1826).

He was born in Bristol, Penna., and died in Burlington, N. J. Joseph McIlvaine was United States Senator in 1823, and was the father of Bishop Charles Pettit McIlvaine, of Ohio. This portrait was painted for his mother and was begun on May 8th, 1837, and finished May 22nd, 1837. Head. Price, $150.00

1158 McILVAINE, JOSEPH.

Portrait painted for Princeton College, begun Dec. 14th, 1818, finished Dec. 31st, 1818. Bust. Price, $100.00

1159 McILVAINE.

Copied from a former picture, begun Oct. 22nd, 1827, finished Nov. 25th, 1827. Bust. Price, $75.00

1160 McILVAINE, MISSES.

Misses Ellen and Mary. Miss Ellen McIlvaine married Dr. William Camac, of Philadelphia. Painting begun Feb. 8th, 1834, finished March 4th, 1834. Busts. Price, $130.00

1161 McKean, Mrs. Thomas (1747–1820).

Was Sarah Armitage, the second wife of the Chief Justice and Governor of Pennsylvania. She was mother of Sally McKean who married Marquis Casa d'Yrujo, for whom this portrait was painted. Begun March 27th, 1819, finished April 19th, 1819. Bust. Price, $100.00

Owned by her grandson the Duke of Sotomayor, in Madrid. The painting has been attributed to Gilbert Stuart.

1162 McLain, William (1806–1873).

A Presbyterian clergyman for the Colonization Society, portrait painted from a photograph, begun April 21st, 1865, finished April 30th, 1865. Size 24" × 20". Price, $80.00

Deposited with Pennsylvania Historical Society.

1163 McLaughlin, Mr. Frank.

Portrait begun May 21st, 1864, finished June 13th, 1864. Size 30 × 25". Price, $50.00

1164 McLaughlin, Mrs. Sally.

Sister-in-law to Mr. McLaughlin. Portrait begun April 27th, 1864, finished May 23rd, 1864. Size 30" × 15". Price, $50.00

1165 McLauthgalen, Mr.

Portrait begun April 13th, 1864, finished April 26th, 1864. Size 25" × 30". Price, $50.00

1166 McLauthgalen, Mrs.

Portrait begun March 31st, 1864, finished April 14th, 1864. Size 25" × 30". Price, $50.00

1167 McLean, John (1785–1861).

Postmaster-General of the United States and Associate-Justice of the Supreme Court. Head facing right, on panel 17" × 19". Signed on front with monogram " TS 1831." Engraved by W. G. Armstrong for the National Portrait Gallery, and lithographed by Albert Newsam. Painted for Benjamin W. Richards, Mayor of Philadelphia. Portrait begun April 6th, 1831, finished April 12th, 1831. Price, $50.00

Owned by Pennsylvania Academy of Fine Arts.

1168 McMichael, Mrs. Meta and child.

(The little girl about a year old being Mrs. Benjamin Chew Tilghman.) Mrs. McMichael wears a low-necked black dress. Portrait painted for her father, Mr. Shaw, begun Oct. 15th, 1866, finished Dec. 8th, 1866. Size 30" × 25". Price, $200.00

Owned by Mrs. Benjamin Chew Tilghman, of Philadelphia.

1169 McMurtrie, James (1784–1854).

An early patron of art in this country and an amateur painter of some ability. Portrait begun May 10th, 1808, finished June 30th, 1808. Bust.

Price, $50.00

1170 McMurtrie, Mrs. James (1791–1870).

Was Miss Rebecca Mifflin Harrison. Portrait painted with her child. Begun Feb. 16th, 1816, finished March, 1818. Size 54" × 45".

Price, $500.00

Owned by John T. Braun, Philadelphia, Pa.

1171 Macaulay, Haynes.

Portrait begun March 1st, 1803, and finished March 20th, 1803. Bust.

Price, $20.00

1172 Macdonough, Commodore Thomas (1783–1825).

Commanded American fleet on Lake Champlain, 1814. Awarded medal by Congress. Portrait begun June 10th, 1815, finished July 16th, 1815. Bust, head to right, in naval uniform, high coat collar. Size 25" × 30".

Price, $80.00

Owned by the State of Delaware and hanging in the capitol at Dover, Del.

1173 Macfarland, Mrs. William H. (1816–1900).

Portrait painted with her daughter Turner (b. 1846). Mrs. Macfarland was Nancy Beime and married Mr. Macfarland, a prominent banker of Richmond, Va. Painting begun June 19th, 1849, finished July 27th, 1849. Signed on back " $\overline{TS}$ 1849." Size 25" × 30". Price, $300.00

Owned by Mrs. John M. Glenn, of New York City.

1174 Mackie, Thomas (1754–1821).

He was a Philadelphia merchant and a member of the St. Andrew's Society, of Philadelphia. Head to right, bust. Size 25" × 30". Portrait painted for Dr. Henry E. Hudson, begun Oct. 21st, 1817, finished Nov. 25th, 1817. Price, $100.00

Owned by Mrs. Rich, of Burlington, New Jersey.

1175 Mackie, Mrs. Joanna Cooke (1763–1845).

Wife of Thomas Mackie. Bust, head to left, with lace cap and collar. Portrait painted for Dr. Henry E. Hudson, begun Oct. 21st, 1817, finished Nov. 25th, 1817. Size 25" × 30". Price, $100.00

Owned by Mrs. Rich, Burlington, New Jersey.

1176 MACLURE, WILLIAM (1763–1840).

Scotch naturalist who became the President of the Academy of Natural Sciences of Philadelphia, for whom the portrait was painted. Bust, seated at table with elbow resting on books with hand to head. Portrait begun Oct. 10th, 1825, finished Dec. 5th, 1825. Bust. Price, $60.00
Lithographed by Albert Newsam.
Owned by the Academy of Natural Sciences of Philadelphia.

1177 MACOMB, GENERAL ALEXANDER (1782–1841).

Entered the army in 1799, and in 1835 was appointed Commander-in-chief. Bust, with arms folded, head to right with dark wavy hair, high military collar and uniform, hills of the Hudson in background. Size 20″ × 24″. Begun May 27th, 1829, finished June 27th, 1829.
Engraved by J. B. Longacre for the National Portrait Gallery (S. ——), also lithographed by Childs.
Painting owned by United States Military Academy at West Point.

1178 MACOMB, GENERAL ALEXANDER (1782–1841).

Congress awarded General Macomb a gold medal, drawing made for the design, Sept., 1817. Size 6″ × 6″. Price, $50.00

1179 MADISON, JAMES (1751–1836).

Fourth President of the United States. Full length, standing, left hand on arm of chair, right hand on " Constitution of the United States, etc." spread on table, globe, etc., to left. Painted by Sully in 1809 and engraved by David Edwin, published by W. H. Morgan, Philadelphia, 1810. Sully received $150.00 for this painting, size 27″ × 20″.
Gift of F. C. Church to Corcoran Art Gallery, of Washington, D. C. (See also Catalogue of Edwin's Engravings, by Fielding, No. 126.)

1180 MADISON, JAMES (1751–1836).

Painted from the portrait by Gilbert Stuart, copy begun June 6th, 1856, finished July 3rd, 1856. Bust. Price, $100.00
Painted for the Virginia Historical Society, Richmond, Va.

1181 MADISON, MRS. (1772–1849).

Deceased, portrait painted from a daguerreotype, begun March 25th, 1857, finished April 18th, 1857. Head. Price, $80.00

1182 MAGRUDER, ELLEN.

Daughter of Richard Magruder, begun Jan. 27th, 1823, finished April 1st, 1823. Bust. Price, $100.00
Owned by Mr. Buckler, Baltimore, Md.

1183 MAGRUDER, HEZEKIAH (1815–1897).

Portrait painted for his aunt, when he was eight years old. Painting begun Sept. 30th, 1823, finished May 17th, 1823. Bust, size 25″ × 30″. Signed " ᴛꜱ 1823." Price, $100.00

Owned by Mrs. F. W. Craighead (née Magruder), Philadelphia.

1184 MAGRUDER, MRS. HEZEKIAH (1820–1885).

(Née Miss Johnston.) Portrait painted in Baltimore, begun Oct. 7th, 1852, finished Oct. 21st, 1852. White low-necked dress, rose-colored curtain, landscape in background. Bust. Size 25″ × 30″. Price, $130.00

Owned by Mrs. F. W. Craighead (née Magruder), Philadelphia.

NOTE.—The name " Magruder " is misspelled " McGruder " in the artist's register.

1185 MALCOLM, MR.

Deceased, painted from a miniature. Begun June 11th, 1810, finished July 24th, 1810. Head. Price, $50.00

1186 MALCOLM, ANGELICA (1792–1834).

Half length, seated, facing right. Size 26″ × 32″. This portrait was painted about the time of her marriage. Miss Malcolm's husband's name was also Malcolm.

It is owned by the estate of Mrs. John Lloyd, of Philadelphia.

NOTE.—It is very doubtful if Sully painted this portrait, but it was exhibited as his work in 1887 at the Pennsylvania Academy af Fine Arts.

1187 MALCOM, REV. HOWARD (1799–1879).

Baptist divine of Philadelphia; one of the founders of the American Tract Society and of the American Sunday-School Union. Portrait begun Feb. 24th, 1864, finished April 13th, 1864. Head. Price, $50.00

1188 MALLON, MRS.

Sister of Mrs. Catherine Matthews. Portrait begun Nov. 12th, 1812, finished Dec. 30th, 1812. Bust. Price, $70.00

1189 MANIGAULT, CHARLES (1795–1874).

Merchant, and a collector of fine paintings. Portrait begun May 11th, 1817, finished June 27th, 1817. Half length, head turned to right, arms folded. Size 27½″ × 35″. Price, $150.00

Reproduced in " One Hundred Early American Paintings." The Ehrich Gallery, New York.

LIST OF PAINTINGS

1190 MANIGAULT, CAPTAIN GABRIEL H. (1788–1834).

Of South Carolina. Served on the staff of General Izard in the War of 1812. Portrait begun March 1st, 1814, finished April 7th, 1814. Size 29″ × 36″.   Price, $100.00

1191 MANSFIELD, COLONEL JARED (1759–1830).

Professor of Natural Philosophy at the Military Academy, West Point. Bust, with hand on book, white stock and frilled shirt. Portrait painted for the Academy, begun May 13th, 1828, finished June 15th, 1828. Bust.
                                                                           Price, $100.00
Reproduced in "Sully portraits" at the United States Military Academy at West Point, by Frank Fowler, Century Magazine.

1192 MARIGNY, COUNT BERNARD MANDEVILLE DE.

A wealthy resident of New Orleans, La. He entertained Louis Phillippe, and Laussat, High Commissioner of Napoleon, in a most lavish manner. Bust, seated, nearly full face, white stock, the hand resting on chair arm is gloved. Panel 25″ × 30″. Signed "TS." Painted in Philadelphia, 1808.
Owned by Dr. Isaac M. Cline, New Orleans, La.

1193 MARIGNY, MRS. BERNARD MANDEVILLE DE.

(Née Mary Jones.) Portrait painted in 1808, half length, seated in chair, holding a book in her hand, head to right, lace collar to neck of dress. She died in Philadelphia, June 4th, 1808, a few months after the painting was finished. Signed "TS." Canvas 25″ × 30″.
Owned by Dr. Isaac M. Cline, New Orleans, La.

1194 MARIS, MRS. RICHARD (1782–1875), AND HER SON MASTER GEORGE (1810–1887).

Mrs. Maris was Rachel Ross, of Philadelphia. Portrait three-quarter seated, head to right, her son stands at her knee with his arm extended. Painted in 1813. Size 39″ × 52″.   Price, $250.00
The original receipt of Sully's is preserved by the owners as well as the sketch for the child's head.
Owned by Mrs. William L. Degn, of Germantown, Philadelphia.

1195 MARKOE, MRS. JOHN.

(Née Hitty Cox.) Portrait begun May 3rd, 1835, finished May 19th, 1835. Head.   Price, $80.00
Owned by Mr. George Wharton Pepper, Philadelphia.

1196 MARSHALL, L. R.

President of Branch Bank of United States at Natchez, Miss. Portrait begun Aug. 19th, 1834, finished Sept. 3rd, 1834. Bust.   Price, $125.00

1197 MARSHALL, L. R.

Of Natchez, Miss. Copy to be worked on by Tom, begun Sept. 11th, 1834, finished Oct. 3rd, 1834. Bust.   Price, $125.00

1198 MASON, MRS. EMMA.

(Née Miss Wheatly.) Painted from a photograph, begun Dec. 5th, 1854, finished March 16th, 1855. Size 29″ × 36″.   Price, $200.00

1199 MASON, JOHN YOUNG (1799–1859).

Born in Virginia and graduated at the University of North Carolina at Chapel Hill in 1816. He was made United States District Judge for Virginia, and he was Secretary of the Navy under Presidents Tyler and Polk. At the time of his death he was United States Minister to France. Portrait begun May 31st, 1847, finished June 18th, 1847. Half length.

Price, $300.00

Painted for University, Chapel Hill, North Carolina.

1200 MASON, JOHN YOUNG (1799–1859).

Finished the sketch Dec. 3rd, 1847. Head.   Price, $50.00

1201 MASON, MRS.

Of Maryland. Portrait painted from a daguerreotype, begun Aug. 29th, 1856, finished Oct. 7th, 1856. Head.   Price, $100.00

1202 MASON, MRS.

(Née Miss McGee.) Portrait begun Sept. 25th, 1856, finished Oct. 7th, 1856. Head.   Price, $80.00

1203 MASON, MRS. AND SON.

Children of General Macomb. Portrait begun June 1st, 1829, finished August 4th, 1829. Size 29″ × 36″.   Price, $200.00

1204 MASON, MRS. JONATHAN (1760–1836).

She was Susanna Powell, and married Mr. Mason, of Boston, Mass., in 1779. The portrait was painted in Boston, begun Aug. 11th, 1836, finished Aug. 22nd, 1836. Head.   Price, $100.00

NOTE.—Mr. and Mrs. Jonathan Mason were both painted by Gilbert Stuart.

1205 MASON, MR.

Portrait begun Sept. 26th, 1856, finished Oct. 7th, 1856. Head.

Price, $80.00

1206 MATTHEWS, MRS. KATHERINE.

Sister of Mrs. Mallon. No. 1188. Figure turned to left, wears a white hood edged with lace, a brown-green dress and brown fur cape, which she holds at the neck with her right hand. Canvas 27″ × 23″. Begun Dec. 1st, 1812, finished Jan. 29th, 1813.   Price, $70.00

Owned by Metropolitan Museum, New York.

1207 MAY, JUDGE.

Portrait painted from a photograph, begun May 12th, 1858, finished July 8th, 1858. Bust.   Price, $100.00

1208 MAY, JUDGE.

Copy made for Mrs. Joyne, begun July 2nd, 1858, finished July 15th, 1858. Bust.   Price, $100.00

1209 MAY, MR.

Of Baltimore, Md. (Father of Mrs. T. Poultney.) Portrait painted from a photograph. Begun Dec. 7th, 1857, finished July, 1858. Head.

Price, $50.00

1210 MAY, MRS.

Of Virginia. Portrait begun April 8th, 1858, finished April 29th, 1858. Bust.   Price, $100.00

1211 MAY, MRS.

Copy of former portrait, begun April 22nd, 1858, finished May 2nd, 1858. Bust.   Price, $100.00

1212 MAY, MRS. JOHN.

Portrait painted for her husband, begun July 12th, 1848, finished July 28th, 1848. Head.   Price, $150.00

1213 MAY, SAMUEL (SR.).

Portrait painted in Boston for his son John, begun July 5th, 1848, finished July 17th, 1848. Head.   Price, $150.00

1214 MAY, MRS. SAMUEL (SR.).

Portrait painted for her son John, begun July 6th, 1848, finished July 27th, 1848. Head.   Price, $150.00

1215 MAYER, C. F.

Portrait begun Aug. 4th, 1840, finished Aug. 14th, 1840. Bust.

Price, $200.00

1216 MAYWOOD, MRS.

(In costume of Roman matron.) Probably wife of the actor Robert Campbell Maywood, who became manager of the Walnut Street Theatre in Philadelphia in 1833. He was a member of the St. Andrew's Society. Portrait begun June 6th, 1835, finished Nov. 2nd, 1835. Bust. Price, $125.00

1217 MEADE, MRS. RICHARD WORSAM.

Was Margaret Coates Butler, she was the mother of General George G. Meade, the hero of Gettysburg. Portrait painted for Mrs. Sansom Levy, begun June 20th, 1811, and finished Sept. 4th, 1811. Size 29" × 36".
Price, $100.00

1218 MEADE, WILLIAM (1789–1862).

Graduated at Princeton College in 1808, and in 1829 was made Assistant P. E. Bishop of Virginia, becoming Bishop in 1841. Portrait painted for Princeton College, begun Oct. 1st, 1808, finished Oct. 6th, 1808. Bust.
Price, $50.00

1219 MEARES, MRS. AND HER SON.

Portrait begun March 6th, 1813, finished July 25th, 1813. Size 25" × 30". Price, $200.00

1220 MEASE, JAMES, M. D. (1771–1846).

Philadelphia physician and surgeon in United States Army in 1812. Portrait painted for his son Pierce, who afterwards changed his name to Butler and married the actress Fanny Kemble. Portrait begun Nov. 24th, 1834. finished Dec. 16th, 1834. Half length, seated, head facing right. Size 28" × 36". Price, $200.00
Owned by Rev. Alfred Elwyn, Philadelphia.

1221 MEIGS, CHARLES DELUCINA (1792–1869).

Prominent Philadelphia physician and professor in the Jefferson Medical College from 1841 to 1861. Head to right, portrait begun June 9th, 1824, finished June 17th, 1824. Size 18" × 20". Signed " TS June 17th, 1824." (Mrs. Charles D. Meigs, see Montgomery.) Price, $30.00
Owned by Anna Ingersoll Meigs, Philadelphia.

1222 MEIGS, CHARLES DELUCINA (1792–1869).
There is a copy or replica of the former portrait owned by Dr. Charles D. Hart, of Chestnut Hill, Philadelphia. Size 18" × 20".

NOTE.—It is said to have been partly the work of Sully's daughter.

1223 MELANCHTHON, PHILIP (1497–1560).

The German reformer, famous as the co-laborer of Martin Luther. Portrait copied from Holbein for Brimmer. Painted 1828. Size 24″ × 28″.

1224 MENDELSSOHN, FELIX (1809–1847).

Portrait painted for the Musician Series, begun Feb. 28th, 1863, finished March 30th, 1863. Head. Price, $30.00

1225 MENGE, MR.

Of James River, Virginia. Portrait noted in register as " a copy," begun June 21st, 1832, finished July 13th, 1832. Bust. Price, $100.00

1226 MENGE, MRS.

Mother of Mrs. Bolling, of Virginia. Portrait begun June 22nd, 1832, finished July 12th, 1832. Bust. Price, $100.00

1227 MERCER, MARGARET (1791–1846).

Was the daughter of John F. Mercer, Governor of Maryland, 1801–1803. After her father's death she freed all her slaves and sent them to Liberia, thereby reducing herself to poverty. Bust, head slightly to left, wearing lace headdress, hair parted in middle and hand supporting head. Portrait painted after her death from a daguerreotype, begun May 16th, 1848, finished June 2nd, 1848. Size 20″ × 24″. Signed on back of canvas " TS 1848."
Price, $80.00

Painted for Colonization Society and now in Pennsylvania Historical Society.

1228 MEREDITH, WILLIAM TUCKEY (1772–1844).

Born in Philadelphia and admitted to the Bar in 1795. He married Gertrude Gouverneur Ogden, a niece of Gouverneur Morris. Head, slightly to left, black stock and high coat collar. Portrait painted for the Schuylkill Bank of which he was president. Begun Aug. 13th, 1833, finished Sept. 2nd, 1833. Head. Price, $60.00
Engraved by Samuel Sartain for Simpson's Eminent Philadelphians.

1229 MEREDITH, WILLIAM TUCKEY (1772–1844).

Portrait painted for Mrs. Ogden, begun Jan. 10th, 1835, finished Feb. 10th, 1835. Bust. Price, $100.00

1230 MEREDITH, MRS. WILLIAM (1777–1828).

(Was Gertrude G. Ogden.) Bust, seated with hands in lap, white low-neck dress with cloak over shoulder. Portrait begun Oct. 28th, 1808, finished Dec. 22nd, 1808. Size 35½″ W. × 29½″ H. Price, $50.00
Gift of Misses Catharine M. and Sarah C. Biddle to the Pennsylvania Historical Society, Philadelphia.

1231 MEREDITH, MRS.

Outline drawn for Tom to continue. Bust, begun Sept. 20th, 1833, finished Oct. 18th, 1833. Price, $60.00

1232 MERREFIELD, MRS. JOSEPH.

(Née Miss Rebe Janney, of Baltimore.) Portrait begun Feb. 1st, 1849, finished March 7th, 1849. Size 29" × 36". Price, $200.00

1233 MESSCHERT, MRS. MATTHEW HINZINGA (1822–1884).

(Née Miss Mary Ann McKenty.) Portrait begun March 2nd, 1859, finished April 7th, 1859. Head. Price, $80.00

1234 MESSCHERT, MRS. MATTHEW HINZINGA.

Second portrait, the first not being approved, begun April 3rd, 1859, finished May 6th, 1859. Head. Price, $80.00

1235 MESSCHERT, MISS ELIZABETH ALBERTINE.

Painted for her father; she married John Blackwood Grant, of Douglasville, Pa. She was the daughter of No. 1233. Portrait begun April 25th, 1871, finished May 10th, 1871. Size 25" × 30". Price, $100.00

1236 MESSCHERT, HINZINGA (SR.) (1808–1871).

A noted Philadelphia bon-vivant; in his latter days he grew to such an enormous size that locomotion was impossible to him. He was the last to drive about the city with a footman standing on a rack at the back of his carriage. Copied from a daguerreotype for his son Hinzinga, begun Feb. 20th, 1871, finished March 1st, 1871. Size 30" × 25". Price, $50.00

1237 METCALF, THOMAS.

Portrait painted for Dr. Dewees, begun Jan. 2nd, 1811, finished Feb. 13th, 1811. Bust. Price, $60.00

1238 MICHAEL-ANGELO.

Painted from an engraving for the Artist Series, begun Jan. 26th, 1872, unfinished. Head. Price, $50.00

1239 MIDDLETON, MISS.

Portrait begun Nov. 27th, 1856, finished Dec. 4th, 1856. Head. Price, $100.00

1240 MIDDLETON, MRS. A.

Of South Carolina. Portrait begun April 6th, 1816, finished Sept., 1816. Size 29" × 36". Price, $150.00

LIST OF PAINTINGS

1241 MIDDLETON, MISS, AND HER SISTER.

Painted for their father, who afterwards countermanded it, begun Dec. 11th, 1856, finished Jan. 6th, 1857. Bust. Price, $150.00

1242 MIDDLETON, MRS. HENRY.

Of Charleston, South Carolina. Portrait painted for her son, it was begun Oct. 10th, 1831, finished Dec. 10th, 1831. Bust. Price, $80.00

This painting with the house in which it hung was burnt during the Rebellion. A copy by an unknown artist is owned by Mr. Evan Kane, of Kane, Penna.

1243 MIDDLETON, MRS. JOHN IZARD.

Half length, head to left, with curls, low-necked dress, holds book in hands. Column and curtain in background. Portrait begun July 1st, 1826, finished on July 25th, 1826. Size 27½" × 36", canvas. Price, $75.00

Reproduced in "One Hundred Early American Paintings," Ehrich Galleries, New York, 1918. Small oil study owned by Mrs. S. H. Thomas, Philadelphia.

NOTE.—Miercken, Miss Catherine. See Mrs. Myers.

1244 MILLER, GENERAL JAMES (1776–1851).

Entered the army in 1808 as Major of the 4th Infantry, and saw important service in the War of 1812. At the battle of Lundy's Lane he captured a British battery; for this service he was brevetted Brigadier General, and received a gold medal from Congress. Drawing made for design of congressional medal Sept., 1817. Size 6" × 6". Price, $50.00

1245 MILLER, GENERAL JAMES (1776–1851).

Design for medal awarded by Congress to General Miller. Size 10" × 12". Begun Oct. 25th, 1822, finished Oct. 8th, 1822. Price, $50.00

1246 MILLER, JOHN L.

(Merchant.) Portrait begun March 24th, 1835, finished April 3rd, 1835. Head. Price, $80.00

1247 MILLER, DR. SAMUEL (1769–1850).

Presbyterian clergyman, associate pastor of First Presbyterian Church of New York City from 1793 to 1813. Afterwards became professor in Princeton Theological Seminary. Portrait begun May 22nd, 1812, finished June 21st, 1812. Size 29" × 36". Price, $100.00

Owned by his grandson, E. Rittenhouse Miller, of Germantown, Philadelphia.

1248 MILLER, GEORGE (d. 1819).

(Or Müller.) He was a German potter, stone-cutter and modeller, he became an Academician of the Pennsylvania Academy of Fine Arts, and produced a bas-relief of Washington in 1798, and of Thomas Jefferson. Portrait begun May 8th, 1815, finished May 30th, 1815. Head. Price, $50.00

1249 MILLER, MRS.

(Née Miss Wheatly.) Of New York. Portrait begun Dec. 2nd, 1854, finished Jan. 15th, 1855. Head. Price, $80.00

1250 MILLER, MRS.

Of Tennessee. Portrait begun Aug. 9th, 1845, finished Aug. 18th, 1845. Size 20″ × 24″. Price, $80.00

1251 MILTON, AND HIS DAUGHTER.

Copied from a smaller picture, executed for Mr. Merredith, Jan., 1816. Engraved by P. Maverick (F. 1030). Price, $50.00

1252 MINIS, SARAH ANNA (1811–1884).

Of Savannah, Georgia. Married Dr. Isaac Hays, of Philadelphia. (Her mother was D. Cohen.) Portrait begun Oct. 14, 1833, finished Nov. 26th, 1833. Head to left, dark hair, low-necked dress. Signed on back " TS 1833." Head, size 17″ × 20″. Price, $80.00
Owned by Mrs. Goodrich, of Princeton, N. J.

1253 MINOR, MISS CATHERINE.

Of Natchez, Miss. Portrait begun June 15th, 1816, finished October 19th, 1816. Size 29″ × 36″. Price, $150.00
Owned by Miss Kate Minor, Southdown Plantation, Houma, La.

1254 MINOR, MISS FANNY.

Of Natchez, Miss. Portrait begun June 15th, 1816, finished Oct. 19th, 1816. Size 29 × 36″. Price, $150.00
Owned by Mrs. Paul Robelot, Sr., New Orleans, La.

1255 MITCHELL, ELIZABETH TYNDALE.

Married Edward P. Mitchell, and their son, James Tyndale Mitchell, was Chief Justice of the Supreme Court of Pennsylvania. Portrait painted for her husband. begun Dec. 20th, 1853, finished Dec. 31st, 1853. Head.
Price, $80.00

1256 MITCHELL, MISS SALLY.

Portrait begun May, 1805, finished June, 1805. Size 12″ × 10″.
Price, $15.00

1257 MITCHELL, WALTON T.

Portrait of a child, copied from a daguerreotype, begun Feb. 2nd, 1854, finished April 10th, 1854. Son of Edward P. Mitchell who died as a child, and a younger brother of Judge James T. Mitchell. Head. Price, $80.00

1258 MITCHELL, WALTON T.

Head of a child, being a copy of the former portrait, begun Feb. 10th, 1854, finished Feb. 24th, 1854. Head. Price, $80.00

1259 MOALE, SAMUEL.

Lawyer. Portrait begun March 13th, 1823, finished March 31st, 1823. Bust. Price, $100.00

1260 MONROE, JAMES (1758–1831).

Statesman and Fifth President of the United States. Married Miss Kortright, of New York. Head to right, white stock, high coat collar. The register states it was painted for the Military Academy at West Point; owned by Monroe's great-granddaughter, begun June 12th, 1829, finished June 17th, 1829. Head. Price, $50.00
Reproduced in Centennial of Washington's Inauguration, by Bowen.

1261 MONROE, JAMES (1758–1831).

Ex-President of the United States, painted for the United States Military Academy at West Point. Portrait begun Feb. 3rd, 1832, finished on Sept. 12th, 1832. Full length, standing in stone entrance, landscape in background, looking to the right, military cloak and sword. Size 58″ × 94″.
Price, $600.00
Reproduced in Centennial of Washington's Inauguration, by Bowen.
Owned by Military Academy of West Point.

1262 MONROE, JAMES (1758–1831).

Study or copy of head, signed "S" or "E. S. 1829." It is recorded as "presented by the Sully family to the Pennsylvania Colonization Society." It has been attributed to Thomas Sully, but is probably largely the work of his daughter Ellen, retouched by her father. It is painted on mill board 20″ × 24″. Head to left, high coat collar and white stock.
Owned by the City of Philadelphia and deposited at Independence Hall.

1263 MONROE, MRS.

(Sister to Mrs. Cruger, of New York.) Portrait begun May 4th, 1843, finished May 13th, 1843. Head. Price, $80.00

233

LIST OF PAINTINGS

1264 MONROE, MISS FANNY.

Portrait painted for her uncle, W. Douglas. Begun Dec. 29th, 1843, finished Jan. 15th, 1844. Bust. Price, $100.00

1265 MONROE, MRS. JAMES.

This portrait is recorded as painted for Mrs. Monroe's brother, Mr. Douglas, and is probably no relative of President James Monroe. Begun Dec. 27th, 1843, finished Jan. 10th, 1844. Bust. Price, $100.00

1266 MONTGOMERY, REV. JAMES, D. D. (1787–1834).

Born at Princeton, N. J. Admitted to the bar, and entered the ministry under Bishop White, whose granddaughter he married. Rector to St. Stephen's Church, Philadelphia. Portrait painted for Dr. Wiltbank, begun June 5th, 1833, finished June 18th, 1833. Bust, nearly full face, in clerical robes, wearing spectacles. Engraved by John Sartain. Bust. Price, $100.00

1267 MONTGOMERY, MISS MARY (1794–1865).

Married Dr. Charles D. Meigs, March 5th, 1815. Bust, facing left. Portrait begun March 2nd, 1815, finished April 27th, 1815. This picture was retouched by Sully in 1837.
Owned by Miss Emily W. Biddle, of Philadelphia.

1268 MONTGOMERY, MR. JOHN CRATHORNE.

Portrait painted for Mrs. Phillips, begun March 6th, 1818, finished on April 24th, 1818. Size 29″ × 36″. Price, $150.00
This portrait was owned by Austin J. Montgomery, of Philadelphia.

1269 MONTGOMERY, MRS. JOHN CRATHORNE.

Portrait begun June 1st, 1815, finished July 3rd, 1815. Bust. Price, $80.00
This portrait was owned by Austin J. Montgomery, of Philadelphia.

1270 MOORE, MRS.

Of Baltimore. Portrait begun April 14th, 1804, finished June 4th, 1804. Price, $12.00

1271 MORDECAI, ALFRED (1804–1887).

Graduated in 1823 at United States Military Academy, West Point. He attained the rank of major and resigned at the breaking out of the Rebellion, being a North Carolinian by birth. Portrait begun March 7th, 1836, finished March 24th, 1836. Painted when he was at the Frankford Arsenal, Philadelphia. Head to right, signed " TS March, 1836." Size 17″ × 20″. Price, $100.00
Owned by the Misses Mordecai, of Philadelphia.

1272 MOREAU, GENERAL JEAN VICTOR (1763–1813).

French soldier, exiled by Napoleon. Came to America and settled at Morrisville, Bucks Co., Penna. Copied from a miniature. Portrait begun Jan. 5th, 1815, finished Jan. 16th, 1815. Bust.   Price, $80.00

1273 MORGAN, BENJAMIN R. (1765–1840).

A prominent lawyer of Philadelphia. Painted for Mr. Rawle, begun March 7th, 1808, finished April 25th, 1808. Bust. (Subscriber.)   Price, $30.00
Owned by Herbert Norris, M. D., of Philadelphia.

1274 MORGAN, MRS. THOMAS GIBBES.

(Née Sarah Fowler.) (Married second time Francis W. Dawson.) The portrait by Sully was cut from the frame during the Civil War, when the house at Baton Rouge, Louisiana, was damaged by the Union troops. Illustrated in " Confederate Girl's Diary," by Sarah Morgan, Dawson, 1913.
The authors have not been able to see the original painting.

1275 MORRIS, GASPER.

Portrait begun Nov. 17th, 1808, and finished Feb. 6th, 1809. Bust. (Subscriber.)   Price, $50.00

1276 MORRIS, GASPER.

Copied from portrait painted in 1809, begun copy May 20th, 1828, finished June 14th, 1828. Bust.   Price, $75.00

1277 MORRIS, MRS. GASPER.

Portrait begun March 24th, 1808, finished May1 2th, 1808. Bust. (Subscriber.)   Price, $30.00

1278 MORRIS, GOUVERNEUR (1752–1816).

Member of Constitutional Convention, 1787. Minister to France, 1792. Elected United States Senator, April, 1800. Portrait seated, head to left, arm extended on table. Begun March 16th, 1808, finished April 19th, 1808. Size 35½" W. × 29½" H.   Subscriber's price, $30.00
This portrait was painted for William T. Meredith, who married a niece of Gouverneur Morris. Engraved by J. B. Longacre (Spark's Life of Morris).
Gift of Misses Catharine M. and Sarah C. Biddle to the Pennsylvania Historical Society, Philadelphia.

1279 MORRIS, GOUVERNEUR (1752–1816).

Half length, seated before table, head nearly full face to right, hand resting on arm of chair. Likeness taken from first portrait, but portrait otherwise entirely different. Begun July 15th, 1808, finished April 19th, 1808. Size 44" × 56".   Price, $100.00
Painting owned by grandchildren at Morrisania, N. Y. Illustrated in Bowen, Centennial Washington Inauguration, 1892.

LIST OF PAINTINGS

1280 MORRIS, ROBERT (1734–1806).

Signer of the Declaration of Independence and financier of the American Revolution. Copy by Bass Otis from Gilbert Stuart's original. Sully's register notes retouching it, but he probably repainted a large part of it as he received $120.00 for it. Painted in 1824. Size 25″ × 30″.

Presented by Miss Nixon to the Pennsylvania Historical Society.

1281 MORRIS, MRS. ROBERT.

Of New Jersey. After the death of his first wife Robert Morris moved to Philadelphia and married a widow named Newman, who had resided in Burlington, New Jersey.

Owned by F. H. Bosworth, of New York, and exhibited at Portrait Exhibition of Women, New York, 1894.

1282 MORRIS, MRS. THOMAS (1778–1853).

(Née Sally Kane.) Married Thomas Morris, second son of Robert Morris, May 28th, 1799. Portrait painted in New York, begun July 21st, 1814, finished August, 1814. Bust, head to left, curls on forehead and headdress.

Owned by C. F. M. Stark, of Dunbarton, New Hampshire.

1283 MORRIS, THOMAS W. (1778–1840).

Philadelphia brewer. Portrait begun Jan. 24th, 1825, finished February 15th, 1826. Bust.   Price, $60.00

Owned by T. Morris Perot, of Philadelphia.

1284 MORRIS, T. B.

Of South Street, Philadelphia. Portrait begun Feb. 14th, 1823, finished March 7th, 1823. Bust.   Price, $100.00

1285 MORRIS, MRS. T. B.

Of South Street, Philadelphia. Portrait begun Dec. 30th, 1822, finished Jan. 11th, 1823. Bust.   Price, $100.00

1286 MORRISON, MRS. ANNE (1798–1866).

Of Arch Street, Philadelphia. She was Miss Anne Dawson. Portrait begun Jan. 16th, 1839, finished Feb. 19th, 1839. Bust, facing right. Size 25″ × 30″.   Price, $200.00

Owned by Mrs. Frederick Collins, Philadelphia.

1287 MORTON, GEORGE.

Painted in Baltimore, begun Dec. 2nd, 1822, finished Dec. 14th, 1822. Bust.   Price, $100.00

LIST OF PAINTINGS

1288 MORTON, WASHINGTON.

Prominent lawyer of New York, married Cornelia Schuyler. Painted for Mrs. Philip Schuyler, begun June 24th, 1807, finished July 10th, 1807. Head. Price, $30.00

1289 MORTON, MRS. WASHINGTON.

Was Cornelia Schuyler, daughter of Philip J. Schuyler, Esq., begun June 26th, 1807, finished July 19th, 1807. Head. Price, $30.00

1290 MOSES, SOLOMON.

Of New York City, married Miss Rachel Gratz, of Philadelphia, in 1806. Portrait begun on Nov. 1st, 1808, and finished Nov. 11th, 1808. Bust. Price, $50.00

1291 MOSHER, MR.

(Son of Mrs. Mosher, of Georgetown, D. C.) Painted in Baltimore, begun Feb. 22nd, 1853, finished March 6th, 1853. Bust. Price, $150.00

1292 MOSHER, MRS. ELIZA.

Portrait painted at Baltimore. (Mother of Mrs. Caperton.) Painting begun Feb. 21st, 1853, finished March 11th, 1853. Bust. Price, $150.00

1293 MOZART, JOHANN (1756–1791).

Celebrated German musical composer. Copied from a print from Teischbein's portrait, begun Oct. 7th, 1862, finished Oct. 8th, 1862. Size 17″ × 12″. Price, $30.00

1294 MUHLENBERG, REV. HENRY MELCHIOR (1711–1787).

Celebrated Lutheran clergyman, born in Hanover, Germany, died at Trappe, Montgomery Co., Penna. Deceased, painted from portrait by C. W. Peale. The copy by Sully begun Jan. 3rd, 1814, finished Jan. 18th, 1814. Bust. Price, $100.00

1295 MUHLENBERG, REV. HENRY MELCHIOR (1711–1787).

Copy made by Sully from his first painting for Mr. Sheaf, begun Jan. 21st, 1814, finished Jan. 28th, 1814. Bust. Price, $100.00

1296 MUMFORD, MRS.

Of Schenectady. For Harding Page. Portrait begun June 5th, 1858, finished June 21st, 1858. Bust. Price, $100.00

1297 MURDOCK, MRS.

Portrait painted at Baltimore (sister of Alexander Trumbull), begun Dec. 6th, 1852, finished Dec. 22nd, 1852. Head. Price, $100.00

1298 MURDOCK, MARGARETTA.
Portrait begun Jan. 26th, 1811, finished Feb. 6th, 1811. Size 29″ × 36″.
Price, $70.00

1299 MUTTER, MRS.
Portrait begun Dec. 15th, 1842, finished Dec. 23rd, 1842. Head.
Subscriber's price, $50.00

1300 MYERS, MR.
Of Norfolk, Virginia. Portrait begun March 18th, 1808, finished April 30th, 1808. Bust. (Subscriber.)
Price, $30.00

1301 MYERS, GUSTAVUS (1801–1869).
Of Virginia. A distinguished lawyer and British Consul, 1861–65. Bust. head to left, long curling hair. Size 21″ × 25″. Signed " TS 1865."
Owned by his granddaughter, Mrs. John H. Morgan, Brooklyn, N. Y.

1302 MYERS, GUSTAVUS (1801–1869).
Portrait painted for his family, begun Nov. 8th, 1850, finished on Jan. 31st, 1851. Head.
Price, $100.00

1303 MYERS, JOHN (——, d. 1844).
Portrait begun Feb. 30th, 1814, finished April 1st, 1814. Size 29″ × 36″.
Price, $100.00

Owned by Mrs. Dr. Laws, Washington, D. C.

1304 MYERS, MRS. JOHN (1796–1874).
Formerly Miss Catherine Miercken, daughter of Captain Peter Miercken. Portrait begun Jan. 23rd, 1814, finished March, 1814. Size 29″ × 36″.
Price, $100.00

Owned by Mrs. Dr. Laws, Washington, D. C.

1305 NAPOLEON.
Copied for William Allston, of Georgetown, begun Dec. 31st, 1825, finished April 6th, 1826. Bust.
Price, $60.00

1306 NEAGLE, ELIZABETH.
Portrait painted for her brother, Garrett C. Neagle. Portrait begun April 12th, 1867, finished April 20th, 1867. Size 20″ × 24″.
Price, $30.00

1307 NEAGLE, GARRETT CROSS.
His mother was the daughter of Thomas Sully's brother Lawrence. Portrait begun Jan. 21st, 1866, finished Feb. 10th, 1866. Head. Price, $30.00

1308 NEAGLE, MARY.

Portrait painted for her brother, Garrett C. Neagle. Painting begun May 9th, 1867, finished May 21st, 1867. Size 20″ × 24″. Price, $30.00

1309 NEAGLE, SARAH SULLY.

Portrait painted for her brother, Garrett C. Neagle. Sarah Neagle married the Rev. S. F. Hotchkin, portrait begun April 8th, 1867, finished Nov. 7th, 1867. Bust, in black dress. Size 20″ × 24″. Signed " TS 1867."
Price, $30.00
Owned by Miss Sarah Sully Rawlins, Philadelphia.

1310 NEAGLE, SUSAN.

Portrait painted for her brother, Garrett C. Neagle. Painting begun April 23rd, 1867, finished May 1st, 1867. Bust, nearly full face. Size 20″ × 24″. Signed " TS 1867." Price, $30.00
Owned by Miss Sarah Sully Rawlins, Philadelphia.

1311 NEILSON, J. C.

Of Baltimore, Md. Portrait begun Nov. 4th, 1818, finished Dec. 4th, 1818. Bust. Price, $100.00

1312 NEILSON, MISS.

Painted for Mrs. Mallon, begun May 9th, 1814, finished May 20th, 1814. Bust. Price, $70.00

1313 NEILSON, MISS.

Deceased, copied from portrait painted in 1814. This copy begun May 20th, 1818, finished May 30th, 1818. Bust. Price, $100.00

1314 NEILSON, MISS.

A second copy, painted for her brother, begun May 20th, 1818, and finished May 31st, 1818. Bust. Price, $100.00

1315 NEWBOLD, MRS. AND HER CHILD.

Portrait begun Feb. 4th, 1813, finished July 25th, 1813. Size 25″ × 30″. Price, $200.00

1316 NEWBOLD, MARY.

And her lap dog, whole length. Portrait begun Jan. 2nd, 1816, finished Jan. 26th, 1816. Size 29″ × 36″. Price, $150.00

1317 NEWMAN, MISS MARY.

(Married John W. Andrews.) Half length, portrait begun Jan. 21st, 1832, finished April 24th, 1832. Price, $200.00
Owned by her granddaughter, Mrs. William Du Pont, Bellevue, Del.

1318 NONES, MISS.

Painted for Miss Mose, begun April 17th, 1815, finished May 22nd, 1815.
Bust.   Price, $80.00

1319 NORRIS, WILLIAM (1802–1867).

Bust, seated, facing right. Similar to portrait in 1830, begun July 21st,
1837, finished August 1st, 1837. Size 25″ × 30″.   Price, $200.00
Owned by Mrs. Frank T. Patterson, Philadelphia.

1320 NORRIS, MRS. WILLIAM (1803–1865).

Bust, in low-necked black dress with white fur or swansdown scarf over
shoulders. Portrait begun Feb. 8th, 1830, finished March 12th, 1830. Size
25″ × 30″. She was Mary Anne Heide, of Baltimore, Md.   Price, $75.00
Owned by G. Heide Norris, of Philadelphia.

1321 NORRIS, MRS. WILLIAM (1803–1865).

She was Mary Anne Heide, of Baltimore, Md. Portrait begun Feb. 23rd,
1839, finished March 9th, 1839 (also painted in 1830). Bust, size 25″ ×
30″.   Price, $200.00
Owned by Mrs. Frank T. Patterson, Philadelphia.

1322 NORRIS, WILLIAM (1802–1867).

Bust, seated facing right. Founder of the Norris Locomotive Works in
Philadelphia. He was a member of the Archery Club of the " United Bowmen." He was formerly of Baltimore. Portrait begun Jan. 18th, 1830, finished Feb. 22nd, 1830. Size 25″ × 30″.   Price, $75.00
Owned by Mr. G. Heide Norris, Philadelphia.

1323 NOTT, MRS.

Wife of Professor Nott, of Wisconsin. Portrait begun April 10th, 1854,
finished Dec. 30th, 1854. Bust.   Price, $100.00

1324 NUGENT, MR.

Painted for Mr. Wagner, begun May 17th, 1827, finished June 26th, 1827.
Bust.   Price, $75.00

1325 OGDEN, SAMUEL G.

(Painted for Beekman and Morton.) Begun Feb. 3rd, 1807, finished
March 10th, 1807. Bust.   Price, $30.00

LIST OF PAINTINGS

1326 O'NEILL, MRS.

Of 424 Coates St. (below 5th St.), Philadelphia. Portrait begun May 31st, 1865, finished Feb. 3rd, 1866. Bust. Price, $50.00

1327 O'NEILL, ELIZABETH (1791–1872).

Actress born in Ireland, withdrew from the stage on marriage with W. Wrixon Becher, M. P. Painted from a sketch. Head, nearly full face, lace scarf head dress, low-necked gown. Size 17″ × 14″. Portrait begun May 17th, 1822, finished May 25th, 1822. Price, $30.00

Owned by the Pennsylvania Historical Society.

1328 ORCUTT, REV. JOHN.

Portrait painted for Colonization Society. Begun Jan. 15th, 1868, finished Jan. 27th, 1868. Size 30″ × 24″. Price, $80.00

NOTE.—Portrait not among the Society's collection at the Pennsylvania Historical Society.

1329 ORNE, JAMES (1790–1852).

Head of the house of J. and B. Orne, on Chestnut Street above Fifth Street, Philadelphia. Painted from a daguerreotype, portrait begun Sept. 22nd, 1853, finished Oct. 22nd, 1853. Bust, head to left, black stock and white shirt front, black coat and black satin waistcoat. Size 24″ × 30″. Price, $100.00

Owned by James Orne McHenry, Esq., Philadelphia.

1330 OSBORNE, MRS.

Of New York, sister to Mrs. Furnace. Portrait begun Dec. 19th, 1826, finished Jan., 1827. Bust. Price, $75.00

1331 OTEY, JAMES HERVEY (1800–1863).

Episcopal Bishop of Tennessee in 1834. He was the founder of the University at Suwanee, Tenn. Portrait begun Oct. 18th, 1844, finished Dec. 5th, 1844. Size 25″ × 30″. Price, $250.00

1332 OTTO, MR.

Portrait begun May 1st, 1809, finished May 11th, 1809. Size 20″ × 24″. Price, $50.00

1333 PAGE, MRS.

The register notes that the " Page " was of the " house of Potter and Page," Portrait begun Oct. 9th, 1808, finished Nov. 1st, 1808. Small size. Price, $40.00

1334 PAGE, MISS MARGARET SARAH.

Married John Grew, of Boston. Sully registers the painting as for Mr. Page, of Potter and Page, of Philadelphia. Begun June 5th, 1810, finished Oct. 4th, 1810. Panel size 25″ × 30″. Bust of young girl, head to right, hands in lap, vase of flowers shown to right.   Price, $70.00

Presented to Pennsylvania Academy of Fine Arts by descendants of the family who recognize the portrait as the Miss Page painted by Sully and noted in the register.

1335 PAGEOT, MADAME.

Portrait of her mother, begun Aug. 2nd, 1845. The register notes " copy put by and another begun." Bust.

1336 PAGEOT, MADAME.

Portrait of her mother, begun Oct, 23rd, 1845, finished Nov. 4th, 1845. Bust.   Price, $150.00

1337 PAINE, THOMAS (1737–1809).

The register notes that it was " copied from Jarvis and sold to him." This was probably a copy from the Romney portrait engraved by William Sharp. Painting begun Nov. 19th, 1807, finished Nov. 23rd, 1807. Bust.
                    Price, $30.00

1338 PARKE, DR. THOMAS.

Eminent Philadelphia physician and a founder of the College of Physicians, he left a bequest to the Philadelphia Library Company. Half length, seated before table holding paper in hand, head three-quarters to left, brown coat, drab background. Size 29″ × 36″. Portrait begun July 8th, 1822, finished July 31st, 1822.   Price, $150.00

Owned by the Library Company of Philadelphia.

1339 PARKER, MISS LIZZIE.

Of Media, Pa, Portrait begun Oct. 6th, 1866, finished Nov. 3rd, 1866. Head.   Price, $80.00

1340 PARSONS, MISS C.

" Lady of the Lake." Painted for James McMurtrie, begun March 4th, 1812, finished April 25th, 1812. Size 52″ × 41″.   Price, $300.00

Exhibited at Artist Fund Society.

1341 PARSONS, MISS C.

Study for " Lady of the Lake." Begun March 14th, 1812, finished April 2nd, 1812. Size 17″ × 20″.   Price, $50.00

NOTE.—Paton, Mary Anne. See Mrs. Joseph Wood.

LIST OF PAINTINGS

1342 PATTERSON, JOSEPH.

Portrait begun April 11th, 1821, finished May 30th, 1821. Bust.
Price, $100.00

1343 PATTERSON, JOSEPH.

Second portrait, begun June 11th, 1821, finished June 19th, 1821. Bust·
Price, $100.00

1344 PATTERSON, MRS. JOSEPH.

(Née Charlotte Graham Nicols.) She married Joseph Patterson the
brother of Mme. Patterson-Bonaparte. Bust, seated in chair, she wears a
low-necked Empire gown, head to left, hair arranged with curls. Portrait
begun June 4th, 1821, finished June 26th, 1821. Bust. Price, $100.00
Reproduced in Century Magazine, Vol. 53, page 817.
Owned by Mrs. Worthington Ross.

1345 PATTERSON, ROBERT MASKELL (1787–1854).

Dr. Patterson was President of the Musical Fund Society, 1838 to 1853.
Portrait begun March 10th, 1856, finished March 17th, 1856. Bust, head
slightly to right, white collar turned down over a black stock. Size 29″ ×
36″, signed on back " TS 1856," and noted as copy from portrait by S. F.
De Bois at American Philosophical Society. Price, $100.00
Owned by Musical Fund Society, Philadelphia.

1346 PATTERSON, WILLIAM (1752–1835).

Merchant of Baltimore, whose daughter Elizabeth married Jerome Bonaparte. Signed and dated as painted in 1821. Bust, head to left, black coat
with brass buttons, white waistcoat. Size 25″ × 30″.
Owned by the Maryland Historical Society, Baltimore, Md. Exhibited in
1921 at Maryland Institute.

1347 PAUL, MRS, JAMES W.

She was Hannah C. Bunker, daughter of Nathan Bunker, of Philadelphia.
and mother of Mrs. William Waldorf Astor. Portrait begun Dec. 2nd, 1844,
finished Dec. 16th, 1844. Head. Price, $80.00
Was owned by Mr. Frank W. Paul, of Villa Nova, Penna.

1348 PAYNE, MR.

Of Warrenton, Va. Portrait begun Feb. 20th, 1854, finished Feb. 26th,
1854. Bust. Price, $100.00

1349 PAYNE, MRS.

(Née Miss Semmes.) Of Warrenton, Va. Portrait painted in Baltimore,
begun March 16th, 1853, finished March 26th, 1853. Head. Price, $100.00

1350 PEACOCK, MR.

Of Germantown, Philadelphia. Begun Aug. 14th, 1832, finished Aug. 24th, 1832. Head. Price, $60.00

1351 PEALE, FRANKLIN (1795–1870).

Son of Charles Willson Peale, was appointed to the United States Mint in 1833, becoming chief coiner in 1839. He was President of the Musical Fund Society, 1869 to 1870. Bust, head slightly to right, wearing full beard. Size 29″ × 36″, begun Feb. 1st, 1868, finished Feb. 21st, 1868.
Price, $100.00
Owned by the Musical Fund Society, Philadelphia.

1352 PEALE, REMBRANDT (1778–1860).

Son of Charles Willson Peale, he showed an early talent for art, and at seventeen painted a portrait of George Washington from life, and numerous other portraits and figure compositions. This portrait was painted for Mr. Joseph Harrison, of Philadelphia, begun April 23rd, 1859, finished June 15th, 1859. Price, $80.00
Owned by Mrs. Sabin W. Colton, of Philadelphia.

1353 PEALE, REMBRANDT (1778–1860).

Painted in Baltimore for the Museum, begun April 10th, 1820, finished April 26th, 1820. Head. Price, $50.00

1354 PEARCE, MRS. G.

Copied from a miniature, begun Sept. 17th, 1807, finished Oct. 14th, 1807. Bust. Price, $50.00

1355 PENDLETON, JUDGE EDMUND (1721–1803).

Statesman and member of the first Continental Congress. Portrait painted from a miniature for Mr. Taylor, begun Feb. 5th, 1854, finished Feb. 14th, 1854. Bust. Price, $100.00
Owned by the Virginia Historical Society, Richmond, Va.

1356 PENN, WILLIAM (1644–1718).

Painted for the Marquis of Townsend, begun Dec. 11th, 1807, finished Jan. 2nd, 1808. Bust. Price, $50.00

1357 PENN, WILLIAM (1644–1718).

Copied from Penn statue in the yard of the Pennsylvania Hospital, Philadelphia. Begun Feb. 10th, 1824, finished Sept. 8th, 1824. Size 29″ × 36″. Price, $80.00

LIST OF PAINTINGS

1358 PENN-GASKELL, ISAAC (1810–1842).

Philadelphia physician, son of Peter Penn-Gaskell. Half length, standing, one hand in trousers pocket, the other gloved, dark brown coat, facing left. Size 28″ × 36″.
Owned by Mrs. James Hancock and Miss Hall, Philadelphia.

1359 PENN-GASKELL, PETER (1763–1831).

Half length, seated, facing right, before a red curtain, he holds a book in his hand. Size 28″ × 36″. Came from England late in the eighteenth century. The Penn-Gaskells were lineal descendants of the founder of Pennsylvania through his eldest son and only child by first wife, Gulielma Maria Springett.
Owned by Mrs. James Hancock and Miss Hall, Philadelphia.

1360 PENN-GASKELL, MRS. PETER (1772–1834).

Was Elizabeth Edwards. Half length, seated, facing front, in red upholstered chair with bible and spectacles, she wears a cap tied under the chin. Size 28″ × 36″.
Owned by Mrs. James Hancock and Miss Hall, Philadelphia.

1361 PENN-GASKELL, MISS JANE (1808–1832).

Daughter of Peter Penn-Gaskell. Portrait painted for Mr. Hall, begun April 17th, 1829, finished May 22nd, 1829. Bust, seated, facing front, low-necked rose-colored bodice, short sleeves, holds a rose at her breast. Size 25″ × 30″.
Owned by Mrs. James Hancock and Miss Hall, Philadelphia.

1362 PENN-GASKELL, WILLIAM.

Portrait painted when a boy about eight years old. On wood panel.
Owned by Mrs. James Hancock and Miss Hall, Philadelphia.

NOTE.—The portrait of Thomas Penn-Gaskell (1796–1847). Half length, size 28″ × 36″, which has been attributed to Thomas Sully, was painted by Henry Inman. It is owned by Mrs. James Hancock, Philadelphia.

1363 PERENNAEN, MR.

Portrait painted for his sister, begun April 18th, 1842, finished April 26th, 1842. Head.   Price, $150.00

1364 PERINE, MR.

Portrait painted for his son Glen, at Baltimore, begun Nov. 5th, 1852, finished Nov. 6th, 1852. Size 20″ × 24″.   Price, $100.00

1365 PERKINS, THOMAS HANDASYDE (1764–1854).

A prominent merchant and philanthropist of Boston and a generous contributor to the Athenaeum where the portrait is now hanging. Whole length, size 58″ × 94″. Portrait begun July 7th, 1831, finished May 18th, 1832.
Price, $600.00
Owned by the Boston Athenaeum.

1366 PERKINS, MRS.

From New Orleans. Portrait begun June 25th, 1846, finished July 9th, 1846. Bust.
Price, $100.00

1367 PETERS, MISS ELIZA W. S.

(Afterwards Mrs. John W. Field.) Bust, facing right. Signed on back " TS 1841." Size 32″ × 44″. Painting begun Jan. 28th, 1841, finished Feb. 11th, 1841.
Price, $200.00
Bequeathed by John W. Field to the Penna. Academy of Fine Arts.

1368 PETERS, RICHARD (1704–1776).

Dr. Peters was born in England and came to Philadelphia, where in 1762 he became rector of the United Churches of Christ and St. Peter's. This portrait was painted for St. Peter's Church, begun Dec. 1st, 1862, finished Dec. 25th, 1862, was copied from an old picture. Size 25″ × 30″.
Price, $50.00

1369 PETIGRU, MISS CAROLINE (1819–   ).

Daughter of James Lewis Petigru, married William A. Carson in 1840, she was an artist of considerable merit. The portrait was painted in Charleston, S. C., begun Dec. 6th, 1841, finished Dec. 21st, 1841. Size 29″ × 36″.
Price, $300.00
Owned by her son, James Carson, and exhibited at Charleston, S. C., 1901.

1370 PETIGRU, JAMES LEWIS (1789–1863).

Statesman and lawyer of South Carolina. Portrait painted for his daughter, Mrs. William A. Carson, begun March 11th, 1842, finished March 19th, 1842. Head.
Price, $150.00
Owned by his grandson, James Carson. (Now in the Gibbes Art Gallery, Charleston, S. C.)

1371 PHILIPS, MISS ELIZABETH HENRIETTA (1797–1850).

She was the daughter of Henry and Sophia Chew Philips, and married J. Montgomery. Portrait begun February 5th, 1812, finished March 14th, 1812. Size 29″ × 36″.
Price, $100.00
Picture was owned by her son, Austin W. Montgomery, of Philadelphia.

LIST OF PAINTINGS

1372 PHYSICK, DR. PHILIP SYNG (1768–1837).

Eminent Philadelphia physician, graduated from the University of Pennsylvania in 1785, and was professor of surgery and anatomy for thirteen years. Portrait painted for Dr. William P. Dewees, begun April 1st, 1809, finished June 7th, 1809. There is a chalk engraving in outline. (Stauffer, 2069.) Size 31″ × 25″. Price, $50.00

Portrait was at the United States Medical War Museum, Washington, D. C., now owned by Ehrich Galleries, New York.

1373 PHYSICK, PHILIP SYNG, M. D. (1768–1837).

He received the degree of Doctor of Medicine from the University of Pennsylvania at the early age of 18. Portrait begun May 8th, 1812, finished May 22nd, 1812. The register notes the price as $100.00, and that "the hands were introduced into the portrait." Bust.

1374 PHYSICK, PHILIP.

(Deceased.) He was the eldest son of Dr. Philip Syng Physick. This painting from a daguerreotype, the hand being introduced in the portrait. Portrait begun Feb. 8th, 1848, finished June 9th, 1848. Bust.

Price, $150.00

Owned by Mrs. Charles P. Keith, Philadelphia.

1375 PHYSICK, ELIZABETH (1773–1820).

Wife of Dr. Philip Syng Physick, was Elizabeth Emlen, this portrait was painted from a miniature, circa 1800, with the costume changed to accord with the period. Begun April 20th, 1844, finished June 18th, 1844. Head.

Price, $80.00

Formerly owned by Philip Syng Physick Conner, of Octorara, Md.

1376 PICKENS, GENERAL ANDREW (1739–1817).

A well-known General in the American Revolution, and after the close of the war he was a member of the South Carolina Legislature. Portrait painted for his grandson, begun Aug. 26th, 1835, finished Dec. 9th, 1835. Bust, in uniform. Price, $125.00

Engraved by J. B. Longacre, in the National Portrait Gallery of Distinguished Americans.

1377 PICKERING, HENRY (1781–1831).

Study of three children. Painting begun Aug. 20th, 1818, finished Sept. 5th, 1818. Bust. Price, $200.00

1378 PICOT, MRS.

Copied from a photograph for her son. Begun Feb. 23rd, 1866, finished May 5th, 1866. Size 29″ × 36″. Price, $150.00

1379 PIKE, MARINUS, W.

A carver, gilder and picture-frame maker at Sixth and North Sts., Philadelphia. Portrait begun April 10th, 1809, finished April 30th, 1809. Bust.
Price, $50.00
Owned by Mr. Snowden Samuel, Philadelphia.

1380 PIKE, MRS.

Portrait begun May 23rd, 1809, finished June 4th, 1809. Bust.
Price, $50.00
Owned by Mr. Snowden Samuel, Philadelphia.

1381 PINCKNEY, MRS. CHARLES COTESWORTH.

Wife of the prominent Episcopal minister of Charleston, S. C., was painted for Mrs. Elliott, begun Oct. 15th, 1827, finished Nov. 23rd, 1827. Size 29″ × 36″, half length, nearly full face, with turban, low-necked gown, hands crossed. Price, $120.00
Reproduced in " Two Centuries of Costumes in America," by Alice Morse Earle. Was owned by Miss M. E. Pinckney, of Blowing Rock, N. C., and exhibited in the Charleston Exhibition of 1901.

1382 PIPKIN, MR.

Deceased, painted from a miniature, portrait begun August 10th, 1826, finished December 3rd, 1826. Bust. Price, $75.00

1383 PIPKIN, MRS.

Wife of Dr. Pipkin, of Murfreesborough, North Carolina. Portrait begun Oct. 24th, 1825, finished Nov. 23rd, 1825. Size 29″ × 36″.
Price, $120.00

1384 PIPKIN, DR.

Of Murfreesborough, North Carolina. Portrait begun Oct. 10th, 1826, finished Nov. 22nd, 1826. Size 29″ × 36″. Price, $120.00

1385 PLANCHÉ, MASTER A. B.

Of New Orleans. Portrait begun for Mr. Constant on May 14th, 1825, finished June 20th, 1825. Bust. Price, $60.00

1386 PLATT, WILLIAM.

An East Indian merchant of Philadelphia and father of Charles Platt, President of the Insurance Company of North America (1878–1909). Portrait begun June 4th, 1841, finished June 14th, 1841. Head,
Price, $150.00

LIST OF PAINTINGS

1387 PLATT, MARIA TAYLOR.

She married William Platt, of Philadelphia. This portrait being painted for her daughter who was Mrs. David Pepper, begun May 4th, 1841, finished May 25th, 1841. Head. Price, $150.00

1388 POE, EDGAR ALLAN (1811–1849).

American poet and novelist. Size about 7″ × 10″. Signed " TS " on panel.

Picture was owned by I. W. Heysinger, M. D., of Philadelphia, from whose possession it passed to Alfred Percival Smith, Esq., of Philadelphia.

NOTE BY DR. H.—This portrait of Edgar Allen Poe was painted by Thomas Sully in 1839 or 1840, while Poe was residing in Philadelphia. George R. Bonfield, the artist, was well acquainted with both Poe and Sully. All three attended social meetings of artists, actors, writers, etc., in the Old Falstaff Hotel, 6th St. above Chestnut, Phila. John Sartain was also a participant. It was the fashion at this time to call Poe the American Byron, and Murray's Childe Harold edition had recently appeared (see Byron portrait), and Sully posed him, for his own pleasure, in the Byron attitude, modified by Poe's dress. James McMurtrie furnished the cloak. John Sartain says of Poe at page 215 of his " Recollections ", " Poe's face was handsome. Although his forehead when seen in profile showed a receding line from the brow up, viewed from the front it presented a broad and noble expanse, very large at and above the temples. His lips were thin and delicately moulded."

This picture alone shows these features. It is strikingly like the sketch of his mother, as shown in Joyce's " Edgar Allen Poe ", page 6. Poe wore no mustache at that time, as shown in Sully's picture.

1389 POINSETT, JOEL R. (1779–1851).

Of South Carolina, was first minister to Mexico from the United States, he was Secretary of War under Van Buren. Painted for Mr. Burns, begun June 10th, 1827, finished July 29th, 1827. Head. Price, $50.00

1390 POINSETT, JOEL R.

Painted for Colonel Pinkney, begun Sept. 27th, 1827, finished Oct. 13th, 1827. Head. Price, $50.00

1391 POINSETT, JOEL R.

This portrait was painted when Poinsett was Secretary of War, the sittings being given in Washington, D. C., begun April 17th, 1840, and finished May 21st, 1840, for the Philosophical Society at Philadelphia. Bust. Size 25″ × 30″. Price, $200.00

Owned by American Philosophical Society, Philadelphia.

1392 POLK, JAMES KNOX (1795–1849).

Eleventh President of the United States. Painted for the University of North Carolina, Chapel Hill. Portrait begun May 30th, 1847, finished June 8th, 1847. Size 25″ × 30″.   Price, $300.00
Engraved by John Sartain and shows a full-length figure standing by a column under an archway with curtain to right.
Owned by the University of North Carolina.

1393 POLK, JAMES KNOX (1795–1849).

Sketch made Dec. 4th, 1847. Head.   Price, $50.00
Owned by Albert Rosenthal, of Philadelphia.

1394 POLLARD, MR.

Of Norfolk, Va. Portrait begun Aug. 17th, 1835, finished Oct. 20th, 1835. Bust.   Price, $125.00

1395 POLLOCK, GEORGE.

Of North Carolina. Portrait begun Nov. 2nd, 1825, finished Nov. 25th, 1825. Bust.   Price, $60.00

1396 POORE, MRS. MARY FORDE.

Bust, standing, hands clasped, white dress, red curtain in background. Size 25″ × 30″. Oval.
Owned by Mrs. Sallie Forde Morris and deposited with the Pennsylvania Academy of Fine Arts, Philadelphia.

1397 PORCHER, MRS. HARRIET.

Sister of the artist, married Professor Porcher, of South Carolina. Portrait painted for the artist's sister Elizabeth (Mrs. Middleton Smith). Head wearing a scarf. Reproduced in Earle's "Two Centuries of Costumes in America." Portrait begun Sept. 13th, 1837, finished Sept. 29th, 1837. Head.   Price, $150.00
Owned by Mrs. Elizabeth W. Hughes and exhibited at Charleston, S. C., 1901–02.

1398 PORE, MR.

(Cabinet maker.) Portrait begun March, 1806, and finished April, 1806, Bust.   Price, $30.00

1399 PORTER, MR.

Portrait begun Aug. 20th, 1807, finished in Sept. Head.   Price, $30.00

1400 PORTER, DAVID (1780–1843).

Distinguished commander of the War of 1812, capturing many British prizes. Congress awarded him a gold medal. Drawing made for the design Sept., 1817. Size 6″ × 6″.   Price, $50.00

LIST OF PAINTINGS

1401 POST, REV.

Rector of the Circular Church in Charleston, S. C. Portrait painted in Charleston, S. C., begun Jan. 8th, 1846, finished Jan. 30th, 1846. Bust.

Price, $200.00

NOTE.—Potestad, Mrs. Louise de. No. 297. (See Carter, Miss Mildred Lee.)

1402 POTTER, MISS ALICE (1846–1894).

Portrait painted when about eighteen months old; she married J. Dundas Lippincott, of Philadelphia. Portrait begun Nov. 18th, 1847, finished Nov. 23rd, 1847. Head.

Price, $80.00

The picture sold at Freeman's Auction, Philadelphia, in 1919, to a Mrs. Coleman.

1403 POTTER, ELIZABETH (1844–1890).

Portrait painted for Dr. Thomas Potter. Head of a little girl about four or five years old. She married Mr. Henry Ashhurst, of Philadelphia. Portrait begun Sept. 3rd, 1849, finished Nov. 2nd, 1849. Size 17″ × 20″.

Price, $100.00

Painting was sold at Freeman Auction Rooms, Philadelphia, in 1919.

1404 POTTER, MR. JOHN (1765–1849).

Of Trenton or Princeton, N. J. Portrait begun March 29th, 1841, finished April 19th, 1841. Canvas size 25″ × 30″. Signed on back "TS 1841." Bust.

Price, $200.00

Owned by Bayard Stockton, Esq., of "Morven," Princeton, N. J.

1405 POTTER, MR. JOHN (1765–1849).

Of Princeton, N. J. (Trenton.) Copy painted for his son, begun Nov. 21st, 1851, finished Dec. 23rd, 1851. Bust.

Price, $100.00

1406 POTTER, MR. JOHN (1765–1849).

Of Princeton, N. J. (Trenton.) Second copy, painted for his son, begun Nov. 22nd, 1851, finished Jan. 7th, 1852. Bust.

Price, $100.00

Owned by James Potter, Esq., Philadelphia.

1407 POTTER, MRS. JOHN (1770–1848).

(Née Catherine Fuller, of South Carolina.) She was the mother of the wife of Commodore Robert Field Stockton, and married John Potter, of Trenton, N. J., in 1791. Portrait begun March 11th, 1841, finished April 1st, 1841. Bust, canvas 25″ × 30″. Signed on back "TS 1841."

Price, $200.00

Owned by Bayard Stockton, Esq., of "Morven," Princeton, N. J.

J S C

LIST OF PAINTINGS

1408 POTTER, MRS. JOHN (1770–1848).

Of Princeton, N. J. (Trenton.) Copy, painted for her son, begun Nov. 17th, 1851, finished Dec. 13th, 1852. Bust. Price, $100.00
Owned by James Potter, Esq., Philadelphia.

1409 POTTER, MRS. JOHN (1770–1848).

Of Princeton, N. J. (Trenton.) Second copy, painted for her son, begun Nov. 19th, 1851, finished Dec. 19th, 1851. Bust. Price, $100.00

1410 POTTER, MASTER JOHN (1842–1864).

John Hamilton Potter of the Georgia Infantry C. S. A., was killed in battle. Portrait painted for his father, begun Aug. 24th, 1849, finished Oct. 30th, 1849. Size 17″ × 20″. Price, $100.00

1411 POTTER, JAMES (1793–1862).

(Married Miss Sarah Jones Grimes.) Bust, nearly full face, black stock and black coat. Portrait begun Sept. 4th, 1849, finished Oct. 22nd, 1849. Size 25″ × 30″. Price, $150.00
Owned by James Potter, Esq., Philadelphia.

1412 POTTER, MARIA AND EMILY.

(Maria Stockton Potter, 1838–1897.) (Emily Charlotte Potter, 1841–1896.) Painted for their father, begun Sept. 7th, 1849, finished Nov. 5th, 1849. Heads. Price, $200.00

1413 POTTER, MARY MARSHALL (1831–1861).

Married John D. Langhorne. Portrait painted at Princeton, N. J. Begun Aug. 10th, 1849, finished Oct. 25th, 1849. Head, nearly full face, with hair parted in middle and drawn down smoothly on each side. Size 17″ × 20″. Oval canvas. Price, $100.00
Owned by James Potter, Esq., Philadelphia, Pa.

1414 POTTER, MISS SARAH JONES (1835–1879).

She married Richard Conover. Head, dark hair arranged in curls. Portrait painted for her father, begun Aug. 20th, 1849, finished Oct. 29th, 1849. Size 17″ × 20″. Oval. Price, $100.00
Owned by James Potter, Esq., Philadelphia.

1415 POTTER, RICHARD.

Portrait begun May 10th, 1814, finished July 4th, 1814. Size 29″ × 36″. Price, $100.00

252

LIST OF PAINTINGS

1416 POTTER, MRS. THOMAS (1818–1877).

(Née Miss Sarah Jane Hall.) She was the mother of Alice Potter (No. 1402). Portrait painted for her husband, begun Aug. 13th, 1849, finished Nov. 13th, 1849. Size 29″ × 36″.   Price, $250.00

1417 POTTER, REV.

Portrait painted for Mr. Tuckerman, begun Sept. 5th, 1831, finished Nov. 5th, 1831. Size 29″ × 36″.   Price, $200.00

1418 POULSON, ZACHARIAH (1761–1844).

Publisher and editor of the "Daily Advertizer," of Philadelphia, and for twenty-one years Librarian of the Library Company of Philadelphia, for whom the portrait was painted and where it now hangs. Begun June 8th, 1843, finished June 18th, 1843. Portrait nearly full face, seated, wearing high hat. Size 20″ × 24″.   Price, $100.00
Engraved by Samuel Sartain. Owned by the Library Company of Philadelphia, Locust Street.

1419 POULTNEY, MRS. (SR.).

Of Baltimore, Md. Portrait begun Nov. 21st, 1857, finished Dec. 2nd, 1857. Head.   Price, $50.00

1420 POULTNEY, MRS. THOMAS.

(Née Susan Carroll.) Of Baltimore, Md. Portrait begun Nov. 15th, 1857, finished Nov. 30th, 1857. Head.   Price, $50.00
Owned by Mr. C. Carroll Poultney, Baltimore, Md.

1421 POWEL, COL. JOHN HARE (1786–1856).

Was originally named John Powel Hare and was own brother to Dr. Robert Hare. He became secretary of the United States Legation in London under William Pinckney. Portrait begun Feb. 28th, 1827, finished April 21st, 1827. Painted after Sir Thomas Lawrence. Bust.   Price, $75.00

1422 POWEL, MRS. SAMUEL (1742–1830).

Née Elizabeth Willing, married Samuel Powel, afterwards mayor of Philadelphia. Portrait painted partly from a miniature by B. Trott, begun Jan. 6th, 1817, finished July 9th, 1817. Bust, head to left, with lace head dress.
       Price, $100.00

1423 PRALE, MISS.

Of No. 3 Broadway, New York. Portrait begun Oct. 26th, 1848, finished Nov. 3rd, 1848. Head.   Price, $80.00

LIST OF PAINTINGS

1424 PRATT, ERASMUS.
Begun Nov. 26th, 1870, finished Dec. 19th, 1870. Size 17" × 20". (A present.)   Price, $80.00

1425 PRATT, HENRY (1761–1838).
Merchant of Philadelphia, and eldest son of Matthew Pratt, the portrait painter. Begun May 3rd, 1815, finished June 5th, 1815. Size 29" × 36".
Price, $100.00
Owned by Mrs. Rosalie V. Tiers Jackson, Jupiter, Florida.

1426 PRATT, MRS.
Portrait painted from a miniature for Mrs. Thompson. Begun Sept. 29th, 1828, finished Oct. 8th, 1828. Bust.   Price, $75.00

1427 PRICE, STEPHEN.
Portrait painted in London; he was the manager of the Park Theatre, New York. Size 29" × 36". Portrait begun Jan. 9th, 1838, finished Feb. 9th, 1838.   Price, $200.00

1428 PRICE, MRS. STEPHEN.
Wife of the manager of the Park Theatre, New York. Portrait begun Feb. 20th, 1807, finished April 13th, 1807. Bust.   Price, $30.00

1429 PRINGLE, MRS. WILLIAM BULL.
(Née Miss Mary Motte Alston.) Of Georgetown. Portrait begun May 2nd, 1842, finished May 7th, 1842. Head.   Price, $150.00
Owned by her granddaughter, Mrs. Mary P. Rhett, of Mobile, Ala.

1430 PRINGLE, MRS. JAMES R.
(Née Miss Ladson.) Portrait begun Jan. 26th, 1846, finished Feb. 16th, 1846. Head.   Price, $150.00
Owned by William Henry Ladson, of Charleston, S. C.

1431 PROSSER, MR.
Portrait begun Feb., 1806, finished the same month. Bust. Price, $30.00

1432 PROSSER, MRS.
Portrait begun Jan., 1806, finished the same month. Bust. Price, $30.00

1433 PROUDIT, MRS. JOHN W. (1801–1847).
Née Abigal Hazard Ralston, youngest daughter of the Philadelphia merchant, Robert Ralston, married Rev. John William Proudit, May 11th, 1830. Bust, head to right, hair parted in the middle, wears a cap or scarf over her head.
Reproduced in " Old Philadelphia Families," by Leach.

1434 PURVIANCE, J.

    Lawyer. Portrait begun June 5th, 1821, finished Dec., 1822. Size 29″ × 36″.   Price, $150.00

    NOTE.—In the register Sully spells the name "Purveyance."

1435 PURVIANCE, MRS. J.

    Portrait begun April 10th, 1821, finished May 28th, 1821. Wife of Lawyer Purviance. Size 29″ × 36″.   Price, $150.00

1436 PYATT, J. F.

    Portrait painted for his mother, begun Feb. 17th, 1864, finished March 4th, 1864. Bust.   Price, $200.00

1437 PYATT, MRS.

    Portrait painted for her daughter, begun March 15th, 1842, finished March 24th, 1842. Head.   Price, $150.00

1438 PYATT, MR.

    Brother of J. F. Pyatt. Portrait begun Feb. 20th, 1864, finished March 5th, 1864. Bust.   Price, $200.00

1439 PYATT, MISS.

    Portrait painted for her mother, begun Feb. 28th, 1842, finished March 24th, 1842. Bust.   Price, $150.00

1440 RALSTON, MISS ELIZABETH ANN.

    Portrait painted for Dr. Dorsey, begun March 12th, 1816, finished March, 1817. Bust.   Price, $100.00

1441 RALSTON, MISS.

    (Deceased.) The register notes hand as introduced in the portrait. Begun Feb. 27th, 1847, finished Dec. 2nd, 1847. Bust.   Price, $150.00

1442 RALSTON, MATTHEW, JUNR.

    Portrait begun May 29th, 1812, finished July 4th, 1812. Size 29″ × 36″.   Price, $100.00

1443 RALSTON, MATTHEW, JR.

    (Deceased, copy made for Mr. Wilcocks.) Portrait begun Dec. 20th, 1842, finished Jan. 31st, 1843. Head.   Subscriber's price, $50.00

1444 RALSTON, MRS. MATTHEW.
Portrait begun Dec. 21st, 1818, finished Dec. 31st, 1818. Bust.
Price, $100.00

1445 RALSTON, ROBERT (1761–1836).
Prominent merchant and philanthropist of Philadelphia. Portrait begun May 26th, 1809, finished June 6th, 1809. Bust. Price, $50.00
Owned by Mrs. Alexander Proudfit, Newcastle, Delaware.

1446 RALSTON, ROBERT (1761–1836).
Portrait seated, head to right, black coat with high collar, white tie and stock, window in background. Begun June 17th, 1846, finished June 22nd, 1846. Size 25″ × 30″. Painted for the Colonization Society.
Price, $100.00
Deposited at the Pennsylvania Historical Society, Philadelphia, Pa.

1447 RANDOLPH, MISS.
Afterwards Mrs. Hackley. Portrait begun May, 1805, finished June, 1805. Size 12″ × 10″. Price, $15.00

1448 RANDOLPH, MRS. THOMAS MANN (1772–1836).
She was Martha Jefferson, daughter of Thomas Jefferson, President of the United States. Bust, nearly full face, in white cap, tied under her chin by lavender ribbon, her curly auburn hair shown in ringlets, portrait begun May 27th, 1836, finished June 6th, 1836. Bust. Price, $150.00
Owned by Ehrich Galleries, New York.

1449 RANDOLPH, MRS. THOMAS M.
Portrait painted for T. J. Randolph, her son, a copy of original picture. Painting begun Oct. 20th, 1836, finished Jan. 19th, 1837. Bust.
Price, $150.00

1450 RANDOLPH, MRS. THOMAS M.
Portrait painted for Mrs. Joseph Coolidge, of Boston, a second copy of original picture. Painting begun Oct. 20th, 1836, finished Dec. 7th, 1836. Bust. Price, $150.00
Owned by Miss Ella W. Coolidge, Boston, Mass.

1451 RANDOLPH, MRS. THOMAS M.
Portrait painted for Mr. Talcot, a third copy of original picture; Sully only painted the outline and then retouched the finished picture; the register does not state who did the rest of the work on the portrait. Painting begun Oct. 20th, 1836, finished Feb. 15th, 1837. Bust. Price, $150.00
Owned by Mrs. Moorfield Storey, of Boston, Mass.

1452 RANDOLPH, MRS. THOMAS M.

Painted for J. Randolph. Portrait commenced by Thomas W. Sully, son of the artist, and finished and retouched by the father, Dec. 30th, 1836. Bust. Price, $150.00

NOTE.—The portrait of Mrs. Thomas Mann Randolph (as a young woman) ascribed to Thomas Sully as published in ''The Republican Court,'' by Rufus W. Griswold, N. Y., 1855, was in the opinion of the authors not painted by Sully, unless it is a copy by him from the work of another artist.

1453 RANKIN, MRS.

Portrait of her father, a copy. Begun April 21st, 1866, finished on April 30th, 1866. Bust. Price, $100.00

1454 RAWLE, MISS REBECCA.

Deceased, painted from a profile, portrait begun Jan. 8th, 1815, finished April 27th, 1815. Bust. Price, $80.00

1455 RAWLE, WILLIAM (1759–1836).

Lawyer of Philadelphia and first President of the Historical Society of Pennsylvania, 1824. Painted Jan. 13th, 1808, finished Feb. 5th, 1808. Size 29" × 36". Price, $50.00
Owned by Theodore Frothingham, Esq., Boston, Mass.

1456 READ, GEORGE (1733–1798).

Signer of the Declaration of Independence from Delaware. He was also the first United States Senator from Delaware. Portrait copied from a painting by Pine. Head, nearly full face, white stock. Size 19½" × 23¾". Painting begun April 18th, 1808, finished Aug. 24th, 1808.
Subscriber's price, $30.00
Owned by the City of Philadelphia, Independence Hall.

1457 READ, GEORGE (1733–1798).

''Copied from my former portrait after Pine.'' Portrait begun February 6th, 1860, finished February 13th, 1860. Bust. Price, $100.00
Portrait painted for Judge John M. Read, of the Supreme Court of Penna.

1458 READ, GEORGE (1733–1798).

''Copied from my former painting after Pine.'' This portrait was painted on order for John M. Read, Jr., of Albany, begun Jan. 1st, 1860, finished Jan. 9th, 1860. Bust. Price, $100.00

LIST OF PAINTINGS

1459 READ, JOHN (1769–1851).

Eminent lawyer; graduate of Princeton, 1787; President Adams appointed him agent-general of the United States under Jay's Treaty. This portrait painted from a miniature for his grandson, John Meredith Read, begun Feb. 8th, 1862, finished Feb. 26th, 1862. Size 30″ × 25″. Bust, head to left, high coat collar, arms crossed on breast. Price, $50.00

1460 READ, MRS.

(Late mother of Mrs. French.) Portrait begun April 2nd, 1847, finished April 24th, 1847. Head. Price, $80.00

1461 REDWOOD, J.

Portrait begun Feb. 24th, 1808, finished March 7th, 1808. Bust. (Subscriber.) Price, $30.00

1462 REEVES, HANNAH SEAGRAVE.

(Mrs. William Pinckney Craig, of Philadelphia.) Her second husband was Judge Randolph, of Tallahassee, Florida. On canvas H. 36 inches, W. 28 inches. Three-quarter length. with low-necked dress and wide-brimmed hat.
Owned by Mrs. A. McLane Hamilton, Philadelphia, shown as the work of Thomas Sully , at Brooklyn Exhibition.

1463 REYNOLDS, SIR JOSHUA (1723–1792).

Eminent English portrait painter. Copy by Sully of the portrait by Reynolds. Canvas 15¾″ × 18¼″. Noted on back of picture " Copy of the portrait of Sir Joshua Reynolds by himself, T. Sully."
Owned by Arthur L. Church, Esq., Philadelphia.

1464 RHOADS, MRS. SAMUEL.

Portrait painted for her daughter, Mrs. Tobias Wagner, begun April 3rd, 1848, finished April 25th, 1848. Bust. Price, $100.00

1465 RICE, MR.

Portrait begun June 19th, 1854, finished June 27th, 1854. Head. The register notes that this portrait was " paid for with books and $10 cash."

1466 RICE, MRS.

Portrait begun Oct. 27th, 1842, finished Nov. 7th, 1842. Head.
Price, $100.00

1467 RICHARDS, SAMUEL (1769–1842).

Ironmaster, with works at Weymouth, N. J. He was a brother of Benjamin W. Richards, Mayor of Philadelphia. Painted for Mr. White, begun Sept. 13th, 1827, finished October 18th, 1827. Bust. Price, $75.00
Owned by the estate of Herbert Dupuy, of Pittsburgh, Pa.

LIST OF PAINTINGS

1468 RICHARDS, SAMUEL.

Copy of first portrait. Painting begun Oct. 2nd, 1829, finished Oct. 15th, 1829. Bust. Price, $75.00

1469 RICHINGS, CAROLINE (d. 1882).

Opera singer and adopted daughter of Peter Richings, actor and manager. She made her debut in Philadelphia in 1852, and in 1867 married Pierre Bernard, operatic tenor, they resided in Richmond, Virginia. Half length, seated with chin resting on hand, low-necked white gown. Portrait begun Sept. 24th, 1845, finished Nov. 9th, 1845. Size 30″ × 25″.
Reduced price, $50.00

Owned by R. C. and N. M. Vose, Boston, Mass.

1470 RICHINGS, MRS.

Portrait begun Oct. 20th, 1845, finished Nov. 5th, 1845. Bust.
Reduced price, $50.00

NOTE.—Sully spells this name " Ritchings.'"

1471 RICKETTS, MR.

Copied from a painting. Portrait begun May 9th, 1807, finished May 27th, 1807. Size 12″ × 10″. Price, $30.00

1472 RICKETTS, MR.

Portrait begun Nov. 11th, 1807, finished Nov. 15th, 1807. Bust.
Price, $50.00

1473 RIDGELY, CHARLES (1762–1829).

Governor of Maryland, 1815–17, was commonly called " General." Painted in Baltimore, begun March 23rd, 1820, finished October 22nd, 1820. Size 25″ × 30″. Price, $200.00

1474 RIDGELY, MISS ELIZABETH (1802–1867).

Of Baltimore, married John Ridgely, of Hampton, Baltimore Co., Md. Full length, standing by harp. Portrait begun May 1st, 1818, finished May 21st, 1818. Size 58″ × 94″. Price, $500.00
Reproduced in Earle's " Two Centuries of Costumes in America," and in the Century Magazine.
Painting at Hampton, Maryland, and owned by her grandson, Captain John Ridgely.

1475 RIDGELY, JOHN.

Of Hampton, Baltimore Co., Md. Portrait begun Jan. 4th, 1841, finished Jan. 16th, 1841. Bust. Price, $200.00
Painting is at Hampton, Maryland, and is owned by Captain John Ridgely.

LIST OF PAINTINGS

1476 RIDGELY, NICHOLAS.

Painted in Baltimore, begun Nov. 25th, 1820, finished Dec. 16th, 1820. Bust. Price, $80.00

1477 RIPLEY, GENERAL JAMES W. (1794–1870).

Graduated at West Point, 1814. Congress awarded him a gold medal. Drawing made for the same, Sept., 1817. Size 6″ × 6″. Price, $50.00

1478 RITCHIE, MRS.

(Daughter of Harrison Gray Otis, of Boston.) Portrait begun May 22nd, 1835, finished May 30th, 1835. Head. Price, $80.00

1479 ROBB, MRS. (AND THREE CHILDREN).

Isabella, Louisa and Mary. From New Orleans, La. Painting begun Aug. 31st, 1844, finished Nov. 21st, 1844. Size 44″ × 56″.
Price, $600.00

1480 ROBB, SAMUEL (1806–1870).

Son of James Robb, was a merchant and lived many years in New Orleans, Louisiana. Head, nearly full face, with high white stock, brown background. Signed " TS." Size of canvas 16½″ × 20″.
Owned by Miss Lloyd, Church Lane, Germantown, Pa.

1481 ROBBINS, LUKE.

Of the theatre. Portrait begun July 10th, 1808, finished July 19th, 1808. Bust. Price, $30.00

1482 ROBERTS, JESSE.

Portrait a present to McDonalds, begun Oct. 11th, 1847, finished Dec. 7th, 1847. Bust. Price, $150.00

1483 ROBERTS, THOMAS PASCHALL (1786–1844).

Treasurer of the Union Canal Company. Bust, nearly full face. Reproduced in " Old Philadelphia Families," by Leach.

1484 ROBESON, MRS.

(Née Rodman, of New Bedford.) Begun Jan. 15th, 1845, finished March 6th, 1845. Size 29″ × 36″. Price, $200.00

1485 ROBERTSON, MISS ANNA.

Sister of Mrs. Barksdale. Portrait begun Jan. 6th, 1851, finished Feb. 15th, 1851. Head. Price, $100.00

LIST OF PAINTINGS

1486 ROBERTSON, MRS.

Nothing further is known of this portrait except the entry in the register of "English lady of Alabama." Painting begun March 10th, 1834, finished March 19th, 1834. Head. Price, $80.00

1487 ROBINSON, MR.

Of Augusta, Georgia. Portrait begun Nov. 4th, 1846, finished Nov. 16th, 1846. Bust. Price, $100.00

1488 ROBINSON, MR.

Owner of the mills near Schuylkill. Portrait begun Nov. 15th, 1827, finished Jan. 22nd, 1828. Bust. Price, $75.00

1489 ROBINSON, MR.

Actor. Portrait begun June 15th, 1807, finished July 5th, 1807. Bust. Price, $50.00

1490 ROBINSON, CONWAY (1805–1884).

Distinguished Virginia lawyer and writer on legal and historical matters. Portrait painted for his brother, Moncure Robinson, begun Nov. 4th, 1850, finished Nov. 30th, 1850. Head. Price, $100.00

1491 ROBINSON, HENRY.

Of Boston. He wears spectacles and holds a pamphlet in his hand, brown background. Portrait begun Sept. 9th, 1846, finished Sept. 17th, 1846. Signed on back " TS 1846." Canvas 20″ × 24″. Head. Price, $80.00 Owned by Mr. Joseph T. Kinsley, of Philadelphia.

1492 ROBINSON, MRS. HENRY.

Of Boston. Black dress, wearing white cap over dark hair, brown background. Portrait begun March 8th, 1849, finished March 29th, 1849. Canvas 20″ × 24″. Head. Price, $80.00 Owned by Mr. Joseph T. Kinsley, of Philadelphia.

1493 ROBINSON, MRS. JOHN.

Portrait painted for her son, Moncure Robinson, begun June 11th, 1849, finished June 18th, 1849. Bust. Price, $150.00

1494 ROBINSON, LOUISA.

(Was Miss Campbell.) Portrait begun April 29th, 1824, finished May 10th, 1824. Head. Price, $20.00

LIST OF PAINTINGS

1495 ROBINSON, MONCURE (1802–1891).

Of Virginia, was an eminent civil engineer and resident of Philadelphia. He was a brother of Conway Robinson, the lawyer and writer on legal and historical subjects. Portrait begun Nov. 28th, 1849, finished Dec. 7th, 1849. Head.   Price, $80.00

1496 ROBINSON, MRS. MONCURE.

Wife of the eminent Philadelphia civil engineer, portrait painted for her husband, begun Nov. 4th, 1845, finished Nov. 18th, 1845. Head.
Price, $80.00

1497 ROBSON, MR.

Father of Mrs. Hughes. Portrait begun Jan. 28th, 1826, finished Sept. 4th, 1826. Size 11½″ × 14½″.   Price, $30.00

1498 ROCKAFELLOW, MISS.

Portrait copied for her aunt, Mrs. George R. Graham, begun Nov. 28th, 1864, finished Jan. 15th, 1865. Head.   Price, $80.00

1499 ROCKAFELLOW, MASTER HARRY.

Portrait painted for Mr. Graham, begun Jan. 16th, 1843, finished March 6th, 1843. Size 29″ × 36″.   Price, $200.00

1500 ROGERS, MRS. CAROLINE.

Daughter of Colonel Gideon Fairman and mother of Professor Fairman Rogers and of Mrs. Horace Howard Furness. Portrait begun Nov. 19th, 1831, finished Jan. 6th, 1832. Bust, wearing hat with feathers, white satin dress and black fur boa. Bust, size 25″ × 30″.   Price, $80.00
Owned by Mr. Horace Howard Furness, Philadelphia.

1501 ROGERS, MRS. TALBOT MERCER.

Of Pittsburgh. Portrait begun Sept. 28th, 1863, finished Oct. 13th, 1863. Head.   Price, $40.00
Owned by Mrs. Talbot Mercer Rogers, of Haverford, Penna.

1502 ROGERS, MRS. HARRIET R. (1810–1889).

Portrait begun Oct. 24th, 1833, finished May 24th, 1834. Bust.
Price, $125.00
Owned by Mrs. Robert C. Drayton, Philadelphia.

1503 ROLANDO, HENRY (b. ——, d. 1869).

Entered the United States Navy in 1836. Attained the rank of Commander. Portrait painted in Baltimore for Dr. Buckler of that city, when he was Lieutenant Rolando. Painting begun Nov. 17th, 1852, finished Dec. 28th, 1852. Bust.   Price, $150.00

1504 ROOTS, MR.

Portrait begun June, 1805, and finished the same month, size 25″ × 30″.
Price, $30.00

1505 ROPER, MR.

Of the Gymnasium. Portrait begun Aug. 18th, 1832, finished but noted as "Erased." Bust. Price, $100.00

1506 ROSE, MISS AMELIA.

Portrait painted for her aunt, begun April 29th, 1846, finished May 8th, 1846. Head. Price, $150.00

1507 ROSS, JAMES (1762–1847).

"Of Pittsburgh, Pa." He was admitted to the Bar in 1784; United States Senator, 1794–1803; President of the Senate during one session. Portrait begun Nov. 15th, 1812, finished Dec. 30th, 1813. Head. Price, $70.00

1508 ROSS, JAMES (1762–1847).

Three-quarter length, standing, facing front, head to left, holds a paper in his hand. Portrait begun Oct. 20th, 1813, and finished Dec. 14th, 1813. Size 40″ × 50″. Price, $150.00
Painted for the Pennsylvania Academy of Fine Arts and owned by them.

1509 ROSS, JOHN.

Portrait begun Oct., 1805, finished Nov., 1805. Size 10″ × 12″.
Price, $15.00

1510 ROSS, J.

Of New Orleans, La., painted in that city about 1815. Bust, seated, arm rests on end of sofa with hand raised to head, high white stock. Painting signed "TS."
Owned by Dr. Isaac M. Cline, New Orleans, La.

1511 ROSSINI, GIOACHINO ANTONIO (1792–1868).

Painted from a daguerreotype for the Musician Series, begun Nov. 10th, 1862, finished March 28th, 1863. Size 17″ × 12″. Price, $30.00

1512 ROTCH, MISS.

Portrait painted for Mrs. Jacob Smith, begun Nov. 12th, 1831, finished but declined. Head. Price, $60.00

1513 ROTCH, MRS.

Copy of former portrait by Sully, commenced by Thomas Jr., and finished by Sully, begun May 2nd, 1832, finished June 13th, 1832. Head.
Price, $60.00

LIST OF PAINTINGS

1514 ROTCH, MISS ELIZABETH.

Portrait painted for Mrs. Smith, begun May 20th, 1833, finished June 27th, 1833. Signed " TS." Head.   Price, $60.00
Owned by Arthur Rotch, 197 Commonwealth Ave., Boston, Mass.

1515 ROTCH, MRS. JOSEPH.

Of New Bedford, Mass. Portrait begun Nov. 7th, 1831, finished Dec. 9th, 1831. Bust.   Price, $80.00

1516 ROTCH, MRS. JOSEPH.

(Née Anne Smith.) Portrait taken from a miniature; this painting was begun by Thomas Sully, Jr., and was completed by the artist, begun June 29th, 1832, finished July 3rd, 1832. Bust.   Price, $60.00
Owned by Mrs. Horatio Lamb, Beacon St., Boston, Mass.

1517 ROTCH, THOMAS.

Of New Bedford, Mass. Portrait begun Dec. 7th, 1825, finished Dec. 14th, 1825. Head.   Price, $40.00

1518 ROTCH, MRS. THOMAS.

Was Miss Ridgway. Portrait begun Sept. 30th, 1816, finished Dec. 4th, 1816. Size 29" × 36".   Price, $150.00

1519 ROTCH, MRS. THOMAS.

(Was Miss Ridgway, of Philadelphia.) Portrait begun May 5th, 1827, finished June 25th, 1827. Bust.   Price, $75.00

1520 ROWBOTHAM, MRS.

The register notes this portrait "as a present for Caddy." Head, begun Dec. 28th, 1832, finished Jan. 5th, 1833.   Price, $60.00

1521 ROYE, EDWARD JAMES (1815–1872).

Chief Justice of the Supreme Court of Liberia. The portrait is of a negro and hangs in the Historical Society in Philadelphia; it is noted in Sully's register under the name of "Boyd." The painting was begun Sept. 6th, 1864, finished Sept. 16th, 1864. Signed " TS 1864," Head, size 20" × 24".   Price, $30.00
Deposited at Historical Society of Pennsylvania.

1522 RUFFIAN, MRS.

(She was Miss Roan, of Richmond, Virginia.) Portrait begun Sept. 7th, 1839, finished Sept. 18th, 1839. Head.   Price, $150.00

1523 RUNDLE, MISS FANNY.

Portrait painted partly from memory, begun on Nov. 27th, 1828, and finished Dec. 27th, 1828. Shows the head of a beautiful young woman, turned slightly to the right, hair in curls arranged with a blue ribbon, open-necked gown indicated. Size canvas 15" × 19". Price, $50.00
Owned by Joseph MacGregor Mitcheson, Philadelphia.

1524 RUNDLE, MISS FANNY.

Deceased, copied from former portrait for James Earle, begun Nov. 25th, 1859, finished Dec. 9th, 1859. Head, 18" × 15". Price, $30.00

1525 RUNDLE, MISS FANNY.

Deceased, copied from former portrait for James Earle, begun Nov. 19th, 1859, finished Dec. 2nd, 1859. Signed " TS, December, 1859." Head. Size 14½" × 18½". Price, $30.00
Owned by Louis A. Biddle, Esq.

1526 RUNDLE, MISS FANNY.

Copy of former portrait. Painted for James Earle, begun Oct. 7th, 1859, finished Oct. 13th, 1859. Size 18" × 15". Price, $30.00

1527 RUSH, DR. BENJAMIN (1745–1813).

Distinguished physician and politician. He was a signer of the Declaration of Independence and Physician General in the Army of the Revolution. Portrait painted for Dr. Dewees, begun April 3rd, 1809, finished May 21st, 1809. Bust. Price, $50.00

1528 RUSH, DR. BENJAMIN (1745–1813).

Head to right, resting on hand; seated, and seen to the knees. Portrait painted for Dr. Hosack, of New York, begun May 7th, 1812, finished July 20th, 1812. Three-quarter length. Price, $100.00

1529 RUSH, DR. BENJAMIN (1745–1813).

" Deceased, painted from my first picture." Full length, seated, head to right, resting on hand. Gray clothing and red curtain in background. Portrait begun Oct. 4th, 1813, finished Dec. 30th, 1813. Size 5' 2" × 6' 11". Price, $400.00
Engraved by David Edwin (see Fielding, No. 170).
Owned by Pennsylvania Hospital, Philadelphia.

1530 RUSH, DR. BENJAMIN (1745–1813).

Portrait painted for his daughter, begun Oct. 12th, 1813, finished Jan., 1814. Half length. Price, $150.00
Owned by the estate of Colonel Alexander Biddle, Philadelphia.

1531 RUSH, DR. BENJAMIN (1745–1813).

Head to right, resting on hand, seated, and seen to the knees, dark clothes and background. Size 40″ × 50″. The register notes "Deceased, copied from my first painting." Begun Sept. 2nd, 1815, finished Sept. 20th, 1815.
Price, $100.00
Owned by American Philosophical Society, Philadelphia, Penna.

1532 RUSH, BENJAMIN.

(Copy of former portrait.) Painted for Judge Black, begun Dec. 14th, 1857, finished Jan. 4th, 1858. Bust. Price, $100.00

NOTE.—A copy of Sully's portrait of Benjamin Rush hangs in Independence Hall. It is a head or bust portrait, size 20″ × 24″. It was catalogued as a Sully, but the painting does not resemble his work.

1533 RUSH, MRS. BENJAMIN (1759–1848).

Was Julia Stockton. This portrait was painted for her son, Richard Rush, Minister to Great Britain, begun Oct. 20th, 1817, finished Dec. 3rd, 1817. Size 25″ × 30″. Price, $200.00

1534 RUSH, MRS. BENJAMIN.

Portrait begun May 7th, 1862, finished May 24th, 1862. Size 25″ × 30″.
Price, $50.00

1535 RUSH, MURRAY.

Portrait painted for his father, R. Rush, begun Dec. 10th, 1857, finished March 25th, 1858. Bust. Price, $100.00

1536 RUSH, MRS. MURRAY.

Deceased, portrait painted from a daguerreotype, begun July 17th, 1857, finished Aug. 20th, 1857. Size 24″ × 20″. Price, $80.00

1537 RUSH, RICHARD.

Of Baltimore, Md. Portrait begun Dec. 19th, 1857, finished Dec. 30th, 1857. Head. Price, $80.00

1538 RUSH, MRS. RICHARD.

Portrait begun Dec. 19th, 1857, finished Jan. 8th, 1858. Head.
Price, $80.00

1539 RUSH, R. (JR.).

Copy of former portrait, painted for his father, begun Feb. 19th, 1858, finished March 1st, 1858. Head. Price, $80.00

LIST OF PAINTINGS

1540 RUSH, MR.

(Late son of the Hon. R. Rush.) Portrait painted from a photograph for Mr. Drayton, begun Oct. 18th, 1856, finished Dec. 6th, 1856. Head.

Price, $80.00

1541 RUSH, MR.

(Late son of the Hon. R. Rush.) Portrait painted from a photograph, begun Oct. 18th, 1856, finished Nov. 13th, 1856. Head. Price, $80.00

1542 RUTHERFORD, MISS EMILY.

Of Richmond, Va. Portrait begun Jan. 4th, 1847, finished Jan. 9th, 1847. Head. Price, $80.00

1543 RUTHERFORD, MISS EMILY.

Portrait begun Nov. 11th, 1850, finished Nov. 25th, 1850. Head.

Price, $100.00

1544 SANDS, MRS.

Of Washington; she was Miss French. Portrait begun Nov. 5th, 1840, finished Nov. 14th, 1840. Head. Price, $150.00

1545 SANFORD, MR.

Cashier of Bank of United States, Fayetteville, North Carolina. Portrait begun July 13th, 1830, finished Sept. 30th, 1830. Bust. Price, $75.00

1546 SANFORD, MRS.

Of North Carolina. Portrait begun July 13th, 1830, finished Aug. 18th, 1830. Bust. Price, $75.00

1547 SARTAIN, MRS. JOHN.

Painted for her relations in England. Susannah Longman Swaine, of London, married John Sartain, the engraver, in 1830, and that year came with him to Philadelphia. Portrait begun Jan. 12th, 1843, finished March 20th, 1843. Bust. Price, $100.00
Owned by Dr. Paul Sartain, of Philadelphia.

1548 SARTAIN, SAMUEL (1831–1909).

Eldest son of John Sartain, the engraver, he followed his father's profession of mezzotinto engraving. Portrait begun May 3rd, 1852, finished May 13th, 1852. Head. Price, $80.00
Owned by Dr. Paul Sartain, Philadelphia.

1549 SAVAGE, JOHN (1790–1834).

He was the son of William and Jane Cooper (Demetris) Savage, of Kingston, Jamaica. Portrait begun June 22nd, 1824, finished Nov. 9th, 1824. Seated, head to left with hand resting in coat front. Size 29″ × 36″.
Price, $60.00
Owned by John Savage, Esq., of Brady, Texas.

1550 SAVAGE, MRS. JOHN.

(Was Jane Allen White.) Head, showing nearly full face with ringlets. Sketch begun March 20th, 1826, finished March 25th, 1826. Head.
Price, $20.00
Reproduced in Lawrence Park's book on " Major Thomas Savage, of Boston, and his Descendants," published 1915.
Owned by John Richards Savage, of Garden City, Long Island.

1551 SAVAGE, MISS.

Portrait shows figure standing by open window with hand resting on sill, white low-necked dress, red turban on head. Painting begun Nov. 17th, 1810, finished Feb. 5th, 1811. Signed " TS November, 1810." Size 29″ × 36″.
Price, $80.00
Owned by D. Fitzhugh Savage, Philadelphia.

1552 SCHOENBERGER, JOHN H.

A prominent philanthropist of Pittsburgh, Pa. Painting begun April 13th, 1841, finished Oct. 20th, 1841. Bust.
Price, $200.00

1553 SCHOENBERGER, MR.

Of Pittsburgh, Pa. Begun April 12th, 1841, finished April 30th, 1841. Bust.
Price, $200.00

1554 SCHOENBERGER, MRS.

Of Cincinnati. Portrait begun August 17th, 1841, finished Sept. 9th, 1841. Bust.
Price, $200.00

1555 SCHOENBERGER, MARY.

(Deceased.) Daughter of Mr. Schoenberger, of Cincinnati, painting begun July 31st, 1844, finished Aug. 7th, 1844. Head.
Price, $80.00

1556 SCHUYLER, PHILIP J. (1768–1855).

Was the son of General Philip Schuyler, and was present at the inauguration of President Washington, April 30th, 1789. This portrait painted for Washington Morton, who married Miss Schuyler, begun April 11th, 1807, finished May 14th, 1807. Bust.
Price, $50.00

LIST OF PAINTINGS

1557 SCHUYLER, MRS. PHILIP J. (1786–1852).

Was Mary Ann Sawyer, of Newburyport, Mass., married Philip J. Schuyler in 1806. This portrait painted for Washington Morton, was begun April 11th, 1807, finished May 14th, 1807. Bust.   Price, $50.00

1558 SCOTT, SIR WALTER (1771–1832).

The Scottish novelist, copied from the portrait painted by Sir Thomas Lawrence. Begun Nov. 5th, 1870, finished Nov. 15th, 1870. Size 20″ × 17½″.   Price, $50.00

1559 SCOTT, GENERAL WINFIELD (1786–1866).

Distinguished soldier; in 1814 he was awarded a gold medal by Congress. Drawing made for the medal Sept., 1817. Size 6″ × 6″.   Price, $50.00

1560 SEABROOK, MISS CAROLINA LA FAYETTE.

Named after General La Fayette who was visiting her father when she was christened. La Fayette added the name "Carolina" before his own. Portrait painted for her mother, begun Sept. 25th, 1843, finished Oct. 29th, 1843. Head.   Price, $80.00
Owned by Francis H. Coffin, Scranton, Pa.

1561 SEARS, DAVID (1782–1871).

The register notes "Drapery, etc., to Stuart's head." Gilbert Stuart painted several portraits of David Sears, of Boston. This portrait is probably the one in the Metropolitan Museum, New York, which has the appearance of work by another hand than Stuart's. Sully must have done considerable work as he commenced painting Aug. 24th and finished Nov. 8th, 1831, receiving for it $150.00
Owned by Metropolitan Museum of New York.

1562 SEARS, ELLEN.

Portrait painted for her father, begun July 22nd, 1831, finished Aug. 15th. 1831. Head.   Price, $100.00

1563 SEDDON, MR.

Portrait painted for Mr. Bruce, begun May 9th, 1849, finished May 15th, 1849. Bust.   Price, $150.00

1564 SERGEANT, JOHN (1779–1852).

Eminent Philadelphia lawyer and member of Congress, and candidate for Vice-President of the United States on ticket with Henry Clay. President of Pennsylvania Constitutional Convention for 1837. Portrait begun Dec. 27th, 1810, finished Feb. 27th, 1811. Bust.   Price, $60.00

LIST OF PAINTINGS

1565 SERGEANT, JOHN (1779–1852).

Half length, seated, facing left. Portrait begun Sept. 28th, 1832, finished Nov. 1st, 1832. Size 29″ × 36″. Painted for the members of the Philadelphia Bar. Price, $150.00

Owned by the "Law Association," of Philadelphia.

1566 SERGEANT, MRS. JOHN.

She was Miss Margaretta Watmough, and married John Sergeant, the well-known Philadelphia lawyer. Portrait begun Jan. 25th, 1819, finished Feb. 20th, 1819. Bust, head to left, hair curled, hand holds drapery at breast with India shawl draped over arm. Signed " TS 1819 " on face of canvas. Price, $100.00

Owned by Miss Katherine S. Smith, of Philadelphia.

1567 SESSIONS, JO. W.

Of Natchez, Miss. Portrait begun Sept. 4th, 1847, finished Sept. 23rd, 1847. Bust. Price, $100.00

1568 SEVIER, MRS.

Of Arkansas. Painted in Washington. Portrait begun April 30th, 1840, finished May 22nd, 1840. Bust. Price, $200.00

1569 SEWEL, MR.

Whe married Miss Janeway; the portrait was painted in Baltimore, being begun Oct. 13th, 1852, finished Jan. 10th, 1852. Bust.

1570 SHAKESPEARE, WILLIAM.

Painted from an engraving, begun Aug. 30th, 1864, finished Sept. 3rd, 1864. Size 17″ × 20″. Price, $30.00

1571 SHAKESPEARE, WILLIAM.

Copied from Chandos. Begun Aug. 19th, 1865, finished Sept. 5th, 1865. Head. Price, $50.00

1572 SHARP, MR. T.

Merchant. Portrait begun May 9th, 1807, finished May 29th, 1807. Bust. Price, $50.00

1573 SHARP, MRS. T.

Portrait begun May 5th, 1807, finished May 27th, 1807. Bust. Price, $50.00

LIST OF PAINTINGS

1574 SHARP, MASTER.

Portrait painted for his mother, begun May 2nd, 1864, finished May 14th, 1864. Head. Price, $50.00

1575 SHAW, MISS CHARLOTTE (b. 1842).

Portrait painted for her father; she married Robert Howell. Head to right, hair parted in middle. Canvas 20″ × 24″. Portrait begun Jan. 8th, 1858, finished Jan. 25th, 1858. Price, $80.00

Owned by Mrs. Benjamin Chew Tilghman, Philadelphia.

1576 SHAW, MISS NANCY.

Portrait painted for her father. Head to right, hair parted in middle. Canvas 20″ × 24″. Portrait begun Jan. 8th, 1858, finished Jan. 25th, 1858.
Price, $80.00

Owned by Mrs. Benjamin Chew Tilghman, Philadelphia.

1577 SHAW, SIR J.

Portrait painted for Mr. W. Douglas, begun Jan. 20th, 1844, finished February 3rd, 1844. Bust. Price, $100.00

1578 SHEAF, MR.

Portrait begun Feb. 14th, 1814, finished April, 1814. Size 29″ × 36″.
Price, $100.00

1579 SHEAF, MRS.

Portrait begun Jan. 28th, 1814, finished March, 1814. Size 29″ × 36″.
Price, $100.00

1580 SHELBY, ISAAC (1750–1826).

Soldier, and first Governor of Kentucky, was voted a medal by Congress in 1818 for the victory at the battle of the Thames. Made for the medal, eight inches in diameter, begun July 26th, 1821, finished July 27th, 1821. Bust. Price, $30.00

1581 SHELTON, MRS.

(Née Miss King.) Portrait begun Nov. 26th, 1844, finished Dec. 3rd, 1844. Head. Price, $80.00

1582 SHERLOCK, MR.

Of Baltimore. Portrait begun July 15th, 1808, finished Sept. 7th, 1808. Bust. Price, $50.00

1583 SHERLOCK, MRS.

Painted in Baltimore, portrait begun Dec. 12th, 1820, finished February, 1821. Bust. Price, $80.00

1584 SHIELDS, MRS. CHARLES W. (1827–1853).

(Née Charlotte Bain.) Deceased, copied from a talbotype, painting begun March 31st, 1854, and finished April 19th, 1854. Head, canvas size 20″ × 25″. Price, $100.00
Owned by Bayard Stockton, Esq., of " Morven," Princeton, N. J.

NOTE.—Portrait damaged by fire and restored.

1585 SHIPPEN, EDWARD (1729–1806).

Deceased, copied from portrait painted by Gilbert Stuart, owned by Corcoran Art Gallery, of Washington, D. C. Copy begun Nov. 15th, 1848, finished Dec. 14th, 1848. Bust. Price, $100.00
Edward Shippen was Chief Justice of the Supreme Court of Pennsylvania, 1795–1805; he was the father of Peggy Shippen, who married Benedict Arnold.
Owned by the Law Association, of Philadelphia.

1586 SHOEMAKER, MRS. EDWARD.

Portrait begun March 8th, 1808, finished April 23rd, 1808. Bust.
Subscriber price, $30.00

1587 SIDDONS, MISS AMY.

Miss Amy Siddons was the sister of Mary Siddons, wife of Israel Whelen, she married Mr. Kintzing. Half length, seated on sofa with arm resting on carved end, head to left with ringlets, Empire gown with low neck.
Owned by the Worcester Art Museum. Painted about 1820–5.

1588 SIGOIGNE, MLLE ADÈLE.

She was of West Indian parentage, and conducted a famous girls school in Philadelphia; she was also prominent as a musician. Portrait begun Oct. 26th, 1829, finished Dec. 26th, 1829. Bust, leaning on harp, large hat with flowers, and low-necked dress. Canvas size 24⅞″ × 30″. Price, $75.00
Owned in 1921 by Knoedler & Co., New York.

1589 SIGOURNEY, MRS. LYDIA H. (1791–1865).

Poetess and philanthropist. Portrait was painted from a photograph. Bust, nearly full face with white cap and white lace at neck of dark dress. Painted for the Colonization Society, begun July 11th, 1865, finished Aug. 22nd, 1865. Size 20″ × 24″. Price, $50.00
Deposited at the Pennsylvania Historical Society.

1590 SILL, JOSEPH (1801–1854).

Philadelphia merchant. Portrait begun July 30th, 1832, finished Aug. 11th, 1832. Head, size 17″ × 20″. Price, $60.00

Owned by Joseph Sill Clark, Esq., Chestnut Hill, Philadelphia.

1591 SILL, MRS. JOSEPH (1801–1877).

(Was Miss Jane Todhunter.) Head to left with lace head-dress. Portrait begun April 6th, 1832, finished April 24th, 1832. Head, size 17″ × 20″. Price, $60.00

Owned by Joseph Sill Clark, Esq., Chestnut Hill, Philadelphia.

NOTE.—Excellent copies of Nos. 1590 and 1591 have been made and are owned by the family.

1592 SILVESTER, MRS. LOUISA.

Painted for E. Gardette, begun Jan. 30th, 1833, finished Feb. 7th, 1833. Head. Price, $60.00

1593 SIMONS, MR.

Of the West Indies. Portrait begun April 29th, 1847, finished May 16th, 1847. Bust. Price, $100.00

1594 SIMONS, MRS.

Daughter of the late Mr. Ball. Portrait begun April 24th, 1846, finished May 6th, 1846. Head. Price, $150.00

1595 SIMONS, MISS.

Daughter of Dr. Simons. Portrait begun April 6th, 1846, finished April 17th, 1846. Head. Price, $150.00

1596 SIMPSON, MR.

Of Pittsburgh, Penna. Portrait begun May 28th, 1841, finished June 12th, 1841. Bust. Price, $200.00

1597 SKINNER, MR.

Of North Carolina. Portrait begun Sept. 27th, 1825, finished Nov. 7th, 1825. Bust. Price, $60.00

1598 SKINNER, MR.

Of North Carolina. Portrait begun Aug. 17th, 1837, finished Sept. 11th, 1837. Bust. Price, $200.00

1599 Skinner, Rev. Thomas H. (1791–1871).

Full bust, nearly full face, portrait begun Aug. 5th, 1816, finished Dec. 1st, 1816. Painted for Mrs. Montgomery. Bust. Price, $100.00 Portrait lithographed by Albert Newsam.

1600 Skinner, Mrs. Thomas H. (1797–1824).

Was Miss Emily Montgomery, married Rev. Thomas H. Skinner, a prominent Presbyterian clergyman. Portrait begun Feb. 9th, 1829, finished Feb. 20th, 1829. Head. Price, $50.00

1601 Skinner, Mrs. Thomas H.

Portrait begun Aug. 5th, 1816, finished Dec. 3rd, 1816. Bust. Price, $100.00

1602 Skinner, Mrs. Thomas H.

Copied from first portrait. Painted for Mr. Meggs, begun Aug. 23rd, 1824, finished Oct. 2nd, 1824. Size 10" × 8". Price, $30.00

1603 Slevin, Mr.

Portrait begun Oct. 23rd, 1856, finished Nov. 11th, 1856. Head. Price, $80.00

1604 Slevin, Mrs.

Portrait begun Nov. 3rd, 1856, finished Nov. 17th, 1856. Head. Price, $80.00

1605 Slevin, Miss Jane.

Portrait painted for her parents, begun Sept. 1st, 1856, finished Sept. 8th, 1856. Head. Price, $80.00

1606 Smith, Charles.

Portrait begun Oct. 27th, 1828, finished Nov. 1st, 1828, for J. B. Smith. Head. Price, $50.00

1607 Smith, Charles.

Portrait copied from first portrait. Painted 1828. Head. Price, $50.00

1608 Smith, Daniel (1755–1836).

Philadelphia merchant. Entered the counting house of Francis Gurney, afterwards Gurney & Smith. He married Elizabeth Shute. Bust, nearly full face, high coat collar and white stock and bow. Portrait begun April 19th, 1808, finished May 2nd, 1808. Size 20" × 24". Subscriber price, $30.00 Owned by J. Somers Smith, Esq., Philadelphia.

1609 SMITH, ELIZABETH.

Elizabeth Sully, sister of the artist, married Middleton Smith, of South Carolina. Head to left, hair parted in middle with lace cap or head-dress. Signed " JS 1828." Size 19⅛" × 15¼". Head. Portrait begun Sept. 19th, 1828, finished Sept. 26th, 1828. Painting has been reproduced in process print. Price, $50.00

Owned by George S. Palmer, Esq.

1610 SMITH, ELIZABETH.

(Sister of the artist.) Inscribed on back "Copied from miniature by Peticolas, by Thomas Sully in 1812." Oval.

Owned by Miss Sarah Sully Rawlins, Philadelphia.

1611 SMITH, MISS EMMA (1825–1879).

Of South Bay. Married William Allston Pringle. Portrait begun March 14th, 1842, finished March 29th, 1842. Head. Size 17" × 20".
Price, $100.00

Owned by her daughter, Mrs. Benjamin Rhett, of Mobile, Ala.

1612 SMITH, MISS FRANCES.

Portrait painted for Mrs. Cresson, Sr. Whole-length portrait, 50" × 37". Painting begun March 25th, 1833, finished April 16th, 1833.
Price, $250.00

1613 SMITH, FRANCIS GURNEY (1784–1873).

Treasurer of the Musical Fund Society, 1820–1864, and for thirty-eight years warden of St. Peter's P. E. Church, Philadelphia. Portrait begun Aug. 14th, 1856, finished Aug. 25th, 1856. Signed on back " JS 1856." Bust. head to right, high collar and block stock. Size 29" × 36".

Owned by the Musical Fund Society, on Locust St., Philadelphia.

1614 SMITH, MRS. GEORGE R.

Was Miss Mary Roberts, and married George Smith, of Philadelphia; her sister married Governor Edward Coles. Portrait begun April 3rd, 1837, finished May 3rd, 1837. Signed on face " JS 1837." Head, 16" × 19".
Price, $150.00

Hanging in rooms of Pennsylvania Historical Society, Philadelphia.

1615 SMITH, MRS. JACOB RIDGWAY (1795–1846).

(Née Rebecca Shoemaker Wharton.) Portrait begun Nov. 24th, 1828, finished Dec. 31st, 1828. Bust, head to left, black dress open at the neck, arm resting on a red book on table. Size 25" × 30". Price, $75.00

Owned by Mrs. William H. Gaw, of Philadelphia, and deposited at the Pennsylvania Academy of Fine Arts.

1616 SMITH, MRS. JAMES.

(Née Elizabeth McEween.) The register notes that the hand was intro-
duced in the portrait, and that it was painted for Miss McEween. Begun
Nov. 24th, 1823, finished Dec. 19th, 1823. Bust.   Price, $75.00
Owned by Oliver B. Judson, Philadelphia.

1617 SMITH, MRS. JOSEPH.

(Née Emily McEween.) Portrait painted for Mrs. Cresson, begun March
5th, 1833, finished April 5th, 1833. Bust.   Price, $100.00

1618 SMITH, MRS. JOSEPH.

(Née Emily McEween.) Copied from first portrait, painted for Miss
McEween, begun June 28th, 1825, finished June 30th, 1825. Head.
     Price, $30.00

Owned by Oliver B. Judson, Philadelphia.

1619 SMITH, J. B.

Of Arch Street near Twelfth Street, Philadelphia. Portrait begun March
3rd, 1828, finished March 22nd, 1828. Size 19" × 15".   Price, $50.00

1620 SMITH, MRS. NEWBURG.

Portrait painted for her husband, begun Feb. 21st, 1848, finished March
18th, 1848. Bust.   Price, $100.00

1621 SMITH, MRS. ROBERT.

Of South Bend. Portrait begun April 23rd, 1842, finished April 29th,
1842. Head.   Price, $150.00
Owned by Mrs. William E. Huger, of Charleston, S. C.

1622 SMITH, REV. SAMUEL STANHOPE (1750–1819).

He was President of Princeton College at the time this portrait was painted
which shows him in cap and gown as a minister of the Presbyterian Church.
Portrait begun Sept. 27th, 1814, finished Nov. 3rd, 1814. Head, size of
panel 27" × 21".   Price, $50.00
Owned by Miss L. P. Bullock, of Lexington, Ky.

1623 SMITH, REV. SAMUEL STANHOPE (1750–1819).

Copy of first portrait, begun Oct. 1st, 1814, finished Nov. 7th, 1814.
Head.   Price, $50.00

LIST OF PAINTINGS

1624 SMITH, WILLIAM (1727–1803).

Provost of the University of Pennsylvania. Copy of the portrait painted by Gilbert Stuart. Sully's painting was for Professor Smith's grandson, begun Dec. 5th, 1855, finished Dec. 21st, 1855. Bust. Size, height 40″, width 50″. Price, $100.00

Owned by William Rudolph Smith, of Philadelphia.

1625 SMITH, MR.

A relative of Mr. Krumbhaar's. Portrait begun June 29th, 1813, finished Sept., 1913. Bust. Price, $70.00

1626 SMITH, MISS.

Painted for Mrs. Allibon, begun Jan. 1st, 1830, finished Jan. 23rd, 1830. Bust. Price, $75.00

1627 SNIDER, JACOB S., JR.

Portrait begun March 18th, 1836, finished March 23rd, 1836. Head. Price, $100.00

1628 SNIDER, JACOB S., JR.

(To cancel a former portrait.) Begun Feb. 24th, 1840, finished March 4th, 1840. Head. Price, $150.00

1629 SNIDER, CHILDREN.

Group of three children of Jacob Snider. Painting begun Feb. 3rd, 1841, finished March 26th, 1841. Signed " TS 1841." (See illustration.) Size 29″ × 36″. Price, $500.00

Owned by John F. Braun, Esq., of Philadelphia.

1630 SNIDER, MRS. JACOB S., JUNR.

Portrait begun April 14th, 1835, finished April 24th, 1835. Head. Price, $80.00

1631 SNYDER, SIMON (1759–1819).

Governor of Pennsylvania, 1808–1817. Half length, seated to right, holding a paper in right hand. Engraved by David Edwin and published in 1809 (Fielding, No. 184). Painting begun Jan. 6th, 1809, finished Jan. 22nd, 1809. Size 30″ × 24″. On wood panel, and signed on back " TS 1809." Price, $50.00

Owned by Albert Rosenthal, of Philadelphia.

Copy by James R. Lambdin, at Pennsylvania Historical Society, Philadelphia.

LIST OF PAINTINGS

1632 SNYDER, MISS.

Portrait begun June 10th, 1812, finished July 17th, 1812. Bust. The register notes that the "hand was introduced," the price being $80.00

1633 SOUTHGATE, MRS.

Of Richmond, Virginia. Portrait begun Oct. 10th, 1814, finished November 5th, 1814. Bust. Price, $80.00

1634 SPANG, MRS. C. F.

Of Pittsburgh, Pa. Head, with hand introduced, portrait begun Sept. 9th, 1845, finished Sept. 15th, 1845. Price, $100.00

1635 SPANG, ROSALIE.

Portrait painted for her parents, of Pittsburgh, Pa., begun Oct. 27th, 1848, finished Nov. 4th, 1848. Head. Price, $80.00

1637 SPARKS, JARED (1789–1866).

Historian, writer and editor. Portrait painted for Mr. Elliot, of Boston. Head, three-quarter to left, hand resting on portfolio. Portrait begun Jan. 25th, 1831, finished March 5th, 1831. Size 29″ × 36″. Price, $100.00
Lithographed by Newsam, and engraved by S. A. Schoff for National Portrait Gallery of Distinguished Americans.
Owned by Mrs. W. J. Clemson, Taunton, Mass.

1637 SPARKS, MRS.

Portrait begun Dec. 4th, 1855, finished Dec. 29th, 1855. Head.
Price, $80.00

1638 SPARKS, MRS. THOMAS (–1865).

Head to right, hair parted in middle and drawn down on sides over ears, black scarf over shoulder. Size 17½″ × 20″. "TS 1856." Price, $80.00
Owned by Miss Sparks, Philadelphia.

1639 STANARD, MRS.

Portrait begun March 12th, 1851, finished April 16th, 1851. Head.
Price, $100.00

1640 STANARD, MRS.

Copy for Mr. Surtees. Painting begun April 11th, 1851, finished April 21st, 1851. Head. Price, $100.00

1641 STERLING, MRS.

Portrait painted at Baltimore, begun Jan. 7th, 1853, finished Feb. 4th, 1853. Bust. Price, $150.00

1642 STERRETT, MRS.

Portrait painted at Baltimore for Mr. Winchester, begun Nov. 31st, 1852, finished Dec. 1st, 1852. Head. Price, $100.00

1643 STETH, MRS. CATHERINE.

(Was Miss Potter.) Portrait begun July 26th, 1824, finished Nov. 22nd, 1824. Head. Price, $30.00

1644 STEVENSON, ANDREW.

Portrait begun April, 1805, and finished the same month, size 25" × 30". Price, $25.00

1645 STEVENSON, MISS FRANCES.

(Niece of McAllisters.) Portrait begun Jan. 27th, 1847, finished Feb. 7th, 1847. Bust. Price, $100.00

1646 STEWART, CHARLES, U. S. N. (1778–1869).

Commodore Stewart, commanded the "Constitution" in the War of 1812; he was voted a gold medal by Congress. His daughter Delia was the mother of Charles Stewart Parnell, the Irish agitator. Portrait full length, standing, left foot forward, hand on sword, white satin breeches, black coat. Begun June 10th, 1811, finished April 13th, 1812. Size 58" × 94". Price, $300.00

Owned by Mrs. Marie T. Garland, and deposited with Museum of Fine Arts, Boston, Mass.

1647 STEWART, CHARLES, U. S. N. (1778–1869).

Portrait painted for a medal awarded him by Congress. Bust painted in olive gray, begun July 10th, 1817, and finished July 29th, 1817. Size 26" × 20". Price, $50.00

Owned by the United States Naval Academy, Annapolis, Md.

1648 STEWART, CHARLES, U. S. N. (1778–1869).

Portrait painted about 1830 when he resided at Bordentown, N. J. Bust, black coat, white stock, nearly full face, side whiskers. Size 25" × 30".

Owned by Daniel H. Carstairs, Esq., Germantown, Philadelphia.

1649 STEWART, DOUGALD (1753–1828).

Sir Henry Raeburn presented the Academy of Fine Arts with a replica of his famous portrait on his election as an honorary member to the Academy. This is the painting Sully copied for Dr. Philip Tidyman in 1825. The picture by Raeburn was destroyed in the fire at the Academy in 1845. Size 44" × 56". Price, $150.00

Owned by the St. Andrew's Society, of Charleston, S. C.

LIST OF PAINTINGS

1650 STEWART, DOUGALD (1753–1828).

    Bust, copied from Sir Henry Raeburn's replica. Size canvas 24″ × 30″. This copy was painted by Sully in 1824 and is owned by John F. Lewis, Esq., of Philadelphia.

1651 STITH, MAJOR.

    (Deceased, copy of a portrait.) Begun Nov. 30th, 1825, finished Dec. 6th, 1825. Size 17″ × 20″.   Price, $30.00

1652 STOCKER, JOHN CLEMENTS (1786–1833).

    Portrait painted for Colonel Louis de Tousard, begun May 12th, 1814, and finished July 5th, 1814, and sent to Colonel Tousard at New Orleans, La. Size 29″ × 36″.   Price, $100.00
Owned by Mrs. Arthington Gilpin, of Philadelphia.

1653 STOCKER, MRS. JOHN CLEMENTS (1788–1877).

    (Née Caroline de Tousard, eldest daughter of Colonel Louis de Tousard.) Portrait begun Nov. 14th, 1814, finished Dec. 29th, 1814. Size 29″ × 36″.   Price, $100.00
Owned by Mr. Arthington Gilpin, of Philadelphia.

1654 STOCKTON, JOHN PETER (1826–1900).

    Of Princeton, N. J.
Owned by Richard Stockton, Esq., Trenton, N. J.

1655 STOCKTON, MRS. JOHN POTTER (1829–1896).

    (Née Sara Marks.) Of Princeton, N. J., portrait begun Oct. 25th, 1847, finished on Nov. 20th, 1847. Oval. Size 29″ × 36″.   Price, $200.00
Owned by Richard Stockton, Esq., Trenton, N. J.

1656 STOCKTON, MRS. PHILIP AUGUSTUS (1816–1908).

    (Née Mary Remington.) Portrait begun Dec. 16th, 1847, noted in artist's register as "Expunged."

1657 STOCKTON, MRS. PHILIP AUGUSTUS (1816–1908).

    (Née Mary Remington.) Portrait painted for her husband, begun March 20th, 1850, finished April 13th, 1850. Bust.   Price, $100.00

1658 STOCKTON, RICHARD (1730–1781).

    Patriot, and signer of the Declaration of Independence. (His daughter Julia married Dr. Benjamin Rush.) Portrait painted for Colonel Alexander Biddle, begun July 7th, 1862, finished July 25th, 1862. Size 30″ × 25″.   Price, $50.00

LIST OF PAINTINGS

1659 STOCKTON, MRS. RICHARD.

(Née Annis Boudinot.)   Portrait painted for Colonel Alexander Biddle, begun July 10th, 1862, finished July 25th, 1862.   Size 30″ × 25″.

Price, $50.00

NOTE.—(Nos. 1658 and 1659.)   The authors are of the opinion that the original portraits were painted by Copley, and that Sully made copies of same.

1660 STOCKTON, ROBERT FIELD (1795–1866).

Of Princeton, N. J.   Entered the United States Navy 1811, and took possession of California for the United States in 1846.   He resigned in 1850, and the next year became United States Senator from New Jersey.   Portrait begun May 2nd, 1851, finished May 7th, 1851.   Head to left.   Bust.   Size 25″ × 30″.   Price, $100.00

Owned by Bayard Stockton, Esq., of " Morren," Princeton, N. J.

1661 STOCKTON, ROBERT FIELD (1795–1866).

Copy for Princeton College, painting begun May 5th, 1851, finished May 18th, 1851.   Head to left.   Bust, size 25″ × 30″.   Price, $100.00

Owned by Richard Stockton, Esq., Trenton, N. J.

1662 STOCKTON, ROBERT FIELD (1795–1866).

Copy for Colonization Society.   Inscribed by Sully on back of painting, " 1851, No. 3."   Copy begun May 9th, 1851, finished May 19th, 1851. Bust, size 25″ × 30″.   Price, $100.00

Colonization Society's Paintings at Pennsylvania Historical Society, of Philadelphia.

1663 STOCKTON, ROBERT FIELD (1847–1891).

Oldest son of John Potter Stockton.   Full-length portrait of a child of three, mischievously upsetting a basket of flowers from a balustrade.   Painting begun Sept. 15th, 1849, finished Nov. 12th, 1849.   Size 29″ × 36″.

Price, $300.00

Owned by Richard Stockton, Esq., Trenton, N. J.

1664 STOCKTON, REV. THOMAS HEWLINGS (1808–1868).

A Methodist minister, for many years chaplain of House of Representatives and to the United States Senate at Washington.   Size 29″ × 36″. Bust, with hand introduced.   Portrait begun Jan. 26th, 1843, finished Feb. 21st, 1843.   Price, $125.00

Purchased by John F. Braun, of Philadelphia, from Mrs. Anna Stockton Allen.

1665 STODDARD, HON.

Deceased, portrait copied from a miniature, begun Feb. 11th, 1851, finished Feb. 27th, 1851. Head.   Price, $100.00

1666 STOTT, MR.

Deceased, portrait painted from an engraving, begun Dec. 17th, 1830, finished March 27th, 1831. Bust.   Price, $75.00

1667 STOTT, MR.

(Deceased.) Copied from a former portrait, begun March 4th, 1831, finished March 16th, 1831. Bust.   Price, $75.00

1668 STOTT, MRS. EBENEZER.

From Scotland. Portrait begun Oct. 5th, 1830, finished Oct. 21st, 1830. Bust.   Price, $75.00

1669 STOTT, SARAH.

Portrait painted for her nephew, Colonel Cooper, London. Painting begun Nov. 4th, 1840, finished Nov. 17th, 1840. Bust.   Price, $200.00

1670 STOTT, MRS.

Copy of her portrait, begun on Feb. 16th, 1831, finished March 4th, 1831. Bust.   Price, $75.00

1671 STOUGHT, R. M. (OR STOUT).

Of Allentown, New Jersey. Portrait begun Dec. 1st, 1830, finished May 12th, 1831. Bust.   Price, $75.00

1672 STOUGHT, MRS. (OR STOUT).

Of Allentown, New Jersey. Portrait begun Nov. 2nd, 1835, finished Nov. 9th, 1835. Bust.   Price, $100.00

1673 STRICKLAND, MR. (SR.).

Portrait begun April 11th, 1809, finished April 22nd, 1809. Size 17" × 20".   Price, $40.00

1674 STRICKLAND, WILLIAM (1789–1854).

Eminent architect of Philadelphia. Portrait begun June, 1820, finished July 3rd, 1820. Bust.   Price, $75.00

1675 STRICKLAND, WILLIAM (1789–1854).

Portrait begun Nov. 27th, 1836, finished Dec. 23rd, 1836. Head.
                    Price, $100.00

1676 STROBIA, FRANK.

(And his father.) Portrait begun April, 1805, and was finished May, 1805. Size 25″ × 30″. Price, $50.00

1677 STROTHERS, MISS THEODOSIA.

Of St. Louis. Portrait begun Aug. 14th, 1844, finished Aug. 21st, 1844. Head. Price, $80.00

1678 STRUTHERS, MRS.

Portrait begun July 25th, 1832, finished August 10th, 1832. Bust. Price, $100.00
Owned by Mrs. Edward S. Dunn, Chestnut Hill, Penna.

1679 STUART, MRS.

Of Jamaica, New Jersey. Portrait begun April 17th, 1837, finished May 2nd, 1837. Bust. Price, $200.00

1680 STUART, MRS.

(Was Miss Calvert.) Portrait begun Sept. 3rd, 1833, finished Sept. 28th, 1833. Head. Price, $60.00

1681 STYLES, MR.

Of Carlisle, Penna. Portrait begun March 20th, 1843, finished April 1st, 1843. Head. Price, $80.00

1682 STYLES, MISS.

(Cousin of Fanny Hayne.) Portrait begun March 22nd, 1843, finished March 14th, 1843. Head. Price, $80.00

1683 SULLY, ALFRED (1820–1879).

Son of the artist. Graduated at West Point in 1841. Served in Indian Wars and the Civil War. Portrait painted for his mother in the uniform of a West Point cadet, begun July 18th, 1839, finished July 20th, 1839. Head, 20″ × 24″. Price, $150.00
Owned by Mrs. Albert Sully, Brooklyn, New York.

1684 SULLY, ALFRED (1820–1879).

Son of the artist, painted as a present for Edward F. Peticolas, miniature painter of Richmond, Va. Portrait begun March 29th, 1830, finished April 5th, 1830. Bust. Price, $50.00

1685 SULLY, ALFRED (1820–1879).

The artist's son, sketch painted for his sister, Blanche Sully, begun Feb. 12th, 1863, finished March 23rd, 1863. Head.   Price, $40.00

1686 SULLY, ALFRED AND JANE.

Son and daughter of the artist, the former aged eight, the latter twenty-two. Jane is shown as reading from a book which she holds in her hand. Alfred's head is shown looking over the book. Engraved by Forrest as "Brother and Sister." Painting begun Oct. 3rd, 1829, finished June 15th, 1831. Size 29" × 36".   Price, $200.00
Owned by Mr. S. S. Spalding, of Buffalo, N. Y.

1687 SULLY, ALFRED AND MANUELLA.

Heads, painted from daguerreotypes of the artist's son Alfred and his first wife, Manuella Zimeno, of Monterey, Cal. Painting begun June 4th, 1851, finished July 8th, 1851. Bust size.   Price, $160.00

1688 SULLY, BLANCHE (1814–1898).

The register states that "this painting was made for Ellen's instruction," begun Nov. 5th, 1834, finished Nov. 13th, 1834. Head.   Price, $80.00

1689 SULLY, BLANCHE (1814–1898).

Head, neck, shoulders and left hand of a young lady holding over her head a feather fan, looking to the right. Panel, size 19¾" × 17", signed on face at left corner " TS 1837." Engraved by John Cheney (K 49).
Owned by Mrs. Mary E. Berens, of Germantown, Philadelphia.

1690 SULLY, BLANCHE.

Bust, head turned to left, wearing a red feather in her black hair. Size of panel 15" × 20". Signed " TS 1840."
Owned by Miss Sarah Sully Rawlins, Philadelphia.

1691 SULLY, BLANCHE (1814–1898).

Bust, nearly full face, smoothly parted hair and wearing a black band across her forehead. Signed " TS 1839." Size 20" × 24".
Owned by Mrs. Albert Sully, of Brooklyn, New York.

1692 SULLY, BLANCHE AND ELLEN.

Daughters of the painter, aged four and two years, painted for their mother, Sarah Sully, begun July 10th, 1818, finished August 30th, 1818. Painted on wood panel 19½" × 14½".   Price, $150.00
Owned by Mrs. Harold M. Sill, Germantown, Philadelphia.

LIST OF PAINTINGS

1693 BLANCHE AND ROSALIE.

Daughters of the painter, aged respectively twenty-eight and twenty-four. Busts, with heads to left, one looks over the shoulder of her sister and rests her hand on her neck. Size 24" high, 30" wide, portrait begun Sept. 1st, 1842, finished Oct. 1st, 1842.   Price, $200.00

Engraved by John Sartain as "The Rose and the Lily." (See illustration.) Was in the possession of the Stanfield family of New York who were friends of the artist's family.

Owned by John D. McIlhenny, Esq., Philadelphia.

1694 SULLY, BLANCHE AND ROSALIE.

Replica of the "Rose and Lily." Painting cut down to a size 17" wide and 20" high, and does not show the girl's arm and shoulder to the right. Signed " TS 1842."

Owned by Albert Rosenthal, artist, Philadelphia, Pa.

1695 SULLY, CHESTER.

The artist's brother, portrait begun July 8th, 1803, finished Aug. 18th, 1803. Painted at Richmond, Va. Size 10" × 12".   Price, $20.00

Owned by Edward W. Hughes, of Charleston, S. C.

1696 SULLY, CHESTER.

Brother of Thomas Sully. Portrait begun May 16th, 1810, finished May 28th, 1810. Bust.   Price, $60.00

1697 SULLY, ELLEN O. (1816–1896).

Daughter of the artist, afterwards Mrs. John H. Wheeler. Portrait sketch begun Jan. 31st, 1824, finished Feb. 6th, 1824. Bust. Size of canvas 16" × 14".   Price, $30.00

Owned by Miss Sarah Sully Rawlins, Philadelphia.

1698 SULLY, JANE COOPER (1807–1877).

She was the daughter of the artist, and also painted portraits. She married in 1833 William Henry Westray Darley, the brother of Felix O. C. Darley, the illustrator, and her son was Francis Thomas Sully Darley, the organist. Half length, seated, low-necked dress with long curl on neck, head to right. Canvas H. 35¾", W. 29". Signed " TS 1838."

Owned by Mr. Luke V. Lockwood.

1699 SULLY, JANE (1807–1877).

Daughter of the artist, sketch painted for Mrs. M. Smith, portrait begun on Dec. 26th, 1828, finished Jan., 1829. Head.   Price, $50.00

LIST OF PAINTINGS

1700 SULLY, JANE (1807–1877).
Sketch of the artist's daughter, painted Oct. 24th, 1824. Head.
Price, $30.00

NOTE.—See " Darley " for portraits of Jane after her marriage.

1701 SULLY, LAWRENCE (1769–1803).
Born in Kilkenny, Ireland, he was the eldest brother of the artist Thomas Sully, who married his widow. Lawrence settled in Charleston, S. C., on his arrival in this country, removing later to Virginia. Portrait begun Nov. 1st, 1803, finished Nov. 16th. Bust. Price, $20.00

1702 SULLY, MARY CHESTER (1802–1845).
Daughter of Lawrence Sully, married John Neagle, the artist, in 1826. Head to right, low-neck white gown, hair drawn down plainly over ears. Size 17½" × 20½". Portrait painted in 1842 and was owned by Blanche Sully, purchased from the descendants by John Hill Morgan, of Brooklyn, N. Y.

1703 SULLY, MARY CHESTER.
(A sketch presented to Mrs. J. Savage.) Head turned to left, black hair with curls. Portrait begun Oct. 4th, 1824, finished Oct. 6th, 1824. Head. Size 14" × 18". Price, $20.00
Owned by Miss Sarah Sully Rawlins, Philadelphia.

1704 SULLY, MATTHEW (–1815).
Father of the artist, portrait painted at Richmond, Virginia. Begun July 8th, 1803, finished Aug. 18th, 1803. Size 10" × 12". Price, $20.00

1705 SULLY, MATTHEW (–1815).
Father of the artist, copied from the portrait painted for his sister Betsey. Begun March 27th, 1829, finished in April. Size 20" × 17".
Owned by Edward W. Hughes, of Charleston, S. C.

1706 SULLY, MATTHEW (–1815).
Father of the artist. Head, nearly full face, gray hair, fur collar to coat. Size 15" × 18". Inscribed on back of canvas " Painted from sketches, TS 1826."
Owned by Miss Sarah Sully Rawlins, Philadelphia.

1707 SULLY, MATTHEW (–1815).
Copied from a miniature, begun May 14th, 1815, finished June 12th, 1815. Bust. Price, $80.00

LIST OF PAINTINGS

1708 SULLY, MATTHEW.

A brother of the artist, who married Elizabeth Robertson, of Virginia, and their son was Robert Matthew Sully, the artist, born in Petersburg, Va., July 17th, 1803. The portrait (size 27" × 23") remained in the family until acquired by the Ehrich Gallery of New York from a granddaughter of Matthew Sully.

1709 SULLY, ROSALIE KEMBLE (1818–1847).

Registered as the "Student," painting intended for Edward Carey, begun Nov. 23rd, 1839, finished Nov. 30th, 1839. Bust, seated, resting crossed hands on portfolio, holding pencil; lamp shade throws the upper part of the face in shadow. Signed "The Student, TS 1839," also " TS 1839." Size 23½" × 29½".   Price, $200.00
Bequest of F. T. S. Darley to Metropolitan Museum of New York.

1710 SULLY, ROSALIE KEMBLE (1818–1847).

This portrait was copied for her sister Blanche, begun June 7th, 1871, finished June 21st, 1871. Size 24" × 32". Signed on back " TS 1871." (Replica of painting of 1839.)   Price, $100.00
Owned by Mrs. Alfred Sully, Brooklyn, New York.

1711 SULLY, ROSALIE (1818–1847).

Sketch of Rosalie reading. Begun Jan. 20th, 1840, finished on Jan. 23rd, 1840. Size 17" × 13".   Price, $20.00
Owned by Miss Sarah Sully Rawlins, Philadelphia, Pa.

1712 SULLY, ROSALIE (1818–1847).

The register states it was painted "to help Hugh Bridport," the English artist who settled in Philadelphia in 1816. Portrait begun Oct. 9th, 1836, finished Dec. 2nd, 1839. Signed " TS 1839." Size 20" × 24". Bust, head to left, with hair parted in middle and ringlets, low-necked dress with rose in corsage.
Owned by Faris C. Pitt, of Baltimore, Md.

1713 SULLY, ROSALIE (1818–1847).

"Prayer." Bust, nearly in profile, of young woman, with eyes and clasped hands uplifted in prayer, pinkish dress. Inscribed on back of canvas " TS 1854." My daughter Rosalie at the age of 18." Size 20" × 24".
Sold at auction of Collection of Mrs. Benjamin Thaw, New York.

287

1714 SULLY, SARAH (1779–1867).

Sarah Annis was born at Annapolis and first married Lawrence Sully, also a painter, after his death she became the wife of the younger brother Thomas. Bust, full face with scarf over her head and shoulders. This portrait painted by Sully for himself. Begun March 22nd, 1830, finished Feb. 22nd, 1832. Bust.   Price, $75.00

1715 SULLY, SARAH (1779–1867).

The artist's wife. Bust, portrait seen full face; she wears a reddish-brown dress, and a cream-colored scarf is over her dark brown hair and held about her shoulders with the left hand. Inscribed on the back, "For my daughter Jane Darley, TS 1851." (Replica of the portrait painted 1832.) H. 29½", W. 22⅝". Canvas, oval. Monogrammed, "TS 1832."
Bequest of Francis T. S. Darley, 1914, to the Metropolitan Museum.

1716 SULLY, SARAH (1779–1867).

Wife of the artist. (See illustration.) Size 25" × 30". Inscribed on back of canvas, "Painted in 1806. Retouched in 1856. Sarah Sully, wife of Thomas Sully. TS."
Owned by the Ehrich Gallery, New York.

1717 SULLY, SARAH (1779–1867).

With Betsy and Mary. Nieces of the artist. Portrait begun Nov. 1st, 1803, finished Nov. 30th, 1803. Size 10" × 12".   Price, $30.00

1718 SULLY, SARAH (1779–1867).

With the artist's sister and Jane and Tom Sully. Painting begun Sept. 25th, 1828. Size 29" × 36".

1719 SULLY, SARAH (1779–1867).

Portrait of the wife of the artist and her dog Ponto. Full length, seated in chair, landscape seen through window and bunch of flowers beside her. Portrait painted for his daughter Blanche, begun Aug. 25th, 1848, finished Oct. 3rd, 1848. Size 5' 2" × 3' 5".   Price, $500.00
Picture owned by Miss Sarah Sully Rawlins, Philadelphia, Pa.

1720 SULLY, SARAH (1779–1867).

(Copy from former portrait, for Sally.) Painting begun Oct. 7th, 1851, finished Oct. 20th, 1851. Head.   Price, $100.00

1721 SULLY, SARAH (1779–1867).

Copy noted in register "to supply one sold to E." Begun Jan. 20th, 1859, finished Jan. 29th, 1859. Size 25" × 30".   Price, $100.00

1722 SULLY, SARAH (1779–1867).

The artist's wife, a copy painted for his daughter Blanche, of the head from portrait painted in 1832. Begun Jan. 20th, 1870, finished Jan. 31st, 1870. Signed "T. Sully." Size 15″ × 13″.   Price, $100.00
Owned by Mrs. Albert Sully, Brooklyn, N. Y.

1723 SULLY, SARAH (1779–1867).

The artist's wife. Deceased, painted for Sarah Neagle, partly from recollection, begun Nov. 15th, 1867, finished Dec. 5th, 1867. Size 21″ × 17″.
                              Price, $50.00

1724 SULLY, SARAH.

Sister of the artist. Portrait begun Nov. 1st, 1803, finished Nov. 20th, 1803. Bust.   Price, $20.00

1725 SULLY, THOMAS (1783–1872).

At the age of 21 years. Painted on a panel 6″ × 7½″.
Owned by Mrs. Albert Sully, Brooklyn, New York.

1726 SULLY, THOMAS (1783–1872).

Painted for Mr. Wadsworth, begun on Nov. 20th, 1807, finished Nov. 29th, 1807. Head. The artist's face is in shadow.   Price, $20.00
Owned by the Wadsworth Athenaeum, Hartford, Conn.

1727 SULLY, THOMAS (1783–1872).

Painted for my brother-in-law, J. B. Le Roy. Begun Oct. 2nd, 1807, finished Oct. 11th, 1807. Head.   Price, $30.00

1728 SULLY, THOMAS (1783–1872).

Bust, as a young man, nearly full face, supporting his hand on a book. "𝕋𝕊 1847, Oct. 25." (See illustration.) Size 25″ × 30″. Inscribed on back of canvas "Painted 1808. Retouched and repainted 1856. 𝕋𝕊."
Owned by Ehrich Galleries, New York.

1729 SULLY, THOMAS (1783–1872).

Head, 14½″ × 20″. Signed "Thos. Sully, Aet. 25, June, 1809." Head to right, eyes to front, dark coat and white neckcloth, auburn hair and blue eyes. The portrait was painted for the artist's sister, Mrs. Middleton Smith, of Charleston, S. C., on the eve of his departure for England on June 10th, 1809. It was the property of Mrs. C. Middleton De Wolf, and is owned by Herbert L. Pratt, Esq., of New York.

1730 SULLY, THOMAS (1783–1872).

Portrait of the artist, painted for his stepson, Chester Sully, begun May 5th, 1815, finished May 20th, 1815. Bust. Price, $80.00

1731 SULLY, THOMAS (1783–1872).

Portrait of the artist. Life-size head and shoulders with the body in profile to the right and face front, he wears a brown coat with velvet collar; a paint brush is held in the right hand. H. 17″, W. 14⅛″. Canvas. Monogrammed, " TS 1821." Painted for H. Robinson, begun May 8th, 1821, finished May 15th, 1821. Price, $50.00

Owned by the Metropolitan Museum, New York.

1732 SULLY, THOMAS (1783–1872).

Drawing in pencil representing him as a young man. Full face, high stock. Signed on face of drawing " T. Sully, by himself, 1823." Size 8½″ × 6½″.

Owned by Charles B. Munn, of New York.

1733 SULLY, THOMAS (1783–1872).

Portrait painted for his sister, Mrs. Harriett Porcher. Begun Sept. 22nd, 1828, finished Sept. 24th, 1828. Size 15″ × 19″. Price, $50.00

1734 SULLY, THOMAS AND WIFE.

Thomas Sully painting the portrait of the lady he afterwards married. Busts. Size 20″ × 24″. (See illustration.)

Owned by Pennsylvania Academy of Fine Arts.

1735 SULLY, THOMAS (1783–1872).

The register notes " my own head for Welfare's child T. S. W." Portrait begun Nov. 27th, 1836, finished Feb. 27th, 1837. Head. Price, $100.00

1736 SULLY, THOMAS (1783–1872).

Bust, head to right, with brushes in hand before canvas on easel. Age 66 years. Portrait painted for the order of Mr. Tyler, begun June 11th, 1850, finished June 27th, 1850. Size 24½″ × 30″. Signed " TS June, 1850." Price, $100.00

Owned by Mr. Walter Jennings, of New York.

1737 SULLY, THOMAS (1783–1872).

Self-portrait, painted about 1855. Bust, nearly full face, with curly hair and black stock. Size 25″ × 30″.

Formerly in private collection of the late W. W. Corcoran and given to the Corcoran Gallery of Art, Washington, in 1869, where it now hangs in the permanent collection.

LIST OF PAINTINGS

1738 SULLY, THOMAS (1783–1872).

The artist, head facing right. Portrait painted for Ferdinand J. Dreer, and presented by him to the Pennsylvania Historical Society. Engraved by John Sartain. (See frontispiece.) Portrait begun March 25th, 1856, finished April 2nd, 1856. Size 17″ × 20″. Price, $100.00
Owned by Pennsylvania Historical Society, Philadelphia.

1739 SULLY, THOMAS (1783–1872).

The artist, head facing right. Portrait painted for the Colonization Society and deposited at the Pennsylvania Historical Society. Portrait begun Dec. 15th, 1860, finished Dec. 31st, 1860. Head, size 20″ × 24″.
Price, $80.00
Owned by Pennsylvania Historical Society, Philadelphia.

1740 SULLY, THOMAS.

Portrait of the artist, painted at reduced size for Garrett C. Neagle, begun June 10th, 1867, finished June 18th, 1867. Size 25″ × 30″. Price, $20.00

1741 SULLY, THOMAS (1783–1872).

The artist, painted from a daguerreotype for Blanche, begun on Sept. 27th, 1867, finished Oct. 4th, 1867. Inscribed on back of canvas "To my daughter Blanche. ℡ 1867, Oct." Size 15″ × 13½″. Price, $50.00
Owned by Mrs. Albert Sully, Brooklyn, N. Y.

1742 SULLY, THOMAS (1783–1872).

The artist, portrait painted on order of Musical Fund Society. Bust, nearly full face, head slightly to right, wears a brown coat with black collar. Size 29″ × 36″. Sully was Vice-President of the Musical Fund Society from 1860 to 1872. Portrait begun May 26th, 1867, finished June 3rd, 1868. Price, $100.00
Owned by Musical Fund Society, Philadelphia.

1743 SULLY, THOMAS (1783–1872).

Portrait of the artist at the age of 51 years, painted by himself in 1834. Head to left, with black stock and dark coat; signed and dated on back of canvas. Size 17″ × 20″. "℡ 1834."
Owned by the Pennsylvania Academy of Fine Arts.

1744 SULLY, THOMAS AND HIS DAUGHTER ROSALIE.

Painted as a present for Vogel, of Dresden, begun Jan. 11th, 1840, finished Jan. 20th, 1840. Size 25″ × 21″. Price, $250.00

LIST OF PAINTINGS

1745 SULLY, THOMAS, JR. (1811–1847).

Son of the artist, who painted a number of excellent portraits. Title, "The Torn Hat." Study, bust of a boy, nearly full face, partly in shadow, and wearing a torn straw hat, collar open at the neck. Signed on hat band "TS 1820." Begun July 11th, 1820, finished July 14th, 1820. Panel, size 19" × 14½".　　　　　　　　　　　　　　　　　　Price, $100.00
Loaned by Miss Margaret Greene to the Museum of Fine Arts, Boston, Mass.

1746 SULLY, THOMAS, JR. (1811–1847).

Son of the artist. Bust, head to right. Size 20" × 24".
Owned by Pennsylvania Academy of Fine Arts.

1747 SULLY, TOM AND JANE (WITH FIDELE).

Children of the artist with their dog. Painting begun Aug. 10th, 1812, finished Aug. 20th, 1812. Size 25" × 30".　　　　　　　　　Price, $200.00

1748 SULLY CHILDREN. (GROUP OF FIVE.)

The artist's children painted for their mother, Sarah Sully, begun Aug. 3rd, 1822, finished May 21st, 1824. Jane, Blanche, Ellen, Rosalie and Alfred. The group has foliage in background and one of the children holds a flute or pipe in his hands. Size 44" × 56".　　　　　　Price, $500.00
Owned by Mrs. Charles A. Klink, Germantown, Pa.

1749 SULLY (FAMILY GROUP).

Ten heads on one canvas of the artist's wife and nine of her children.
Owned by Miss Sarah Sully Rawlins.

1750 SULLY (FAMILY GROUP).

Sketch of members of the artist's family, begun July 4th, 1859, finished July 6th, 1859. Size 12" × 19½".　　　　　　　　　　　Price, $10.00

1751 SUMPTER, THOMAS (1734–1832).

Soldier, served in the Revolution and present at Braddock's defeat. He was born in South Carolina. The portrait by Sully, a bust in uniform, is probably a copy of the painting by Charles W. Peale, at Independence Hall, Philadelphia. The Sully painting was formerly owned by General Sumpter's granddaughters, the Misses Brownfield. Reproduced in Bowen's History of Centennial Celebration of Inauguration of Washington.

1752 SWAN, MRS. JAMES (1801–1838).

(Née Elizabeth Donnell, eldest daughter of John and Anna T. Donnell.) Bust.
Owned by Mrs. Henry Barton Jacobs. Exhibited at Maryland Institute, Baltimore, 1921.

1753 SWANN, MISS AND MISS BRYAN.

Portrait begun May 9th, 1831, finished June 14th, 1831. Bust.

Price, $100.00

1754 SWIFT, JOSEPH GARDNER (1783–1865).

Painted for Engineers Department at West Point; he was the first graduate of the United States Military Academy at West Point. Bust, facing front, heavy gray army cloak over uniform showing one gold epaulette, and gold buttons, this insignia is beautifully shown, the gilt lighting up the entire portrait. Portrait begun April 17th, 1829, finished Nov. 20th, 1829. Size 25″ × 30″.   Price, $85.00

Owned by United States Military Academy, West Point.

1755 TALCOTT, MRS. HARRIET RANDOLPH.

Portrait nearly full face, turned slightly to the right, low-necked gown. Painted for Mrs. Hackley, of Richmond, Va., begun Nov. 26th, 1832, finished Dec. 12th, 1833. Bust.   Price, $100.00

1756 TALIAFERRO, MISS.

(Toliver.) Painted for Mr. Seddon, portrait begun May 21st, 1849, finished May 31st, 1849. Head, size 20″ × 17″.   Price, $100.00

1757 TAYLOR, MR.

Deceased, painted from a portrait by Ford. Begun Sept. 3rd, 1845, finished Sept. 12th, 1845. Bust.   Price, $100.00

1758 TAYLOR, MRS. CHARLES.

Of Chestnut St., Philadelphia. Mary Howell Taylor was the mother of the children No. 1767. Portrait begun Jan. 27th, 1837, finished Feb. 11th, 1837. Size 17″ × 19″, on millboard. Head to right, with curls at side of face, cloak edged with fur drawn over shoulders. Signed on back " TS 1837."   Price, $100.00

Owned by Mrs. Edward Smith.

1759 TAYLOR, MRS. E.

(Deceased.) Portrait painted from a miniature, painting begun Sept. 30th, 1844, finished Jan. 9th, 1845. Head.   Price, $80.00

1760 TAYLOR, MISS FANNY.

Daughter of William E. Taylor, of Virginia. She was one of the belles of Richmond, and known as one of the " Richmond Graces." Bust, nearly full face, and wearing a large oval brooch. Portrait begun June 10th, 1835, finished June 16th, 1835. Head.   Price, $80.00

Reproduced in Peacock's Famous American Belles.

Owned by Randolph Harrison, Amherst, Va.

1761 TAYLOR, MISS.

Portrait begun March 20th, 1862, finished April 14th, 1862. Size 30″ × 25″.   Price, $50.00

1762 TAYLOR, HENRY.

Portrait painted for his nephew, begun Jan. 4th, 1845, finished Jan. 19th, 1845. Copy. Head.   Price, $80.00

1763 TAYLOR, JAMES.

Pastor of Unitarian Church. Portrait begun Jan. 6th, 1818, finished Feb. 21st, 1818. Size 20″ × 24″.   Price, $100.00

1764 TAYLOR, MR. J.

Portrait begun June, 1817, finished June 28th, 1817. Size 20″ × 24″.
                                                                        Price, $100.00

1765 TAYLOR, JAMES.

Unitarian clergyman. Portrait begun Jan. 1st, 1830, finished Jan. 26th, 1830. Size 20″ × 24″.   Price, $75.00

1766 TAYLOR, R.

The register notes " Mr. Taylor, his wife and two children" on separate canvases, 12″ × 10″. Portraits begun May 6th, 1803, finished July 10th, 1803.   Price, $40.00

1767 TAYLOR, SALLY AND MARIA.

Daughters of Charles and Mary H. Taylor. Sally H. Taylor born 1832, died 1837. Maria Taylor, born 1835, died 1840. Portraits of two little girls, one having her arms clasped around the neck of her sister. Inscribed on back of canvas " From a daguerreotype, TS 1857." Size 25″ h., 30″ w. Owned by Mrs. George C. Gillespie, Moorestown, New Jersey.

NOTE.—The portrait of the Taylor children was not entirely completed by Sully, which would account for his not having entered it in his register of paintings. He gave the picture to an artist friend. A copy of this picture was sold at Freeman'a Auction Rooms in March, 1920, Chestnut St., Philadelphia.

1768 TAYLOR, T.

Portrait begun May, 1805, and finished the same month, size 25″ × 30″.
                                                                        Price, $30.00

1769 TEACKLE, JOHN (1753–1817).

A wealthy Virginia planter who liberated his slaves and went to Burlington, N. J., to live. Portrait was painted for his daughter, Mrs. Montgomery, begun Aug. 10th, 1815, finished Aug. 21st, 1815. Bust.   Price, $80.00
Owned by John Cadwalader, Esq., Philadelphia.

LIST OF PAINTINGS

1770 TEACKLE, JOHN (1753–1817).

Portrait copied from first painting, begun Jan. 7th, 1818, finished Feb. 13th, 1818. Bust. Price, $100.00

1771 TEACKLE, MISS REBECCA.

Daughter of John Teackle, of Virginia. Portrait begun Sept. 3rd, 1812, finished Sept. 19th, 1812. Bust. Price, $70.00

1772 TERRY, MRS.

Painted for Daniel Wadsworth, Esq., begun Sept. 10th, 1807, finished Sept. 17th, 1807. Bust. Price, $50.00

Owned by Richard B. Post, of New York.

1773 TESERE, MADAME.

Portrait begun Dec. 1st, 1814, finished Dec. 21st, 1814. Bust.
Price, $100.00

1774 TEVIS, MR.

Salesman and Philadelphia auction house. Portrait begun Jan. 23rd, 1822, finished March 1st, 1822. Bust. Price, $100.00

1775 TEVIS, MRS.

(Was Miss Hunter.) Portrait begun Sept. 17th, 1827, finished Dec. 25th, 1827. Bust. Price, $75.00

1776 THAYER, COLONEL SYLVANUS (1785–1872).

Graduated at the United States Military Academy at West Point in 1808, and assigned to the Engineer Corps. He was Superintendent of the Military Academy at West Point from 1817 to 1833. Portrait begun Sept. 25th, 1831, finished Jan. 27th, 1832. Bust. Price, $85.00

Original owned by Dartmouth College, Hanover, N. H., and a copy of it by the West Point Military Academy.

1777 THOURON, MONSIEUR.

Painted for his son, begun July 6th, 1818, finished July 13th, 1818. Bust. Signed " TS 1818." Price, $100.00

Owned by Nicholas Thouron, Esq., Philadelphia.

1778 THOMAS, GEORGE GRAY (1798–1854).

Son of Evan William Thomas and Martha Gray, married first Jane H. Graff, and second, Ann Gray Leiper. Portrait begun Feb. 21st, 1844, finished March 26th, 1844. Bust. Price, $100.00

Owned by Mrs. Mary Stanley Liddell, of West Lafayette, Indiana.

1779 THOMAS, JAMES C. AND ELIZA.

Brother and sister; children of Jacob and Ann Johnson Thomas, of Philadelphia. Eliza married Isaac Elliott. Painting begun March 1st, 1811, and finished July 25th, 1811. The children are seen as looking out of a window, the brother's hand on his sister's shoulder. Size 29″ × 36″. Price, $120.00
Owned by Mrs. Seabury Johnson, Jr., New York.

1780 THOMAS, WILLIAM B.

Collector of the port of Philadelphia and Colonel of the 20th afterwards the 192nd Regiment Pennsylvania Volunteers in the Civil War. Portrait begun May 8th, 1865, finished May 28th, 1865. Size 36″ × 44″.
Price, $300.00

1781 THOMAS, MRS. W.

Of Baltimore. (Whethered.) Portrait begun Jan. 2nd, 1841, finished Jan. 9th, 1841. Bust. Price, $200.00

1782 THOMPSON, MR.

Son of Edward Thompson. (Deceased, copied from a miniature.) Begun Oct. 19th, 1824. (Rejected.) Bust. Price, $60.00

1783 THOMPSON, MR.

Portrait painted from a picture by William James Hubard (1807–1862). Hubard began his artistic career by cutting silhouettes. He came to Philadelphia in 1826, and put himself under Sully's instruction. He became noted for his cabinet whole-length portraits in oil. Portrait begun April 14th, 1847, finished May 7th, 1847. Bust. Price, $100.00

1784 THOMPSON, MR.

Of New Orleans, La. Portrait painted for Mr. Lewis, begun Aug. 25th, 1835, finished Sept. 16th, 1835. Head. Price, $80.00

NOTE.—A portrait of a Mr. Samuel Thompson, painted by Thomas Sully, was lithographed by A. Newsam.

1785 THOMPSON, JONAH.

Portrait begun April 9th, 1809, finished April 21st, 1809. Bust.
Price, $50.00

1786 TICKNOR, GEORGE (1791–1871).

Distinguished author and one of the founders of the Boston Public Library. Half length, seated, resting his arm on end of sofa and holds manuscript in hand. Portrait painted on order of Mr. Ticknor and reproduced in " Life and Letters of George Ticknor." Portrait begun July 8th, 1831, finished Aug. 25th, 1831. Size 29″ × 36″. Price, $200.00
Owned by Boston Public Library.

1787 TIDYMAN, DR. PHILIP (1777–1850).

A distinguished physician of Charleston, S. C., and member of the American Philosophical Society. Bust, head to right with high stock and velvet collar to coat. Portrait begun June 17th, 1826, finished July 10th, 1826. Size 20″ × 24″. Engraved by Thomas B. Welch.

Portrait owned by the St. Andrew's Society, of Charleston, South Carolina.

1788 TIDYMAN, DR. PHILIP (1777–1850).

Small half-length portrait, painted for the German Friendly Society, of Charleston, S. C., begun June 24th, 1829, finished July 28th, 1829. Small whole length size. Price, $120.00

1789 TIERMAN, FRANK.

Portrait begun June 20th, 1837, finished July 5th, 1837. Bust.
Price, $200.00

1790 TIFFANY, MRS.

Of Baltimore, Md. Portrait begun July 6th, 1847, finished December, 1847. Bust. Price, $150.00

1791 TIFFANY, MRS.

Of Baltimore, Md. Copy of portrait begun at Providence, R. I. Painting begun on Dec. 9th, 1847, finished December, 1847. Bust. Price, $150.00

1792 TILGHMAN, MRS. BENJAMIN (d. 1872).

Bust, head to left, with curls, blue low-necked dress. Mrs. Tilghman was Anna McMurtrie, portrait begun Jan. 9th, 1816, finished Jan. 17th, 1816. Size of canvas was 24″ × 20″, but has been cut down to 18″ × 24″.
Price, $100.00

Owned by Mr. B. C. Tilghman, of Philadelphia.

1793 TILGHMAN, MRS.

Portrait begun Oct. 4th, 1815, finished Nov. 10th, 1815. Bust.
Price, $100.00

1794 TILGHMAN, EDWARD (1750–1815).

Eminent lawyer of Philadelphia, who studied in London; on the completion of his legal education he returned to Philadelphia and was admitted to the Bar of that city. Half length, head to left, holds a book in hand, signed on back of book " $\mathbb{TS}$ 1809." Size 25″ × 30″. Picture lithographed by Max Rosenthal.

Portrait owned by Mr. B. C. Tilghman, of Philadelphia.

297

1795 TILGHMAN, MRS. JAMES (1797–1872).

(Née Miss Ann Caroline Shoemaker.) Bust, with arm resting on table, her hand supporting her head, wearing a low-necked dress. Portrait begun on Oct. 4th, 1815, finished Dec. 30th, 1815. Size 29½″ × 24″.

Price, $100.00

Owned by her grandson, Mr. F. B. Tilghman, of New York.

1796 TILINGHAST, MRS.

Portrait begun June 16th, 1842, finished June 27th, 1842. Head,

Price, $100.00

1797 TODD, MISS.

Of Harrisburg, Pa. Portrait begun May 21st, 1845, finished May 29th, 1845. Head.

Price, $80.00

1798 TODD, MRS.

Portrait begun May 14th, 1808, finished June 29th, 1808. Size 20″ × 24″. (Subscriber) Price, $30.00

1799 TODD, MRS.

Portrait begun April 2nd, 1808, finished July 1st, 1808.

(Subscriber) Price, $30.00

1800 TODD, MR., SR.

Portrait begun March 6th, 1808, finished May 14th, 1808. Bust.

(Subscriber) Price, $30.00

1801 TODHUNTER, JOHN.

East India merchant of London, where the portrait was painted, begun Dec. 5th, 1837, finished Dec. 26th, 1837. Son of Joseph Todhunter. Bust.

Price, $250.00

Portrait is owned in England.

1802 TODHUNTER, JOSEPH (1767–1833).

Mr. Joseph Sill was Mr. Todhunter's son-in-law. Portrait begun Jan. 28th, 1831, finished Feb. 24th, 1831. Size 30″ × 24″. Bust, head to left, nearly full face, high coat collar, white stock, florid complexion, white hair and side whiskers. Price, $75.00

Portrait owned by Mrs. Harold M. Sill, Germantown, Philadelphia.

1803 TOMKINS, MR.

A grocer. Portrait begun July, 1805, and finished the same month, size 25″ × 30″. Price, $30.00

1804 TOMPKINS, DANIEL D. (1774–1825).

He was Governor of New York State and Vice-President of the United States. He was one of the founders of the New York Historical Society. Portrait painted for Dr. Gillespie, begun Sept. 23rd, 1816, finished Feb., 1818. Half length, seated, head to left. Size 40″ × 50″. Price, $100.00 Owned by the "Brook Club," of New York.

1805 TOMKINS, DANIEL D. (1774–1825).

Vice-President of the United States and Governor of New York. Painted for Delaplaine and engraved by W. R. Jones. Portrait begun July 24th, 1813, finished Oct. 2nd, 1813. Size 25″ × 30″. Price, $150.00

1806 TOMKINS, DANIEL D. (1774–1825).

Copied for Jarvis, begun Nov. 28th, 1807, finished Dec. 2nd, 1807. Bust. Price, $20.00

1807 TOWNE, MISS SARAH.

Portrait begun Jan. 14th, 1845, finished Jan. 31st, 1845. Bust. Price, $100.00

1808 TRASK, ISRAEL.

Of Gloucester, Mass., he was a ship owner, and came to Philadelphia in 1840 to have his portrait painted by Sully. Bust, wears a black coat with white stock. Size 20″ × 24″. Owned by the Macbeth Gallery, N. Y.

1809 TRIECHEL, MR.

Deceased, portrait painted from a daguerreotype. Painting begun Oct. 4th, 1855, finished Nov. 12th, 1855. Head. Price, $100.00

1810 TRIECHEL, MRS.

Portrait painted from a photograph for her son, begun Aug. 6th, 1849, finished Aug. 15th, 1849. Head. Price, $80.00

1811 TROTTER, MRS. W. H.

Bust, facing front, 20″ × 24″. Was owned by Mrs. John Farr, who loaned it to Philadelphia Academy Loan Exhibition, 1887.

1812 TRUMBULL, JONATHAN (1740–1809).

Governor of Connecticut and brother of the artist, Colonel John Trumbull. Portrait begun Oct. 2nd, 1807, finished Oct. 13th, 1807. Size 20″ × 24″. Bust, seated, head to right, holding a letter in his hand. Price, $50.00 Owned in 1889 by Mrs. Harriet C. Stickney (née Trumbull), of New York, a grandniece of the subject.

LIST OF PAINTINGS

1813 TUCKER, MRS.

Wife of lawyer Tucker, of Norfolk, Va. Portrait begun April, 1805, finished the same month, size 25″ × 30″.   Price, $25.00

1814 TUDOR, WILLIAM (1779–1830).

Was one of the founders of the Boston Athenaeum and the projector of the North American Review. This portrait was copied by Sully from a portrait by Gilbert Stuart, for Colonel Perkins; it was begun Sept. 13th, 1831, finished Sept. 19th, 1831. Bust.   Price, $120.00
Owned by the Boston Athenaeum, Boston, Mass.

1815 TURNBULL, MR. (SENR).

Portrait copied from painting by Rembrandt Peale, begun May 13th, 1850, finished May 20th, 1850. Oval, 25″ × 30″. Bust, black coat and stock, head to right.   Price, $100.00
Owned by Bayard Turnbull, Esq., and exhibited in 1921 at Maryland Institute, Baltimore.

1816 TURNBULL, MR.

Portrait begun June 29th, 1852, finished July 21st, 1852. Bust.
                    Price, $100.00

1817 TURNBULL, MR.

Copy of former portrait. Painted for Mr. Krumbhaar, begun Jan. 9th, 1855, finished Jan. 22nd, 1855. Oval, 25″ × 30″.   Price, $100.00

1818 TURNBULL, MRS.

Of Cincinnati or Tennessee. Portrait begun June 28th, 1852, finished July 17th, 1852. Bust.   Price, $100.00

1819 TURNBULL, MR. (JR.).

Portrait begun June 29th, 1852, finished July 22nd, 1852. Bust.
                    Price, $100.00

1820 TURNBULL, MISS.

Of Baltimore. Portrait begun April 24th, 1850, finished May 8th, 1850. Bust.   Price, $100.00

1821 TURNBULL, NESBIT.

Portrait painted at the age of two and a half years, painting begun April 8th, 1850, finished May 28th, 1850, for his parents. Size 3′ 5″ × 2′ 7″.
                    Price, $300.00

1822 TURNBULL, MISS SARAH.

Portrait begun June 28th, 1852, finished July 20th, 1852. Bust.
                    Price, $100.00

J S C

INTAGLIO GRAVURE CO, PHILA.

1823 TURNER, CHARLES.

Of Virginia. Portrait begun July 23rd, 1846, finished July 31st, 1846. Bust. Price, $100.00

1824 TURNER, MRS.

Of Fredericksburg, Virginia. Portrait begun Oct. 13th, 1847, finished Nov. 6th, 1847. Bust. Price, $150.00

1825 TURNER, MISS.

Of Fredericksburg, Virginia. Portrait noted as having the hand introduced, begun Oct. 13th, 1847, finished Nov. 3rd, 1847. Bust.
Price, $150.00

1826 TURNER, MISS ABBY ANN.

Married Peter Van Pelt. Portrait was painted for Mrs. Van Pelt, begun April 12th, 1852, finished July 4th, 1852. Size 29" × 36". Price, $150.00
Owned by Dr. Van Pelt, Chestnut Hill, Philadelphia.

1827 TWAITS, WILLIAM (1781–1814).

An English actor who first played at the Grove Theatre, New York, on June 21st, 1805. Portrait painted for Thomas A. Cooper, of the Park Theatre, N. Y., begun Nov. 3rd, 1806, finished Dec. 9th, 1806. Bust.
Price, $30.00

1828 TWELLS, MARY.

Portrait painted at two and a half years of age, begun May 2nd, 1831, finished May 21st, 1831. Size 10" × 16". Price, $50.00

1829 TYLER, MRS. (SENR.).

Of Brattleboro, Vt. Portrait painted for her son, begun Aug. 29th, 1851, finished Sept. 6th, 1851. Head. Price, $80.00

1830 UNKNOWN WOMAN.

Head of a lady, painted for Edward Carey for publishing in his annuals. Begun March 11th, 1839, finished April 8th, 1839. Head. Price, $150.00

1831 UNKNOWN WOMAN.

Portrait of a young lady, head to left, hair parted in middle and arranged with ribbon, low-necked gown indicated.
Sold in Henkel's Auction Room, Philadelphia.

1832 UNKNOWN WOMAN.

Small half-length, copied for Ravises. Portrait begun Oct. 10th, 1817, finished Oct. 17th, 1817. Size 18" × 15". Price, $100.00

LIST OF PAINTINGS

1833 UNKNOWN WOMAN.

The painting came from a descendant of James Reid Lambdin, a pupil and close friend of Sully. It was a canvas about 10″ × 12″, and has been inlaid to 25″ × 30″, and the lines of the shoulders added.

Called "Aunt Sabina," and is owned by the Ehrich Galleries, of New York.

1834 UNKNOWN MAN.

Life-size, seated figure, seen to the waist, a framed miniature is in his left hand and the right is held inside his black coat. H. 30¼″, W. 25⅛″. Canvas. Gift of George H. Story, 1906. Attributed to Thomas Sully.

Owned by the Metropolitan Museum, New York.

1835 UNKNOWN MAN.

Unfinished portrait of a young man with long brown hair, head to right, with dark stock. Size 20″ × 24″.

From collection of Mrs. Benjamin Thaw, 1916; sold at auction of pictures 1920, of the late Frank Bulkley Smith.

1836 VALUE, VICTOR R

And his daughter Charlotte (painted as a child). Portrait begun Jan. 11th, 1828, finished July 30th, 1828. Size 50″ × 40″.   Price, $175.00

Owned by Mrs. Henry Stackpole, and has been loaned to Boston Museum of Fine Arts.

1837 VANBRUN.

A child, son of the Governor of Batavia. Portrait begun May 9th, 1808, finished May 18th, 1808. Bust.   Price, $50.00

1838 VANDERKEMP CHILDREN.

(Group.) Pauline, Bertha and John. Pauline married Bernard Henry and founded the Bethesda Home, Chestnut Hill; John Vanderkemp settled in France and followed sculpture as a profession. Busts, painting begun Feb. 25th, 1832, finished May 3rd, 1832. Size 28″ × 36″. Signed "TS 1832." Three children holding a folio between them.   Price, $150.00

Owned by the Ehrich Gallery, New York.

NOTE.—Sully's original sketch for the painting of the Vanderkemp group of children is owned by the artist's great-granddaughter, Miss Blanchet. It is a panel 12″ × 10″, signed on back "TS," and has the color notes for the original portrait on the back of the panel.

1839 VAN RENSSELAER, MRS.

Of Albany, N. Y. Portrait begun March 9th, 1840, finished March 23rd, 1840. Head.   Price, $150.00

302

LIST OF PAINTINGS

1840 VAN RENSSELAER, MRS.

Copy made for her daughter, begun March 30th, 1840, finished April 13th, 1840. Bust. Price, $200.00

1841 VAN RENSSELAER, EUPHEMIA.

Portrait begun March 24th, 1840, finished April 4th, 1840. Head.

Price, $150.00

1842 VAUGHAN, JOHN (1765–1841).

Born in England; he came to Philadelphia about 1790 and was Treasurer and Librarian of the American Philosophical Society. Bust, facing left, seated, hand resting on upright folio volume. Portrait begun July 29th, 1823, finished Sept. 13th, 1823. (Picture has been engraved by J. W. Steel.) Size 25″ × 30″. Price, $100.00

Owned by American Philosophical Society, Philadelphia, Penna.

1843 VAUGHAN, JOHN (1765–1841).

Portrait copied from the first picture, begun Aug. 20th, 1823, finished Sept. 12th, 1823. Size 25″ × 30″. Price, $100.00

Presented by Mrs. E. F. Wistar to Pennsylvania Historical Society, Philadelphia.

1844 VAUGHAN, JOHN (1765–1841).

Portrait begun July 1st, 1815, finished August, 1815. Bust. The register notes this painting as being "for myself" (Sully), and the price as $80.00

1845 VAUGHAN, JOHN (1765–1841).

Copied from portrait of 1815, begun Jan. 10th, 1822, finished Jan. 28th, 1822. Bust. Price, $100.00

Lithographed by Hugh Bridport, the engraver, painter and friend of Sully.

1846 VAUGHAN, JOHN (1765–1841).

Portrait copied from first picture, begun Sept. 17th, 1823, finished Sept. 20th, 1823. Size 10″ × 8″. Price, $30.00

1847 VAUGHAN, JOHN (1765–1841).

"Copied from my first portrait," begun Aug. 18th, 1823, finished Sept. 17th, 1823. Size 17″ × 20″. Price, $50.00

1848 VER BRYCK, CORNELIUS (1813–1844).

Artist, and a member of the National Academy, he studied under Samuel Morse, and in 1839 he visited London. Bust, oval canvas 22″ × 25½″, signed on back " $\overline{\text{S}}$ " and is dated " 1833 or 1838 (Jan.)."

Owned by the Brooklyn Museum, New York.

LIST OF PAINTINGS

1849 VERRIER, MRS.

Portrait painted from a photograph for her son, begun Sept. 4th, 1865, finished Sept. 12th, 1865.　Head.　　　　　　　　Price, $50.00

1850 VERRIER, MRS.

Copied from former painting for her brother, begun Sept. 14th, 1865, finished Sept. 22nd, 1865.　Head.　　　　　　Price, $50.00

1851 VERRIER, MRS.

Copied from a former portrait, begun Oct. 3rd, 1865, finished Oct. 17th, 1865.　Head.　　　　　　　　　Price, $50.00

1852 VETHAKE, HENRY (1792–1866).

He was a graduate of Columbia College, N. Y., in 1808, was Professor of Mathematics in the University of Pennsylvania, afterwards Vice-Provost and Provost.　Seated at Table, three-quarter length in gown, full face, hand resting on open book.　Size 50″ × 40″.　Painting begun April 28th, 1859, finished May 24th, 1859.　　　　　　　　Price, $300.00
Owned by University of Pennsylvania.

1853 VICTORIA, QUEEN (1819–1901).

Queen of Great Britain and Ireland and in 1877 Empress of India; she succeeded to the throne in 1837 and her coronation took place June 28, 1838; in 1840 she married Albert, Prince of Saxe-Coburg and Gotha.　Bust portrait in vignette on a stained canvas; she is looking over her right shoulder with the face turned three-quarters front; a jeweled crown rests on her parted brown hair and she wears a jeweled necklace and pendent earrings; there is light drapery about her bare shoulders with a touch of red at the left; brown background behind the head; two studies for jewelry are at the right.　Price noted as $500.00.　This is the original study, begun March 22nd and finished May 15th, 1838, according to Sully's own register, for the three-quarter-length portrait now in the Wallace Collection in London, for the whole-length painted for the St. George's Society in Philadelphia, where it still hangs, and for the whole length given by the artist to the St. Andrew's Society in Charleston, S. C.　This sketch is known to be the first portrait of the Queen by Sully made after her accession to the throne; it was painted before her coronation.　H. 35$\frac{15}{16}$″, W. 28$\frac{5}{16}$″.　Canvas.　Inscribed " TS, London, May 15th, 1838.　My original study of the Queen of England, Victoria I. Painted from life, Buckingham House."　Engraved by T. Johnson for the Century Magazine.
Owned by the Metropolitan Museum.

LIST OF PAINTINGS

1854 VICTORIA, QUEEN.

In robes of state. Her Majesty Queen Victoria (1819–1901) in her robes of state ascending the throne in the House of Lords. Inscribed on the back " TS June, 1838, London." Canvas 54½" × 43½". This is the original picture, it is in the Wallace Collection, Hertford House, London. Engraved by Wagstaff. Painting begun May 25th, 1838, and finished June 24th, 1838. Price, $1000.00

NOTE.—A beautiful water-color copy of Sully's painting by S. P. Denning is also in the Wallace Collection.

1855 VICTORIA, QUEEN (1819–1901).

In robes as noted above, whole length, begun Sept. 30th, 1838, finished Jan. 14th, 1839, size 58" × 94". Painted for the St. George Society, Philadelphia, and now hanging in their rooms. Sully was paid $1000.00 for the picture. Signed " TS 1838." (See illustration.)
Owned by St. George Society, Philadelphia.

1856 VICTORIA, QUEEN (1819–1901).

In robes as noted above, whole length, begun Oct. 2nd, 1838, and finished Dec. 20th, 1838. Size 58" × 94". Presented by Sully to the St. Andrew's Society, of Charleston, S. C. The register notes Price, $2000.00
Owned by the St. Andrew's Society, of Charleston, S. C.

1857 VICTORIA, QUEEN (1819–1901).

Copy of former painting, begun Dec. 7th, 1839, finished Dec. 23rd, 1839. Bust. Price, $150.00

1858 VICTORIA, QUEEN (1819–1901).

Copy of former painting, begun July 31st, 1871, finished Sept. 6th, 1871. Size 30" × 25". Price, $100.00
Owned by Dr. John B. Roberts, Philadelphia.

1859 VILLARS, MRS.

Actress. Painted in character, sketch for Thomas A. Cooper. Portrait begun Feb. 5th, 1807, finished the same day. Whole length. Price, $10.00

1860 VILLARS, MRS.

Actress, in the character of Lady Macbeth. Portrait begun Feb. 19th, 1807, finished July 5th, 1807, size 29" × 36". Painted for Thomas A. Cooper. Price, $60.00

305

LIST OF PAINTINGS

1861 VINCENT, MR.

"Painted for Norfolk." Portrait begun May 2nd, 1816, finished May 29th, 1816. Size 20″ × 24″. Price, $100.00

1862 VON SPRECKELSEN, GEORGE H.

Portrait copied from a daguerreotype. Begun Nov. 19th, 1853, finished Dec. 12th, 1853. Head. Price, $80.00

1863 WADSWORTH, DANIEL (1771–1848).

He was the founder of the Wadsworth Athenaeum of Hartford, Conn. This portrait was painted when the artist was 24 years old, and is signed and dated "1807, ae 24," begun Sept. 4th, 1807, finished Sept. 15th, 1807, painted on a panel 14″ × 17″. Bust. Price, $50.00
Owned by the Wadsworth Athenaeum, of Hartford, Conn.

1864 WADSWORTH, MRS. DANIEL (1769–1846).

She was Faith Trumbull, daughter of Governor Trumbull, of Connecticut. Portrait begun Sept. 18th, 1807, finished Oct. 16th, 1807. Bust.
Price, $50.00

1865 WADSWORTH, MISS ELIZABETH.

Sister of General James S. Wadsworth, of Geneseo, N. Y. She married the Honorable Charles Augustus Murray, of England. The portrait was painted for the wife of Judge Joseph Hopkinson, begun March 31st, 1834, finished April, 1834. On panel with monogram "TS." Head looking to right, with low-necked dress. Price, $80.00
Reproduced in "Salons Colonial and Republican." By Ann Hollingsworth Wharton. The picture is now in England.

1866 WADSWORTH, MRS. JEREMIAH.

(Née Mehitabel Russell, was the mother of Daniel Wadsworth.) Portrait begun Sept 28th, 1807, finished Oct. 15th, 1807. (Reproduced in Bowen's History of the Centennial Celebration of Inauguration of George Washington.) Bust, nearly full face, she holds an open book in both hands.
Price, $50.00
Owned by Charles A. Brinley, Philadelphia.

1867 WAGNER, MR.

Portrait painted for Mr. Nugent, begun July 1st, 1836, finished July 19th, 1836. Bust. Price, $150.00

1868 WALDBURG, MR.

Of Savannah, Ga. Portrait begun Oct. 11th, 1822, finished Nov. 5th, 1822. Bust. Price, $100.00

LIST OF PAINTINGS

1869 WALKER, MRS. JOHN K.

Mrs. Walker lived in Philadelphia where the portrait was painted. Portrait begun Feb. 18th, 1859, finished March 22nd, 1859. Size 27″ × 20″.

Price, $80.00

1870 WALLACE, MRS. JOHN BRADFORD (1778–1849).

She was Susan Binney and was the mother of John William Wallace, President of the Historical Society of Pennsylvania. Portrait begun May 7th, 1839, and finished June 1st, 1839. Bust, black dress, nearly full face, dark hair with cap or head dress. Signed " TS 1839." Size 25″ × 30″.

Price, $200.00

Reproduced in "Old Philadelphia Families." By Leach.
Owned by Willing Spencer, Philadelphia.

1871 WALLACE, MRS. JOHN BRADFORD.

This portrait was painted for the Honorable Horace Binney, and was copied from the former portrait. Begun June 19th, 1840, finished Aug. 31st, 1840. Signed on back of canvas " TS 1840." Bust. Price, $200.00
Owned by Archibald R. Montgomery, Esq., Bryn Mawr, Pa.

1872 WALLACK, MRS. JAMES WILLIAM (d. 1851).

Susan Johnstone, daughter of " Irish Johnston," married James W. Wallack in 1817 and came to America with her husband in 1818; she died in London. Portrait begun Jan. 12th, 1819, finished Jan. 24th, 1819. Bust.

Price, $100.00

1873 WALLSCOURT, LADY.

Copy of the portrait painted by Sir Thomas Lawrence. Half length, seated playing the guitar, dark hair in short loose curls. Painted in 1826. Copy by Thomas Sully, begun July 28th, 1850, finished Sept. 6th, 1850. Size 29″ × 36″.

Price, $200.00

Owned by Mrs. John Cadwalader, Philadelphia.

1874 WALN, MRS. ROBERT.

Miss Phoebe Lewis married the Honorable Robert Waln, of Philadelphia. Portrait begun Nov. 17th, 1849, finished Dec. 11th, 1849. Head.

Price, $80.00

NOTE.—One of the portraits of Mrs. Robert Waln is owned by Mrs. Rebecca Waln Tutt Wood, of Colorado Springs, Colorado, the owner of the other portrait is unknown to the authors.

LIST OF PAINTINGS

1875 WALN, MRS. ROBERT.

Miss Phoebe Lewis, married the Honorable Robert Waln, of Philadelphia. Portrait begun April 22nd, 1845, finished May 15th, 1845. Head.

Price, $80.00

1876 WALN, MISS.

Portrait begun March 23rd, 1808, and finished May 12th, 1808. Bust.

(Subscriber) Price, $30.00

1877 WALSH, ROBERT (1784–1859).

He was United States Consul in Paris and the founder of " American Review of History and Politics," in 1811. Admitted to the Philadelphia Bar in 1808, but prevented by deafness from practising. Half length, seated, with hand supporting head, his elbow rests on a large open volume on a writing table. Portrait begun April 3rd, 1814, finished July 4th, 1814. Size 25" × 30". Price, $70.00

Sold by H. C. Walsh to F. B. Smith. His collection sold in New York, 1920, this picture was bought by William Kane, Esq., of New York. Portrait was lithographed by Albert Newsam, at Childs', Philadelphia.

1878 WALSH, THE MISSES.

Group of the four daughters of Robert Walsh, of Philadelphia, two being seated in foreground with two standing to left reading letter. Size 54" wide, 34" high. Elizabeth married Henry Beckett and died in 1882; Anna married Mr. Laffan and died young; Mary married Mr. McBlair and also died young; Isabella, the eldest of the group, never married and died in 1896. Portrait begun Dec. 10th, 1834, finished March 5th, 1835. Price, $600.00

Was owned by Miss Katherine Walsh, Philadelphia.

1879 WALSH, MISS GRACEY.

Portrait begun April 7th, 1803, finished June 9th, 1803. Bust.

Price, $20.00

1880 WALTON, MISS.

Of Pensacola. Portrait begun Oct. 25th, 1833, finished Dec. 12th, 1833. Whole length. Price, $300.00

1881 WALTON, MR.

Portrait begun July 21st, 1817, finished Sept. 19th, 1817. Bust.

Price, $100.00

1882 WARD, JOSHUA.

Of Georgetown, S. C. (Brother of Miss Penelope, No. 1883.) Portrait begun Oct. 9th, 1845, finished Oct. 22nd, 1845. Bust. Price, $100.00

LIST OF PAINTINGS

1883 WARD, MISS PENELOPE BENTLEY.

(Afterwards Mrs. Flag.) Of Georgetown, S. C. Half length, seated, head slightly to right, hair parted in middle. Portrait begun Oct. 8th, 1845, finished Oct. 22nd, 1845. (Painted at the age of nineteen.) Bust 25″ × 30″. The register notes the "hand introduced" in the portrait.

Price, $150.00

Sold by Macbeth Gallery to Mrs. E. H. Harriman, of New York.

1884 WARD, R. I.

Of Lexington, Kentucky. Portrait begun Feb. 11th, 1833, finished Feb. 20th, 1833. Bust. Price, $100.00

Owned by Mrs. Matthew F. Ward, Lexington, Ky.

1885 WARLEY, MRS.

Deceased, copied from a daguerreotype, portrait begun June 9th, 1853, and noted in the register as condemned. Head. Price, $80.00

1886 WARNER, DANIEL BASTRIAL (1815–1880).

Negro. President of Liberia in 1863–65. Portrait painted from a photograph for the Colonization Society, begun April 13th, 1864, finished May 12th, 1864. Signed "TS 1864." Head, size 20″ × 24″. Price, $50.00

Owned by Pennsylvania Historical Society, Philadelphia.

1887 WARREN, JOHN COLLINS (1778–1856).

Distinguished surgeon of Boston and nephew of General Joseph Warren, who fell at the battle of Bunker Hill. Portrait begun Aug. 13th, 1836, finished Aug. 23rd, 1836. Bust Price, $200.00

1888 WARREN, WILLIAM (1767–1832).

For many years manager of the old Chestnut Street Theatre, Philadelphia. This portrait was engraved by David Edwin for the "Mirror of Taste" (F 195). Painting begun by Sully Dec. 4th, 1808, finished Dec. 8th, 1808. Head. (Subscriber) Price, $30.00

1889 WARREN, MRS. WILLIAM (1769–1818).

An English actress (Ann Brunton), she married Robert Merry and came to this country in 1796, later she married Thomas Wignell, manager of the theatre, and at his death William Warren, the actor, of the Philadelphia theatre. Portrait begun March 7th, 1807, finished March 17th, 1807. Bust.

Price, $30.00

1890 WARREN, MRS. WILLIAM (1769–1818).

In character as Calister in Fair Penitent. Painting begun July 25th, 1808, finished Sept. 6th, 1808. Bust. Price, $50.00

LIST OF PAINTINGS

1891 WARREN, MRS. WILLIAM AND INFANT.
Portrait begun Jan. 28th, 1811, finished Feb. 21st, 1811. Head.
Price, $60.00

1892 WASHINGTON, GEORGE.
Copied from Stuart's whole-length portrait at Hartford, Conn. Painting begun Aug. 25th, 1807, finished Oct. 10th, 1807. Size 29″ × 36″.
Price, $100.00

1893 WASHINGTON, GEORGE.
Copied from No. 1892. Painting begun Aug. 30th, 1807, finished Oct. 10th, 1807. Size 20″ × 24″.
Price, $50.00

1894 WASHINGTON, GENERAL GEORGE.
Copied from portrait by Gilbert Stuart. Painted for State of North Carolina, begun Oct. 17th, 1817, finished Feb. 7th, 1818. Size 9 ft. × 6 ft.
Price, $400.00

1895 WASHINGTON, GEORGE.
From Gilbert Stuart's painting, begun copy July 11th, 1820, finished July 20th, 1820. Size 20″ × 24″.
Price, $80.00

1896 WASHINGTON, GEORGE.
Copied from the portrait by Gilbert Stuart. Painted for J. Waln, begun Nov. 30th, 1827, finished Dec. 10th, 1827. Bust.
Price, $50.00

1897 WASHINGTON, GENERAL GEORGE.
Equestrian portrait, the register notes it as "a study, presented to Colonel John Wheeler." The painting was begun May 3rd, 1841, finished on Nov. 22nd, 1841. Signed "TS 1842." Size 27″ × 36″.
Price, $150.00
Owned by Daniel Carstairs, Esq.

1898 WASHINGTON, GENERAL GEORGE.
Equestrian portrait, begun Sept. 12th, 1842, finished Nov. 21st, 1842. Size 12′ 6″ × 9′ 6″. Purchased by subscription of the members of the Union League of Philadelphia.
Price, $2000.00

1899 WASHINGTON, GENERAL GEORGE.
Copy of Gilbert Stuart's portrait, begun by Thomas Sully, Jr., and finished by his father. Size 8 ft. by 5 ft. Portrait begun Nov. 24th, 1842, finished Dec. 10th, 1842.
Price, $200.00

LIST OF PAINTINGS

1900 WASHINGTON, GEORGE.

Copied from painting by Stuart for the Historical Society of Wisconsin, painting begun March 31st, 1854, finished April 19th, 1854. Bust.

Price, $100.00

Owned by the Historical Society of Wisconsin at Madison.

1901 WASHINGTON, GEORGE (1732–1799).

Copied from original portrait by Gilbert Stuart, owned by Colonel Wesley P. Hunt, of Trenton, N. J. Bust, head to left, size 25″ × 30″. Copy begun Oct. 19th, 1855, finished Nov. 2nd, 1855. Price, $100.00

Thomas Sully considered this portrait by Stuart as next in point of merit to the head in the Boston Athenaeum.

Presented to the Pennsylvania Historical Society by Thomas Sully, Nov. 12th, 1855.

1902 WASHINGTON, GEORGE.

Copied from a portrait by Gilbert Stuart, owned by Colonel Hunt, of Trenton, N. J. Painting begun Oct. 19th, 1855, finished Nov. 1st, 1855. Head. Painted for the artist's own collection. Price, $80.00

1903 WASHINGTON, GEORGE.

Painted for the Virginia Historical Society, Richmond, Va. Portrait begun June 6th, 1856, finished July 5th, 1856. Bust. Price, $100.00

Owned by the Historical Society of Virginia (Richmond, Va.).

1904 WASHINGTON, GEORGE.

Copy fourth of Stuart's. Begun Jan. 17th, 1856, finished March 3rd, 1856. Bust. Price, $100.00

1905 WASHINGTON, GEORGE.

Copy of portrait by Gilbert Stuart, begun June 13th, 1863, finished June 19th, 1863. Size 21″ × 25″. Signed on back of canvas " TS 1863." Formerly in collection of James Claghorn.

Owned by Joseph Y. Jeanes, of Philadelphia.

1906 WASHINGTON, GEORGE.

Painted after Healy's copy, begun June 26th, 1868, finished July 6th, 1868. Size 20″ × 24″. Price, $100.00

1907 WASHINGTON, GEORGE.

No. 2. Painted after Healy's copy. Begun June 30th, 1868, finished July 10th, 1868. Size 20″ × 24″. Price, $100.00

1908 WASHINGTON, GEORGE.

    No. 3. Painted after Healy's copy. Begun July 9th, 1868, finished Aug. 3rd, 1868. Size 20″ × 24″.   Price, $100.00
Sold at sale of Harrison paintings, Philadelphia.

1909 WASHINGTON, GEORGE.

    No. 4. Painted after Healy's copy. Begun July 10th, 1868, finished August 8th, 1868. Size 20″ × 24″.   Price, $100.00

    NOTE.—(Nos. 1906–1907.) Washingtons copied by Sully, 1868, after Healy's copy were sold in collection of estate of Mr. F. Dreer, of Philadelphia, June, 1813.

1910 WASHINGTON, GEORGE.

    Copy begun Nov. 8th, 1869, finished Nov. 18th, 1869. Size 5″ × 9″.
    Price, $20.00

1911 WASHINGTON, GEORGE.

    Copy of Stuart's whole-length. Begun June 20th, 1870, finished July 17th, 1870. Size 27″ × 30″.   Price, $100.00

1912 WASHINGTON, GEORGE.

    Bust, copied from the portraits painted from life by Gilbert Stuart and Trumbull, and reproduced in the photograph made for Mr. Dreer of the artist in his studio. It stands on the easel; it was begun Oct. 4th, 1871, finished Nov. 28th, 1871. Size 25″ × 30″.   Price, $100.00
Owned by Herbert L. Pratt, Glen Cove, L. I.

1913 WASHINGTON, MARTHA.

    Copy begun Nov. 8th, 1869, finished Nov. 18th, 1869. Size 5″ × 9″.
    Price, $20.00

1914 WASHINGTON FAMILY.

    Original composition, begun July 9th, 1850, finished July 26th, 1850. Size 29″ × 36″.   Price, $200.00

1915 WATERMAN, MRS.

    The register notes this portrait as " condemned, declined," and that it was begun on Jan. 14th, 1845, finished Jan. 21st, 1845, and the price as $80.00 for the painting. Head.

1916 WATERMAN, MRS.

    This portrait was painted in lieu of an earlier one that was condemned and declined, begun April 22nd, 1845, finished May 2nd, 1845. Head.
    Price, $80.00

LIST OF PAINTINGS

1917 WATMOUGH, MRS. EDMUND C. (1800–1864).

(Was Maria Chew Nicklin.)   Portrait begun Oct. 3rd, 1825, finished Jan. 4th, 1828.   Bust.   Price, $60.00
Owned by M. Russell Thayer, of Philadelphia.

1918 WATTS, HENRY MILLER (1805–1885).

United States Attorney for Pennsylvania and United States Minister to Austria.   Portrait begun April 11th, 1843, finished April 25th, 1843.   Head.
Price, $67.00

1919 WATTS, MRS. HENRY MILLER.

(Née Miss Schonenberger.)   Portrait begun Feb. 27th, 1843, finished April 6th, 1843.   Head.   Price, $67.00

1920 WATTS, MR. DAVID.

Portrait was painted from a small picture.   Begun March 1st, 1843, finished April 29th, 1843.   Inscribed "Copied from Wollet, TS 1843, April."
Head, size 17″ × 20″.   Price, $67.00
Owned by Charles A. Watts, Esq., Philadelphia.

1921 WEIGHTMAN, MR.

Of Georgetown.   Portrait begun Sept. 27th, 1812, finished Oct. 8th, 1812.   Size 29″ × 36″.   Price, $100.00

1922 WEIR, SILAS.

Auctioneer.   Portrait begun March 9th, 1815, finished April 29th, 1815.
Size 29″ × 36″·   Price, $100.00

1923 WEIR, SILAS.

Auctioneer.   Portrait begun Jan. 13th, 1813, finished March 6th, 1813.
Bust.   Price, $100.00

1924 WELLFORD, MRS.

Portrait begun Feb. 12th, 1811, finished on June 14th, 1811.   Head.
Price, $50.00

1925 WELLFORD, MR.

Portrait begun Feb. 17th, 1811, finished June 14th, 1811.   Head.
Price, $50.00

1926 WEST, BENJAMIN (1738–1820).

Copied from Leslie's copy of Lawrence's portrait of West, painted for the Artists' Fund Society, begun July 2nd, 1864, and finished July 16th, 1864.
Half length.   Price, $50.00
Owned by the Pennsylvania Academy of Fine Arts.

313

LIST OF PAINTINGS

1927 WETHERED, MR.
Portrait painted in Baltimore, begun April 4th, 1853, finished April 22nd, 1853. Bust. Price, $150.00

1928 WETHERED, MRS.
(Née Miss Evans.) Portrait painted in Baltimore, begun March 4th, 1853, finished March 25th, 1853. Bust. Price, $150.00

1929 WETHERILL, DR. CHARLES.
Portrait begun March 20th, 1855, finished March 31st, 1855. Head.
Price, $80.00

1930 WETHERILL, CHARLES (1798–1838).
Portrait copied from painting by John Grimes, begun Oct. 25th, 1853, finished Nov. 4th, 1853. Head. Price, $80.00

1931 WETHERILL, CHARLES (1798–1838).
Bust, head to left, high white collar and white bow tie. Portrait painted for his son, begun Nov. 7th, 1853, finished Nov. 19th, 1853. No. 2. Copy. Head, size 20″ × 24″· Inscribed on back of canvas " From Grimes, ℟ 1853." Price, $80.00
Owned by Mrs. Christopher Wetherill, Germantown, Philadelphia.

1932 WETHERILL, CHARLES (1798–1838).
(Deceased.) Third copy of former portrait. Begun Jan. 18th, 1854, finished Feb. 16th, 1854. Head. Price, $80.00

1933 WETHERILL, CHARLES (1798–1838).
Fourth copy of former portrait, painted for their son, begun April 7th, 1854, finished April 22nd, 1854. Head. Price, $80.00

1934 WETHERILL, MRS. CHARLES (1804–   ).
Portrait copied from the painting by Eichholtz, begun Oct. 25th, 1853, finished Nov. 4th, 1853. Head. Price, $80.00

1935 WETHERILL, MRS. CHARLES (1804–   ).
(Née Margaretta Sybilla Mayer.) Bust, head slightly to left, dark hair and curls. Portrait begun Jan. 18th, 1854, finished Feb. 2nd, 1854. No. 2 copy. Inscribed on back of canvas " No. 2 from Eichholtz, ℟ 1854." Size 20″ × 24″. Head. Price, $80.00
Owned by Mrs. Christopher Wetherill, Germantown, Philadelphia.

LIST OF PAINTINGS

1936 WETHERILL, MRS. CHARLES.

Third copy of former portrait, painted for their son, begun April 7th, 1854, finished May 11th, 1854. Head. Price, $80.00

1937 WETHERILL, MRS. CHARLES.

(Two copies of the former portrait reduced to ovals.) Fourth copy. Begun Nov. 13th, 1854, finished Nov. 15th, 1854. Each Price, $30.00

1938 WETHERILL, CHARLES (JR.).

Portrait begun March 6th, 1854, finished March 24th, 1854. Head. Price, $80.00

1939 WETHERILL, MRS.

(Was Miss Bloomfield.) Portrait begun March 5th, 1833, finished March 22nd, 1833. Head. Price, $60.00

1940 WETHERILL, DR.

Portrait begun Jan. 30th, 1833, finished Feb. 9th, 1833. Head. Price, $60.00

1941 WETHERILL, MRS. DR.

Portrait given in place of the one condemned, begun Feb. 27th, 1834, finished March 11th, 1834. Head. Price, $80.00

1942 WETHERILL, JOHN PRICE (1794–1853).

He succeeded his father, Samuel Wetherill, in the manufacture of chemicals and white lead. Bust, seated with arm over chair back, blue coat with brass buttons, size 25" × 30". Begun May 13th, 1822, finished June 25th, 1822. Signed " TS 1822." Price, $100.00

Owned by Mrs. Paul L. Tiers, Germantown, Philadelphia.

1943 WETHERILL, MRS. JOHN PRICE (1797–1877).

(Née Maria Kane Lawrence.) Bust, the head to left, white low-necked dress with blue cloak. Signed on belt " TS 1822." Portrait begun Feb. 26th, 1822, finished March 19th, 1822. Size 25" × 30". Price, $100.00

Owned by Mrs. Paul L. Tiers, Germantown, Philadelphia.

1944 WETHERILL, PRICE.

From a former portrait, begun April 25th, 1854, finished June 28th, 1854. Head. Price, $60.00

1945 WETHERILL, JOHN PRICE.

Portrait begun April 20th, 1854, finished June 28th, 1854. Head. Price, $60.00

Painted for one of a group of five heads.

LIST OF PAINTINGS

1946 WETHERILL, MRS. JOHN PRICE.
Portrait begun April, 1854, finished June 28th, 1854. Head.
Price, $60.00
Painted for one of a group of five heads.

1947 WETHERILL, JOHN PRICE, JR.
Portrait begun April 25th, 1854, finished June 28th, 1854. Head.
Price, $60.00

1948 WETHERILL, MRS. HENRY MAYER (1830–1914).
(Wife of Price Wetherill's son.) (Née Rebecca Price Wetherill.) Head, nearly full face, black hair parted in the middle. Signed " TS 1853." Portrait begun Sept. 27th, 1853, finished Oct. 4th, 1853. Head, size 20″ × 24″.
Price, $80.00
Owned by Mrs. Paul L. Tiers, Germantown, Philadelphia.

1949 WETHERILL, MISS MARGARITE.
Portrait begun Sept. 29th, 1851, finished Oct. 16th, 1851. Head.
Price, $80.00

1950 WETHERILL, MISS RACHEL.
Portrait begun April 19th, 1854, finished June 26th, 1854. Head.
Price, $60.00
Painted for one of a group of five heads.

1951 WETHERILL, SAMUEL (SR.).
Copied from a portrait painted by Eichholtz for Dr. Wetherill. Begun Jan. 19th, 1833, finished Jan. 29th, 1833. Bust, seated to left. Size 25″ × 30″.
Price, $100.00
Owned by Dr. Richard Wetherill, La Fayette, Ind.

1952 WHARTON, MRS. GEORGE M. (b. ——, d. 1873).
(Née Maria Markoe, of Philadelphia.) Portrait begun March 30th, 1837, and finished April 7th, 1837. Head, facing to right. Panel, signed " TS 1837."
Price, $150.00
Owned by Mrs. Benjamin Allen, Colorado Springs, and deposited with Mrs. George Boker, Philadelphia.

1953 WHARTON, MRS. ISAAC (1760–1831).
She was Margaret Rawle, daughter of Francis Rawle, of Laurel Hill, Philadelphia, and married Isaac Wharton, merchant, in 1786. Portrait begun Jan. 24th, 1825, finished May 30th, 1825. Bust, seated, nearly full face, wearing a cap tied under her chin and has a fringed fichu across her bust.
Price, $60.00

316

LIST OF PAINTINGS

1954 WHARTON, MRS. ISAAC (1760–1831).

A copy of the first portrait, made for her daughter Rebecca, who married Jacob Ridgway Smith, of Philadelphia. Begun Aug. 12th, 1833, finished Oct. 22nd, 1833. Bust, size 25″ × 30″. Price, $100.00
Owned by Mrs. William H. Gaw and deposited at the Pennsylvania Academy of Fine Arts, Philadelphia.

1955 WHARTON, MISS MARY CRAIG.

Married General James S. Wadsworth, and her portrait is reproduced in "Salons Colonial and Republican," by Ann Hollingsworth Wharton. Portrait begun May 6th, 1834, finished May 16th, 1834. Head. Price, $80.00
Owned by Charles P. Wadsworth, of Geneseo, N. Y.

1956 WHARTON, THOMAS I. (1791–1856).

Solicitor for the Philadelphia Saving Fund Society. Bust, head to right. Reproduced in "History of Philadelphia Saving Fund Society," by J. M. Willcox; it is there recorded as by Thomas Sully, but it has also been attributed to Henry Inman by members of the Wharton family.
Portrait owned by Mrs. Wharton Sinkler, Philadelphia.

1957 WHEATLY, MRS.

Portrait begun Dec. 5th, 1854, finished March 16th, 1855. Size 29″ × 36″. Price, $200.00

1958 WHEELER, ELLEN OLDMIXON (1816–1896).

Daughter of the artist, who married John H. Wheeler, portrait painted for her mother, Sarah Sully, begun June 14th, 1848, finished June 21st, 1848. Head. Price, $80.00

1959 WHEELER, MRS. JOHN H. AND HER TWO SONS.

The artist's daughter Ellen and her sons Charles and Woodbury, portrait begun July 3rd, 1844, finished July 25th, 1844. Signed on back "July 25th, 1844, TS." Size 4′ 3¾″ × 5′ 1¾″. Price, $1000.00
Loaned by the artist's great-grandson to the National Gallery, Washington, D. C.

1960 WHEELER, JOHN H.

Married the artist's daughter Ellen on Nov. 8th, 1838. Portrait begun March 31st, 1845, and finished April 11th, 1845. Bust. The register notes the painting "as a present," and the price as $100.00

LIST OF PAINTINGS

1961 WHEELER, WOODBURY.

Portrait of the artist's grandson, painted as a present for his daughter, Mrs. John H. Wheeler (née Ellen Sully). Begun April 29th, 1868, finished June 5th, 1868. Oval. Price, $30.00

1962 WHELEN, MARY SIDDONS (1788–1867).

Wife of Israel Whelen and grandmother of Henry Whelen, Jr., a former President of the Pennsylvania Academy of Fine Arts. Three-quarter length, facing to left, with arm resting on broken branch, landscape in the background. Portrait begun Nov. 19th, 1812, finished Dec. 20th, 1812. Size 37″ × 49″.

Owned by Miss Emily Whelen, Philadelphia.

1963 WHITE, WILLIAM, D. D. (1748–1836).

First Episcopal Bishop of Pennsylvania. Chaplain of the Continental Congress and United States Senate under Washington. Three-quarter length, seated in robes, facing left, left hand in book. Signed " TS 1814 " on band of sleeve. Engraved by Pekenino (S-2455). Portrait begun Oct. 7th, 1814, finished Nov. 10th, 1814. Size 40″ × 50″. Price, $200.00

Was owned by Judge William White Wiltbank, of Philadelphia.

1964 WHITE, WILLIAM.

Bishop of Pennsylvania. Copied from portrait by Gilbert Stuart and painted for Mrs. McMurtrie, begun Feb. 24th, 1827, finished Feb. 28th, 1827. Size 19″ × 15″. Price, $30.00

Owned by the Pennsylvania Historical Society; gift of Miss Nixon.

1965 WHITE, WILLIAM.

Bishop of Pennsylvania. Copied from the portrait by Gilbert Stuart for Joseph Harrison. Begun Nov. 26th, 1827, finished Dec. 17th, 1827. Size 17″ × 20″. Price, $50.00

1966 WHITE, WILLIAM.

Bishop of Pennsylvania. At the age of 80. Head facing right, on panel 15″ × 16″. Portrait painted for George Harrison, begun Feb. 12th, 1828, finished March 24th, 1828. Price, $50.00

Owned by George Harrison Fisher, of Philadelphia.

1967 WHITE, WILLIAM.

Bishop of Pennsylvania. Portrait painted for Dr. Montgomery, begun Jan. 19th, 1829, finished March 24th, 1829. Size 19″ × 15″. Price, $50.00

LIST OF PAINTINGS

1968 WHITE, WILLIAM.

Bishop of Pennsylvania. Copy of head painted in 1828. Portrait begun Jan. 20th, 1829, finished Jan. 31st, 1829. Picture signed " TS 1829," and engraved full size by John Sartain.

1969 WHITE, WILLIAM (1748–1836).

Bishop of Pennsylvania. A copy of the head, signed "E. S., 1836," hangs in the Pennsylvania Historical Society. It is recorded as " Painted and presented by the Sully family to the Pennsylvania Colonization Society." It has been attributed to Thomas Sully but is probably the work of his daughter Ellen, who is mentioned in family letters about this time as " copying in a most creditable way a number of portraits " of her father's.

1970 WHITE, MRS. JUDGE.

Portrait begun April 17th, 1837, finished April 28th, 1837. Bust.

Price, $200.00

1971 WHITEHEAD, MR.

Portrait begun May 18th, 1813, finished July 2nd, 1813. Size 29″ × 36″.

Price, $100.00

1972 WICKHAM, MRS.

Portrait begun March, 1805, and finished the same month. Size 10″ × 12″.

Price, $15.00

1973 WIGGIN, MRS. BENJAMIN.

Formerly Charlotte Fowle. Mrs. Wiggin resided in Boston. Portrait begun Oct. 20th, 1814, finished March 12th, 1815. Size 29″ × 36″.

Price, $80.00

Owned by H. T. Durant, of Boston.

1974 WIGNAL, ELIZABETH.

Painted for William Warren. Portrait begun Dec. 1st, 1813, finished Jan. 13th, 1814. Size 17″ × 20″.

Price, $70.00

1975 WILCOCKS, MISS ANN (1781–1831).

Married Joseph Reed Ingersoll in 1813. Bust, seated with hands folded in lap, low-necked high-waisted white dress with brown cloak over shoulder with yellow lining. Portrait begun on Nov. 22nd, 1808, finished Jan. 29th, 1809. Size 25″ × 30″.

Price, $50.00

Owned by the Misses Hutchinson, Philadelphia.

1976 WILCOCKS, MISS ANN (1781–1831),

Painted for her brother, Benjamin Wilcocks, begun Dec. 9th, 1807, finished Dec. 28th, 1807. Bust.

Price, $50.00

1977 WILCOCKS, BENJAMIN CHEW (1776–1845).

Of Philadelphia; a liberal friend of the fine arts and Sully's first patron in Philadelphia. Portrait painted for J. Beekman, begun June 20th, 1807, and finished July 24th, 1807. Bust. Price, $50.00

1978 WILCOCKS, BENJAMIN C. (1776–1845).

Portrait begun Dec. 20th, 1807, finished on June 10th, 1808. Bust.
Price, $50.00

1979 WILCOCKS, MISS MARY.

Afterwards Mrs. Kirk B. Wells. She was the niece and adopted daughter of Joseph R. Ingersoll, of Philadelphia. Portrait begun Nov. 4th, 1844, finished Dec. 13th, 1844. Size 29″ × 36″. Price, $200.00

1980 WILCOCKS, MARY WALN AND HELEN JULIA.

Children of Benjamin Chew Wilcocks, begun Oct. 22nd, 1846, finished Dec. 19th, 1846, portraits painted for Mrs. Wilcocks. Busts, size 25 h. by 30 w. Two little girls, one with her arms around her sister's neck. Mary married Alexander D. Campbell and Helen married Chandler Robbins.
Price, $200.00

Owned by Mrs. Alexander D. Campbell, Philadelphia.

1981 WILEY, MRS.

Of New York, painted for her sister, Mrs. Campbell. Bust, head to left, white transparent bodice, coral earrings and a pink ribbon around neck. Portrait begun Nov. 29th, 1862, finished Dec. 9th, 1862. Size 24″ × 20″. Signed on back of canvas " TS 1862." Price, $40.00

Owned by the Pennsylvania Historical Society, Philadelphia.

1982 WILKES, CAPTAIN CHARLES (1798–1877).

United States naval officer who made important explorations of the Southern hemisphere for which he received the gold medal of the Royal Geographical Society of London. Portrait painted for the United States government, begun Sept. 5th, 1843, finished Sept. 21st, 1843. Bust. Engraved by Richard W. Dodson. Price, $100.00

1983 WILLIAMS, COLONEL JONATHAN (1750–1815).

Head to right, his right arm rests on a book and the hand holds a partly unrolled plan, military coat with gold epaulettes. Painted for the City of New York; begun Nov. 19th, 1813, finished Dec. 13th, 1813. Size 30″ × 26″. Price, $100.00

Hanging in City Hall, New York.

LIST OF PAINTINGS

1984 WILLIAMS, COLONEL JONATHAN (1750–1815).

Full length, facing front, seated in uniform. The register notes "Copied from my 1st picture intended for West Point; begun by my pupil West." (This was William E. West, 1788–1857, known as "Kentucky West.") Portrait begun Aug. 14th, 1816, finished Sept. 30th, 1816. Size 58" × 81".
Price, $250.00
Owned by estate of Colonel Alexander Biddle, of Philadelphia.

1985 WILLIAMS, COLONEL JONATHAN (1750–1815).

Organizer and first superintendent of West Point Military Academy. General of New York Militia, 1812. Whole length, seated in uniform by a table, on which are his hat and sword. A sturdy figure with ruddy complexion. Portrait begun Feb. 14th, 1815, finished May, 1815. Size 58" × 94".
Price, $300.00
Owned by the United States Military Academy at West Point. Engraved by R. W. Dodson. See "Sully Portraits at the Military Academy, West Point," by Frank Fowler, Scribners Magazine, 1908.

1986 WILLIAMS, T. H.

Of Natchez. Miss. Portrait begun Aug. 23rd, 1834, finished Sept. 2nd, 1834. Bust.
Price, $125.00

1987 WILLIAMS, MR.

Of Georgetown. Portrait begun Sept. 21st, 1812, finished Nov. 17th, 1812. Size 29" × 36".
Price, $100.00

1988 WILLIAMS, MRS. B.

Portrait begun May 19th, 1821, finished June 13th, 1821. Size 20" × 24".
Price, $100.00

1989 WILLIAMS, MRS.

Of Baltimore (was Miss Beck). Portrait begun May 21st, 1817, finished Aug. 5th, 1817. Size 20" × 24".
Price, $100.00

1990 WILLIAMSON, ISAIAH VANSANT (1803–1889).

Of 73 Market Street, Philadelphia. Founder of the Williamson Trades School, of Philadelphia. Portrait begun July 3rd, 1837, finished July 15th, 1837. Bust.
Price, $200.00

1991 WILLING, RICHARD (1775–1858).

He was President of the Mutual Assurance Company of Philadelphia, a member of the First City Troop and connected with the firm of Willing and Francis. Portrait painted for Mutual Assurance Company, begun Jan. 24th, 1845, finished March 15th, 1845. Bust.
Price, $100.00
NOTE.—The only portrait now owned by "The Mutual Assurance" of Richard Willing is painted by G. A. P. Healy.

LIST OF PAINTINGS

1992 WILMOT, MRS.

(Of the Theatre, Virginia.) Begun July, 1805, finished the same month. Size 25" × 30". Portrait painted from a miniature. Price, $30.00

1993 WINTHROP, THOMAS LINDALL (1760–1841).

Lieutenant-Governor of Massachusetts from 1826 to 1832. Portrait begun July 20th, 1831, finished Sept. 6th, 1831. Half length. Signed and dated 1831. Price, $350.00
Owned by his grandson, Thomas Lindall Winthrop, Esq., of Beacon St., Boston.

1994 WISTAR, DR. CASPAR (1761–1818).

Well-known Philadelphia physician and founder of the Wistar parties. Portrait begun Aug. 13th, 1830, from Woods' drawing. Bust. (Erased.) Price, $75.00

1995 WISTAR, CASPAR (1761–1818).

Copied by Sully from the original painting by Bass Otis, in the possession of Mrs. Caspar Wistar, who allowed it to be copied for the American Philosophical Society, begun Sept. 16th, 1830, finished Dec. 14th, 1830. Bust to left. Size 25" × 30".
Owned by the American Philosophical Society, Fifth Street, Philadelphia.

1996 WITHERS, MISS CAROLINE AND MISS CORNELIA.

Painting begun Nov. 1st, 1858, finished Nov. 15th, 1858. Heads. Price, $150.00

1997 WOLCOTT, OLIVER (1760–1833).

Secretary of Treasury under Washington and Governor of Connecticut, 1817–1827. Engraved by A. B. Durand (Stauffer 669). Portrait begun Sept. 10th, 1814, finished Sept. 12th, 1814. Size 20" × 24". Price, $100.00
Owned by Wadsworth Athenaeum, of Hartford, Conn.

1998 WOOD, JAMES FREDERIC (1813–1863).

Roman Catholic Archbishop of Philadelphia. He was born a Quaker and joined the Roman Catholic Church at the age of twenty-three and began to study for the priesthood, to which he was ordained at thirty-one. Painted for the Propaganda at Rome. Painting begun Aug. 25th, 1859, finished Sept. 10th, 1859. Bust. Price, $100.00

LIST OF PAINTINGS

1999 WOOD, MARY ANNE (1802–1854).

Mary Anne Paton, an English opera singer was married in 1824 to Lord William Pitt Lennox; she procured a divorce in 1831 and the same year married Joe Wood, tenor singer and actor, with whom she came to America in 1833 and sang in opera in New York, Philadelphia and other cities. Portrait painted from recollection for the artist's own collection, begun Feb. 27th, 1836, finished March 7th, 1836.   Head.   Price, $100.00

2000 WOOD, MARY ANNE (1802–1854).

In character of Amina in opera of " Somnambula," last scene. Portrait begun March 6th, 1836, and finished Aug. 5th, 1836. Size 6′ 6″ by 4′ 6″.
Price, $600.00

Exhibited in 1837 at Artists Fund Society and then owned by R. Maywood & Co., managers of the Chestnut Street Theatre, Philadelphia.

2001 WOOD, MARY ANNE (1802–1854).

Mrs. Joseph Wood, née Mary Anne Paton. In the character of Amina in opera of " Somnambula," last scene. Bust, study for No. 2000. Nearly full face, with eyes raised, hair hanging down loose on neck, hands crossed on breast. Portrait reduced to 29″ × 39″ size, begun March 11th, 1836, finished Aug. 5th, 1836.   Price, $300.00

Owned by the National Portrait Gallery, London, England.

2002 WOOD, MARY ANNE (1802–1854).

Copy of portrait painted by John Neagle, begun April 27th, 1836, finished May 7th, 1836. Bust.   Price, $100.00

Owned by William McHale, Esq., Cleveland, Ohio.

2003 WOOD, WILLIAM B. (1779–1861).

Popular actor and theatrical manager, head to left. In character as " Charles de Moor." Painted from a study in 1810, begun April 12th, 1860, finished April 27th, 1860. Size of panel 12″ × 10½″. Engraved by D. Edwin (F. 220).   Price, $10.00

Owned by Pennsylvania Historical Society, Philadelphia.

2004 WOOD, WILLIAM B. (1779–1861).

In character as " Charles de Moor." Full length, reclining on rocks, with arm outstretched, figures and landscape in background. Painting begun Aug. 10th, 1810, and finished in June, 1811. Size 43″ × 30″.
Price, $300.00

Owned by the Misses Hutchinson, Philadelphia.

2005 WOOD, WILLIAM B. (1779–1861).

In character as "Charles de Moor." Water-color sketch 18″ × 14″, signed on back of painting "TS." Composition similar to large painting No. 2004.

Owned by Mrs. John Thompson Spencer, Philadelphia.

2006 WOOD, MRS.

Of Arch Street, Philadelphia. Portrait begun Dec. 17th, 1835, finished Feb. 1st, 1836. Size 29″ × 36″.   Price, $300.00

2007 WOOD, WILLIAM.

Surveyor. Portrait begun July 18th, 1810, finished on June 11th, 1811. Bust.   Price, $60.00

2008 WOODALL, REV. DR.

Of Burlington, N. J. Portrait begun May 17th, 1822, finished July 22nd, 1822. Size 29″ × 36″.   Price, $150.00

2009 WOODROUGH, REV. G.

Painted for Lady Houston, begun Dec. 16th, 1819, finished Dec. 30th, 1819. Bust.   Price, $100.00

2010 WOODROUGH, MRS.

At Oakville, Trenton, N. J. Portrait begun Aug. 14th, 1819, finished Oct. 2nd, 1819. Bust.   Price, $100.00

2011 WOOLCOT, MRS.

Retouching a copy by Dunlap. Begun Aug. 21st, 1814, finished Sept. 10th, 1814. Bust.   Price, $50.00

2012 WRIGHT, MRS. GROVE.

Painted with her two children, begun July 10th, 1807, finished July 23rd, 1807. Size 44″ × 56″.   Price, $200.00

2013 YATES, REV. H.

Rector of the Bethel Church, of Charleston, S. C. Portrait begun Jan. 2nd, 1846, finished Jan. 20th, 1846. Bust.   Price, $200.00
Portrait at the Gibbes Art Gallery, Meeting Street, Charleston, S. C.

2014 YATES, JASPER (1745–1817).

Associate-Justice of the Supreme Court of Pennsylvania. Judge Yates was of Lancaster, Penna. Portrait begun March 25th, 1808, finished May 12th, 1808. Size 20″ × 23″.   Subscriber Price, $30.00

LIST OF PAINTINGS

2015 YOUNG, J. T.

Of Mississippi. Portrait begun Oct. 1st, 1855, finished Oct. 15th, 1855.
Bust. Price, $100.00

2016 YOUNG, MRS.

The register notes that the hand was introduced in the painting and that the portrait was begun on Sept. 3rd, 1835, and finished Sept. 12th, 1835, for Mr. Young, of Mississippi. Bust. Price, $150.00

2017 ZANTZINGER, MRS.

Of Lancaster, Penna. Portrait begun Nov. 14th, 1808, finished Nov. 29th, 1808. Size 20″ × 24″. Price, $40.00
Portrait owned by William F. Zantzinger, of New York.

MINIATURES

Thomas Sully's painting of Miniatures is not as generally well known as his life-size portrait painting. The following catalogue of his work is the first complete list attempted.

2018 ALLISON, MISS MARIA.

For T. Armistead, of Richmond, Va. Miniature, painted in 1802, being begun on Jan. 5th, and finished Jan. 10th.   Price, $15.00

2019 ARMSTEAD, THOMAS.

(Miniature.) Painted from a sketch, begun Aug. 25th, and finished Aug. 29th, 1801. Richmond, Va.   Price, $15.00

2020 BATES, MISS ANTOINETTE.

Sister of Mrs. De Silver. Painted in Philadelphia. Ivory. Rectangle. Owned by Mr. P. F. Kernan, of Philadelphia. Exhibited Loan Collection of Miniatures, Pennsylvania Academy of Fine Arts, Philadelphia, 1911.

2021 BILLS, CAPTAIN.

Miniature, begun July 22nd, 1801, and was finished on July 25th, 1801. The price was $15.00

2022 BLYTHE, MRS.

Miniature, begun Sept. 2nd, 1802, finished Sept. 10th, 1802.
     Price, $15.00

2023 BUCCANON, REVD.

Miniature, painted in 1804.

2024 BURR, D., ESQ.

Miniature, begun Jan., 1805, and finished same month.   Price, $20.00

2025 COOK, MRS. REBECCA.

Miniature, painted in Richmond, Va. Begun Decr. 7th, 1801, finished Decr. 14th, 1801.

2026 COLE, MR.

Miniature on ivory. Was exhibited at the Metropolitan Museum. Owned by Mrs. Richard T. Harriss, who received it from Miss Blanche Sully's family.

MINIATURES

2027 COLUMBUS.

Miniature on ivory, owned by Mrs. Albert Sully, Brooklyn, N. Y.

2028 COOPER, MRS.

Evidently at whose boarding house the Sully's stayed in Norfolk, Va. Miniature, begun on Sept. 8th, 1802, and finished Sept. 21st, 1802.

2029 CUSHMAN, CHARLOTTE (1816–1876).

In the "Taming of the Shew." Miniature on ivory. Painted about 1840. Owned by Mrs. Richard T. Harris, who received it from Blanche Sully's family.

2030 CUSHMAN, CHARLOTTE (1816–1876).

In the character of "Joan of Arc." Miniature on ivory. Owned by Mrs. Richard T. Harriss, New York.

2031 DABNEY, I.

Miniature, begun April, 1806, finished May, 1806.   Price, $20.00

2032 DAVIS, MR.

Collector of the port of Norfolk, Va. Miniature, begun April 5th, 1803, finished April 15th, 1803.

2033 DAVIS, I.

Miniature, begun June 30th, 1804, finished July 10th, 1804.   Price, $20.00

2034 DE SILVER, MRS. EMILY BATES.

Bust, head to right, white low-necked dress with red mantle lined with gold over shoulder and arm. Painted in Philadelphia about 1830. Ivory, rectangle. Owned by Miss. A. M. Archambault, of Philadelphia. Exhibited at Loan Collection of Miniatures, Pennsylvania Academy of Fine Arts, Philadelphia, 1911.

2035 FARLOW, MRS.

Miniature, begun on Oct. 10th, 1802, and finished Oct. 13th, 1802.

Price, $15.00

2036 FALCON, MR.

Miniature, begun May 18th, 1804, finished June 12th, 1804.

Price, $20.00

2037 FARRAR, EZRA (1763–1845).

Bust, head to right, high coat collar and white stock with bow tie. Miniature is signed on right of figure " TS." Owned by Miss Grace Edwards, of Boston, Mass.

MINIATURES

2038 GIBBON, LIEUTENANT.

Miniature, begun July, 1805, and finished the same month.   Price, $20.00

2039 GILMORE, MRS.

Of Baltimore, Md.   Miniature, signed " TS."   Owned by the Ehrich Galleries, New York.

2040 GREEN, JOHN.

(Son of William Green, actor.)   Miniature, begun March 10th, 1804, finished April 11th, 1804.   Price, $15.00

2041 GREEN, WILLIAM.

Actor.   Miniature, begun September, 1804, and finished the same month.
                                                                Price, $20.00

2042 GREY, JOHN.

Miniature, begun Aug., 1805, and finished the same month.   Price, $20.00

2043 GRIMES, CHANCELLOR.

Miniature, begun May 6th, 1804, finished May 20th, 1804.   Price, $20.00

2044 HIOTT, MRS.

(Deceased, from a sketch.)   Miniature, begun Decr. 23rd, 1802, finished Janr. 14th, 1803.

2045 HOLMES, JOHN.

Of the Bowling Green.   Miniature, begun May 31st, 1804, finished June 10th, 1804.   Price, $20.00

2046 HOPKINS, MRS.

Miniature, begun July 23rd, 1803, finished Aug. 13th, 1803.   Price, $15.00

2047 JENNINGS, MRS.

Miniature, begun June 5th, 1803, finished June 10th, 1803.
                                                                Price, $15.00

2048 JACKSON, EDWARD DRAKE.

Of Clarksburg, West Virginia.   Oval, 2⅜" × 1⅞".

NOTE.—This miniature in its original gold frame was sold in auction, Philadelphia, 1920.

2049 JOHNSTON, DAVID, ESQ.

Miniature, begun June 21st, 1804, finished July 10th, 1804.   Price, $20.00

MINIATURES

2050 JOHNSTON, MRS. JAMES MCCONNELL.

Miniature, painted after death partly from description, begun June 8th, 1803, finished June 13th, 1803. The miniature is painted on a white metal, and was owned in Richmond, Va., in 1918.   Price, $15.00

2051 KEMBLE, FRANCES ANNE (1809–1893).

Portrait painted as "Beatrice Cenci." Miniature on ivory. Owned by Mrs. Richard T. Harriss, New York.

2052 LADY.

Miniature painted from description for Mrs. William Southerwood, begun Dec. 6th, 1801, finished Dec. 12th, 1802.   Price, $20.00

2053 MALCOLM, MISS ANGELICA (1792–1834).

Miniature painted about 1813. Owned by Mrs. John Lloyd, Philadelphia.

2054 MATTHEWS, MARY.

Miniature, begun Jany. 2nd, 1803, finished Jany. 14th, 1803.
                                                                     Price, $15.00

2055 MCCLERG, WALTER.

Miniature, begun March, 1805, and finished the same month.
                                                                     Price, $20.00

2056 MCKENSIE, MRS.

Miniature, begun August, 1804, finished the same month.   Price, $20.00

2057 NEMO, MR.

Lawyer. Miniature, begun June 2nd, 1803, finished June 13th, 1803.
                                                                     Price, $15.00

2058 NEW, ELIZABETH.

Miniature, painted in Norfolk, Va., being begun on March 7th, 1802, and finished March 13th, 1802.   Price, $15.00

2059 OTT, MONSIEUR.

Jeweler. Miniature, begun Aug. 5th, 1801, and finished on Aug. 10th, 1801. According to the register this was the fifth miniature painted by Sully, and on the back is noted "T. Sully, Miniature and Fancy Painter, Norfolk, 1801." The miniature is signed "T. Sully 5." Owned by Miss Penrose, Philadelphia, Pa.

MINIATURES

2060 RUTH.

Thomas Sully's conception of the Biblical character. Miniature on ivory, owned by Mrs. Albert Sully, Brooklyn, N. Y.

2061 SHOEMAKER, CAROLINE.

Of Baltimore. Miniature painted from remembrance, begun May 5th, 1804, finished May 10th, 1804. Price, $15.00

2062 SOLAGE, MADAME.

Of Norfolk, Va. Miniature begun on May 5th, 1801, and finished June 8th, 1801. The price was $15.00

2063 SULLY, ALFRED (1820–1879).

Miniature, copied from portrait painted for his mother in the uniform of a West Point cadet. On ivory. Owned by Mrs. Albert Sully, Brooklyn, New York.

2064 SULLY, BLANCHE (1814–1898).

Miniature on ivory, owned by Mrs. Albert Sully, Brooklyn, N. Y.

2065 SULLY, CHESTER.

This miniature was painted in Norfolk, Virginia, being begun on May 13th, 1801, and finished on June 1st, 1801. It was Thomas Sully's first attempt in painting from life. The miniature was painted for Mary Lee, and the price received being $15.00

2066 SULLY, JANE (1807–1877).

Miniature on ivory, owned by Mrs. Albert Sully, Brooklyn, N. Y.

2067 SULLY, MANUELLA.

Manuella Zimeno, of Monterey, Cal., was the first wife of the artist's son Alfred. Miniature on ivory, owned by Mrs. Albert Sully, Brooklyn, N. Y.

2068 SULLY, MANUELLA.

Manuella Zimeno, of Monterey, California. Miniature painted on copper. Owned by Mrs. Alfred Sully, Brooklyn, N. Y.

2069 SULLY, MATTHEW (–1815).

Miniature of the artist's father. Bust, red coat, head to right. Oval, ivory 1¼" × 1". Owned by Mrs. E. O. Bolling, of Virginia.

MINIATURES

2070 SULLY, ROSALIE KEMBLE (1818–1847).

Miniature, copied from the portrait painted for her sister Blanche in 1871. On ivory. Owned by Mrs. Albert Sully, Brooklyn, New York.

2071 SULLY, SARAH (1779–1867).

Wife of the artist, painted as a young woman of about thirty. Formerly owned by Garrett Neagle. Ivory, circular, and purchased from him by Gilbert S. Parker and exhibited at Loan Collection of Miniatures, Pennsylvania Academy of Fine Arts, Philadelphia, 1911.

2072 SULLY, SOPHIA.

She was the daughter of Matthew Sully, Jr., and married Mr. Bolling at Richmond, Va., Oct. 17th, 1819. The register notes the miniature " was begun June 8th, 1801, and finished June 19th, 1801," also that the hands were introduced. Bust, head to right, dark hair, low-necked white dress, green shawl over left shoulder. Oval ivory 2½" × 2¼". Owned by Mrs. E. O. Bolling, of Virginia.   Price, $20.00

2073 SULLY. (MEMORIAL.)

To the artist's wife, Sarah Sully. Weeping woman in white dress with long black veil, standing by tomb under a willow tree. Ivory circle 1½" diam. Owned by Mrs. E. O. Bolling, of Virginia.

2074 TOME, MRS.

Of Norfolk, Virginia. Miniature, begun Feb. 5th, 1803, finished Feb. 13th, 1803.   Price, $10.00

2075 WHITE, MR.

A glass merchant of Norfolk, Va. Miniature, begun on June 20th, 1801, and finished on July 20th, 1801. The price was $15.00

2076 WILSON, MR.

Miniature, begun March 11th, 1803, and finished April 1st, 1803.

Price, $15.00

2077 WOODWORTH, DUDLEY.

Miniature, begun August 1st, 1801, and finished August 5th, 1801. The price was $15.00

2078 WORSELY, MRS.

Miniature, begun August, 1805, and finished the same month.

Price, $20.00

MINIATURES

2079 UNKNOWN LADY.

Miniature, painted from description for Mr. Southerwood, begun Decr. 6th, 1801, finished Decr. 12th, 1801.   Price, $20.00

2080 UNKNOWN CHILD.

(Deceased.) Miniature, painted in Norfolk, Va., begun August 12th, 1802, finished August 20th, 1802.   Price, $15.00

2081 UNKNOWN MAN.

Miniature, painted from a sketch of a gentleman by Lawrence Sully, begun on March 4th, 1804, finished March 5th, 1804.   Price, $15.00

2082 UNKNOWN MAN.

Miniature on ivory. Owned by Mrs. Albert Sully, Brooklyn, N. Y.

SUBJECT PAINTINGS

2083 ADIEU, THE.

Noted in register of paintings as " subject suggested by King." This was Charles B. King who was Sully's fellow student in London. Painting begun Nov. 21st, 1839, finished June 13th, 1840. Size 35″ × 28″. Price, $250.00

2084 AGES, THE THREE.

Past, Present and to Come. Painting begun May 4th, 1869, finished May 29th, 1869. Size 20″ × 24″. Price, $50.00

Sold at executor's sale of artist's paintings, Dec. 20th, 1872, Thomas & Sons, Fourth St., Philadelphia.

2085 ALFRED THE GREAT, IN THE PEASANT'S HUT.

Painted from an engraving of the picture by Sir David Wilkie. Begun Aug. 8th, 1854, finished Sept. 12th, 1854. Size 4′ 10″ × 3′ 2″.
Price, $300.00

This painting was owned for many years by Mrs. Bridport, Philadelphia.

2086 AMERICA.

America Wresting the Trident from Neptune. Design ordered by the State of New York for an enamelled box presented to Commodore Perry. Size 18″ × 13″.

2087 ANATOMICAL DRAWINGS.

Six drawings made for Dr. Gibson, each 6″ × 3½″. Jan. 12th, 1824.
Price, $60.00

2088 ANDRE, CAPTURE OF MAJOR.

Painted for the engraver, Francis Kearney, begun Jan. 2nd, 1812, and finished April 1st, 1812. Size 31″ × 32″. Price, $200.00

Exhibited in 1812 at the Second Exhibition of the Society of Artists of the United States at the Pennsylvania Academy, Philadelphia.

2089 ARIADNE (LADY HAMILTON).

After painting by Sir Joshua Reynolds. Picture is noted as "begun by Jane Sully and finished by Thomas Sully for James Earle" (the Philadelphia picture dealer). Bust, size 20″ × 24″. Price, $40.00

Painted March 30th, 1837 (the date is evidently the time that Thomas Sully finished the picture). Owned by Mr. Joseph MacG. Mitcheson, Philadelphia.

2090 ARIADNE (LADY HAMILTON).

After the painting by Sir Joshua Reynolds. Copy begun April 28th, 1860, finished May 7th, 1860. Head. Price, $50.00

2091 ARIADNE (LADY HAMILTON).

Painted from an engraving of the picture by Sir Joshua Reynolds. Begun May 10th, 1861, finished May 18th, 1861. Size 12" × 17". Price, $50.00

2092 ARIADNE (LADY HAMILTON).

Copy of the painting by Sir Joshua Reynolds. Painting begun Sept. 15th, 1864, finished Sept. 24th, 1864. Size 20" × 17". Price, $30.00

2093 ARIADNE (LADY HAMILTON).

Copied from painting of Sir Joshua Reynolds, begun Dec. 24th, 1864, finished May 25th, 1865. Head. Price, $30.00

2094 ARIADNE (LADY HAMILTON).

Copy from painting of Sir Joshua Reynolds, begun Oct. 27th, 1870, finished Nov. 3rd, 1870. Size 20" × 16½". Price, $50.00

2095 ARIADNE.

Copy from painting by Vanderlyn for James Earle, picture dealer of Philadelphia. Begun June 28th, 1825, finished Jan. 26th, 1826. Bust.

2096 ARIADNE.

(Original composition.) Begun Oct. 26th, 1861, finished Dec. 6th, 1861. Size 9" × 6". Price, $15.00

2097 ARISTOPHANES.

Design for Works of Aristophanes. Begun Oct. 10th, 1822, finished Oct. 22nd, 1822. In sepia, for Mr. Laval. Size 8" × 4". Price, $15.00

2098 ASSUMPTION OF THE VIRGIN.

By Titian. Copy begun Feb. 13th, 1829, finished April 3rd, 1830. Size 39" × 22". Price, $75.00

2099 ATALLA.

Copied from Gerard. Begun Oct. 18th, 1823, finished Nov. 1st, 1823. Size 17" × 20". Price, $30.00

2100 BACCHANTE (LADY HAMILTON).

Copy of the painting by Romney. Head of a young girl with long hair. Painting begun April 7th, 1860, finished April 19th, 1860. Signed on back of canvas " TS 1860." Size 20" × 24". Price, $80.00
Owned by Mrs. John Thompson Spencer, Philadelphia.

SUBJECT PAINTINGS

2101 BANK NOTE DESIGN.

Sketch drawn for the engraver George Murray, of the firm of Murray, Draper, Fairman & Co., of Philadelphia, the large bank-note engravers. Size 17″ × 9″. Aug. 19th, 1810. Price, $30.00

2102 BANK NOTE DESIGN.

Sketch drawn for the engraver, W. H. Tappan. Size 6″ × 4″. Jan. 23rd, 1830. Price, $20.00

2103 BANK NOTE DESIGN.

Sketch drawn for the engraver, Cephas G. Childs. Size 6″ × 4″. Feb. 22nd, 1830. Price, $20.00

2104 BANK NOTE DESIGN.

Sketch drawn for the engraver, Cephas G. Childs. Size 10″ × 8″. June, 1830. Two children: " Prayer." Price, $25.00

2105 BATH, THE.

(A copy from a picture.) Begun Jan. 26th, 1847, finished Feb. 1st, 1847. Size 18″ × 12½″. Price, $30.00

2106 BEATRICE CENCI.

After the painting by Guido, copied in 1822. Size 17″ × 14″. Signed " TS." Owned by the Ehrich Gallery, New York.

2107 BEATRICE CENCI.

After Guido. This picture was begun by Jane Sully and finished by Thomas Sully, painted for Sturgess of Boston, begun June 10th, 1828, finished June 14th, 1828. Size 17″ × 20″. Price, $50.00

2108 BOWMEN, THE.

India-ink wash drawing of three bowmen standing by target stringing and shooting bows and arrows. Designed and presented to the " United Bowmen Association." Drawn on July 20th, 1829. Signed " T. Sully, 1829." In records of United Bowmen, Pennsylvania Historical Society, Philadelphia.

2109 BOY AND CAT.

Painted from a sketch made in 1810, begun July 20th, 1859, finished July 28th, 1859. Size 20″ × 24″. Price, $100.00

2110 BOY AND DOG.

Painted from a former sketch. Begun June 8th, 1860, finished June 16th, 1860. Painted for Mr. and Mrs. Thomas Sparks. Size 20″ × 24″. Head. A curly-headed blond boy of six or eight years with a large black spaniel.
Price, $50.00
Owned by Miss Hannah Sparks, of Philadelphia, Pa.

2111 BOY AND DOG.

Picture begun June 20th, 1862, finished June 21st, 1862. Size 9″ × 6″.
Price, $10.00

2112 BOY AT PRAYER.

A copy, begun Jan. 13th, 1871, finished Jan. 16th, 1871. Size 11″ × 9″.
Price, $10.00

2113 BOY AT WINDOW.

Painting begun Jan. 26th, 1857, finished Feb. 2nd, 1857. Size 20″ × 24″.
Price, $100.00

2114 BOY SAILING BOAT.

Picture begun June 23rd, 1862, finished June 28th, 1862. Sketch. Size 9″ × 6″.
Price, $10.00
Sold at executor's sale of artist's paintings, Dec. 20th, 1872, Thomas & Sons, Fourth St., Philadelphia.

2115 BOY AND CONCH SHELL.

The register notes the size as 29″ × 36″, the price as $400.00, and that the painting was started Dec. 3rd, 1839, and was "Expunged." It also records a second design, slightly varied.

2116 BOY'S HEAD.

Copy of painting by Sir Thomas Lawrence, noted in register of paintings as "Romantic Boy," copy begun Sept. 26th, 1861, finished Oct. 9th, 1861. Size 11″ × 7½″.
Price, $20.00

2117 BOY'S HEAD.

By Sir Thomas Lawrence. Second copy, begun March 2nd, 1852, finished March 6th, 1852.
Price, $30.00

2118 BOY'S HEAD.

By Sir Thomas Lawrence. Copy begun Feb. 28th, 1852, finished March 2nd, 1852. Size 16″ × 20″.
Price, $20.00

2119 BOY'S HEAD.

Copy from painting by Julien, begun Dec. 14th, 1869, finished Jan. 6th, 1870. Size 17″ × 12″.
Price, $50.00

SUBJECT PAINTINGS

2120 Boy's Head.

Copied from painting by Julien, begun Dec. 8th, 1869, finished Dec. 13th, 1869. For Garrett C. Neagle. Size 18½″ × 14″.   Price, $30.00

2121 Boy's Head.

Copy from Julien. Begun Sept. 6th, 1867, finished Sept. 11th, 1867. Size 20″ × 16″.   Price, $30.00

2122 Boy's Head.

Copy from Julien. Begun Dec. 18th, 1867, finished Dec. 19th, 1867. Size 20″ × 16″.   Price, $30.00

2123 Boy's Head.

In half shadows. Begun Dec. 20th, 1867, finished Dec. 28th, 1867. Size 12″ × 14″.   Price, $10.00

2124 Brothers.

Painting begun April 26th, 1869, finished May 3rd, 1869. Size 20″ × 16″.   Price, $50.00
Sold at executor's sale of artist's paintings on Dec. 20th, 1872.

2125 "Brunette" (Ideal Head).

Painting begun March 5th, 1850, finished March 13th, 1850. Size 20″ × 24″.   Price, $50.00

2126 Brunetta, La.

Bust of a young woman seated, her head resting en her hand, neck and shoulders undraped, head to left with hair surrounding her face. Inscribed on back of canvas "La Brunetta, $\overline{TS}$, 1854, September." Painted for Mrs. Caperton, of Georgetown, D. C., begun Aug. 29th, 1854, finished Sept. 22nd, 1854. Size 20″ × 24″.   Price, $60.00
Owned by Mrs. Hugh Caperton, Baltimore, Md.

2127 Capuchin Chapel.

Copied from the original painting by Granet that was owned by Benjamin Wiggins, of Boston, who allowed Sully to copy it for exhibition purposes. The copy was begun Aug. 7th, 1821, and finished Oct. 9th, 1821, Sully working for ten hours daily. The size was 5′ 8″ × 4′ 3″, and the copy so admirable that it was confused with the original. The register notes the price or valuation as $800.00, and Sully's correspondence records it was sold in Mexico, about 1828, through Joel R. Poinsett.   Price, $800.00

339

SUBJECT PAINTINGS

2128 CASTLE IN A STORM.

Original composition, begun Jan. 11th, 1871, finished Jan. 23rd, 1871. Size 11″ × 9″.   Price, $10.00

2129 CERTIFICATE DESIGN.

For membership in the Washington Benevolent Society.   July, 1813.
Price, $100.00

2130 CERTIFICATE DESIGN.

For membership in the Agriculturist Society.   August, 1823.   Size 10″ × 14″.   Price, $40.00

2131 CHARITY.

An original composition.   Begun Jan. 11th, 1838.   Size 29″ × 36″. Erased.   Price, $300.00

2132 CHARITY.

Painting begun April 19th, 1839, and finished July 21st, 1839.   (A reduced half-length of original.)   Size 20″ × 17″.   Price $150.00

2133 CHILD.

Studying her lesson, begun Oct. 12th, 1867, finished Oct. 17th, 1867. Size 20″ × 16″.   Price, $50.00

2134 CHILD.

Child reposing.   Head and shoulders of a child about two years old. Blond hair.   Signed on face " TS 1859."   Panel 10″ × 12″.
Gibson collection, The Pennsylvania Academy of Fine Arts.

2135 CHILD.

In contemplation.   Painting intended for Edward Carey, begun Jan. 6th, 1840, finished Jan. 13th, 1840.   Head.   Price, $150.00

2136 CHILD.

Sketch, whole length, begun Sept. 18th, 1810, finished Sept. 24th, 1810. Size 44″ × 56″.   Price, $50.00

2137 CHILD ASLEEP.

(The Rosebud.)   Sleeping child with golden curly hair lies in a crib, half covered with a yellow coverlet, with red curtain background; a pink rosebud is on the pillow.   Painting begun June 7th, 1841, finished June 21st, 1841. Size 24″ × 36″.   Engraved by John Sartain.   Signed " TS 1841."
Price, $150.00
Bequest of Frank T. S. Darley to the Metropolitan Museum, New York.

SUBJECT PAINTINGS

2138 CHILD, SLEEPING.

Painting begun Feb. 27th, 1857, finished March 10th, 1857. Bust.
Price, $100.00

2139 CHILD, SLEEPING.

Copied from an English publication, begun Feb. 15th, 1867, finished Feb. 23rd, 1867. Size 30″ × 25″. The register notes the painting as afterwards erased. Price, $100.00

2140 CHILD, SLEEPING.

Copy from painting by Sir Joshua Reynolds, begun Jan. 28th, 1865, finished Feb. 28th, 1865. Size 30″ × 25″. Price, $50.00

2141 CHILD, SLEEPING.

After Sir Joshua Reynolds. Copy begun April 29th, 1870, finished May 30th, 1870. Size 23″ × 19″. Price, $50.00
Sold at executor's sale of artist's paintings on Dec. 20th, 1872.

2142 CHILD'S HEAD.

"Devotion." Painting begun Sept. 8th, 1851, finished Sept. 16th, 1851. Size 17″ × 20″. Price, $80.00

2143 CHILD'S HEAD.

In half shadow, begun Sept. 1st, 1859, finished Sept. 24th, 1859. Size 8½″ × 7″. Price, $10.00

2144 CHILD'S HEAD.

(Ideal.) Painting begun June 1st, 1863, finished June 12th, 1863. Size 17″ × 20″. Price, $30.00

2145 CHILD'S HEAD.

Copied from painting by Du Bois, begun March 6th, 1856, finished March 10th, 1856. Size 13″ × 10″. Price, $50.00

2146 CHILD'S HEAD.

(Ideal.) Painting begun July 28th, 1864, finished Aug. 5th, 1864. Size 17″ × 14″. Price, $30.00

2147 CHILD'S HEAD.

(Ideal.) Copied from painting by Drummond, begun Aug. 20th, 1864, finished Aug. 29th, 1864. Size 20″ × 24″. Price, $30.00

2148 CHILD PRAYING.

Ideal composition, begun Dec. 14th, 1848, finished Dec. 27th, 1848. Head. Price, $50.00

341

SUBJECT PAINTINGS

2149 CHILD'S HEAD.

Water-color sketch of little girl with golden hair, copied from painting by Sir Thomas Lawrence. Size 6″ × 6″.

Purchased from sale of artist's grandson. Owned by Mantle Fielding, Germantown, Philadelphia.

2150 CHILD'S HEAD.

Copy from Broadbent. Begun Oct. 19th, 1867, finished Oct. 24th, 1867. Size 17″ × 14″. Price, $50.00

2151 CHILD'S HEAD.

Painted for Mrs. Jones on April 1st, 1864. Size 18″ × 14″.
Price, $50.00

2152 CHILD AND BOOK.

Painting begun Nov. 8th, 1869, finished Nov. 18th, 1869. Size 5″ × 5″.
Price, $20.00

2153 CHILD LISTENING TO A BIRD.

Painting begun Oct. 20th, 1869, finished Oct. 29th, 1869. Size 18″ × 14″. Price, $50.00

Sold at executor's sale of artist's paintings, Dec. 20th, 1872.

2154 CHILD.

(After Sir Joshua Reynolds.) Copy begun by Ellen and finished by Thomas Sully. Painting begun on March 24th, 1835, finished April 9th, 1835. Bust. Price, $125.00

2155 CHILD WITH FLOWERS IN HAT.

Painting begun Jan. 10th, 1860, finished Jan. 21st, 1860. Sketch 7″ × 5½″. Price, $10.00

2156 CHILD WITH DOG.

Study for a portrait, begun Aug. 2nd, 1859, finished Aug. 3rd, 1859. Size 7″ × 4″. Price, $10.00

2157 CHILD AND DOG.

Third picture, a copy of former painting, begun Aug. 26th, 1852, finished Sept 7th, 1852. Size 20″ × 17″. Signed on back of canvas " TS 1852." Price, $100.00

Owned by Mrs. John Thompson Spencer, Philadelphia.

2158 CHILD AND DOG.

Sketch for fancy picture, begun June 26th, 1852, finished June 28th, 1852. Size 9″ × 7″. Price, $20.00

SUBJECT PAINTINGS

2159 CHILD AND DOG.

Painted for James S. Earle, of Philadelphia, begun June 28th, 1852, finished June 30th, 1852. Size 20″ × 17″. Price, $30.00

2160 CHILD AND DOG.

Second picture, a copy of former painting, begun Aug. 25th, 1852, finished Sept. 7th, 1852. Size 20″ × 17″. Price, $30.00

2161 CHILD AND DOG.

Painted on order of James S. Earle, picture dealer, Philadelphia, begun Feb. 6th, 1852, finished Feb. 14th, 1852. Size 17″ × 20″. Price, $30.00

2162 CHILD AND DOG.

Full-length seated figure with dog, the child holds in one hand a large hat filled with flowers, landscape in background. Size H. 27½″, W. 36″. Signed " JS 1839." Engraved by John Sartain.
Formerly owned by F. T. S. Darley, Philadelphia, and later by Joseph T. Kinsley, who sold the picture by auction in New York.

NOTE.—Child and Dog (No. 2162). A replica, but not signed or dated on face of canvas is owned by the Pennsylvania Academy of Fine Arts, Philadelphia.

2163 CHILD AND DOG.

Fancy picture, begun Dec. 3rd, 1855, finished Dec. 27th, 1855. Size 17″ × 20″. Price, $50.00

2164 CHILD, THE LOST.

A composition painted for Cephas G. Childs, the engraver. A boy is seated in the woods and his dog looks up in his face, evidently lost. Painting begun Oct. 24th, 1829, finished March 7th, 1837. Panel 27″ × 21½″. Signed on back of panel " JS 1837." Price, $100.00
Owned by the Ehrich Gallery, New York.

2165 CHILD, THE LOST.

Painting begun in 1829, finished March 7th, 1837. Bust. Price, $150.00

2166 CHILD, THE LOST.

A child lost in the woods with a hungry dog looking up in his face. Painting begun Dec. 19th, 1846, finished Jan. 21st, 1848. Size 25″ × 30″. Price, $150.00
Owned by estate of Colonel Thomas Fitzgerald, Philadelphia, Pa.

2167 CHILD, THE LOST.

Copy of the former painting, begun July 23rd, 1867, finished Aug. 7th, 1867. Size 21″ × 17″. Price, $50.00

2168 CHILD, THE LOST.

Water-color drawing, begun June 26th, 1830, finished July, 1834. Size 10″× 12″.

2169 CHILD, THE LOST.

Copy in oil of the water-color painting. Small half-length, begun Nov. 25th, 1833, finished March 8th, 1837. Price, $200.00

2170 CHILD IN HIGH WIND.

Head and shoulders of a child with both arms raised, holding on its head a broad brim hat. Signed on back "Too much wind, TS 1856." Noted in register as a "Fancy picture, child overtaken by a high wind," begun April 12th, 1856, finished April 18th, 1856. Size 17″ × 20″.
Price, $80.00
This picture was in collection of John Neagle, and was sold by Thomas & Sons in 1866. Owned by Mr. Lucien Phillips, of Radnor, Penna.

2171 CHILD IN HIGH WIND.

(Too much wind.) Begun May 10th, 1860, finished May 29th, 1860. Head. Price, $50.00

NOTE.—A small study or sketch for this painting is owned by Mrs. Albert Sully, Brooklyn, New York.

2172 CHILD IN HIGH WIND.

(Rather Windy.) Painted from a magazine illustration, begun April 2nd, 1869, finished April 19th, 1869. Size 15″ × 12″. Price, $30.00
Owned by Mr. A. H. Peiffer, Philadelphia.

2173 CHILD AT COTTAGE WINDOW.

Painting begun Jan. 22nd, 1847, finished Jan. 29th, 1847. Size 22″ × 17″. Price, $50.00

2174 CHILD AT WINDOW WITH BASKET OF FLOWERS.

A little girl sits at a window or balcony and holds in her hands a basket of flowers, head to right, hair parted in the middle, low-necked waist with black velvet bracelets. Signed " TS 1847." Painted and presented to fair for Musical Fund Society, begun Nov. 5th, 1847, finished Nov. 16th, 1847. Size 25″ × 30″. Price, $50.00
Owned by the John Levy Galleries, Fifth Ave., New York, in 1920.

2175 CHILD ON THE SEASIDE.

(Ideal.) Full-length figure of little girl wading on the sea beach, white dress, hair blowing in wind, hat at her side, one hand holding up her skirt, coast and figures in background. Painting begun April 24th, 1828, finished May 20th, 1828. For Dr. Tidyman. Size 58″ × 38″. (Was engraved by J. W. Steel.) Price, $200.00

2176 CHILD AT THE SEASHORE.

(Long Branch, N. J.) Begun Jan. 25th, 1860, finished Jan. 28th, 1860. Size 14″ × 9″. Price, $10.00

2177 CHILD.

Ideal head. Painting begun Dec. 27th, 1858, finished Dec. 31st, 1858. Size 12½ ×″ 10½″. Price, $50.00

2178 CHILD (HEAD).

Copy from Sir Joshua Reynolds. Begun June 15th, 1861, finished July 5th, 1861. Size 12″ × 10″. Price, $50.00

2179 CHILD (HEAD).

Second copy from Sir Joshua Reynolds, painting begun June 29th, 1861, finished July 6th, 1861. Size 12″ × 10″. Price, $50.00

2180 CHILD.

Copy from Reynolds. Begun May 27th, 1861, finished June 14th, 1861. Size 12″ × 17″. Price, $50.00

2181 CHILD SAVED FROM DROWNING.

A copy, begun Oct. 14th, 1871, finished Nov. 3rd, 1871. Size 20″ × 11″. Price, $50.00

2182 CHILDREN.

Ideal subject, two children. Begun Jan. 24th, 1856, finished Feb. 22nd, 1856. Size 17″ × 20″. Price, $100.00

2183 CHILDREN.

Group of two (ideal). Painting begun Oct. 17th, 1866, finished Nov. 14th, 1866. Size 30″ × 25″. Price, $50.00

2184 CHILDREN'S HEADS.

Group of eleven (ideal). Painting begun Oct. 19th, 1866, finished Oct. 29th, 1866. Signed " TS 1866, Novem." Size 30″ × 25″. Price, $50.00 Owned by J. Edwin Megargee, Brooklyn, N. Y.

SUBJECT PAINTINGS

2185 CHILDREN.

From painting by Sir Joshua Reynolds, begun June 3rd, 1863, finished June 11th, 1863. Size 17″ × 20″.   Price, $50.00

2186 CHILDREN.

(Two.) By Sir Joshua Reynolds. Copy of painting begun June 1st, 1830, finished July 10th, 1830. Size 20″ × 24″.   Price, $75.00

2187 CHILDREN.

(Group.) A sketch, begun June 27th, 1859, finished July 2nd, 1859. Size 8″ × 9″.   Price, $10.00

2188 CHILDREN.

Two heads, in an oval 17″ × 20″. Begun May 12th, 1866, finished May 21st, 1866.   Price, $30.00

2189 CHILDREN BATHING.

Painting begun April 19th, 1861, finished May 3rd, 1861. Size 10″ × 12″.   Price, $20.00

2190 CHILDREN AT THEIR MORNING DEVOTIONS.

Original composition, painting begun March 17th, 1845, finished March 29th, 1845. Size 29″ × 36″.   Price, $150.00

2191 CHILDREN IN THE STORM.

Painting begun Feb. 12th, 1861, finished Feb. 16th, 1861. Size 14″ × 20″.   Price, $20.00

2192 CHIP GIRL.

Painted for Mr. B. Heyward, begun Jan. 29th, 1856, finished Feb. 18th, 1856. Size 17″ × 20″. Head to right, wearing hood or shawl on head and carrying a basket of chips on arm.   Price, $100.00

Owned by John F. Braun, Esq., of Philadelphia.

2193 CHIP GIRL.

Painting begun Dec. 2nd, 1843, finished Dec. 9th, 1843. Size 24″ × 20″.   Price, $80.00

2194 CHRIST.

Head after Guido. Copy begun May 30th, 1870, finished June 13th, 1870. Size 20″ × 30″.   Price, $50.00

Sold at executor's sale of artist's paintings, Dec. 20th, 1872.

SUBJECT PAINTINGS

2195 CHRIST BLESSING LITTLE CHILDREN.

Painted for Mrs. Caperton, of Georgetown, D. C.   Begun Sept. 27th, 1854, finished Nov. 14th, 1854.   Size 4′ 6″ × 3′ 6″.   Price, $400.00
Owned by the Caperton family, of Baltimore, Md.

2196 CHRIST BLESSING LITTLE CHILDREN.

Painting begun July 15th, 1854, finished Aug. 20th, 1854.   Size 25″ × 30″.   Price, $300.00
Painted for the artist's sister Elizabeth (Mrs. Middleton Smith, of Charleston, S. C.).

2197 CHRIST BLESSING LITTLE CHILDREN.

Painting begun Sept. 22nd, 1853, finished July 12th, 1854.   Original composition.   Size 4′ 2″ × 3′ 4″.   Price, $300.00

2198 CHRIST, "SUFFER LITTLE CHILDREN TO COME UNTO ME."

Painting begun Nov. 14th, 1849, finished Dec. 26th, 1849.   Size 25″ × 30″.   Price, $500.00

2199 CHRIST HEALING THE SICK.

Copy of painting by Benjamin West for the Pennsylvania Hospital, Philadelphia.   Copy made Jan., 1818, size 37″ × 17″, for an engraving (noted as being unfinished).

2200 CHRIST HEALING THE SICK.

Drawing of Benjamin West's painting, Feb. 5th, 1828.   Size 13″ × 10″.
Price, $10.00

2201 CHRIST REJECTED.

Drawing of Benjamin West's painting, Oct. 30th, 1817.   Size 18″ × 15″.
As an illustration and key for the original painting.   Price, $50.00

2202 CINDERELLA AT THE KITCHEN FIRE.

A young girl, in ashes-of-roses gown, on the floor at whole length playing with a kitten, in the kitchen.   Fireplace, crane and big iron pot in the rear to left, while through a doorway on the right the two sisters are seen dressing for the ball as in the Fairy tale.   Engraved by Sartain.   Signed in front "TS 1843."   Begun Aug. 10th, 1843, finished Nov. 28th, 1843.   Size 51″ × 58″.   Price, $200.00
Sale of property of Mrs. Benjamin Thaw.

2203 CINDERELLA AND THE FAIRY DISGUISED AS A BEGGAR.

Painting begun Feb. 24th, 1867, finished March 4th, 1867.   Size 17″ × 17″.   Price, $50.00

SUBJECT PAINTINGS

2204 CINDERELLA.

(An incident in the story.) Painting begun Oct. 13th, 1858, finished Dec. 10th, 1858. Bust. Price, $100.00

2205 CINDERELLA.

And her sisters. Painting begun June 26th, 1867, finished July 9th, 1867. Size 25" × 30". Price, $50.00

2206 CINDERELLA.

Copy of Legane. Begun Aug. 8th, 1867, finished Aug. 24th, 1867. Size 17" × 14". Price, $50.00

2207 COINAGE DESIGN.

Liberty. (Size 8 in. by 10 in.) Design begun Oct. 1st, 1835, finished Oct. 5th, 1835. Price, $50.00

2208 CONFLAGRATION OF THE THEATER RICHMOND, VIRGINIA.

Sketch begun Jan. 28th, 1812, finished Jan. 30th, 1813. Size 16" × 12". Price, $40.00

2209 CONNECTICUT.

Arms of the State of Connecticut. Drawing made for Mr. J. Binns, begun March 7th, 1817, finished March 10th, 1817. Size 6" × 6". Price, $30.00

2210 CONTEMPLATION.

An ideal composition. Bust of a young girl with head supported by hand, an open book lies before her. Painting begun July 7th, 1846, finished August 12th, 1846. Signed on back of canvas " TS 1846." Size 20" × 24". Price, $100.00
Owned by Mrs. John Thompson Spencer, Philadelphia.

2211 CONTEMPLATION.

Lady in contemplation. After the painting by Gavin Hamilton. Presented to Mr. Beckert, of London. Begun Jan. 21st, 1840, finished Feb. 8th, 1840. Size 25" × 21". Price, ———

2212 CONTEMPLATION.

Lady in contemplation. Painting begun Jan. 21st, 1840, finished Jan. 24th, 1840. Size 25" × 21". Price, $150.00

2213 CONTEMPLATION.

Painting begun April 14th, 1852, finished April 21st, 1852. Size 24" × 26". Price, $30.00

SUBJECT PAINTINGS

2214 COTTAGE DOOR.

Painted from a sketch, begun April 6th, 1852, finished April 13th, 1852. Size 14″ × 11″.   Price, $20.00

2215 COUNTRY GIRL.

Painted in 1839 and noted in his register. (See Miss Elizabeth Cook.) Afterwards Mrs. Benjamin Franklin Bache.

2216 CROSSING A STREAM.

From an engraving, begun June 4th, 1867, finished June 25th, 1867. Size 25″ × 30″.   Price, $100.00

2217 DAISY MAID.

Copied from an engraving, painting begun June 22nd, 1855, finished June 23rd, 1855. Size 18″ × 15″.   Price, $50.00

2218 DANAE.

After the painting by Titian. Copied from a copy, begun Sept. 1st, 1811, finished Nov. 24th, 1811. Painted for James Earle, art dealer of Philadelphia. Size 58″ × 94″.   Price, $300.00

2219 DEJANIRE (ABDUCTION OF).

After Guido. Copy of the head, begun Sept. 27th, 1847, finished Oct. 2nd, 1847. Signed " JS 1847," on front of canvas. Size 20″ × 24″. Head.   Price, $50.00
Owned by the Vose Galleries, Boston, Mass.

2220 DEPARTURE, THE.

Original composition. Painting begun Dec. 24th, 1839, finished Dec. 30th, 1839. Size 20″ × 24″.   Price, $100.00

2221 DEPARTURE OF THE CONSCRIPT.

Copied from Dr. Bouse, begun Sept. 26th, 1870, finished Oct. 16th, 1870. Size 25″ × 30″.   Price, $100.00

2222 DEVOTION.

Painted from an engraving, begun June 18th, 1864, finished July 23rd, 1864. Head.   Price, $30.00

2223 DESIGN FROM AN OLD BALLAD.

Painting begun March 15th, 1865, finished March 22nd, 1865. Size 20″ × 12″.   Price, $30.00

2224 DIPLOMA.

Design of the Diploma of the Pennsylvania Academy of Fine Arts, Philadelphia. Oct. 3rd, 1817. Size 8" × 8". Price, $50.00
Another design made on Jan. 17th, 1831.

2225 DIPLOMA.

Design for the Diploma of the "Wig Society," of Princeton College. June 2nd, 1819. Size 24" × 18". Price, $100.00

2226 DOGS.

Copied from Rademaker. Painted Aug. 13th, 1815. Size 10" × 12".
Price, $50.00

2227 "DOMESTICITY," MOTHER AND TWO CHILDREN.

Curtain in background with sky showing. Mother has a rose-lined green mantle over left shoulder, child leans against her at her right, a boy unclothed is on her lap. Noted as "fancy subject." Painting begun Sept. 23rd, 1836, finished Dec. 12th, 1841. Size 43" × 36". Signed " TS 1840." Price, $500.00
Owned by Mrs. O. A. Parker, and loaned to Cleveland Museum of Art.

2228 DUBOIS.

(Study from life.) Copy begun July, 1832, finished August 1st, 1832. Size 29" × 36". Price, $30.00

2229 DUNSMORE VOLUNTEER LIGHT INFANTRY.

A study of colors. Painted in Richmond, Virginia. Begun July 4th, 1803, finished July 15th, 1803. Size 5 feet, four inches. Price, $30.00

2230 ERIN.

Ideal composition. Painting begun March 25th, 1852, finished March 27th, 1852. Size 11" × 14". Price, $20.00

2231 EXPECTATION OR THE LOOKOUT.

Bust of a young girl with her hand raised shading her eyes. Painting begun on March 8th, 1852, finished March 23rd, 1852. Signed on back of canvas " TS 1852." Size 20" × 24". Price, $50.00
Owned by Mrs. John Thompson Spencer, Philadelphia.

2232 FAIRIES FROLICKING.

Painting begun Jan. 13th, 1868, finished March 11th, 1868. Size 20" × 24". Price, $50.00

J S C

SUBJECT PAINTINGS

2233 FANCY SUBJECT.

Copied from Harper's Weekly for Garrett Neagle. Begun Oct. 1st, 1866, finished Oct. 6th, 1866. Size 18″ × 14″. Price, $30.00

2234 FAREWELL.

Painting begun March 28th, 1861, finished March 30th, 1861. Size 11″ × 7″. Price, $10.00

2235 "FAREWELL."

A lady leaving home. Painting begun Dec. 16th, 1865, finished Dec. 31st, 1865. Size 20″ × 24″. Price, $50.00

2236 FARMER'S BOY.

Picture begun Aug. 4th, 1841, finished Sept. 15th, 1841. Size 20″ × 24″. Price, $150.00

2237 FAUST.

Copied from a photograph after the painting by Ary Scheffer, begun March 1st, 1865, finished March 13th, 1865. Size 30″ × 25″. Price, $100.00

2238 "FIDELIO."

Painted from a cosmographic, begun June 5th, 1867, finished June 12th, 1867. Size 21″ × 17½″. Price, $80.00

2239 FISH GIRL.

Sketch begun April 26th, 1871, finished May 7th, 1871. Size 12″ × 10″. Price, $30.00
Sold at executor's sale of the artist's paintings, Thomas & Sons, Fourth St., Philadelphia, Dec., 1872.

2240 FISHERWOMAN'S DAUGHTER.

Painting begun July 28th, 1870, finished Aug. 12th, 1870. Size 20″ × 24″. Price, $50.00
Sold at executor's sale, Dec. 20th, 1872, by Thomas & Sons, Fourth St., Philadelphia.

2241 FLAGELLATION OF CHRIST.

By Titian. Copy begun Feb. 20th, 1829, finished April 3rd, 1830. Size 19″ × 15″. Price, $20.00

2242 FLEMISH PICTURE.

"Copy for myself" (Sully). Noted from the register as being 20″ × 24″, begun Aug. 8th, 1825, finished Aug. 29th, 1825. Price, $100.00

2243 FLIGHT, THE.

Painting begun March 2nd, 1840, finished June 13th, 1840. Size 17″ × 20″. Price, $150.00

2244 FLOWERS.

A copy, painting begun Aug. 4th, 1862, finished Aug. 13th, 1862. Size 12″ × 14″. Price, $10.00

2245 FLOWERS.

A copy, painting begun July 28th, 1843, finished July 30th, 1843. Size 10″ × 8″. Price, $15.00

2246 FLOWER GIRL, THE.

Copy after Murillo. Begun June 15th, 1868, finished June 29th, 1868. Size 20″ × 24″. Price, $100.00
Sold at executor's sale of artist's paintings, Dec. 20th, 1872, by Thomas & Sons, Philadelphia.

2247 FORAGING IN VIRGINIA.

Copied from drawing by F. O. C. Darley. Begun Dec. 18th, 1863, finished Jan. 15th, 1864. Size 29″ × 36″. Price, $150.00

2248 FRANKLIN INSTITUTE OF PHILADELPHIA.

Two designs, presented June 7th, 1830. Size 10″ × 8″. Price, $20.00

2249 FRANKLIN INSTITUTE OF PHILADELPHIA.

Design in water color. Painted Nov., 1830. Size 10″ × 12″.
Price, $15.00

2250 "FUN."

Copy, begun Sept. 8th, 1868, finished Sept. 29th, 1868. Size 20″ × 24″.
Price, $100.00

2251 GANYMEDE.

(After Guido Reni.) Bust, partly draped, holding cup in hand, head to left nearly in profile. Inscribed on back in center of panel " Guido. Ganymede. Copy by TS 1855." Panel 16⅞″ × 21⅝″. Begun July 20th, 1855, finished Aug. 3rd, 1855. Head. Price, $80.00

NOTE.—The original canvas by Guido is owned by the Pennsylvania Academy of Fine Arts, and this copy by Sully, by Arthur L. Church, of Philadelphia.

SUBJECT PAINTINGS

2252 GANYMEDE.

(Copied from painting by Guido for the artist's own collection. Begun Oct. 29th, 1822, finished Nov. 11th, 1822. Head. Price, $80.00 Owned by Mrs. Richard T. Harriss, of New York.

2253 GANYMEDE.

Copied from Guido Reni. Begun Oct. 27th, 1822, finished Nov. 9th, 1822. Size 17" × 20". Price, $50.00

2254 GANYMEDE.

Copied from painting by Guido for the artist's own collection. Begun Sept. 24th, 1859, finished Oct. 1st, 1859. Size 17" × 20". Price, $100.00

2255 GANYMEDE.

Copied from the painting by Guido, begun June 15th, 1869, finished Sept. 2nd, 1869. Size 24" × 30". Price, $100.00

2256 GATHERING OF THE CLANS.

Sold at executor's sale of artist's paintings, Dec. 20th, 1872, Thomas & Sons, Fourth St., Philadelphia.

2257 GENTLE SHEPHERD, THE.

By Sir David Wilkie. Copied from an engraving, begun June 25th, 1842, finished July 21st, 1842. Size 29" × 36". Price, $200.00

2258 GEORGIA.

Arms of the State of Georgia. Drawing made for Mr. Binns, begun Dec. 15th, 1818, finished Dec. 16th, 1818. Size 6" × 6". Price, $30.00

2259 GIL BLAS.

Composition copied from Opie's painting. Begun Nov. 20th, 1812, finished Dec. 4th, 1812. Size 58" × 94". Price, $150.00

2260 GIPSY GIRL.

An original composition, designed in England and finished in Philadelphia, for Edward Carey. Girl reclining on ground, head supported on her hands, a hood falls over the shoulders and she wears a bead bracelet and ring. Foliage and tree in background with tent in distance. Begun Feb. 24th, 1839, finished Sept. 9th, 1839. Size 25" × 30". Signed " JS." Price, $300.00 Engraved by John Cheney for the " Gift," 1842. Owned by A. H. Halberstadt, Pottsville, Pa.

2261 GIPSY AND CHILD.

>Copied from an engraving. Begun August 1st, 1828, finished August 11th, 1828. Size 20″ × 24″. Price, $75.00

2262 GIPSY.

>Second copy, painting begun May 29th, 1854, finished July 18th, 1854. Head. Price, $50.00

2263 GIPSY.

>Copy from French painting for Mr. Robert De Silver, begun Jan. 31st, 1859, finished Feb. 14th, 1859. Size 25″ × 30″. Price, $100.00
>Owned by Wilstach Collection, Fairmount Park, Philadelphia.

2264 GIPSY.

>Painted from a former picture. Begun July 25th, 1861, finished Aug. 5th, 1861. Size 12″ × 10″. Price, $20.00

2265 GIPSY.

>(The young Gipsy, a copy from the French.) Painting begun July 28th, 1866, finished July 23rd, 1866. Signed " TS 1866." Size 30″ × 25″.
>Price, $100.00
>Owned by Mr. Franklin Skinner, Philadelphia.

2266 GIPSY OR TAMBOURINE PLAYER.

>Copy, begun April 28th, 1868, finished June 22nd, 1868. Oval.
>Price, $50.00

2267 GIPSY OR TAMBOURINE PLAYER.

>Copy by Revier, size 20″ × 24″. Painting begun Aug. 10th, 1868, finished Aug. 24th, 1868. Price, $100.00

2268 GIRL.

>Bust, nude, with arms crossed on breast, head to right. Signed " TS 1839." Size 25″ × 30″.
>Ehrich Gallery, New York.

2269 GIRL.

>Bust of an English peasant girl, copied from Inskipp. Head, nearly full face, wearing a large hat, holding her hands before her. Size of canvas 20″ × 25″. Inscribed on back " Copied from Inskipp, TS 1867, September." Begun Sept. 12th, 1867, finished Sept. 21st, 1867. Price, $80.00
>Sold at executor's sale 1872 of Sully's paintings. Owned by Mrs. Clement Wainwright, Chestnut Hill, Philadelphia.

SUBJECT PAINTINGS

2270 GIRL.

Copy of painting, begun Feb. 23rd, 1866, finished March 28th, 1866. Size 17" × 14". Price, $30.00

2271 GIRL.

Resting against a beech tree. Painting begun Dec. 28th, 1869, finished Jan. 18th, 1870. Size 18" × 14". Price, $50.00

2272 GIRL BATHING.

Sketch painted for Colonel Allston, begun July 4th, 1828, finished July 6th, 1828. Size 15" × 19". Price, $50.00

2273 GIRL AND BIRD.

After Sir Joshua Reynolds. Copy begun April 21st, 1838, in London. The original was in the possession of Samuel Rogers. Size 17" × 20". Price, $300.00

2274 GIRL AND BIRD.

Sketch after the painting by Sir Joshua Reynolds. Painting begun June 22nd, 1843, finished June 24th, 1843. Size 12" × 12". Price, $30.00

2275 GIRL AND BIRD.

After Sir Joshua Reynolds. Copy begun Feb. 20th, 1860, finished March 16th, 1860. Bust. Price, $100.00

2276 GIRL AND BIRD.

After Sir Joshua Reynolds. Painting begun Feb. 1st, 1869, finished Feb. 17th, 1869. Size 25" × 30". Price, $150.00
Sold at executor's sale of artist's paintings, by Thomas & Sons, Fourth St., Philadelphia, on Dec. 20th, 1872.

2277 GIRL AND DOG.

Painting begun Jan. 13th, 1869, finished Feb. 13th, 1869. Size 17" × 21". Price, $50.00

2278 GIRL AND DOG.

Girl standing, in a low-necked yellow dress, holding up in her arms a white terrier. Signed "TS."
From collection of Mrs. Theodore Linke and J. C. McNerney; owned in 1919 by Knoedler & Co., New York.

2279 GIRL AND KITTEN.

Copy from painting by Greuze for the artist's own collection, begun June 7th, 1859, finished June 25th, 1859. Bust. Price, $150.00
Sold at executor's sale of artist's paintings, Dec. 20th, 1872, by Thomas & Sons, Fourth St., Philadelphia.

355

2280 GIRL AND MACAW.

Full-length figure of a young girl seated, low-necked blue dress, beside a large red macaw, landscape in background. Signed " TS 1832." Canvas 30″ × 38½″.
Owned by the Redwood Library, of Newport, R. I.

2281 GIRL AND MACAW.

A sketch, begun June 30th, 1859, finished July 4th, 1859. Size 8″ × 9″.
Price, $10.00

2282 GIRL AND POTTLE.

After Sir Joshua Reynolds. Painting begun March 19th, 1860, finished March 28th, 1860. Bust.   Price, $100.00

2283 GIRL FILLING HER PITCHER.

Copy from picture by William Owen, begun Aug. 18th, 1868, finished Aug. 29th, 1868. Size 20″ × 24″.   Price, $100.00

2284 GIRL WITH PITCHER.

Presented to Mr. Brown, of Richmond, Va., painting begun June 29th, 1850, finished July 6th, 1850. Head.   Price, $80.00

2285 GIRL SLEEPING.

After Sir Joshua Reynolds. Girl asleep, seated figure with head pillowed in her arms. Painting noted as reduced in size. Copy 17″ × 20″, begun June 13th, 1841, finished June 18th, 1841.   Price, $50.00

2286 GIRL SLEEPING.

After Sir Joshua Reynolds. Copied by Sully from painting of Miss Ross. Begun Dec. 8th, 1826, finished Dec. 24th, 1826. Size 20″ × 24″.
Price, $75.00

2287 GIRL SLEEPING.

After Sir Joshua Reynolds. Copy begun March 13th, 1838, finished in June, 1838. Size 25″ × 30″.   Price, $300.00
Exhibited in Artist Fund Society 1840. Owned by Francis Fisher Kane, of Philadelphia.

2288 GIRL AT THE SEASHORE.

Painting begun Aug. 14th, 1862, finished Aug. 20th, 1862. Size 14″ × 10″.   Price, $10.00

2289 GIRL AND SHELL.

Young girl holding a shell to her ear, begun Jan. 17th, 1871, finished Jan. 20th, 1871. Size 11″ × 9″.   Price, $10.00

SUBJECT PAINTINGS

2290 GIRL AND SHELL.

Copy of former painting with slight variation, begun April 7th, 1871, finished May 9th, 1871. Size 12″ × 10″. Price, $30.00

2291 GIRL AT A COTTAGE WINDOW.

Painting begun Aug. 29th, 1848, finished Sept. 4th, 1848. Head.
Price, $50.00

2292 GIRL'S HEAD.

Ideal head to left, hair parted in middle with ringlets, column in background to right with vine leaves. Robe covers shoulders but shows neck at back. Size 25″ × 30″.
Owned by the Corcoran Art Gallery, Washington, D. C.

2293 GIRL'S HEAD.

Head of a young girl about nine years of age with golden hair parted in middle and blue eyes. Size 12″ × 17″.
Owned by Mrs. R. T. Harriss, New York.

NOTE.—On back of canvas is inscribed by restorer who backed canvas that it was signed " TS 1863."

2294 GIRL'S HEAD.

Copied from Frank Leslie's Weekly Painting begun Oct. 10th, 1866, finished Dec. 15th, 1866. Size 12″ × 15′. Price, $50.00

2295 GIRL LAUGHING.

Painting begun Feb. 5th, 1861, finished Feb. 13th, 1861. Head.
Price, $80.00

2296 GIRL.

From North Holland. Copy, painting begun April 1st, 1861, finished April 3rd, 1861. Size 11″ × 7″. Price, $20.00
Sold at executor's sale of artist's paintings, Dec. 20th, 1872, Thomas & Sons, Fourth St., Philadelphia.

2297 GIRLS.

Two girls. Copied from a French engraving. Sketch begun Oct. 18th, 1859, finished Oct. 22nd, 1859. Size 15″ × 12″. Price, $20.00

2298 GIRLS BATHING.

Painting begun Nov. 23rd, 1869, finished Nov. 30th, 1869. Size 11½″ × 9½″. Price, $20.00

SUBJECT PAINTINGS

2299 GREEK GIRLS.

After the painting by Gavin Hamilton. Presented to Mr. Beckert, of London. Begun Jan. 31st, 1840, finished Feb. 27th, 1840. Size 26″ × 21″.
Price, $300.00

2300 GREUZE.

Copy of painting, begun by Jane, March, 10th, 1831, finished March 15th, 1831.
Price, $75.00

2301 GREUZE.

Second copy for the artist's own collection, begun June 2nd, 1855, finished June 25th, 1855. Bust size.
Price, $150.00

2302 GREUZE.

Copy for Mr. Vanderkemp, begun May 21st, 1855, finished June 17th, 1855. Bust size.
Price, $150.00

2303 GUARDIAN ANGELS.

Copy from painting by Sir Joshua Reynolds, begun Jan. 17th, 1865, finished Jan. 27th, 1865. Size 30″ × 25″.
Price, $100.00

2304 GUARDIAN ANGELS.

Copy from painting by Sir Joshua Reynolds. Begun Dec. 9th, 1871, finished Dec. 15th, 1871. Size 30″ × 25″.
Price, $100.00

2305 HEAD OF YOUNG GIRL.

Begun Feb. 19th, 1845, finished April 19th, 1845. Head. Price, $150.00

2306 HEAD OF YOUNG GIRL.

Bust, broad-brimmed hat with flowing ribbons. Size 20″ × 24″. Signed " 1859."
Owned by S. G. Hooper, of New York.

2307 HEAD.

Of an old man, painted in the style of Rembrandt, to instruct Charles Leslie, Oct. 4th, 1811. Size 12″ × 10″.

2308 HEAD.

Presented to the Academy of Fine Arts, Philadelphia. Begun Aug. 11th, 1845, finished Sept. 19th, 1845. Size 20″ × 24″.
Price, $80.00

2309 HEAD.

Old man, painted for Thomas A. Cooper. Begun June 18th, 1807, finished July 11th, 1807. Size 20″ × 24″.
Price, $3.00

SUBJECT PAINTINGS

2310 HEAD.

Painted for the Fair for the Blind. Painting begun Feb. 9th, 1837, finished Feb. 17th, 1837. Head. Price, $100.00

2311 HEAD.

Ideal composition, painted for Mr. Paine, of Charleston, S. C., begun Nov. 5th, 1855, finished Nov. 15th, 1855. Price, $100.00

2312 HEAD.

(Ideal.) Painting begun May 4th, 1861, finished May 10th, 1861. Size 12″ × 17″. Price, $50.00

2313 HEAD.

Copy from painting by Julien, begun March 29th, 1860, finished April 6th, 1860. Head. Price, $80.00

2314 HEAD.

Copy from painting by Julien. Begun Aug. 14th, 1861, finished Aug. 22nd, 1861. Size 12″ × 10″. Price, $20.00

2315 HEAD.

Copy from Julien for H. Price. Begun Nov. 10th, 1867, finished Nov. 20th, 1867. Size 20″ × 19″. Price, $30.00

2316 HEAD.

An ideal painting from a vignette, begun Jan. 23rd, 1867, finished Jan. 30th, 1867. Size 21″ × 17″. Price, $50.00

2317 HEAD.

Copy from painting by Julien. Begun Oct. 14th, 1861, finished Oct. 24th, 1861. Size 11″ × 7½″. Price, $20.00

2318 HEAD.

(From Guido.) Painted for James Earle in March, 1824, size 17″ × 20″. Price, $20.00

2319 HEAD.

(From Guido.) Copy of first painting, begun April, 1824. Size 17″ × 20″. Price, $20.00

2320 HEBE.

Painted for Mr. Paine. Begun Jan. 28th, 1856, finished Feb. 8th, 1856. Size 17″ × 20″. Price, $100.00

2321 HILTON, WILLIAM.

Historic sketch from the painting by Hilton, begun Aug. 23rd, 1822, finished Sept. 10th, 1822.   Size 29″ × 36″.   Price, $100.00

2322 HOGARTH'S " GATE OF CALAIS."

From Leslie's copy, painted by Sully, Jan. 26th, 1820, and finished May 19th, 1822.   Size 29″ × 36″.   Price, $150.00
Sully notes in his book "Hints to Young Portrait Painters," published in 1873, that the colors in this painting "were mostly tempered with wax."

2323 HOLY FAMILY.

After Corregio.   Copy begun Sept. 18th, 1809, in London, and finished Sept. 23rd, 1809.   Size 20″ × 24″.   Price, $200.00

2324 HOLY FAMILY.

After Corregio.   Copy is noted in the register as painted for the artist's own collection, begun Sept. 23rd, 1809, finished Nov. 14th, 1809.   Size 20″ × 24″.   Price, $200.00

2325 HOLY FAMILY (MADONNA DELLA SEDIA).

Copied from Raphael's original painting in Benjamin West's collection, London.   Begun Dec. 6th, 1809, finished on Dec. 30th, 1809.   Size 35″ × 35″.   Price, $200.00
Owned by Mrs. Alexander D. Campbell (née Wilcocks), of Philadelphia.

2326 HOLY FAMILY, RAPHAEL.

Small study 14½″ square.   Begun Feb. 2nd, 1812.   Price, $100.00

2327 HOLY FAMILY, RAPHAEL.

(Copied from Sully's first painting.)   Painting begun Feb. 17th, 1812, finished August 20th, 1812.   Size 30″ × 30″.   Price, $200.00

2328 HOLY FAMILY, RAPHAEL.

Copied from Sully's first painting.   Begun Jan. 26th, 1812, finished December, 1813.   Size 30″ × 30″.   Price, $200.00

2329 HOLY FAMILY.

By Raphael.   Lloyd of Boston.   Copy begun Sept. 3rd, 1820, finished October 12th, 1820.   Size 32″ × 32″.   Price, $200.00

2330 HOLY FAMILY.

By Raphael.   Copied by Jane Sully and retouched by Sully.   Begun Dec. 21st, 1825, finished Jan. 10th, 1826.   Size 32″ × 32″.   Price, $100.00

2331 HOLY FAMILY.

By Raphael. Painted by Jane Sully and retouched by Thomas Sully on May 10th, 1827. Size 32″ × 32″. Price, $80.00

2332 HOLY FAMILY.

By Raphael. Painting begun Dec. 27th, 1828, finished Feb. 13th, 1829. Size 32″ × 32″. Price, $150.00
Owned by Mrs. William D. Winsor, Philadelphia.

2333 HOLY FAMILY.

Copy of Sir Joshua Reynold's painting begun in London, Jan. 2nd, 1810, and finished March 1st, 1810. Size 42″ × 33′. Price, $200.00

2334 HOPE.

Copied from painting by Guido. Copy made in 1869. Noted as sold at executor's sale of the artist's paintings, Thomas & Sons, Fourth St., Philadelphia, Dec. 20th, 1872.

2335 HOPE AND DESPAIR.

A sketch begun May 17th, 1869, finished June 14th, 1869. Size 20″ × 24″. Price, $150.00
Sold at executor's sale of artist's pictures, Thomas & Sons, Fourth St., Philadelphia, Dec. 20th, 1872.

2336 HORSEMAN.

Copied from Swebach, begun Oct. 1st, 1845, finished Oct. 6th, 1845. Size 20″ × 24′. Price, $20.00

2337 HORSES FIGHTING.

Copy from Stubbs. Painting begun May 6th, 1809, finished May 14th, 1809. Size 29″ × 36″. Price, $25.00

2338 HOURS, THE.

(After Shelly.) Copied from an engraving and presented to Ellen Sully, painting begun Feb. 19th, 1850, finished Feb. 24th, 1850. Size 20″ × 24″.

2339 IDEAL COMPOSITION.

Painted for Garrett Neagle. Begun Feb. 24th, 1866, finished March 12th, 1866. Size 18″ × 14″. Price, $30.00

2340 IDEAL COMPOSITION.

Painted on order of James S. Earle, picture dealer, Philadelphia. Picture begun July 19th, 1851, finished Aug. 4th, 1851. Size 17″ × 20″.
Price, $80.00

SUBJECT PAINTINGS

2341 INDIAN MOTHER.

Painting begun April 27th, 1839, finished Sept. 13th, 1839. Noted in register as "a dream." Size 29" × 36". Price, $500.00

2342 INDIAN SQUAW.

Painting begun Oct. 30th, 1869, finished Nov. 6th, 1869. Size 18" × 16". (Noted as erased.) Price, $50.00

2343 INDOLENCE.

Copy after Chapman, painted in 1867. Noted as sold at executor's sale of artist's paintings, Dec. 20th, 1872, by Thomas & Sons, Fourth St., Philadelphia.

2344 INFANT ACADEMY.

After Sir Joshua Reynolds. For Mr. J. Craig. Copy begun Nov. 24th, 1823, finished Dec. 6th, 1823. Size 20" × 24". Price, $40.00

2345 INFANT HERCULES.

After the painting by Reynolds, begun Oct. 9th, 1863, finished Oct. 13th, 1863. Size 17" × 14". Price, $30.00
Sold at executor's sale of artist's paintings, Dec. 20, 1872, by Thomas & Sons, Fourth St., Philadelphia.

2346 "ISABELLA," IN "MEASURE FOR MEASURE."

Bust, standing dressed as a Nun and holding a cross in her hand. Signed on back with monogram " TS 1836." Engraved by John Cheney for the Gift of 1840, published by Edward L. Carey. Presented by him to Pennsylvania Academy of Fine Arts. Size 28" × 36".
Owned by Pennsylvania Academy of Fine Arts, Philadelphia.

2347 "ISABELLA."

(Shakespeare illustration.) From "Measure for Measure." Copy of former painting for Mr. Joseph Harrison, of Philadelphia. Begun Nov. 23rd, 1860, finished Dec. 15th, 1860. Size 29" × 36". Price, $200.00

2348 "ISABELLA."

(Shakespeare illustration.) From "Measure for Measure." Study made for the first painting. On a wood panel 10½ × 12, on the back of panel another sketch and inscribed "Painted by T. Sully."
Owned by Francis Fisher Kane, of Philadelphia.

2349 "JOE ANDERSON, MY JOE."

Noted in the register as painted for steamboat, copy begun Feb. 22nd, 1828, finished March 6th, 1828. Size 4′ 6″ × 24″. One of a set of four paintings noted in the register as for steamboat, for which he received

$300.00

2350 JULIET.

Study for picture of "Juliet," Romeo and Juliet. The register notes it as "erased," and the size as 12″ × 10″, and the price as $50.00

2351 JULIET.

(Vide Romeo and Juliet.) Painted for E. Carey, Philadelphia. Painting begun Dec. 14th, 1836, finished June 2nd, 1840. Size 44″ × 56″.

Price, $350.00

2352 JULIET. ARISEN FROM THE TOMB.

(Vide Romeo and Juliet.) Act 5, Scene 8. Painting presented to Mr. Carey, of Philadelphia. Begun Jan. 7th, 1836, finished Jan. 11th, 1836. Head originally on 19″ × 16″ panel, now inlaid to 25″ × 30″, with drapery added. Signed " TS 1836."
Owned by Ehrich Galleries, New York.

2353 JUVENILE AMBITION.

Copied from picture of Charles King, Washington, D. C. Begun Dec. 19th, 1824, finished Jan. 12th, 1825. Size 29″ × 36″. Price, $50.00

2354 KAUFMAN, ANGELICA.

Copy from a painting by Kaufman for Mr. Tucker, a lawyer of Norfolk, Virginia.

2355 LADIES.

(Group of three.) Busts, seen as if in an opera box. Canvas about 12″ high, 18″ wide. Signed " TS 1866, March 12th."
Owned by Miss Sarah Sully Rawlins.

2356 LADIES.

(Three.) A sketch, partly a copy. Begun Dec. 11th, 1861, finished Jan. 10th, 1862. Size 9″ × 8″. Price, $20.00

2357 LADY.

Copy from painting by Greuze. Begun Feb. 7th, 1870, finished March 10th, 1870. Size 21″ × 17″. Price, $100.00

SUBJECT PAINTINGS

2358 LADY.

Copied from an engraving, begun July 9th, 1870, finished July 25th, 1870 Size 14″ × 17″.   Price, $50.00

2359 LADY PREPARING TO BATHE.

Painting begun Nov. 14th, 1863, finished Nov. 30th, 1863. Size 27″ × 21″.   Price, $50.00

2360 LADY PREPARING TO BATHE.

Painting begun Nov. 28th, 1863, finished Jan. 8th, 1864.   Size 21″ × 17″.
Price, $50.00

2361 LADY PREPARING TO BATHE, ARETHUSA.

Painting begun March 6th, 1867, finished March 13th, 1867. Size 24″ × 18″.   Price, $50.00
Sold at executor's sale, Dec. 20th, 1872, at Thomas & Sons, Fourth St., Philadelphia.

2362 LADY WITH HAND AT THROAT.

Fancy subject, begun Feb. 1st, 1870, finished Feb. 9th, 1870.   Size 17″ × 15″.   Price, $100.00

2363 LADY WITH HOLLY.

Begun Dec. 30th, 1867, finished Dec. 31st, 1867.   Size 20″ × 24″.
Price, $30.00

2364 LADY READING.

Copy from Chiney. Begun Aug. 31st, 1861, finished Sept. 9th, 1861. Size 13″ × 9½″.   Price, $20.00

2365 LADY READING.

Painting begun Sept. 1st, 1870, finished Sept. 9th, 1870.   Size 18″ × 15″.
Price, $30.00

2366 LADY WALKING WITH HER DOG BY THE SEA.

Painting begun March 4th, 1869, finished March 30th, 1869. Size 24″ × 27″.   Price, $60.00
Sold at executor's sale of artist's paintings, Dec. 20th, 1872, by Thomas & Sons, Fourth St., Philadelphia.

2367 LADY.

(Music.) Copy for Wiseman. Begun Dec. 28th, 1871, finished Jan. 8th, 1872. Size 20 ″ × 24″.   Price, $80.00

2368 LADY.

Portrait painted for James Earle, of Philadelphia, begun Oct. 12th, 1860, finished Nov. 26th, 1860.   Bust.   Price, $50.00

2369 LADY AND FAN.

Head and shoulders of a young girl holding a feather fan over her head. Painted for James Earle (the Philadelphia picture dealer) begun May 13th, 1856, and finished June 3rd, 1856.   Signed on back of canvas " TS 1856," size 20" × 24".   Engraved by Cheney.   Price, $30.00
Owned by Mrs. John Thompson Spencer, Philadelphia.

2370 LADY AND FAN.

Head and shoulders of a young girl holding a feather fan over her head. Painted for James Earle, copy of former picture, begun May 13th, 1856, finished July 1st, 1856.   Size 20" × 24".
Owned by Albert Rosenthal, of Philadelphia.

2371 LADY AND FAN.

"Elenora."   Begun April 30th, 1868, finished June 18th, 1868.   Size 20" × 24".   Price, $100.00

2372 LADY, WITH LAMP STAND.

Copied for Blanche Sully, begun Oct. 20th, 1859, finished Dec. 3rd, 1859. Size 20" × 17".   Price, $30.00

2373 LADY, LOOKING AT THE MOON.

Original composition, begun April 29th, 1868, finished June 13th, 1868. Size 20" × 24".   Price, $100.00

2374 LADY, LOOKING OVER BATTLEMENT.

Painting begun Oct. 14th, 1859, finished Oct. 17th, 1859.   Size 10" × 18".
Price, $10.00

2375 LADY, ON THE BATTLEMENTS OF A CASTLE.

Painting begun Sept. 1st, 1868, finished Sept. 3rd, 1868.   Size 22 × 14".
Price, $100.00

2376 LADY AND GIRL.

Copied from an engraving.   Picture begun June 13th, 1862, finished June 19th, 1862.   Size 9½" × 8".   Price, $20.00

2377 LADY READING.

Painting begun Aug. 2nd, 1842, finished Aug. 9th, 1842.   Size 20" × 24". Price, $150.00

SUBJECT PAINTINGS

2378 LADY READING.

Study of a female head, begun Aug. 20th, 1859, finished Sept. 20th, 1859. Size 24″ × 20″. Price, $50.00

2379 LADY READING IN BED.

Painted for Mr. Carey, begun July 10th, 1834, finished Jan. 8th, 1835. Bust. Price, $100.00

2380 LADY READING IN BED.

(Fancy subject). Copy of former painting, begun July 10th, 1834, finished Dec. 14th, 1834. Bust. Price, $125.00

2381 LADY RESTING ON A HARP.

Painting begun July 26th, 1862, finished August 2nd, 1862. Size 20″ × 16″. Price, $20.00

2382 LADY OF THE LAKE.

See portrait of Miss C. Parsons.

2383 LANDSCAPE AND FIGURES.

Painting begun Feb. 14th, 1808, finished July 17th, 1808. Size 20″ × 24″. Price, $30.00

2384 LANDSCAPE.

Sketch from Turner. Painting begun Jan. 8th, 1820. Size 12″ × 9″. Price, $10.00

2385 LANDSCAPE.

By Beck. Copied by Sully, May, 1809. Size 10″ × 12″. Price, $10.00

2386 LANDSCAPES.

The register of painting in 1809 notes "five different English views," four being 10″ × 12″, and one 20″ × 24″.

2387 LANDSCAPES.

Four views painted for Birch in Philadelphia, Jan., 1818. Size 7″ × 10″. Owned by Mrs. Albert W. Sully, Brooklyn, N. Y.

NOTE.—Landscape studies. A number of small landscapes painted evidently as studies for backgrounds. Oil colors on paper and mounted on canvas.

2388 LEON COGNIET.

(Copied from Art Union.) Begun March 22nd, 1849, finished March 26th, 1849. Size 18″ × 14″· Price, $50.00

SUBJECT PAINTINGS

2389 LISTLESS.

Copied from an engraving. Begun May 20th, 1861, finished May 27th, 1861. Size 12″ × 17″. Price, $50.00

2390 LISTLESS.

(A fancy subject.) Painting begun Sept. 18th, 1856, finished Sept. 24th, 1856. Head. Price, $80.00

Sketch of above painted Sept. 20th, 1856. Size 10″ × 12″.
Price, $10.00

2391 LITTLE NELL ASLEEP.

(The Old Curiosity Shop.) Child with golden hair asleep on a bed, interior of the old curiosity shop, canary bird in gilt cage. Painting begun July 7th, 1841, and finished on Aug. 3rd, 1841. Signed " TS 1841." Size 44″ × 56″. Price, $500.00

Owned by Mrs. Custis, of Philadelphia.

2392 "LITTLE NELL ASLEEP."

Dickens' novel, "Old Curiosity Shop." Painting begun July 10th, 1867, finished July 19th, 1867. Size 21″ × 17″. Price, $50.00

Sold in executor's sale of the artist's pictures, Thomas & Sons, Fourth St., Philadelphia, Dec. 20th, 1872.

2393 LITTLE NELL.

Copy of former picture with variations, her hair in paper. Painted for Mr. Whitney. (By Furness.) Begun Aug. 25th, 1867, finished Sept. 2nd, 1867. Size 19″ × 16″. Price, $80.00

2394 "LONG TOM COFFINS."

Water color, copied from a former study for Mr. Childs. Painted March 12th, 1824. Size 12″ × 10″. Price, $15.00

2395 LOVE ME, LOVE MY DOG.

Painting begun May 6th, 1856, finished May 12th, 1856. Size 20″ × 24″.
Price, $80.00

2396 LOVE LETTER, THE.

A young girl reading a letter in bed, one hand supports her head, the other holds the letter. Her hair is parted in the middle and one long ringlet falls over her neck. Size of canvas 25″ × 30″, signed on back "TS 1835."

Owned by Mrs. Gilmore, Philadelphia.

SUBJECT PAINTINGS

2397 LOVE LETTER, THE.

Copy of the painting of 1835. Signed "丅S 1837."
Sold at auction of paintings of Cooper Estate, at Davis & Harveys, Philadelphia, May, 1891.

2398 LOVE LETTER, THE.

A composition. Size 20" × 24". Begun July 29th, 1828. Price, $100.00.

2399 LOVE LETTER, THE.

Painted from an engraving by John Cheney, of the artist's former picture.
Begun Feb. 19th, 1857, finished Feb. 26th, 1857. Bust.   Price, $100.00

2400 LOVE LETTER, THE.

A sketch 10" × 8", begun July 6th, 1859, finished July 12th, 1859. Size
10" × 8".   Price, $10.00

2401 LOVE LETTER, THE.

A sketch begun Feb. 19th, 1861, finished March 14th, 1861. Size 12"
× 17".   Price, $30.00

2402 LOVE LETTER, THE.

Copied from former paintiug, on order of Mr. Robt. DeSilver, begun April
20th, 1861, finished April 30th, 1861. Size 30" × 25".   Price, $150.00
Owned by Mrs. Mary H. Levis, Mt. Airy, Philadelphia.

2403 LOVE LETTER, THE.

Copy from former picture, begun Jan. 17th, 1867, finished Jan. 29th, 1867.
Size 30" × 25".   Price $100.00
Sold at executor's sale, December 20th, 1872, by Thomas & Sons, Fourth
St., Philadelphia.

2404 MACBETH.

Painted from a Shakespearean sketch made in 1822. Painting begun Oct.
9th, 1840, finished Oct. 18th, 1840. Size 29" × 24".   Price $100.00

2405 MACBETH, LADY.

Picture painted for Edward Carey, President of the Pennsylvania Academy
of Fine Arts. Painted in Philadelphia on Sully's return to the city in 1836.
Picture begun Aug. 29th, 1836, and finished Sept. 5th, 1836. Bust.
                                                             Price, $200.00

2406 MAGDALENE.

After the painting by Corregio, copied from a photograph, begun April
7th, 1859, finished May 6th, 1859. Size 17" × 20".   Price, $50.00

SUBJECT PAINTINGS

2407 MAGDALENE.

A young woman with light hair, and eyes upraised, hands clasped on her breast, an open book before her. Painted on order of Mr. Tyler, begun May 31st, 1850, finished June 8th, 1850. Bust. Size 25" × 30". Price, $150.00 Owned by Mrs. Fanny Goodwyn Dreyspring.

2408 MAGDALENE.

Full length, Jane Sully's copy retouched, begun Aug. 23rd, 1828, finished Aug. 23rd, 1828. Size 20" × 24". Price, $100.00

2409 MAGDALENE.

Painted for James Earle the Philadelphia picture dealer, begun May 13th, 1827, finished June 10th, 1827. Size 17" × 20". Price, $30.00

2410 MAP DESIGNS.

Two designs for an engraving of the map of Kentucky. Size 10" × 12". 1818. Price, $60.00

2411 MARMION.

Designed for James Earle, Philadelphia, art dealer. Painting begun Feb. 1st, 1811, finished March 15th, 1811. Size 12" × 18". Price, $30.00

2412 MASK, THE.

Young lady holding a mask in her hand, begun Dec. 10th, 1859, finished Dec. 17th, 1859. Head. Price, $80.00

2413 MARRIAGE FEAST OF CANA.

Copy by Sully.
Sold at executor's sale of artist's pictures, Dec. 20, 1872, by Thomas & Sons.

2414 MASSACHUSETTS.

Arms of the state of Massachusetts. Drawing made for Mr. J. Binns, begun March 10th, 1817, finished March 12th, 1817. Size 6" × 6". Price, $30.00

2415 MASSACRE OF THE INNOCENTS.

Group from the painting by Cogniets. Begun Aug. 6th, 1861, finished Aug. 13th, 1861. Size 12" × 10". Price, $20.00

2416 MATCH GIRL.

A copy, begun April 28th, 1868, finished May 21st, 1868, and presented by the artist to Mrs. William D. Lewis (No. 1091). Size 20" × 24". Price, $100.00 Owned by Mr. Lewis Neilson, St. David's, Philadelphia.

2417 MERMAID (ON A WAVE).

Painting begun Jan. 26th, 1836, finished Sept. 12th, 1836. Signed " TS September, 1836." Size 29″ × 36″. Price, $300.00

Girl swimming, with wave in distance, the head with long hair, and the nude shoulders, bust and arms showing above the water. She wears a coral necklace. A small engraving was made of this painting by J. B. Forrest.

Painting owned by R. T. Harris, New York.

2418 MERMAID.

Girl swimming, the head with long hair, and the nude shoulders, bust and arms showing above the water. Coral necklace. Sketch 10½″ × 13″, begun July 6th, 1859, finished July 11th, 1859. Price, $10.00

Sketch is owned by Mrs. Albert Sully, Brooklyn, New York.

2419 MERMAID.

Painted as a present for Mr. Fitzgerald, begun Jan. 24th, 1862, finished Feb. 22nd, 1862. Size 17″ × 12½″. Price, $30.00

2420 MILK GIRL.

Copy from the painting by Gainsborough. Begun Aug. 23rd, 1861, finished Aug. 30th, 1861. Size 12″ × 10″. Price, $20.00

2421 MIRANDA.

Head to left, with long hair blowing in the wind with a stormy sea in background. The girl wears a low-necked gown and has her hands clasped. Studies for the painting, begun Dec. 11th, 1835, finished Jan. 7th, 1836. Bust. Price, $200.00

Engraved by R. W. Dodson. (See American Engravers. By Fielding, No. 346.)

2422 MIRANDA.

Shakespeare. "The Tempest." Painting begun March 22nd, 1861, finished March 26th, 1861. Size 10″ × 12″. Price, $20.00

2423 MIRANDA.

First of series. (Shakespeare.) Painting begun April 17th, 1868, finished May 8th, 1868. Size 24″ × 20″. Price, $100.00

2424 MISCHIEF.

Original composition, painted in 1866.

Sold at executor's sale of artist's paintings, Dec. 20th, 1872, Thomas & Sons, Fourth St., Philadelphia.

SUBJECT PAINTINGS

2425 MISSOURI FALLS.

Painted for Lewis & Clark. Painted Aug. 12th, 1810. Size 22″ × 17″.
Price, $30.00

2426 MOONLIGHT SCENE.

Studied from Allston, begun Dec. 18th, 1826, finished Dec. 28th, 1826.
Size 27″ × 24″.   Price, $50.00

2427 MOSES WITH TABLES (RESURRECTION).

Two designs, size 10″ × 8″, begun Nov. 30th, 1823, finished Dec. 30th,
1823.   Price, each $50.00

2428 MOTHER, TEACHING HER CHILD TO PRAY.

Painting begun Nov. 17th, 1854, finished Feb. 24th, 1855. Head.
Price, $70.00

2429 MOTHER AND CHILD.

From the Greek story. Sketch begun Nov. 21st, 1870, finished Dec. 6th,
1870.   Price, $20.00

2430 MOTHER AND CHILD.

An original composition, painting begun Feb. 24th, 1870, finished the
same day, size 18″ × 14″.   Price, $30.00

2431 MOTHER AND CHILD.

Sketch, size 10″ × 12″, begun Oct. 3rd, 1859, finished Oct. 7th, 1859.
Price, $10.00

2432 MOTHER AND CHILD.

Study painted for Mr. Stevens. Begun Dec. 4th, 1826, finished March,
1827. Size 18″ × 36″.   Price, $200.00
Sold by the Macbeth Gallery in 1912.

2433 MOTHER AND CHILD.

An ideal subject, painting begun Dec. 15th, 1858, finished Dec. 25th,
1858. Size 29″ × 36″.   Price, $200.00

2434 MOTHER AND CHILD.

By Sir Joshua Reynolds. Copied by Sully. Painting begun Jan. 8th,
1820. Size 20″ × 24″.   Price, $20.00

2435 MOTHER AND CHILD.

Copy made for Dr. Philip Tidyman, begun Feb. 10th, 1827, finished Aug.
3rd, 1827. Size 44″ × 27″.   Price, $200.00

2436 Heads, after Gerard's painting.   Begun July 26th, 1843, finished July 28th, 1843.   Head.   Price, $50.00

2437 MOTHER, CHILD AND BOOK.
Ideal composition, begun Dec. 21st, 1848, finished Dec. 30th, 1848. Signed " TS 1849."   Size 20" × 24".   Price, $100.00
Owned by Mrs. John Thompson Spencer, Philadelphia.

2438 MUSIC PARTY.
After Titian.   Copy begun March 19th, 1829.   Size 30" × 25".
Price, $20.00

2439 MUSIDORA.
By Benjamin West.   This picture was painted from a copy made by Leslie, begun April 2nd, 1813, finished May 4th, 1813.   Size 17" × 20".
Price, $150.00

2440 MUSIDORA.
After Benjamin West.   Copy of former painting, begun in 1813, and finished 1835.   Signed on face of picture " TS 1835."   Size 25" × 30".
Price, $200.00
A beautiful young woman who formed the subject of an episode in the poem on " Summer" in Thomson's " Seasons."   Full-length figure, nude, seated on red cloak by woodland stream, one foot in water.
Owned by Metropolitan Museum, New York.

2441 MYSTERIES OF UDOLPHO.
(Two copies.)   Design for (India ink sketch).   Begun July 5th, 1861, finished July 16th, 1861.   Size 10" × 12".   Price, $50.00
Sold at executor's sale, Dec. 20th, 1872, by Thomas & Sons, Philadelphia.

2442 NARCISSUS.
From Michael Angelo.   Study painted in two colors to show as a specimen of work.   Begun July 3rd, 1809, finished July 31st, 1809.   Size 17" × 20".   Price, $5.00

2443 NATURAL BRIDGE, VIRGINIA.
Landscape, begun June 13th, 1808, finished June 30th, 1808.   Size 17" × 20".   Price, $25.00

2444 NAOMI, ORPHA AND RUTH.
Painting begun Aug. 28th, 1862, finished Aug. 30th, 1862.   Size 9½" × 7½".   Price, $15.00

SUBJECT PAINTINGS

2445 NAOMI, ORPHA AND RUTH.
Painting begun Sept. 1st, 1862, finished Sept. 13th, 1862. Size 20″ × 24″. Price, $50.00

2446 NAPOLEON AT ST. HELENA.
Copy from the painting by Paul Delaroche. Begun Aug. 2nd, 1861, finished Aug. 4th, 1861. Size 11″ × 7″. Price, $20.00

2447 NEW JERSEY.
Arms of the State of New Jersey. Drawing made for Mr. J. Binns, begun March 2nd, 1817, finished March 4th, 1817. Size 6″ × 6″. Price, $30.00

2448 NEW YORK.
Arms of the State of New York. Drawing made for Mr. J. Binns, begun Jan. 26th, 1817, finished Jan. 28th, 1817. Size 6″ × 6″. Price, $30.00

2449 NIAGARA FALLS.
Table Rock and the American side. Copy from Wilcocks' picture for Mr. Brewster, begun Feb. 9th, 1847, finished March 15th, 1847. Size 20″ × 30″. Price, $50.00

NOTE.—Sully records making small copies for himself of the Niagara paintings.

2450 NIAGARA FALLS.
Copy from Wilcocks' picture for Mr. Brewster, begun Feb. 9th, 1847, finished April 3rd, 1847. Size 29″ × 36″. Price, $50.00

2451 NIAGARA FALLS.
Table Rock. Painting begun July 12th, 1843, finished July 17th, 1843. Size 30″ × 20″. Price, $25.00

2452 NIAGARA.
Table Rock, from sketch made in 1843. Begun March 29th, 1852, finished April 2nd, 1852. Size 20″ × 13″. Price, $20.00

2453 NIAGARA FALLS.
Painting begun July 12th, 1843, finished July 20th, 1843. Size 30″ × 20″. Price, $25.00

2454 NIAGARA FALLS.
Painting begun July 12th, 1843, finished July 20th, 1843. Size 30″ × 20″. Price, $25.00

2455 NIAGARA FALLS.
Taken from Sully's sketch from Goat Island. Painting begun July 1st, 1843, finished July 19th, 1843. Size 29″ × 36″. Price, $50.00

2456 NIAGARA FALLS.

Copied from Murray. Begun June 26th, 1808, finished June 30th, 1808. Size 17″ × 20″. Price, $25.00

2457 NORTH CAROLINA.

Arms of the State of North Carolina. Drawing made for Mr. J. Binns, begun March 23rd, 1817, finished March 25th, 1817. Size 6″ × 6″.
Price, $30.00

2458 NORTHCOTE'S CHILDREN.

Children of the artist James Northcote, a copy in part, begun Feb. 8th, 1828, finished March 7th, 1828. Size 4′ 6″ × 24″. One of a set of four paintings noted in the register as for steamboat, for which he received
$300.00

2459 NUN'S HEAD.

A copy from Julien, begun Sept. 6th, 1871, finished Sept. 19th, 1871. Size 20″ × 24″. Price, $80.00

2460 NURSE AND CHILD.

Painted for Edward Carey. A vignette, size 20″ × 24″. Painting begun Feb. 18th, 1839, finished April 2nd, 1839. Price, $250.00

2461 NYMPH.

Half length of young woman, hands clasped, resting on elbows. Neck and shoulders undraped, head to left, hair parted in middle with scarf head-dress. Inscribed on back of canvas "A Nymph, copied from Andre, TS 1851." Size 29″ × 36″, in oval. Painting begun Nov. 24th, 1851, finished Dec. 31st, 1852. Price, $100.00
Owned by Mrs. Hugh Caperton, Baltimore, Md.

2462 NYMPH.

Copy begun Feb. 11th, 1853, in Baltimore, Md., finished in Philadelphia, May 23rd, 1854. Size 26″ × 36″. Price, $100.00

2463 NYMPH.

Copied from Westall. Begun Aug. 5th, 1865, finished Aug. 18th, 1865. Bust. Price, $50.00

2464 NYMPH.

Full-length figure dancing, landscape background, and lyre at foot of figure. Size 13″ × 9″.
Sold at Henkel's Auction Rooms, Philadelphia.

SUBJECT PAINTINGS

2465 OBSERVATION.

(A study.) Painting begun July 14th, 1856, finished July 17th, 1856. Head.

Price, $80.00

2466 OSSIAN AND MALVINA.

Painting begun May 13th, 1835, finished Nov. 18th, 1840. Size 29" × 36".

2467 OVERTAKEN.

Copied from a photograph, begun Jan. 28th, 1871, finished Feb. 9th, 1871. Size 13½" × 9".

Price, $30.00

2468 "PAPA'S COMING."

Copied from Harper's Weekly. Begun Aug. 17th, 1866, finished Aug. 25th, 1866. Size 30" × 23".

Price, $100.00

2469 PALLAS AND THE MUSES.

Design for the Society Belles Lettres of Carlisle. Vignette, begun May, 1815. Size 18" × 12".

Price, $50.00

2470 PASSAIC FALLS.

Painted for I. P. Davis, of Boston. Begun Oct. 27, 1807, finished Dec., 1807. Size 20" × 24".

Price, $25.00

2471 PASSAIC FALLS.

Two views, painted for Thomas A. Cooper, begun Feb. 4th, 1807, finished July 5th, 1807. Size 20" × 24".

Price, $50.00

2472 PEACE.

(Ideal head.) Canvas 25" × 30". Signed on back of canvas in center "Peace, TS 1862, December."
Owned by Arthur L. Church, Philadelphia.

2473 PEASANT BOY.

Copied from picture of a German artist. Begun Nov. 14th, 1822, finished Nov. 21st, 1822. Size 17" × 20".

Price, $50.00

2474 PEASANTS.

Sketch of American. Begun July 5th, 1866, finished July 23rd, 1866. Size 18" × 14".

Price, $50.00

2475 PEASANT.

Copy from a French painting for the artist's collection, begun Feb. 22nd, 1859, finished April 25th, 1859. Size 25" × 30". Price, $100.00

375

2476 PEASANT GIRL (FRENCH).
Painting begun Sept. 11th, 1850, finished Sept. 17th, 1850. Size 17′ ×
20″.   Price, $50.00

2477 PEASANT, FRENCH.
Copy from a painting, begun June 18th, 1852, finished June 23rd, 1852.
Size 13″ × 10″.   Price, $30.00

2478 PEASANTS.
Group in French cottage. Copy from painting, begun Sept. 18th, 1850,
finished Sept. 27th, 1850. Size 17″ × 20″.   Price, $100.00

2479 PEASANT GIRL.
(From a French sketch.) Painting begun Sept. 9th, 1856, finished Sept.
17th, 1856. Head.   Price, $80.00

2480 PEASANT GIRL AT A SPRING.
Painting begun Aug. 10th, 1846, finished Aug. 21st, 1846. Bust.
Price, $100.00

2481 PEASANT GIRL.
Painted for James Earle the Philadelphia picture-dealer, begun March
21st, 1854, finished May 19th, 1854. Head.   Price, $30.00

2482 PEASANT GIRL.
After the painting by Rembrandt. Copy begun Jan. 3rd, 1866, finished
Jan. 17th, 1866. Bust.   Price, $50.00

2483 PEASANT GIRL.
After the painting by Rembrandt. Copy begun Oct. 20th, 1865, finished
Oct. 27th, 1865. Bust.   Price, $50.00

2484 PEASANT GIRL.
After the painting by Rembrandt. Copy begun Nov. 6th, 1865, finished
Nov. 13th, 1865. Bust. Painted for Mr. Hamilton, of New York.
Price, $50.00

2485 PEASANT GIRL.
After Rembrandt, painted for Henry Carey, begun Feb. 3rd, 1857, finished
Feb. 11th, 1857. Bust, size 24″ × 30″. " TS 1857 " (signed).
Price, $100.00
Owned by the Wilstach Collection, Fairmount Park, Philadelphia.

2486 PEASANT GIRL.
After Rembrandt. Copy begun Sept. 24th, 1847, finished Sept. 28th,
1847. Bust.   Price, $100.00

2487 PEASANT GIRL.

After Rembrandt. Copy made by the artist's daughter Ellen, and re-touched by Thomas Sully, begun June 20th, 1837, finished June 30th, 1837. Bust. Price, $150.00

2488 PEASANT GIRL.

After Rembrandt. Begun Feb. 15th, 1844, finished July 27th, 1844. Bust. Price, $50.00

2489 PEASANT GIRL.

Copy after Rembrandt. Begun Dec. 27th, 1838, and finished Jan. 2nd, 1839.

2490 PEASANT GIRL.

(Rembrandt.) Copy sold to James Earle, Philadelphia. Begun April 28th, 1847, finished Sept. 20th, 1847. Size 30″ × 25″. Price, $100.00

2491 PEASANT GIRL.

(Rembrandt.) Small copy 8″ × 10″. Painting begun Feb. 14th, 1850, finished Feb. 18th, 1850. Price, $30.00

2492 PEASANT GIRL.

(Rembrandt.) Copied from an engraving. Painting begun Jan. 1st, 1847, finished Jan. 14th, 1847. Size 25″ × 30″. Price, $100.00

2493 PEASANT GIRL.

(Rembrandt.) Copy begun Jan. 28th, 1859, finished Feb. 4th, 1859. Painted for Robert De Silver. Size 25″ × 30″. Price, $100.00

2494 PEASANT GIRL.

(Rembrandt.) Painting begun by Rosalie and retouched by Thomas Sully, begun July 13th, 1839, finished July 19th, 1839. Bust. Price, $150.00

2495 PEASANT GIRL.

After Rembrandt. Copy, painting begun Feb. 11th, 1857, finished Feb. 18th, 1857. Bust. Price, $100.00

2496 PEASANT GIRL.

After the painting by Rembrandt. Copy begun Aug. 16th, 1860, finished Aug. 28th, 1860. Bust. Price, $100.00

2497 PEASANT GIRL.

Copy of Rembrandt's painting for the artist's own collection, begun Feb. 25th, 1859, finished May 7th, 1859. Size 25″ × 30″. Price, $100.00

SUBJECT PAINTINGS

2498 PEASANT GIRL.

After the painting by Rembrandt. Copy made for Garrett Neagle, begun Oct. 9th, 1866, finished Oct. 17th, 1866. Size 18" × 14". Price, $30.00

2499 PEASANT GIRL.

After Rembrandt's painting. Copy for James Earle, begun May 17th, 1860, finished May 28th, 1860. Bust. Price, $50.00

2500 PENNSYLVANIA.

Arms of the State of Pennsylvania. Rough sketch made for the engraver G. Fairman. Size 5" × 4". Drawing begun Jan. 10th, 1818, finished Jan. 11th, 1818. Price, $5.00

2501 PERRY'S VICTORY.

Two drawings about 17" × 12", begun April 4th, 1814. Price, $20.00

2502 PERSIAN LADY.

Painted for the artist's own collection, begun Feb. 25th, 1859, finished May 30th, 1859. Size 25" × 30". Price, $100.00

2503 PERSONIFICATION OF PEACE.

Painting begun Nov. 18th, 1862, finished Dec. 9th, 1862. Size 25" × 30". Price, $50.00
Sketch made Nov. 15th, 1862. Size 17½" × 12½". Price, $30.00

2504 PHILADELPHIA.

Arms of the City of Philadelphia. Painted for the architect, William Strickland, for the triumphal arch erected for General La Fayette's reception. Painted in September, 1824. Size 8ft. by 6 ft. Price, $80.00
Owned by the City of Philadelphia and still in good condition.

2505 PICTURE.

Painted for Mr. Claghorn, of Philadelphia. Begun Jan. 12th, 1855, finished Feb. 3rd, 1855. Size 25" × 30", oval. Price, $150.00

NOTE.—The authors could find no details beyond the above entry in the artist's register.

2506 PILOT, THE.

Composition from the novel by J. Fenimore Cooper, it shows the dungeon or prison scene. The painting was begun Sept. 22nd, 1841, and was finished Oct. 5th, 1841. Size 37" × 28". Price, $150.00
Owned by Dr. Daniel Strock, Camden, N. J.

SUBJECT PAINTINGS

2507 PILOT, THE.

Illustrating Cooper's novel "Tom Coffin." Begun Dec. 2nd, 1865, finished Dec. 11th, 1865. Size 20" × 24". Price, $30.00

2508 PIRATE, THE.

Composition from the novel by Sir Walter Scott, "Minna and Brenda Troil." Painting begun Aug. 21st, 1862, and finished Aug. 27th, 1862. Size 10" × 14". Price, $15.00

2509 PLYADES AND ORESTES.

Copy from the painting by Benjamin West. Painting begun Aug. 11th, 1809, in London, and finished Sept. 11th, 1809. Size 49½" × 39½". Price, $200.00

Was exhibited at the Artists Fund Society in 1811. Sold in auction of paintings belonging to Joseph T. Kinsley, of Philadelphia.

2510 POCAHONTAS.

Ideal portrait, from an engraving. Bust, head to left, hair down and low-necked gown, arms crossed. She wears a bead necklace and bracelet. Painting begun May 17th, 1852, finished Aug. 24th, 1852. Size 29" × 36". Price, $200.00

Painted for the Historical Society of Virginia. Illustrated in "Old Time Belles and Cavaliers." By Edith Tunis Sale, Philadelphia, 1912.

2511 PONTO (DOG'S HEAD).

Sketch of pet dog belonging to the artist's wife. Painting begun May 12th, 1848, finished May 13th, 1848. Size 10" × 12". Price, $20.00
Owned by Mrs. Albert Sully, of Brooklyn, New York.

2512 PORTRAIT OF A LADY.

Study for a whole-length, begun July 28th, 1859, finished Aug. 1st, 1859. Size 14" × 9". Price, $10.00

2513 PORTRAIT OF A LADY AND HER SON.

Study for a whole-length portrait, begun Aug. 5th, 1859, finished August 7th, 1859. Size 13" × 9". Price, $20.00

2514 PORTIA AND SHYLOCK.

Painted for Edward Carey, of Philadelphia. Portia, nearly full face with long hair, holds in her hand the bond or document, Shylock with his scales stands beside her. Begun Nov. 14th, 1835, finished Dec. 4th, 1835. Size 29" × 38½". Signed "TS." Price, $400.00

Engraved by J. B. Forrest for book illustration. Owned by A. H. Halberstadt, Pottsville, Pa.

SUBJECT PAINTINGS

2515 PORTIA AND SHYLOCK.

Study for a large painting, the record notes it as abandoned. Painted in June, 1835. Size 17" × 20".   Price, $20.00

2516 PROSPERO AND MIRANDA.

Second of series. Painting begun April 22nd, 1868, finished June 18th, 1868. Size 24" × 20".   Price, $100.00

2517 PSYCHE.

Copy from Dubony. (Head.) Painting begun Aug. 22nd, 1843. The register notes it as " Expunged " and the price as $50.00

2518 PYRAMUS AND THISBE.

Copied from Brammer. Painting begun Aug. 20th, 1815. Size 12" × 10".   Price, $50.00

2519 PYRAMUS AND THISBE.

Picture, copy of a former painting. Begun Oct. 30th, 1865, finished Dec. 13th, 1865. Bust.   Price, $50.00

2520 READING IN WARM WEATHER.

From a sketch by Chapman, copy begun Sept. 21st, 1861, finished Sept. 25th, 1861. Size 9" × 6".   Price, $15.00

2521 RED RIDING HOOD.

Copy from an engraving, painting begun May 28th, 1857, finished June 4th, 1857. Size 17" × 20".   Price, $50.00

2522 RED RIDING HOOD.

Bust of a little girl with a red hood. Size 17" × 20". Signed on back of canvas " TS 1846, November."
Owned by Mr. John Thompson Spencer, Philadelphia.

2523 RED RIDING HOOD.

Painting begun Jan. 27th, 1866, finished March 17th, 1866. Size 17" × 20".   Price, $30.00

2524 RED RIDING HOOD.

Original painting, begun Jan. 1st, 1859, finished Jan. 10th, 1859. Size 17" × 20".   Price, $80.00

2525 RED RIDING HOOD.

Painting begun June 28th, 1865, finished July 7th, 1865. Bust size.
Price, $50.00

SUBJECT PAINTINGS

2526 RED RIDING HOOD.

Painting begun Sept. 30th, 1864, finished Nov. 12th, 1864. Size 20″ ×
16″. Price, $50.00

2527 RED RIDING HOOD.

Copy of former original composition, begun Jan. 31st, 1859, finished Feb.
19th, 1859. Painted for Mr. Robert De Silver. Size 17″ × 21″.
Price, $100.00

2528 RED RIDING HOOD.

Painting begun Oct. 23rd, 1863, finished Nov. 6th, 1863. Size 22″ × 12″.
Price, $50.00

2529 REFLECTION.

Painting begun April 21st, 1856, finished May 3rd, 1856. Size 20″ ×
24″. Price, $80.00

2530 REFLECTION.

(Ideal head.) Painting begun March 18th, 1861, and finished March
29th, 1861. Canvas 9½″ × 13″. Signed on back " TS 1861, Pxtr."
(Painted on top bar of the stretches " Reflection.") Price, $30.00
Owned by Arthur L. Church, Philadelphia.

2531 REFLECTION.

(Copied from Julien.) Head and shoulders with supporting arm and
hand to head. Painting begun March 15th, 1867, finished March 25th,
1867. Signed "Copied from Julien, TS 1867, March." Size 21″ × 17″.
Price, $50.00
Owned by J. Edwin Megargee, Brooklyn, N. Y.

2532 REMBRANDT.

Copy of Ord's sketch. Begun Aug. 11th, 1832, finished Aug. 22nd, 1832.
Head, 17″ × 20″. Price, $50.00

2533 REMBRANDT PAINTING.

Copied from a copy by Robert Sully, begun Oct. 23rd, 1830, finished
April 13th, 1831. Size 20″ × 18″. Price, $50.00

2534 REMBRANDT.

Painted by Ellen and retouched by Thomas Sully, begun Feb. 12th, 1837,
finished March 1st, 1837. Bust. Price, $100.00

381

2535 RETURN, THE.

Half-length of a young woman waving a greeting to someone outside the picture. Painted on the order of Dr. Tyler, of Alabama, begun July 15th, 1851, finished July 29th, 1851. Size 29″ × 36″. Signed on back of canvas " ⊺S 1851." Price, $200.00
Owned in 1920 by Scott & Fowles, of New York.

2536 RETURN OF THE SOLDIER.

Copied from De Boufe, begun Sept. 12th, 1870, finished Sept. 25th, 1870. Size 30″ × 25″. Price, $100.00

2537 REYNOLDS.

Copy from a picture painted by Sir Joshua Reynolds, begun Aug. 17th, 1859, finished Aug. 27th, 1859. Size 8½″ × 7″. Price, $10.00

2538 RHODE ISLAND.

Arms of the State of Rhode Island. Drawing made for Mr. J. Binns, begun March 23rd, 1817, finished March 25th, 1817. Size 6″ × 6″.
Price, $30.00

2539 ROBINSON CRUSOE.

(Shipwrecked.) Painted for the artist's own collection, begun May 20th, 1857, finished July 11th, 1857. Size 48″ × 34″. Price, $300.00
This series of ten pictures were exhibited at Earle's gallery and were all destroyed by fire; the studies for the painting are owned by Mrs. Albert Sully, of New York.

2540 ROBINSON CRUSOE.

(Taking articles from the ship.) No. 2. Painting begun Aug. 21st, 1857, finished Sept. 29th, 1857. Size 48″ × 34″. Price, $300.00

2541 ROBINSON CRUSOE.

(Third incident of the shipwreck.) Painting begun Oct. 3rd, 1857, finished Oct. 26th, 1857. Size 48″ × 34″. Price, $300.00

2542 ROBINSON CRUSOE.

(Fourth incident of the shipwreck.) Painting begun Oct. 28th, 1857, finished Nov. 11th, 1857. Size 48″ × 34″. Price, $300.00

2543 ROBINSON CRUSOE.

(Fifth incident of the shipwreck.) Painting begun Nov. 12th, 1857, finished May 17th, 1857. Size 48″ × 34″. Price, $300.00

SUBJECT PAINTINGS

2544 ROBINSON CRUSOE.

(Sixth incident of the shipwreck.) Painting begun May 18th, 1857, finished June 1st, 1857. Size 48" × 34". Price, $300.00

2545 ROBINSON CRUSOE.

(Seventh incident of the shipwreck.) Painting begun June 2nd, 1857, finished Aug. 7th, 1857. Size 48" × 34". Price, $200.00

2546 ROBINSON CRUSOE.

(Eighth incident in his life.) Painting begun Aug. 3rd, 1858, finished August 14th, 1858. Size 48" × 34". Price, $300.00

2547 ROBINSON CRUSOE.

(Ninth incident in his life.) Painting begun Aug. 21st, 1858, finished Sept. 9th, 1858. Size 33½" × 29½". Price, $300.00

2548 ROBINSON CRUSOE.

(Tenth incident in his life.) Painting begun Aug. 24th, 1858, finished Oct. 9th, 1858. Size 33½" × 29½". Price, $300.00

2549 ROBINSON CRUSOE.

Sully painted ten sketches, size 11" × 9", during the months of February and March of 1871. The compositions are very similar to the illustrations in the edition published by Cadell & Co.
A number of the sketches are owned by Mrs. Albert Sully, New York.

2550 ROBINSON CRUSOE.

Copied for Fraser. Size 29" × 36". Painting begun March 30th, 1858, finished May 8th, 1858. Price, $100.00

2551 ROCKY COAST.

View begun June 26th, 1871, finished July 6th, 1871. Size 12" × 10".
Price, $20.00

2552 ROMAN GIRL.

Copy from the painting by Daniel Huntington, begun Feb. 1st, 1867, finished Feb. 11th, 1867. Size 22" × 26". Price, $100.00
Sold at executor's sale, Dec. 20th, 1872, at Thomas & Sons, Fourth St., Philadelphia.

2553 ROMAN GIRL.

Copy from painting by Daniel Huntington, begun July 31st, 1856, finished Aug. 9th, 1856. Bust. Price, $100.00
Owned by Wilstach Collection, Fairmount Park, Philadelphia.

SUBJECT PAINTINGS

2554 ROMAN GIRL.

Copy from painting by Julien. Begun Oct. 6th, 1870, finished Oct. 22nd, 1870. Size 17" × 14". Price, $50.00

2555 ROMEO AND JULIET.

Copy of Northcote's painting. Begun Oct. 9th, 1808, finished Nov. 10th, 1808. Size 40" × 30". Price. $25.00

2556 SAILOR'S RETURN.

Noted in register as painted for steamboat. Copy 4' 6" × 24". Painting begun Feb. 3rd, 1828, finished Feb. 28th, 1828.

One of a set of four paintings for which the artist received $300.00

2557 SAVED.

Painted in 1871.

Sold at executor's sale of artist's paintings, Dec. 20th, 1872, by Thomas & Sons.

2558 SHIPWRECKED SAILOR.

Noted in register as painted for steamboat. Copy 4' 6" × 24". Begun Feb. 2nd, 1828, finished Feb. 8th, 1828.

One of a set of four paintings for which the artist received $300.00

2559 SHIPWRECKED SAILOR.

Painting begun April 5th, 1861, finished April 8th, 1861. Size 11" × 7". Price, $20.00

2560 SHIPWRECKED SAILOR.

Copy of former painting. Begun July 11th, 1861, finished July 13th, 1861. Size 11" × 7". Price, $20.00

2561 SHIPWRECKED SAILOR.

Sketch begun Nov. 21st, 1870, finished Nov. 23rd, 1870. Price, $20.00

2562 SCOTT'S LADY OF THE LAKE.

Scene from the poem. Painting begun July 17th, 1861, finished July 24th, 1861. Size 12" × 10". Price, $30.00

2563 SENTRY BOX, THE.

" Uncle Toby and the Widow," from Tristam Shandy. Copied from the painting by Charles Robert Leslie. Copy begun March 12th, 1871, finished May 24th, 1871. Size 20" × 24". Price, $100.00

SUBJECT PAINTINGS

2564 SIBILLA PERSICA.

After Guercino. Female figure, three-quarter length, seated with elbow on table with books and hand supporting head. Copy begun Sept. 30th, 1869, finished Oct. 18th, 1869. Size 25″ × 30″. Price, $100.00

Sold at executor's sale of artist's paintings, by Thomas & Sons., Fourth St., Philadelphia, Dec., 1872.

2565 SIGN.

(Of an eagle.) Painted for the Eagle Tavern of Richmond, Va. Begun in January, 1805, and finished in March, 1805. Size 8 feet by 5 feet.

Price, $50.00

2566 SKATER, THE.

From Thompson's "Seasons—Winter." Begun Jan. 9th, 1872, finished Jan. 26th, 1872. Size 20″ × 24″. Price, $50.00

Noted as sold at executor's sale of the artist's paintings, by Thomas & Sons, Fourth St., Philadelphia, Dec., 1872.

2567 SKETCH.

For experiment in varnish, begun Aug. 7th, 1846, finished Aug. 8th, 1846. Size 14½ × 10″. Price, $10.00

2568 SKETCH OR STUDY FOR PICTURE.

Painted for Mr. Claghorn, of Philadelphia. Sign 12″ × 17″. Begun Jan. 8th, 1855, finished Feb. 6th, 1855. Price, $20.00

2569 SLAUGHTER OF THE INNOCENTS.

A copy begun April 16th, 1869, finished April 24th, 1869. Size 18″ × 15″. Price, $50.00

2570 SNAKE IN THE GRASS.

From the painting by Sir Joshua Reynolds. Copy begun Sept. 23rd, 1865, finished Oct. 10th, 1865. Size 29″ × 36″. Price, $50.00

2571 SOUTH CAROLINA.

Arms of the State of South Carolina. Drawing made for Mr. Binns, begun March 25th, 1818, finished March 27th, 1818. Size 6″ × 6″.

Price, $30.00

2572 SPANISH BOY.

A copy, begun Feb. 17th, 1870, finished March 12th, 1870. Size 10″ × 8″. Price, $20.00

SUBJECT PAINTINGS

2573 SPANISH BOY.

A copy, begun Oct. 20th, 1870, finished Nov. 3rd, 1870. Size 10″ ×
7½″. Price, $30.00

2574 SPANISH BOY.

No. 2. A copy, begun Jan. 13th, 1870, finished Jan. 31st, 1870. Size
10″ × 8″. Price, $20.00

2575 SPANISH BOY.

No. 3. A copy, begun Feb. 23rd, 1870, finished April 2nd, 1870. Size
10″ × 8″. Price, $20.00

2576 SPANISH BOY.

Painting begun Jan. 24th, 1871, finished Jan. 31st, 1871. Size 11″ × 7″.
Price, $30.00

2577 SPANISH GUITAR AND MANTILLA.

An ideal composition painted by Sully on an order. It was purchased
from the original owner by Dr. Charles D. Meigs, of Philadelphia, and exhibited by Miss Sarah T. Meigs in 1917, and by the Vose Brothers of Boston
in 1919. Painting begun Feb. 10th, 1840, finished Feb. 27th, 1840. Size
29″ × 36″. Signed " TS 1840." Price, $300.00
Engraved by John Sartain, of Philadelphia. Owned by R. C. and N. M.
Vose, Boston, Mass.

2578 SPANISH MANTILLA (THE).

Similar to the picture painted in 1840 with slight variations, the shoulder
and neck showing through the lace of the mantilla, and the lower portion of
the guitar is not shown. Size 20″ × 24″.
Painting owned by the artist, William M. Chase, now property of John F.
Braun, Philadelphia.

2579 SPANISH LADY WITH GUITAR.

Painting begun July 19th, 1856, finished July 29th, 1856. Head.
Price, $80.00

2580 SPANISH LADY.

Copied from painting by Sir Edwin Landseer, the English animal painter
(1802–1873). Copy begun Oct. 2nd, 1871, finished Oct. 9th, 1871. Size
16″ × 20″. Price, $50.00

2581 SPANISH LADY.

Painting begun April 8th, 1870, finished April 25th, 1870. Size 16″ ×
20″. Price, $100.00

2582 SPANISH MOTHER.

Heads, copied from painting by Sir David Wilkie, copy begun Feb. 13th, 1852, finished Feb. 28th, 1852. Size 17″ × 20″. Price, $50.00

2583 SPRINGTIME.

Three-quarter length standing, young woman holding little girl in her arms. The child is bareheaded, her mother wears a felt hat and is partly enfolded in a maroon cloak. Painted from an illustration in Harper's Weekly. Begun May 25th, 1866, finished June 7th, 1866. Size 18″ × 14″. Inscribed "Springtime Harper's Weekly, TS 1866." Price, $30.00

Sold at auction, Philadelphia, March, 1920. Price, $330.00

2584 SPRINGTIME.

(Second picture.) Copy for Garrett Neagle. Begun June 7th, 1866, finished June 30th, 1866. Size 18″ × 13½″. Inscribed on back of canvas "Springtime Harper's Weekly, TS 1866." Price, $30.00

Sold in auction of American Art Association, New York, April, 1920.
Price, $275.00

2585 SPRINGTIME.

Third picture, copy for Mrs. Griffin, begun June 8th, 1866, finished June 30th, 1866. Size 18″ × 14″. Price, $50.00

2586 ST. ANDREW'S CHURCH.

Size 10″ × 12″. Price, $15.00

2587 ST. JEROME.

Copy. Begun Jan. 16th, 1829, finished Feb. 8th, 1829. Size 28″ × 17″.
Price, $50.00

2588 ST. PANTELEON.

Sketch of. Painted for ——— in 1822. Size 48″ × 36″. Price, $80.00

2589 STATE ARMS.

Drawings made of the arms of six different states for Mr. J. Binns, April, 1817. Price, $180.00

2590 STORY OF A BATTLE (THE).

Copy from a design by F. O. C. Darley. Begun June 30th, 1863, finished July 18th, 1863. Size 20″ × 24″. Price, $50.00

2591 STRAWBERRY GIRL.

After Sir Joshua Reynolds. Copy begun April 5th, 1838, finished April 20th, 1838. The original was in the possession of Samuel Rogers. Size 17″ × 20″.   Price, $300.00

2592 STUDENT (THE).

An ideal head, begun Nov. 5th, 1848, finished Dec. 18th, 1848. Size 24″ × 20″.   Price, $50.00

2593 STUDENT.

(Or Weak Eyes.) Copied from a former picture, begun Dec. 19th, 1859, finished Dec. 30th, 1859. Head.   Price, $80.00

2594 STUDENT.

(Or Fair Student.) See Sully, Rosalie.

2595 SUMMER.

A child hugging a rose to bosom. Painting begun Dec. 10th, 1843, finished Dec. 15th, 1843. Size 17″ × 20″.   Price, $80.00

2596 SUMMER INDOLENCE.

Painting begun Oct. 30th, 1867, finished Nov. 9th, 1867. Size 20″ × 16″.
                                                                            Price, $50.00

2597 SUTTERMANS, JUSTUS.

Copy of a bust, after Suttermans, painted for Chapman, begun July 7th, 1834, finished Sept. 10th, 1834.   Price, $125.00

2598 SWEDISH LUTHERAN CHURCH.

View of "Old Swedes" Church with figure and graveyard in foreground, and view in distance of house and woods. Engraved by C. C. Childs, 1828.

2599 TELEMACHUS ON THE ISLAND OF CALYPSO.

Copy of Benjamin West's painting. Begun in London, Jan. 13th, 1810, and finished March 2nd, 1810. Size 56″ × 33″.   Price, $200.00
Exhibited at Academy of Fine Arts, 1811.

2600 THEATRE SCENE, CURTAIN.

The register notes on Sept. 23rd, 1815. A frontispiece for the Chestnut Street Theatre, 8 ft. by 8t. "The Gem of Comedy and Tragedy."
                                                                            Price, $200.00

SUBJECT PAINTINGS

2601 TOILET, THE.

Copied from an engraving with slight variations. Painting begun June 9th, 1862, finished June 12th, 1862. Size 9½" × 8". Price, $20.00

2602 TITIAN.

Picture by Titian, entered in the register as painted May 10th, 1813. Size 25" × 30". Price, $100.00

2603 TITIAN.

Copy of a painting by Titian, begun April 3rd, 1867 finished, May 8th, 1867. Size 25" × 30". Price, $100.00

2604 TRENTON FALLS.

Painted from an earlier sketch by the artist. The register notes it as begun Sept. 5th, 1845, and as " erased."

2605 TRIBUTE MONEY.

By Rubens (copied from a small picture). Painting begun Sept. 20th, 1813, finished May 1st, 1814. Size 84" × 60". Price, $600.00
Owned by the Pennsylvania Academy of Fine Arts, Philadelphia.

2606 TURK'S HEAD.

Copied from Mr. Allston's, begun Sept. 22nd, 1845, finished Sept. 23rd, 1845. Size 24" × 20". Price, $80.00

2607 UNITED STATES.

Arms of the United States. Drawing made for Mr. Binns, begun Dec. 25th, 1818, finished Dec. 27th, 1818. Size 8" × 12". Price, $30.00

2608 VAN DYCK.

Copy of Philip II, of Spain, by Van Dyck. Formerly owned by Joseph Harrison, of Philadelphia, and exhibited in his gallery of paintings on Rittenhouse Square, and sold at auction of Harrison pictures. Price, $250.00

2609 VAN DYCK SKETCH.

Fancy portrait in Van Dyck dress, painted for the actor, Thomas A. Cooper, of the New York Theatre. Picture begun March 29th, 1807, finished April 28th, 1807. Price, $30.00

2610 VENUS.

Small full-length figure for Thomas A. Cooper, begun June 19th, 1807, finished July 23rd, 1807. Size 20" × 24". Price, $20.00

SUBJECT PAINTINGS

2611 VENUS.

From Sir Joshua Reynolds' painting. Begun Aug. 25th, 1865, finished Sept. 18th, 1865. Painted for Miss Siddalls. Size 29″ × 36″.

Price, $50.00

Sold at executor's sale, Dec. 20th, 1872, Thomas & Sons, Fourth St., Philadelphia.

2612 VENUS AND CUPID.

(A design for a large picture.) Painting begun Aug. 14th, 1816, finished Sept. 17th, 1816. Size 17″ × 20″. Price, $100.00

2613 VIRGIN.

Copied from Salva Ferrata. Painted in 1822. Size 17″ × 20″.

Price, $30.00

2614 VIRGINIA.

Arms of the State of Virginia. Drawing made for Mr. J. Binns, begun June 20th, 1817, finished June 21st, 1817. Size 6″ × 6″. Price, $30.00
Additions and corrections $15.00.

2615 VOYAGE (MOTHER AND CHILD).

Painting begun Aug. 13th, 1870, finished Sept. 1st, 1870. Size 22″ × 17″. Price, $50.00
Sold at executor's sale of artist's paintings, at Thomas & Sons, Fourth St., Philadelphia, Dec. 20th, 1872.

2616 WASHINGTON'S PASSAGE OF THE DELAWARE.

Painted for the State of South Carolina, begun Aug. 7th, 1819, finished Dec. 15th, 1819. Size 17 ft. by 12 ft. Signed " TS Dec., 1819."

Price, $1000.00

Owned by the Boston Museum of Fine Arts.

2617 WASHINGTON'S PASSAGE OF THE DELAWARE.

Study for the large historical picture intended for the State of North Carolina, was begun Sept. 10th, 1818, and finished February, 1819. Size 48″ × 36″. Price, $500.00

2618 WASHINGTON'S PASSAGE OF THE DELAWARE.

A copy made from the study for the large picture, begun July 28th, 1823, finished April 24th, 1825, for Sir James Wright, of Scotland. Size 36″ × 51″. Price, $400.00
Owned in Edinburgh, Scotland.

SUBJECT PAINTINGS

2619 WASHINGTON'S FAREWELL ADDRESS.
Design, vignette, size 17" × 20". Painting begun May 8th, 1820, finished May 17th, 1820.   Price, $200.00

2620 WASHINGTON MEMORIAL.
Water-color sketch done by Sully for a book or portfolio of Philadelphia Artists for the Philadelphia Sanitary Fair of 186–. The sketch is signed " TS 1816."
Owned by John F. Braun, Philadelphia.

2621 WESTALL.
Historic group from the painting by Westall, begun Feb. 11th, 1808, finished Feb. 21st, 1808. Size 29" × 36".   Price, $25.00

2622 WISSAHICKON CREEK.
(View.) Painted from a former sketch, begun Nov. 15th, 1845, finished Nov. 21st, 1845. Size 24" × 29½".   Price, $50.00

2623 WISSAHICKON CREEK.
(View.) Painting begun Dec. 6th, 1870, finished Jan. 5th, 1871. Size 17" × 20".   Price, $20.00

2624 WISSAHICKON CREEK.
(View near.) Sketch No. 2. Begun Jan. 6th, 1871, finished Jan. 13th, 1871. Size 12" × 9".   Price, $10.00

2625 WREATH OF PALMS.
Design 2" circle. Feb., 1837.   Price, $10.00

2626 WRECKED SAILOR.
Painting begun Nov. 11th, 1867, finished Nov. 23rd, 1867. Size 20" × 14".   Price, $50.00
Sold at executor's sale of artist's paintings, Dec. 20th, 1872, by Thomas & Sons, Fourth St., Philadelphia.

2627 YOUTH, OR SPRINGTIME.
Painting begun April 7th, 1869, finished April 19th, 1869. Size 15" × 12".   Price, $30.00

2628 YOUTHFUL ATTACHMENT.
Painting begun June 29th, 1862, finished July 5th, 1862. Size 9" × 8".
Price, $10.00

SUBJECT PAINTINGS

2629 YOUNG WOMAN.

Bust, seated, lightly draped with bosom exposed. Head to left, dark hair, with long ringlet held by upraised hand. Coral necklace and jewels arranged in hair. Seated before a dressing mirror. Size 25″ × 30″.

Owned by Mrs. Alexander Campbell (née Wilcocks), of Philadelphia.

2630 YOUNG WOMAN.

Bust, profile to right, long dark hair falling down at back and side, blue dress with yellow border, low at the neck. Size 20″ × 24″, oval.

Owned by John Frederick Lewis, Philadelphia, Pa.

2631 ZERLINA AT HER TOILET.

(Fra Diavolo.) Painting begun July 5th, 1841, finished Sept. 19th, 1841. Size 29″ × 36″. Price, $300.00

Exhibited at Artists Fund Society in 1844.

APPENDIX

I. LETTERS

MAY 30, 1831.

Dear Sir:

At the last meeting of the Directors of the Penna. Academy of the Fine Arts I presented your letter tendering your resignation as a Member of the Board. Altho' we are unwilling to press upon you a continuance of your services to the Academy at the expense of your own convenience and wishes, we hope you will consent to a postponement of your retirement from office, at least for another year. The organization of the schools and the arrangements to be put in operation during the ensuing year, will render your knowledge and experience peculiarly important to us. I am therefore directed by the unanimous desire of the Board to ask your assent to be put on the ticket for Directors at the approaching election. Very Truly & Respectfully

Yr. very obed. Servant

JOS. HOPKINSON.

T. SULLY, ESQ.

(Sully's Answer to Mr. Hopkinson on back of letter.)

MAY 31.

HON. JUDGE HOPKINSON.

My dear Sir:

Since it was after mature deliberation that I determined upon resigning my place on the Board of Directors of the Academy of Fine Arts, I would by no means be dissuaded from this step at the present juncture.

393

My engagements at Boston will oblige me to leave home by the middle of June, and will detain me until late in the Fall; so that at all events I should be precluded from rendering any assistance in the arrangements to be made in the schools of the Academy, but I am fully persuaded that I could not offer a single idea to improve the views already embraced on the subject.

I consider the reluctance of the Board to accept my resignation as a testimonial of their friendly feelings towards me, for which I beg through you to make them my grateful acknowledgments.

With sincere esteem,

Your obt. Servt

PENNSYLVANIA ACADEMY OF FINE ARTS.

PHILADA: FEBRUARY 9TH, 1842.

Dear Sir:

At a stated meeting of the Board of Directors held on Wednesday Evening the 9th Inst.; you were elected a Director of the Academy, and immediately afterwards you were Elected President of the Academy in the place of the late Judge Hopkinson.

Very respectfully yours,

F'RA HOPKINSON, Secy.

MR. THOMAS SULLY.

PHILADELPHIA,

16TH FEBRUARY 1842

THOMAS SULLY, ESQR.

Dear Sir:

You have no doubt long ere this heard of the death of our much lamented fellow citizen Joseph Hopkinson Esquire, late President of the Pennsylvania Academy of the Fine Arts, who departed this life on the 15th of January last.

394

APPENDIX

In his death that institution has met with a very serious loss, for since its first establishment, he upon every occasion exercised a most active and untiring zeal in furtherance of its best interests.

The directors of the Academy on whom it devolves to fill the vacancy made by the death of their highly esteemed late President, held a special meeting on the evening of the 10th inst. for that purpose, when you were unanimously chosen to fill that station, and in accordance with the following Resolution we take pleasure in communicating the same to you.

RESOLVED, that Charles Graff, Hyman Gratz and Thomas C. Rockhill be a Committee to inform Thomas Sully, Esq. of his election as President of the Pennsylvania Academy of Fine Arts.

We are with great regard and esteem,

Dear Sir, Your m. obedt. St.

CHARLES GRAFF

HYMAN GRATZ

T. C. ROCKHILL

(Answer.)

To Messrs.

C. GRAFF

H. GRATZ

T. C. ROCKHILL.

Gentlemen :

I am greatly impressed with the honor conferred upon me by the Directors of the Academy of the Fine Arts in electing me President of the Institution ; particularly so when I consider the talents and high standing of our late friend Joseph Hopkinson Esquire whose vacated place I was expected to fill.

Yet I am constrained to decline the distinction you have proffered me ; I have long since resolved to avoid all situations of official rank, and especially one of such responsibility as that in question.

395

With heart felt thanks for the favor you have done me, and in confidence of still possessing your friendly regard,

I am with great respect

Gentlemen,

Yr Friend &

Feby. 22.

II. "CAPUCHIN CHAPEL"

STORY OF THE PICTURE

It is related that in July of the year 1821, Sully first became personally acquainted with Washington Allston.

Portrait painting being temporarily under an eclipse, it was suggested by Allston that a well executed copy of Granet's picture of the " Capuchin Chapel " (the choir of the Capuchin Monastery in the Piazza Barberini at Rome. Painted by François Marius Granet), at that time owned by a wealthy Bostonian, might prove profitable as an exhibition picture. Permission having been gained from the owner of the picture, Sully at once set about executing a copy. His indefatigable industry is again emphasized, when we find him completing the picture in two months' time, after brother artists had expressed the view that it would take very much longer. Allston allowed five months for its completion, while Gilbert Stuart predicted it would involve six months' labor.

The entry in Sully's "Account of Pictures" shows that he began it on "Aug. 7" aud finished it "Oct. 9", or in just about two months. It was a large canvas, measuring 5 ft. 8 in. by 4 ft. 3 in. An anecdote is related that when he informed Allston of its completion, the latter remarked, "You have made a sketch." "No; a carefully finished copy—come and see."

APPENDIX

That it must have been well executed and a spirited reproduction of the original, there is evidence in correspondence, which the writer has been fortunate in having had access to. In the Hopkinson (MSS) Collection, letters are extant referring to the picture and its ultimate history. Under date of July 7, 1825, the Hon. Joel R. Poinsett writes from Mexico City to Judge Joseph Hopkinson, in Philadelphia:

"I saw a bad copy of the 'Capuchin Chapel' in the cabinet of the Bishop of Puebla; it cost him an enormous sum. If Mr. Sully thinks the public curiosity exhausted in the United States, and will send me his copy, I will hang it in my house and sell it for him if I can get the price he shall fix upon it."

To which Judge Hopkinson replied under date of September 27, 1825:

"Mr. Sully is very grateful for your thinking so kindly of him, the copy of the 'Capuchin Chapel' produces from $120 to $150 dollars a year;* and it would be imprudent to part with it. On my suggestion, however, he will make another copy equally good, and send it to you. It will be ready for some vessel in the Spring."

Then, on December 27, 1825, Sully himself writes Mr. Poinsett:

"Our mutual friend, Mr. Hopkinson, read to me a passage in one of your letters to him last Fall, in which you kindly invited me to adventure in your charge the sale of my picture of the 'Capuchin Chapel.' I promptly replied to the message from you, but find that the vessel I wrote by has been lost at sea. I would now assure you that I intend to send the picture to you by the first spring ship; at the same time will also send one or two other subjects with the limit price attached." In accepting your benevolent invitation, I am fully sensible of your kind intention and hope my feelings of grateful acknowledgment will be acceptable to you."

* Sully's copy of the "Capuchin Chapel" was brought to Norfolk. It received in two weeks' exhibition upwards of $200." Under date of March, 1822, in Dunlap's Autobiography, p. 540.

APPENDIX

From the foregoing, it would appear that Sully decided to send the picture he had been exhibiting, rather than delay matters by executing a second copy, as suggested by Mr. Hopkinson.*

Under date of October 20, 1826, Mr. Poinsett writes Judge Hopkinson:

"I enclose you a letter for Mr. Sully, which I will thank you to deliver to him. I have chosen this channel because the letter contains an order for $500. I sold his picture for $550. The expenses of carriage rather exceeded $50."

This is confirmed by Sully himself, who addresses "His Excellency Joel R. Poinsett, Minister of U. S. to Mexico" from Philadelphia, February 27, 1827:

"I have received the draft you sent me for Five hundred dollars, some months ago by the hand of Mr. Hopkinson. I took it for granted he would tell you so in his next communication. I have since received the duplicate and your kind letter, which obliges me to feel ashamed of my remissness. *I am well satisfied to learn that the 'Capuchin Chapel' has come safe to hand.*"

The language of this last paragraph raises a doubt whether the picture reported sold by Mr. Poinsett under date of *October 20, 1826*, refers to the canvas under discussion or a different one. It is possible that the "Capuchin Chapel" might have been purchased and paid for before arrival, in consideration of Mr. Poinsett's responsibility. But that the picture did sell and found a home in Mexico is clearly proven by the following letter from Sully, which we give in full:

* July 8th, 1826. "Finished the retouching of copy of 'Capuchin Chapel,' $100, 5' 8" × 4' 2"." From Sully's own "Account of Pictures." This was probably preparatory to shipping it to Mexico.

APPENDIX

"PHILADELPHIA, APRIL 20TH, 1828.

"HON'L' J POINSETT,

Minister of U. S. in Mexico.

Dear Sir:

I received yesterday by the hand of Mr. Vaughan your letter of February 23rd, inclosing a draft on the Govt. for $500 as part payment of the sale of 'Capuchin Chapel.'

The amount is beyond my expectations and our obligation to you very great for the trouble you have so kindly undertaken; indeed the reflection of having taken up so much of your valuable time is the only alloy to the pleasure I have received in the termination of the business.

You will be pleased to hear that the Arts follow in the train of success and encouragement that has lately been given to every branch of industry in the U. S. I am persuaded that it only requires the aid of wealth and fashion to prove that the Fine Arts is one strong point of character in the people of this country.

I am, dear Sir, with high esteem and gratitude,

Yr. friend and Ob't servant,

T. S."

The close of this letter shows Sully in happy and optimistic mood, as he had every reason to be.

III. PASSPORT

(Copied from original, in possession of Mrs. Albert Sully, grand-daughter by marriage, Brooklyn, N. Y.)

54 years	Thos. Sully
5 ft. 6 inches	of the City of Philada.
Forehead, high	Portrait-painter
Eyes, blue grey	accompanied by his daughter
Nose, prominent	Blanche, aged 21 yrs.
Mouth, moderate size	
Chin, round	3rd day of October, 1837.
Hair, brown mixed with grey	
Complexion, pallid	
Face, long	

NOTE.—The above furnishes a very reliable record of our artist's physical appearance, and has its importance. (A biographer writing of him shortly before the English voyage, puts his height at five feet eight inches.)

J S C

APPENDIX

IV. SULLY'S "HINTS"

Hints to Young Portrait Painters
And the Process of Portrait Painting
As practiced by the late
Thomas Sully

———

J. M. Stoddart & Co.
Phila., 1873

———

PREFACE

These "Hints to Young Painters" were prepared for the press by the late Thomas Sully in the year 1851, and revised by him in 1871, but were not during his lifetime placed in the hands of any publisher. Their merit lies in their brevity and clearness, and they are addressed especially to young artists, who will find in them much useful information. Knowing the deep interest that was felt by the profession in every word spoken or written by the artist, it has been deemed best to add a few notes on the preparation of canvas and vehicles, gleaned from his memoirs. This will interest the accomplished professor as well as the inexperienced amateur and may prove of service to both.

FRANCIS THOMAS SULLY DARLEY.

December, 1872.

NOTE.—The authors note the above-mentioned *brochure* as containing valuable suggestions for the guidance of young artists. It also contains a colored reproduction of the setting of Sully's palette.

ADDENDA AND CORRIGENDA

Page   5. The statement made that both the artist's parents were dead at the date named (1799) is an error.   The father survived until 1815, living to about ninety years of age.

Page 21. 1910 to read 1810.

Page 99. No. 136.   1892 to read 1792.

Page 117. No. 294.   Owned by the Carroll family at Carrolton.

Page 117. Carpenter, Samuel.   The original portrait of Samuel Carpenter was in the possession of his great-granddaughter, the late Mrs. Isaac C. Jones, and an excellent copy by Thomas Sully was owned by a descendant at Salem, N. J.

Page 125. No. 354.   (Born 1782, died 1861.)

Page 231. No. 1242.   For Mr. Evan Kane, read Dr. Evan O'Neill Kane.

Page 235. No. 1275–1276.   Gasper or Casper.

Page 235. No. 1277.   Elizabeth Giles (1774–1832).

INDEX OF OWNERS OF PORTRAITS

BY NUMBERS

405

Bullock, Miss L. P., 1622
Butler Insane Asylum, Providence, R. I., 211, 261

Cadwalader, John, Philadelphia, 81, 532 533, 1769, 1873
Campbell, Mrs. Alexander D., 368, 528, 1980, 2325
Campbell, Benjamin H., 827
Caperton, Mrs. Hugh, Baltimore, 285, 2126, 2195, 2461
Carson, James, 1369, 1370
Carstairs, Daniel H., 1648, 1897
Cassidy, Gilbert H., 301
Charleston, St. Andrew's Society, 1649, 1787, 1856
Chauncey, Elihu, 317
Chicago Art Institute, 1098
Church, Arthur, 1018, 1463, 2251, 2472, 2530
Clark, Joseph S., 1590, 1591
Clarke, Thomas B., New York, 147
Clay, Mrs. Thomas, 669, 670, 675
Clemenson, Mrs. W. J., 1637
Cleveland Museum of Fine Arts, 436, 437, 2227
Cline, Dr. Isaac M., New Orleans La., 12, 1192, 1193, 1510
Cochran, A. S., Phillipse Manor, Yonkers, N. Y., 4
Coffin, Francis H., 1560
Collins, Mrs. Frederick, 1286
Collins, Dr. Stacy B., 919
Colman, Mrs., 1402
Colt, Lyman R, Seattle, 359
Colton, Mrs. Sabin W., 1352
Connor, Philip Syng P., 1375
Coolidge, Miss Ella W., 1450
Cope, Eliza Kane, Mrs., 562
Corcoran Art Gallery, Washington, D. C., 882, 1179, 1737, 2292
Coxe, Charles B. (Mrs.), 689
Cox, John Lyman, 380, 381
Craighead, Mrs. F. W., 1183, 1184
Cushing, Mrs. Robert M., 469

Custis Mrs., 2391
Cutts, Mrs. Richard D., 712

Dale, Edward C., 412
Dallas, Miss Sophia, 417
Dartmouth College, N. H., 812, 1776
Davis, Sussex D., 444
Day, Newton H., 448
Degn, Mrs. William L., 1194
Delaware, State of, 933, 1172
Dewees, Mr. H. M., 462
Dixon, Mrs. Thomas. F., Philadelphia, 132
Drayton, Mrs. Robert C. 1502
Dreer, F. J. (Sale), 1909
Drew, John, 485
Dreyspring, Mrs. Fanny Goodwyn, 2407
Dunn, Mrs. Edward S., 1678
Du Pont, Alexis I., 505, 506
Du Pont, Mrs. Elizabeth G. 473, 474
Du Pont, Mrs. William, 1317
Dupuy, Herbert, 1467

Edwards, Miss Grace, 2037
Ehrich Galleries, New York City, 51, 110, 250, 735, 879, 843, 925, 926, 1189, 1243, 1372, 1448, 1708, 1716, 1728, 1833, 1838, 2039, 2106, 2164, 2268, 2352
Ellis, Col. Thomas A., 323
Elwyn, Rev. Alfred, 1220
Etting, Frank M., 538

Farr, Mrs. John, 1811
Field, John W., 1367
Fielding, Mantle, 2149
Findlay, Mrs. James, 823
Fisher, Geo. Harrison, 1966
Fisher, Miss Sally W., 1128
Fitzgerald, Mrs. Hildebrand, 577
Fitzgerald, Mrs. James R., 731
Fitzgerald, Col. Thomas (estate of), 566, 569, 570, 572, 573, 574, 576, 581, 2166
Forney, James (Estate of), 598

INDEX OF OWNERS OF PORTRAITS

Forrest Home, Holmesburg, Pa., **886,** 917
Fox, William H., 1005
Freeman Auction Rooms, 1403
Frothingham, Theodore, 1455
Furness, F. R., (Estate), 628
Furness, Horace Howard, 544, 545, 547, 629, 1500

Garland, Mrs. Marie T., 1646
Gaw, Mrs. William H., 1615, 1954
George, Mrs. H. E., 637, 638
Gibbes Art Gallery, Charleston, S. C., 1370, 2013
Gillespie, George C., 1767
Gilmore, Mrs., 2396
Gilpin, Mrs. Arthington, 1652, 1653
Glenn, John M., 657, 1173
Glover, Mrs. W. B., 213
Gonzales, Ambrose E., 521
Goodrich, Mrs., 1252
Graff, Miss, 1141
Grant, Mrs. Harriet, 714
Green, Miss Margaret, 1745
Gribbel, John, 674
Griffith, Manuel Eyre, 361

Halberstadt, A. H., 2260, 2514
Hamilton, Mrs. A. McLane, 1462
Hamilton, Charles, 770
Hancock, Mrs. James and Miss Hall, 721, 1358, 1359, 1360, 1361, 1362
Hanson, Benedict H., (Mrs.), 911
Hare, Mrs. Horace Binney, 151, 738
Harriman, Mrs. E. H., 1883
Harris, C., New York City, 7, 809, 810
Harris, Rev. John Andrews, Philadelphia, 39
Harriss, R. T., 2026, 2029, 2030, 2051, 2252, 2293, 2417
Harrison, Joseph (Sale), 959, 1908
Harrison, Randolph, 1760
Hart, Dr. Charles D., 1222
Harvard College, Cambridge, Mass., 6
Hawkes, Hon. McDougall, 1031

Hayward, Mrs. Nathan, 831
Heard, Mrs., Pittsburgh, Pa., 145
Henkel, Stan V., (Auction Rooms), 849, 947, 1831
Henry, William Hamilton, 772
Hewson, Dr. Addinell, 775, (also 777)
Hinckley, Mrs. Frank, 807
Hodder, Mrs. Alfred, 920
Hodge, Mrs. G. Woolsey, 291
Hoffman, Mrs. John W., 980
Hoffman, Miss Frances H., 795
Hoffman, George, New York, 109
Hoffman, R. C., 791, 793, 796
Hooper, S. G., 2306
Hopkins, William, 808
Hopkinson, Edward, 811
Horst, Vander, Mrs. Arnoldus, 27
Howard, B. B., New Orleans, La., 254
Howell, Mrs. Arthur W., 830
Howell, Henry W., 828
Howell, Mrs. Joshua L., 829
Hubbard, Mrs. A. H., 579
Huger, Mrs. William E., 1621
Hughes, Edward W., 1695, 1705
Hughes, Mrs. Elizabeth W., 1397
Hunt, Mrs. A. D., 988
Hunt, Miss Ellen R., 893
Hutchins, Stitson, 922
Hutchinson, Misses, 858, 1975, 2004
Hutchinson, Charles Hare, 852
Hutchinson, Mrs. James H., 193

Ingersoll, Mrs. Henry, 853

Jackson, Anne T. H., Maryland, 752
Jackson, Mrs. Oswald, 103, 892, 894
Jackson, Mrs. R. T., 1425
Jacobs, Mrs. Henry Barton, 1752
Janeway, J. J., 903
Janeway, Miss Maria, 902
Jeanes, Joseph Y., 1905
Jenkins, J. Foster, 439, 440
Jennings, Walter, 1736
Jessup, W. D., 824, 1078, 1079, 1083
Johnson, Mr., Uniontown, Pa., 245

INDEX OF OWNERS OF PORTRAITS

INDEX OF OWNERS OF PORTRAITS

411